THE SHAPE OF THE NEW

THE SHAPE OF THE NEW

Four Big Ideas
and How They Made
the Modern World

SCOTT L. MONTGOMERY AND DANIEL CHIROT

PRINCETON UNIVERSITY PRESS
Princeton & Oxford

Copyright © 2015 by Princeton University Press
Published by Princeton University Press, 41 William Street, Princeton, New Jersey 08540
In the United Kingdom: Princeton University Press, 6 Oxford Street, Woodstock,
    Oxfordshire OX20 1TW

press.princeton.edu

Jacket photograph ©Rachael Wright

LIBRARY OF CONGRESS CATALOGING-IN-PUBLICATION DATA
Montgomery, Scott L.
    The shape of the new : four big ideas and how they made the modern
        world / Scott Montgomery and Daniel Chirot.
                pages cm
    Includes bibliographical references and index.
    ISBN 978-0-691-15064-2 (hardback : alk. paper) 1. Civilization, Modern. 2. Intellectual life—
        History. 3. Philosophy, Modern—History. I. Chirot, Daniel. II. Title.
    CB358.M66 2015
    909.4—dc23   2014037906

British Library Cataloging-in-Publication Data is available

This book has been composed in Garamond Pro

Printed on acid-free paper. ∞

Printed in the United States of America

10 9 8 7 6 5 4 3 2

TO PETER DOUGHERTY

who has done so much to promote and enhance scholarly publishing
and to whom so many of us are indebted

CONTENTS

It is important to understand what this book is about and what our strategy has been in writing it. Briefly put, it is about key ideas that have built the modern world. Not all of them, to be sure (space and competence being limited), but those that have been and that remain among the most central to modern understanding about the nature and working of human society and also how it might be changed. These ideas, and the history of their epochal influence, we have chosen from the domains of politics, economics, science, and religion. This may not seem particularly original or pathbreaking. Indeed, that is not our intent. Our principal theme—that ideas have made the world we live in and still direct our conceptions, even our imagining, of it, for better and for ill—has been stated before, though in different form. Our principal effort, then, has been to illustrate and clarify this theme by looking at particular thinkers and their systems of thought. It is absolutely clear that in various ways and at various times these thinkers and their ideas have impacted the great majority of lives from the late 1700s until today and will continue to do so for a long time to come. It is thus our second but no less important theme that these particular intellectuals very much need to be read and discussed today. We would go so far as to suggest that they are essential to any real understanding of modernity and contemporary global society.

Our strategy in this book has therefore been mainly instructional, not theoretical. We cannot claim that we have found new facts or even that we have as yet undiscovered insights about the individuals we have examined. Of course we have consulted their works, in translation if necessary, but this is not a book based mostly on primary sources. Each chapter synthesizes the pertinent scholarship about a particular thinker or group of thinkers, including their chief writings, and then uses this knowledge to reveal, analyze, and evaluate the forms of influence each has had and continues to have.

We have assumed little knowledge on the reader's part in every case. Thus our discussions on figures like Adam Smith, Karl Marx, and Charles Darwin will likely appear introductory to scholars in relevant disciplines. This we view not as an occupational hazard but as a necessity. Our hope is to introduce these key people, and their immeasurable impacts, to a large and diverse audience. We also wish to argue, forcefully if needed, for the importance of studying them in any program of higher learning, not least in the humanities.

In conclusion we will argue that if we are to comprehend the complexities of the world as it has come to exist, reading the actual texts of these and other major thinkers who have shaped our world is necessary. Intellectual history and the analysis of these most important writings are an important part of the humanities because of their emphasis on the powers of thought and expression. The humanities should in their own way be no less compulsory than the social and natural sciences, and to dismiss them, as too many do today, is to diminish our capacity to know and understand the ideas that have shaped how we think and what we believe.

ACKNOWLEDGMENTS

We would like to thank Jim Wellman, our colleague, for having carefully read and commented on some of our manuscript. Sabine Lang, Joel Migdal, and Sunila Kale, three other colleagues, gave us helpful advice. We are grateful for the suggestions made by two anonymous reviewers who read this work for Princeton University Press and to the members of the Press's editorial board who made valuable recommendations. Mashary Balghonaim, a friend, carefully went over the entire work and made good suggestions. We owe a great debt to many other friends, colleagues, former students of ours, and our own teachers. We particularly want to thank Steve Bailey of Knox College, whose courses on the history of ideas left a lasting impression on one of us.

We have both received unstinting support and advice from Reşat Kasaba, the director of the Jackson School of International Studies at the University of Washington where we teach. We have been helped by the material support provided by the Herbert J. Ellison Professorship that one of us holds. The late Professor Ellison was one of our most esteemed colleagues. Our research assistant, Nicola Castle-Bauer, proved invaluable in the later stages of work. We also wish to offer our deep appreciation to the devoted staff at Princeton University Press, whose professionalism and commitment to excellence set an exemplary standard.

Finally, we would like to thank our respective families, who have patiently helped us in so many ways. This book is also for them.

THE SHAPE OF THE NEW

Ideas as Historical Forces

On résiste à l'invasion des armées; on ne résiste pas à l'invasion des idées.
(Invading armies can be resisted; invading ideas cannot be.)
VICTOR HUGO'S ESSAY ON NAPOLEON III'S 1851 COUP
D'ÉTAT, *THE HISTORY OF A CRIME*

Arguably the three most powerful men of the twentieth century never lived to see it. Adam Smith, Karl Marx, and Charles Darwin could hardly have imagined the forms of wealth, revolution, and science that would emerge in their names during the decades after 1900 or the ugly dogmatism, pseudoscience, and staggering brutality. It would surprise them no less to find that their names were familiar to every well-educated person in a world of billions. Had each of them lived only a few decades longer, they might have seen inklings of this. What they could not have guessed was that their formative role in modern history would only grow with time.

Smith, Marx, and Darwin were not kings or military commanders. Nor were they political leaders or religious prophets. They were intellectuals. Their field of effort and the origin of the influence they exerted after their deaths lie in the realm of ideas. The ideas they articulated in the hands of followers, detractors, and many others provided the radioactive substance of transformation. It is impossible to talk about the rise of modern economics and the capitalist system—a system that profoundly changed the nature of the world and that is now fully global—without referring to Adam Smith. Marx set loose ideas that sought to destroy this system, that became the inspiration for revolutions and wars that swept away entire societies, changing and also ending the lives of many millions of people. And Darwin? His thought redefined the universe of living things and their relation to human beings, while both radically weakening the explanatory power of religion and radicalizing its reactive response to modernity.

Needless to say, these are not minor developments. They must be considered essential to the "modern," however defined. Moreover, the conflicts and debates that led to these developments, and the struggles over them, are far from over. If the past two hundred years have revealed anything, it is that engagements over fundamental ideas—those elemental to the building of institutions, to changes in governments and the organization of society, to concepts like individualism and human rights—have not at all receded and show no prospect of an end. The battle over free markets and government power can hardly be called settled. The collapse of the Soviet Union has not erased state control from the globe and turned the world democratic by default. Modern biology has not destroyed fundamentalist religion. The confrontations waged over these primary matters have a continuing history to them that is still lived—in extreme as well as moderate form, today as much as a century ago. No group, nation, or party has definitively won the battle of ideas.

Contemporary society, in short, has been built over time from the materials of thought. We live within institutions and under political systems created and shaped by ideas that often began in the imagination of major thinkers. When first made public, many of these seemed in their time to be so original, sometimes so daring, that they were dismissed as implausible or even dangerous. For a great many of us, meanwhile, it is easy to assume that the society we inhabit has long been in place and sits on firm foundations. We are not quite prepared to accept that fundamentally new ways of looking at the world might come to reshape the reality we inhabit. But they have. Indeed, they are largely the source of our social existence and even a fair part of our beliefs about it. By this is meant not only grand theories about economics, history, and life but ideas concerned with liberty, the individual, the role of religion, education, and, not least, the nation-state. Concepts about these and similar institutions are often called by other names: policies, principles, schemes, plans; but they all come back to basic, underlying philosophies about the nature of society and how it should work. Ideas, therefore, are not mere mental substance. Operating through leaders, the public, interest groups, and ordinary individuals, they are a determining factor in the creation of social reality.

We are hardly the first to argue such a position. One of the twentieth century's great economists, John Maynard Keynes, completed his most ambitious work, *The General Theory of Employment, Interest and Money*, with these pointed words:

> The ideas of economists and political philosophers, both when they are right and when they are wrong, are more powerful than is commonly understood. Indeed the world is ruled by little else. Practical men, who believe themselves to be quite exempt from any intellectual influence, are usually the slaves of some defunct economist. Madmen in authority, who hear voices in the air, are distilling their frenzy from some academic scribbler of a few years back. I am sure that the power of vested interests is vastly exaggerated compared with the gradual encroachment of ideas. . . . [S]oon or late, it is ideas, not vested interests, which are dangerous for good or evil. (1936/2009, 383)

We agree with Keynes in most respects. But as we inhabit a later time and have seen a good deal more of history unfold, we would amend his conclusion in a significant way. We would emphasize that economists and political philosophers, important as they are (and as close to Mr. Keynes's heart as they undoubtedly were), do not compose the entire taxonomy of thinkers who have delivered us to the present. We should not leave out the ideas from such pivotal domains as science and religion, for example. And in this book, we do not. Nor do we ignore the dangers that Keynes refers to, meaning dangers that have come from extreme and often violent interpretations of key ideas.

Our title states that "four big ideas" shaped the modern world. At the risk of being accused of oversimplification, we want to emphasize that we are speaking here in broad, all-encompassing terms. It should be apparent from what has already been said that we will be dealing not only with single concepts and beliefs but whole systems of thought that have touched every level of social experience. Taken together, these can be grouped into four encompassing themes than can be summarized as follows.

From Adam Smith came the idea that individuals should have the freedom to make all essential decisions affecting their material and moral lives, and that if they were allowed to do so, the resulting society would be the most efficient, prosperous, and free. This was a very big idea that opposed both communal tradition and the prevailing forms of authority in his time.

Humanity had dreamed of universal equality long before Karl Marx came along. What Marx did, however, was to show that utopian dreams were insufficient to bring this about. An egalitarian world would arrive as the result of "scientific laws" governing history, but for this to happen revolutionary parties based on the solid material interests of the downtrodden majority would have to be organized. Only then would inequality and injustice be vanquished forever.

Charles Darwin turned the idea of evolution into a true scientific theory, one that came to give all life a secular history and that, through the essential mechanism of natural selection, was applied by others to a great many aspects of society and, more recently, to human behavior and culture. This was hugely controversial in his time and continues to be so because it raises such difficult questions about our purpose on Earth. Darwin insisted that these issues have to be faced through open inquiry, not denied or evaded as his enemies in his time and ours claim.

And the fourth "big idea"? Modern democracy first came into being through the efforts of the founders of the United States, most of all those we have chosen to discuss, Thomas Jefferson and Alexander Hamilton. It was these two brilliant but also flawed men, more than any others, whose fierce debates set the patterns for how to imagine, implement, and institutionalize this new political system that, in various shapes, would come to influence so much of the world.

These define our four "big," thematic ideas: freedom, equality, evolution, and democracy. We are concerned not only with each of them in and of themselves but also with the forms of reaction that rose against them. These, too, are critical to understand. We are aware, of course, that the thinkers we have chosen were not the sole inventors of each thematic idea or the only ones to have written important works about them. But as we will explain, they were far and away the most influential. Indeed, it is an integral part of our effort to show how complex and many-sided their thoughts were, how they have spawned many followers, and how they have been resisted and fought over time and again, down to the present.

Our intent, then, is to pursue a different type of intellectual history. In simple terms, we wish to show that ideas have been among the primary forces behind modern history during the past three centuries. Ideas, that is, do not merely matter; they matter immensely, as they have been the source for decisions and actions that have structured the modern world. We offer, therefore, an interpretation of history that begins with this premise. It is one we feel is amply shown by an examination of the choices and motives of leaders, in the past and present, but still more by tracing the particular influences of ideas themselves and the specific ways in which they have been the agents of historical events. The untold number of human lives that have been bettered and saved, but also imprisoned and annihilated, in the name of one or another political philosophy, theory of history, concept of national destiny, or other vision convinces us that a more direct approach to understanding the power of ideas is warranted. The chapters that follow take up some of the most influential thinkers and concepts that shaped the twentieth century and that are now shaping the twenty-first century. Our aim has been to synthesize what is known about these thinkers and concepts into a coherent set of discussions about their diverse, long-term impact.

There is a venerable debate between "idealist" and "materialist" explanations of history. Do new ideas cause social, political, and economic change, or is it the reverse, that such ideas are products of their time period? Erudite philosophers who eschew crude generalizations have debated this issue for more than a century. We do not propose to do so. Rather, we take the position that ideas have often come before material changes that they then help explain and propel. Adam Smith's economics turned out to further the cause of capitalist development and to explain it even though he did not realize that the Industrial Revolution was about to transform the world. Marx wanted to cause change, and his ideas certainly did. Darwin, who was more modest, feared that his ideas would change much, and he was right. We are far from wanting to use such examples as evidence for a single, dogmatic interpretation of history. At the same time, it seems irrefutable to us that certain ideas have indeed shown transformational power over the span of the last few centuries. This is not a unique perspective; important analysts in the social sciences and philosophy have also adopted it (Nisbet 1980; Hirschman 1977; Berlin 2013).

The first set of ideas we have chosen had their birth and early maturation during the seventeenth- and eighteenth-century European Enlightenment and its expansion into the nineteenth century. These are necessary choices. The Enlightenment was a critical period for the birth of modernity, an era of deep separation from all that had gone before, a period of enormous creativity and destruction, most of all in the realm of thought. It was when, in the words of Jonathan Israel, one of the period's most knowledgeable students, everything known became available for questioning, skepticism, and, in many cases, rejection and replacement (Israel 2001, 2006, 2011). Not every received idea was attacked; not all forms of authority and privilege were challenged. But many of the most fundamental concepts about the nature of human beings and society were indeed contested, placed in doubt, and then, over time, supplanted. If earlier upheavals of the social order sought their legitimacy in theology, law, and tradition, from the eighteenth century onward such changes were powered by ideas that were secular and that looked to found society and its institutions on concepts presumably anchored in an evidence-based, reason-led "scientific" understanding of man and the universe.

To state things plainly: it was in the late seventeenth, eighteenth, and early nineteenth centuries when most of the fundamental ideas of modernity were born.

And it was in the late nineteenth and twentieth centuries when these ideas were tested, expanded, and institutionalized but also brutally resisted. Among them are to be counted the ideas of democratic freedom, economic self-determination, individual liberty and equality, and religious tolerance, as well as those of communism, nationalism, racial "science," and violent revolution. The Enlightenment, that is, brought forth the terms for both its fulfillment and its own annihilation—a Counter-Enlightenment, which came frighteningly close to destroying it in the twentieth century and which has been revived in different forms in the 2000s. Inasmuch as liberal democracy can be considered a product of Enlightenment thought, so can trends that eventually led toward its opposite, totalitarian communism and fascism, and more recently a reaction rooted in religious beliefs.

We do not, in other words, present the development of ideas as a straightforward march to enlightened progress. Such is no more in evidence today than in the 1930s or the 1890s. Nor have we ignored criticisms of Enlightenment thought that seek to point out other troubling elements: its relationship to colonialism, its misguided utopianism, its mechanization of and disenchantment with the natural world, its emphasis on abstract and instrumental reason, and the powers of rational and bureaucratic control it supposedly set loose upon humanity.

We agree with some of the criticisms of the Enlightenment but hardly all, and the reader will see why in the pages that follow. We are strong supporters of the conclusion that real, concrete progress has taken place, that many of the restrictions on freedom and life existing in the eighteenth and nineteenth centuries—the institution of slavery, disenfranchisement of women, religious intolerance, constraints on free expression, the ability of the authorities to come to your house at any time of their pleasing and do just about anything they liked—have been eliminated in most democratic states, along with a great many cruel practices that used to be common such as drawing and quartering, public hangings for petty crimes, and others. No less, the Enlightenment created standards by which its own legacy could be measured. In the United States, for instance, there was originally the great gap between stated ideals of liberty ("we the people") and actual limits to such liberty when the Constitution was adopted. Along with the constitutional acceptance of slavery there was an acceptance of the laws of various states that denied voting rights to those without property as well as to most Blacks, Native Americans, and women. Over time, however, through great struggles that kept on referring back to the original ideas of the Enlightenment, these limits have been removed. Had the original impetus of these ideas not been present, the struggle for improvement would have been far more difficult, perhaps even impossible. We can still see in parts of the world where Enlightenment ideas are rejected that the freedoms and rights accepted as commonplace in democracies are far from being practiced.

Nor can we overlook the legacy of the Enlightenment in the enormous scientific advances and technological innovations made possible by the new freedom of thought. These are now so taken for granted that it is easy to forget how gradual and often resisted such advances were before the eighteenth century.

But for all its eventual progress, the twentieth century also saw epic revolutions, wars, genocides, and suffering on a monstrous scale, as the Enlightenment and Counter-Enlightenment battled for supremacy in many parts of the world. This may seem a crude or mythic way to put things, as if two great colossi had fought for the soul of humanity. Historians, however, have themselves often described these events, and the twentieth century as a whole, as representing the period of "great ideological struggle." We certainly agree, though we also take care to show that the reality was immensely complex, not least on the plains of thought where it all began. It is also our view that much of the conflict never ended. It would be exceedingly foolish, that is, to believe that such struggles are over. The new century will continue to see large-scale struggle in the realm of ideas, though its precise forms and its principle actors will no longer be exactly the same. Such is yet one more pressing reason why it remains imperative to comprehend and analyze ideas, for they are as much involved in the making of the present and future as they were in the past.

This Book

Accepting, then, that specific ideas have been key forces behind events in modern history provides the principal theme of our book. The chapters that follow each take up one key domain of idea-making and trace its origins, invention, rhetoric, logic, and relevance to debates going on today. For this, we have drawn on the work of many excellent authors and specialists in each area. Our effort is not one of original scholarship but of synthesis built around our theme.

We have structured the book in a straightforward manner. Part 1, including chapters 1–4, examines the thought of the three authors already mentioned, Smith, Marx, and Darwin, as well as the invention of modern democracy in the thoughts of Thomas Jefferson and Alexander Hamilton and the often bitter debates they had about how to construct the new United States. Their views were essential to the creation of the world's first large-scale democratic republic based on Enlightenment thinking. Studying these, however, also reveals deep conflicts within Enlightenment thought that remain unresolved and a source of instability in that same republic and elsewhere in the world.

Part 2 then turns to key ideas, less tied to single authors, that rose to combat the Enlightenment, those that have rejected the very core of its liberalism and free thought as well as much of, if not all of, its science. With chapter 5, we meet the Counter-Enlightenment, whose specific and varied forms of reaction grew through the nineteenth and early twentieth centuries, reaching a peak in the phenomenon of fascism.

In chapters 6 and 7 the subject turns to fundamentalist religion in Christianity and Islam, which have seen a surging influence in many parts of the globe during the late twentieth and early twenty-first centuries. We have chosen to focus on these two religions, in particular, because they are both the largest and the most widespread internationally in terms of their adherents. These two faiths have also produced the most far-reaching versions of what we refer to as "fundamentalist," a term we use to designate a set of characteristics that includes strict, literal interpretation of Scripture, a claim to the one pure and true faith, and denial of worth and legitimacy to all other beliefs. The religious "turn" in general but specifically in its fundamentalist forms, it is now evident, has produced a deep reaction against liberal modernization whose ultimate political impact and potential for further violence is still far from clear.

Finally, in a concluding chapter, we summarize the major findings of the book and take up the matter of their implications. It should come as no surprise that our principal theme of posing ideas as primary historical forces brings with it some major implications for scholarship and teaching. This applies to both the humanities and the social sciences. Our discussion of these implications is brief and straightforward but also strongly worded. It is our feeling that too much is at stake to pedal lightly.

Readers will inevitably ask why we have chosen to speak of "ideas" and not "ideologies." Mainly it is a matter of focus and clarity. Though originally an Enlightenment term itself, coined by Count Destutt Tracy in his book on political economy (1817) to signify a "science of ideas," the meaning of "ideology" later underwent many adaptations. For Karl Marx, as we will see, ideologies were reflections of the class positions of those who expounded them, and thus, rather than being independent ideas that influenced society directly, they were by-products of various economic classes in conflict with each other. This is ironic, since the history of his own ideas in creating a whole new kind of society proves the exact opposite: first came the ideas, then the resulting political programs, and only after that the creation of an entirely novel social form. Karl Mannheim, whose *Ideology and Utopia* (1936) tried to overcome this particular Marxist bias, essentially failed. He, too, felt that ideas were a product of the social situation from which they emerged and thus were ideologies, incapable of acting as forces that could produce change. In the mid- and late twentieth century, Daniel Bell and Francis Fukuyama defined "ideology" to mean political ideas and policies that had become obsolete, particularly those on the left of the political spectrum (Bell 1960; Fukuyama 1992).

We accept none of these ways of understanding with regard to the ideas we discuss. First of all, we insist that these ideas are major influences on their own, indeed influences of primary importance. Obviously they were somewhat a product of their times, but the most important among them have enormous originality and have been able to ultimately transform societies by generating whole sets of belief systems and programs. Whereas "ideology" has come to suggest a fixed worldview that is self-referential and even inescapable, a kind of mental prison from which believers cannot exit, the ideas we are studying were anything but this. Moreover, applying "ideology" to such concepts as liberal democracy, free trade, religious fundamentalism, or biological evolution does not seem to us especially helpful or illuminating. It serves more to confuse the matter with appeals to what we have just described.

Second, we reject any notion that the ideas we are looking at are obsolete or have lost their power. We do not deny that they have produced different kinds of interpretations, conflicting schools, both acceptance and resistance—on the contrary, such is precisely the point. This degree of argument and controversy continues today. Consider the example of Darwinian evolution and the battles that continue to be waged over it, battles that have lost none of their vehemence or complexity. The very fact that such ideas remain so contemporary in their impact, so much a part of sociopolitical reality, is the reason why we believe they need to be studied and understood by a wide array of people. For this it is necessary to take the valuable work of many scholars who have written about them and put this work into a more general context that shows how the transcendent power of these ideas has spread and continues to be pervasive today. The notion that somehow powerful ideas have ceased to strongly influence the present, or will do so in the future, is dangerously wrong. In the twenty-first century, ideas that run counter to the Enlightenment are, if anything, growing once more in power. While they may not yet be as coherent or persuasive as liberal democracy, they are generating their own political realities. To understand this, we need to look at the source of these ideas, too, and take them seriously, even if we do not find them congenial.

The term "idea," therefore, takes us back to the importance of particular concepts and their creators, concepts that are not at all static but have been altered over time by different spokespeople and schools of thought that claim a common origin. For an example, we might return to Marxism, which was originally conceived as a "scientific" model that would free humanity but was turned instead into something that denied the possibility of such freedom and worked entirely against the Enlightenment liberalism that made possible Marx's own analysis and career. Ideas, that is, suggest a far more dynamic universe of thought than does "ideology." This is a universe where individuals can be the leaders or followers of an intellectual credo, even its "victims" in a sense, but may modify its principles (to the point of altering the Founders' intentions) in order to try to seize the historical moment.

This leads us to the need to say something about "responsibility." In our perspective, there is a great deal of inescapable complexity here. For example, while it is wrong to say that Marx was the sole dark father of Stalinism, Maoism, and the atrocities of the Khmer Rouge, it is also evident that his writing acted to help inspire communism and its abuses.

Adam Smith was by no means the only Enlightenment philosopher to praise markets and legitimize capitalism, but his ideas regarding "self-interest" and the "invisible hand" came to be exploited by those favoring a rigid free market system that allowed tragedies such as the Irish potato famine of the 1840s and 1850s to be so devastating and the Great Depression of the 1930s to persist as long as it did. As for Darwin, we can hardly ascribe to him the multitude of positive and negative creations that have come from selective application of his principal theory. Linking Darwinian evolution directly to the Holocaust, for instance, by way of "unfitness" and "inferior races" makes no more sense than blaming Adam Smith for the Great Depression. And yet there are connections in both cases that cannot be avoided.

What the reader will see repeatedly in the pages that follow is that powerful concepts like "mode of production," "invisible hand," "natural selection," and "true religion" have been appropriated by others and given enormous force and utility. Often later thinkers stretched and deformed these ideas into rationales for certain types of political or economic action, government policy, racial laws, educational systems, and so on. Some of these impacts have been hugely beneficial; some have been the opposite. In short, we can and indeed we must credit the profound order-making force, emotional draw, and problematic universalism of the thought that emerged from the pens of Smith, Marx, Darwin, and the others we have examined.

In short, we agree with Victor Hugo's quote cited at the start of this introduction. The powerful ideas that we will be studying may be fought against, they may be distorted, and they may be repressed, but in the end, they survive and continue to impact the world.

The Enlightenment

Our book is not an attempt to say anything new about the Enlightenment, a topic so richly studied and debated for over two centuries and recently rethought in a most profound way by Jonathan Israel. Anything that we might add could only seem superficial. But as it forms a central point of reference for every chapter, we are obliged to at least summarize clearly our understanding of it and to ask why it has produced such varying responses, from adoration to virulent hatred.

Immanuel Kant wrote his well-known short essay, "Beantwortung der Frage: Was ist Aufklärung?" (An Answer to the Question: What Is Enlightenment?), in 1784 as a direct response to a query posed by Prussian clergyman and official Friedrich Zöllner. In a footnote to one of his essays, Zöllner had written: "What is enlightenment? This question, which is nearly as important as 'What is truth?' should be answered before one begins to enlighten." Kant did not merely provide a response but a call to arms: "Enlightenment is man's exit from his self-incurred immaturity. Immaturity is the inability to make use of one's intellect without the direction of another. . . . 'Sapere aude! (Dare to know!)' . . . 'Have the courage to make use of your own intellect!' is hence the motto of enlightenment" (Kant 1784/2006, 17). Free thought, rather than dependence on received tradition or official texts, was a better guide to understanding the natural and social worlds. Such understanding could liberate people from past constraints on progress and make them better individuals—that is, more creative and ethical. Kant meant to free humanity from religious dogma and to convince his readers that the new science and moral philosophy he championed would bring an enlightened, rational society.

Politically, the desired outcome was what came to be called classical liberalism. This term has been considerably obscured by its use in contemporary American political discourse. There, "liberalism" means something closer to what the Europeans call social democracy, a position that believes government should be active in pursuing political and social change for greater equality but without taking over too much of the economy that is best served by open and free market forces. Economically, this has meant direct involvement in markets and limiting the power of private wealth. But originally, the Enlightenment liberalism that flourished in the late eighteenth and nineteenth centuries had very little if anything to do with such intentions; it was a call for freedom, tolerance, and democracy. Later, in the nineteenth century, after the ideas of Adam Smith had taken hold, this kind of liberalism was given an economic sense as well, such that the core concept of freedom was extended to mean minimal government control over the free market. True Enlightenment liberalism is well expressed in the American Constitution (1787) and Bill of Rights (1791) and in the French "Declaration of the Rights of Man and of Citizens" (1789). The legitimacy given to slavery in the Constitution, as well as the Reign of Terror in the French Revolution, sullied those ideals. Yet they remained intact for a growing portion of the United States and Europe, and they ultimately came to guide a major share of political and legal action in democracies everywhere. Indeed, by the late twentieth century, they had spread as ideas if not always as institutionalized facts throughout the world and attained enormous importance in promoting individual liberty, as well as human rights.

Freedom of thought and expression, including freedom to practice any religion, are inherent in classical liberal thinking. So is personal liberty as defined by John Locke, that is, the freedom to choose where one lives, what work one does, and with whom one associates. Government's task is to safeguard security and property rights but to interfere as little as possible to do this. Impartiality of laws, transparency of government, and the right of all citizens to participate in choosing those who govern and make laws will guarantee the preservation of a just and liberal order (Locke 1690/1980). As put by Stephen Holmes, who has given us an excellent history of reactionary responses to the Enlightenment:

> Concerning equality, the liberal attitude is traditionalism turned upside down. In traditional societies, as liberals understood them, inherited inequalities were accepted, while new economic inequalities [particularly those that made successful commoner entrepreneurs rich] were unwelcome. Liberals wanted to reverse this pattern, banning aristocracy while considering new inequalities of wealth as perfectly legitimate. (1993, 3–4)

As far as economies were concerned, both free markets and the security of property from arbitrary confiscation were liberal. Unjustified taxation and, later on, constraint by either monopolistic practices or traditional privileges were to be eliminated, while barriers to trade were to be minimized and put to use only on a highly selective basis. In other words, the economics of liberalism were those recommended by Adam Smith.

Enlightenment liberalism also embraced the huge transformation that natural science brought to human knowledge. This meant accepting several key principles: first, the mechanization of the natural world, whose truths could be revealed not through religious texts but through close observation, experiment, and mathematical explanation; second, ordinary human experience was an inadequate guide to understanding nature, so that scientists were free to test and accept findings that might contradict "common sense" or existing explanations; third, the removal of scientific thought as much as possible from emotional and ideological passions; and finally, the acceptance of the idea that science ought to be a disinterested force for good and the improvement of mankind, even if it contradicted traditional ideas (Shapin 1996).

For a great many Europeans in the eighteenth century, this was powerful medicine. Actual, hard truth about nature and the world could no longer be gained from existing and older sources; it now had to be established and proved. All prior understanding, including sacred teachings, was available for testing and falsification. Certainly there was an ultimate order to the universe, but it was an order man could fathom and discover (Baker 1975). Furthermore, the reality of discovery meant scientific knowledge would advance and thus always be partial. The "truth" of one era could well be amended, improved, even replaced by the era that followed. Science thus brought the promise and the threat of remaking human knowledge about the universe, challenging divinely ordained certainties, placing human beings at the center of truth. The exchange of discovery for revelation proved to be an enormously profound transformation, one that added fully to a desacralization of the social and political spheres (Gellner 1992, 80–84). One measure of how profound this transformation became, and how unsettling, is that it continues to generate enemies in many parts of the world, including not least of all in the United States.

This continued opposition, in other words, is itself an element in the legacy of Enlightenment thought. While it has diminished in some parts of the world, in others it has expanded and remains very much alive where antiliberalism has had a long and successful history, even (but should we be surprised?) within a number of nations where modern science was born. Where political antiliberalism and science clash, as we will see in the chapters on Darwin, on fascism, and on fundamentalist religion, science itself has been attacked, along with its commitment to free thought and insistence on questioning received ideas. Such attack, moreover, has not in the least been confined to religious fanatics or worshipers of spiritual truths.

Indeed, it is not only Enlightenment ideas that were originally formulated by intellectuals. At every step of the way, opposition to these ideas has depended just as much on thinkers who have made their position known through books, essays, speeches, and more recently various modern media. This theme will come up repeatedly in our book as well: intellectuals have always been the inventors and key agents for the Counter-Enlightenment as well as the Enlightenment itself. We will propose, in fact, that Immanuel Kant's hope for reason and freedom to prevail remains as contested and uncertain as ever. The conflict between supporters and enemies of these ideas continues, as it has since the late eighteenth century, to be the key struggle of our present and our future.

PART I

INVENTORS OF MODERNITY AND
WHAT BECAME OF THEIR IDEAS

CHAPTER 1

Adam Smith

The Science of Man, Morality, and Money

> It is the highest impertinence and presumption, therefore, in kings and ministers, to pretend to watch over the economy of private people. . . . Let them look well after their own expence, and they may safely trust private people with theirs.
>
> ADAM SMITH, *AN INQUIRY INTO THE NATURE AND CAUSES OF THE WEALTH OF NATIONS*

> Man does not live by GNP alone.
>
> PAUL SAMUELSON, *ECONOMICS*

Adam Smith is known worldwide as the founder of modern economics. However, though he knew French well, he seems never to have uttered or written the phrase "laissez-faire." Like "free enterprise," "entrepreneur," and even "capitalism," it is a term that does not appear in any of his writings, which amount to over a million words. Born in 1723, Smith died in July 1790, four years before the firm of Boulton and Watt produced the first advanced steam engine. Smith thought, lectured, and wrote, that is, before the full advent of the Industrial Revolution, a development of which he knew neither the reality nor the name. Important as this may be, it has never counted against his reputation. Erudite, eccentric, generous but intensely private, living at a time when wood and animals still powered the globe, this eighteenth-century Scotsman nonetheless composed a book destined to explain a modern world of machines, corporations, and global markets running on oil and electricity, powering unimaginable industrial, military, and financial might that would alter the human prospect forever.

Smith himself was not wealthy and was no apologist for the rich. The man who lived quietly in the small town of Kirkcaldy, where *Wealth of Nations* was composed, who breathed the wet sea air from the Firth of Forth and often absentmindedly strolled its mist-laden shores, became a key and in some part radical figure of the Scottish Enlightenment, arguing as much on behalf of working-class laborers as manufacturers and free trade. To be sure it was Adam Smith who wrote that the object of every country's economy is to increase the riches and power of that country. No less did he claim that in a law-abiding state, those who seek to maximize their own gain serve the benefit of all, being "led by an invisible hand to promote an end which was no part of his intention" (Smith 1776 in Cohen and Fermon 1996, 326). Here is the true Adam Smith, economists have often said. But "invisible hand" appears only once in a book of over eight hundred pages, and only three times in all of his writing, leading at least one scholar to suggest it may have been nothing more than a sarcastic phrase (Rothschild 2001, 117). This does create a problem for economists who have made it the center of his thought. It was this same Adam Smith, after all, not his presumed opposite, Karl Marx, who wrote that when "regulation is in support of the workman, it is always just and equitable" (Smith 1776, 143). It was Smith, too, whom Thomas Malthus charged with confusing the wealth of a state with the happiness of its lower classes.

This complex thinker is not the Adam Smith so many have come to believe in. Indeed, anyone with knowledge of Smith's reputation who reads *An Inquiry into the Nature and Causes of the Wealth of Nations* today with a clear eye will be struck by the subtlety of his thought and by the gap between what has been most often said about Smith and what he actually said. They may also find it surprising that he has a sense of humor, dry as gin. "By nature, a philosopher is not in genius and disposition half so different from a street porter, as a mastiff is from a greyhound," he tells us (1776, 18). The literature dealing with his thought would by now fill a well-endowed public library, and this includes much excellent historiography that takes this literature as subject of inquiry, critique, and correction (Winch 1978; Jones and Skinner 1992; Rothschild 2001; Milgate and Stimson 2009).

It is the real Smith that deserves our interest. As economists who have studied him carefully know, the varied strands of his thinking remain even today the basis of most schools in the field, even those that seem to oppose each other.

He wrote only two books, but the range of his mind revealed in these works was vast, his interests spacious, his thought many-layered. This helps explain the complexities of *Wealth of Nations* in particular. Like all great works, it has many levels and is more wide-ranging, diverse, and bewildering than any one group of ideas. In addition to the division of labor and trade, it takes up matters of education, colonialism, the nature of sovereignty, civil society, natural resources, and a great deal more. It endorses certain trade restrictions and taxes on transportation, it favors universal schooling for the poor, and it expresses a healthy distrust of merchants at all times. But it is also a plea for the right of individuals to make their own decisions about how to conduct their lives, and it is in favor of eliminating the many restrictions on trade that were then current in Britain and even more on the European continent. Allowing markets to operate freely was part of this, if not the only part. In other words, the Adam Smith of the eighteenth-century Scottish Enlightenment can be interpreted by the fervid apostles of total free market thinking that some economists have favored only if they look at one side of his writing, ignoring much else that he stood for. One thing, perhaps, we can say for certain: as a man in some anxiety about his future legacy, who on his deathbed had close friends burn his remaining manuscripts, Smith would have been pained to see what some have made of him but perhaps pleased that he remains so important and the source of study.

There are other ironies to contemplate. Smith's real goal was to map out human nature, yet his own life remains largely an outline. To biographers, he "lacks visibility"; he left no journal, autobiography, or other record of his detailed existence (Phillipson 2010). We are fairly sure that he visited many workplaces and markets, discussed the things he saw, and wrote down what he learned. But there is no documentation of this. To those who would ask for more, Smith offers only negative advice: "The character of a man is never very striking . . . [but] a dull and lifeless thing, taken merely by itself" (Smith 1976–87, vol. 4, 132). Though he lectured about trade and wage labor, about law and politics, about military matters and industrial production, Smith partook little in any of these areas himself. He was highly conscientious, doing much administrative work while teaching at Glasgow, and was no less involved in his work as customs commissioner. But he was no public figure; he even shunned debates about his books. Intensely private, Smith was physically small and unattractive, internally directed. He never married and never seems to have had extended amorous experiences of any kind. He was, instead, a teacher who lived with his mother for many years in the same seaside town of 2,300 where he was born.

Yet, from a certain perspective, the lack of drama can only be called appropriate. Nearly everything Smith had to say he girded with his own keen observation and his brilliant, intense powers of deduction, sharpened by a deep scholarship of and sympathy for Greek and Roman antiquity. He seems to have had a remarkable memory that he plied with unending study, without limits as to subject or depth. Intellectual commerce with so many domains of learning no doubt helped fuel his lifelong ambition to unlock the principles of human nature. But in seeking this, Smith remained cerebral above all. He preferred observation to participation, contemplation to exploit, scholarship to leadership. We perceive that his life was mainly a vehicle for his thought.

THE WORLD OF ADAM SMITH

Adam Smith was born on June 5, 1723, just a few months after the death of his father. Sickly and infirm as a child, he "required all the tender solicitude of his surviving parent" to continue in life, as Dugald Stewart, Smith's first biographer, puts it (Stewart 1858, 5). Never spoiled by such attentions, and prevented by physical frailty from ever engaging in the normal pursuits of active boys, he was nonetheless much-loved by his schoolmates "on account of his temper, which, though warm, was to an uncommon degree friendly and generous" (Stewart 1800, 6). He spent much time alone, often talking to himself, developing the absentmindedness for which he would one day be famous. There is a story Stewart tells that baby Smith was stolen one night by a troop of Roma and that an uncle raced out into the darkness to recover him. Whether the tale be true or not, it is amusing to think of how poor a Gypsy the father of economics would have made.

His parents were comfortably middle class. His mother, Margaret Douglas, came from a family of landowners; his father, Adam, was a lawyer with connections to Scottish political circles. Adam senior came of age in an uncertain period for Scotland, whose fate as a nation was undecided until the 1707 Treaty of Union that created the kingdom of Great Britain. The elder Smith profited considerably in the new era, however, gaining significant positions in the administration, ending up as Controller of Customs at Kirkcaldy. He died of unknown causes when his wife was three months pregnant with their son, whom she named Adam. The father's success left the family well-off, and Margaret was able to live comfortably in Kirkcaldy near friends and relatives for many years, greatly indulging her gifted son and developing a special bond that would trump—indeed take the place of—all other female companionship.

What were the outlines of his career? Adam the son left home at fourteen to attend the University of Glasgow but returned for his vacations, both as a student and later as a professor. He did his studies here and at the University of Oxford, where his reading was broad, deep, and incessant. He afterward launched himself in entrepreneurial fashion by giving a series of public lectures at Edinburgh on rhetoric, literature, and jurisprudence. These gained him a following and led to a post at his alma mater in Glasgow, where he remained for thirteen years, teaching topics related to moral theory, history, Greek and Latin authors, and, eventually, political economy. He then left university life, first to become tutor for a young aristocrat, the Duke of Buccleuh, on a Grand Tour of Europe, and then, after moving back with his mother and publishing *Wealth of Nations*, to accept appointment as Commissioner of Customs, a position he held until his death.

From humanist professor, to tutor for the wealthy, to tax collector— such was the angular trajectory of Adam Smith's professional life. He was certainly open to opportunities for advancement but did not seem particularly concerned to acquire riches. He joined the world of commerce only at the very end, well after *Wealth of Nations* was published.

Tutoring the young duke gave him the chance to visit France and talk with the most important thinkers on economic matters of the day and Switzerland, for a brief and disappointing meeting with his intellectual idol, Voltaire. His first book, published in 1759, *The Theory of Moral Sentiments*, was based on his lectures at Glasgow. It established a reputation for him but was followed by very little over the next twenty-five years. *Wealth of Nations* appeared in 1776 and became, in time, the source of the worldwide fame he now enjoys but of which he saw only a little in his own lifetime. There are a few other essays on the history of science and jurisprudence, plus a meager correspondence, little else. Well-known in his own time as a moral philosopher, not a scientist or economist, Smith was hardly prolific. Today's university tenure committees might well view him with a skeptical or unkind eye.

Smith, in fact, strikes us as neither a heroic figure nor a tragic one. His life had few outward signs of excitement, and his ending speaks only softly of pathos. It was in his Kirkcaldy home where he composed the major part of *Wealth of Nations* and where, alongside his aging mother, he himself grew prematurely old, worn down by long hours of work, a frail constitution, and hypochondria. His mother's death at ninety proved to be devastating. Indeed, it marked a true loss of vigor and the beginning of his own end, which came only six years later after a protracted invalidism. By the age of sixty-seven, the man whose ideas would shift the axis of the modern world's understanding of trade and economic well-being was spent. He would not live to complete even half of the grand project to which his intellectual life had been devoted. As he never married and had no sons or daughters, no legacy existed for him except his writings. His life seems to have been a source of curiosity to others. He was said to speak to himself on his walks and to have fallen into a tanner's pit while engaged in a lecture to a friend. Alexander Carlyle, a conservative church leader in Scotland, recounts that Smith's voice "was harsh and in enunciation thick, approaching to stammering. His conversation was not colloquial, but like lecturing. . . . He was the most absent man in company that I ever saw, moving his lips, and talking to himself, and smiling. . . . If you awaked him from his reverie and made him attend to the subject of conversation, he immediately began a harangue, and never stopped till he told you all he knew about it, with the utmost philosophical ingenuity" (Carlyle 1860, 279).

If Carlyle can be trusted, it would appear that Adam Smith found society a difficult proposition, though an infinite subject of intellectual interest. This brings us back to his grand project. What was this project, whose ambition was so vast? It was nothing less than a complete and "genuine Science of Man based on the observation of human nature and human history; a science which would not only explain the principles of social and political organization . . . but [those] of government and legislation that ought to be followed by enlightened rulers" (Phillipson 2010, 2). It was thus a project that went even beyond the goals of the great French *Encyclopédie*, which sought to collect all knowledge in the sciences, arts, and professions as the foundation of Enlightenment progress (*Des sciences, des arts et des métiers* 1751–72). Smith was after more: the elemental natural laws of human behavior and social existence.

The World as Adam Smith Knew It

Smith was a member of a small but special group of thinkers born in the last decades of the seventeenth and the first quarter of the eighteenth century. Scotland at the time remained one of the poorest, most backward nations in all of western Europe. Yet from its soil issued the likes of Francis Hutcheson, James Steuart, David Hume, Adam Ferguson, James Watt, James Hutton, Joseph Black, and Smith himself. This group added to Western thought in nearly every major domain of knowledge, from politics and economics to science and belles lettres. Each man pursued, in varied fashion, an embrace of reason and individual autonomy. All believed in the power of a scientific frame of mind to penetrate both the material and mental realms (Oz-Salzberger 2003).

Much of the outlook of these Scottish thinkers was both intellectual and practical. They sought to delineate what was important to know and how it could be applied toward daily life. It was an outlook that received impetus from the Treaty of Union with England passed in 1707, which, by midcentury, had altered Scotland from an agrarian realm of fields and clans to a center of trade and traders. Progress in this setting meant buying and selling no less than learning and discovering. It was to define a paradigm of political, moral, and social guidance for the new Scotland that this group of intellectuals, inventors, and scientists labored (Merikoski 2002; Berry 1997; Haakonssen 1996).

The preceding century, meanwhile, had seen enormous turmoil in England, beginning with the Civil War (1642–51) and ending with the Glorious Revolution of 1688. Catholic France under Louis XIV and his successors, the most powerful nation in Europe, acted as the great threat to Protestant nations. Confrontation with Britain eventually erupted into what some historians have characterized as the first true world conflict, the Seven Years' War, fought round the globe, particularly in the New World (where it was called French and Indian War, 1756–63) and in India. British victory in this great struggle seemed to guarantee advantage, despite subsequent defeat in the American Revolution (1776–81). India became the key possession of England's imperial domain, while the Royal Navy secured a dominion over the seas that would last until the middle of the twentieth century.

Political events did not retard the coming of a market transformation impacting all of western Europe. This commercial revolution involved an expansion powered by colonialism, the growth not only of trading empires, such as the Hudson's Bay and East India companies, but also of joint stock enterprises modeled on those originated by the Dutch, launching many new overseas ventures and flooding Europe with new goods and raw materials. If, in Shakespeare's day, people in Britain relied on local farms and artisans for their necessaries and luxuries, a century and a half later they were buying tobacco from America, nails from Germany, wine from France, linen from Belfast, spices and silks from India, and sugar from the West Indies. Britain was now a major exporting nation, too, taking in raw materials from its colonies and turning them into expensive manufactured goods. Merchants and retailers, storekeepers and company managers were now rising members of society. This transformation was fully in evidence by the years 1740 to 1780, when Adam Smith was at the height of his powers (Mokyr 2010).

It was also when the Enlightenment as a whole, and specifically in Scotland, reached a certain peak of intellectual activity and production (Broadie 2001). A deep change in the idea of "wealth" and its meaning was about to take place. Ever since the classical period, that is, pursuit of riches for their own sake was considered a base activity, particularly in comparison to seeking honor, glory, and virtue, all noble ends. By the eighteenth century, however, as Albert Hirschman has argued, this view had come to be increasingly questioned. Commerce and the peaceful quest of gain were now being rethought as antidotes to the unending wars waged in the name of honor, religion, and the sheer lust for power (Hirschman 1977, 9–66).

One of the most powerful and respected minds to promote this view was the Frenchman Charles Louis de Secondat, Baron de Montesquieu. His widely read and highly influential 1748 work, *Spirit of the Laws*, argued with calm elegance that the creation of wealth by commerce had its own reality, its own demand for liberty, and its own impact upon the state. "Peace is the natural effect of commerce," he wrote. "Two nations that trade with each other become reciprocally dependent; if one has an interest in buying, the other has an interest in selling, and all unions are founded on mutual needs" (Montesquieu 1989, 338). Montesquieu also speaks of the individual: an overdeveloped desire for wealth can render all one's actions mercenary. But "the spirit of commerce," of exchange among equals, "produces in men a certain feeling of exact justice [and fairness]." It compels "those moral virtues that make it so that one does not always discuss one's own interests alone [but] can neglect them for those of others" (Montesquieu 1989, 339).

Here was a vital concept that Adam Smith would later adapt to his own advantage. Indeed, that private interest could lead to larger benefit was an idea held by other writers of varied type, as Albert Hirschman (1977) has pointed out. In 1725 Giambattista Vico in his *New Science* stated that "the passions of men entirely occupied by the pursuit of their private utility are transformed into a civil order" (cited in Hirschman 1977, 17). David Hume in 1752 and James Steuart in 1767 had expressed similar thoughts, that self-interest and a passion for enrichment were forces for general social prosperity (Hirschman 1977). All of these works predated Smith's writing of *Wealth of Nations*.

But the most well-known version of the concept came in a very different form. Bernard Mandeville (1670–1733), a Dutch doctor living in London, created a storm with his poetic satire, *The Fable of the Bees: or,*

Private Vices, Publick Benefits, published in 1714. Provocatively, Mandeville utterly denied any positive role for Christian virtue in social progress. All public advantage, he said, came from selfishness and avarice, and this applied to matters economic, too: "Luxury employ'd a Million of the Poor / And odious Pride a Million more: / Envy itself, and Vanity / Were Ministers of Industry" (Mandeville 1924, vol. 1, 25). The conceit was neither jest nor jibe. The author made fun of moral pedantries yet was dead serious in his claim that greed and pride and the endless ambitions they impel drive people to success: "Bare Virtue can't make Nations live in Splendor" (1924, vol. 1, 35). The idle rich who care little for others still spend money on clothes, food, art, and travel and thus put to work tailors, cooks, painters, coachmen. Mandeville sees this as human nature. When humanity is placed under the lens, like a bee, what appears is original sin channeled into productivity. Progress will happen as long as vice-like passions have an outlet, a goal that government can best serve. If Montesquieu saw commerce as a cultivating force, Mandeville conceived it as a paradox—uncivilized urges yoked to a civilizing purpose.

The other piece of eighteenth-century sensibility that Smith had to contend with was the French school of economic thought known as Physiocracy. Leadership of the school rested with François Quesnay (1694–1774), a royal physician in the court of Louis XV and contributor to the great *Encyclopédie*. In 1759, Quesnay privately published *Tableau Économique*, a type of stylish flowchart, showing monetary movements through the French economy. This became the acknowledged basis of the Physiocratic system. The chart is drawn as a balanced, mathematical diagram, with nodes and diagonals that resemble schema showing the organization of the heavens, the hierarchy of life, the structure of the human body, and other scientific images. Quesnay conceived the major economic actors as farmers, landlords, and manufacturers. Farmers were "productive" and landlords acted as the holders of cash. Manufacturers, however, were "sterile," as they made use of materials produced by others, did not generate a surplus, and lived off the farmers. This reflected something of the situation in France, which remained more agrarian and less commercial than England. What was truly new in Quesnay's scheme, however, was his proposal of interdependence at every level and that money was only one type of asset: the farmer had capital in his grain, the landlord in land, the manufacturer in goods. These forms of capital, with money as a carrier of value, flowed efficiently and productively only if exchange was allowed to operate naturally, with "complete liberty," as the Physiocrats put it. Individuals, too, must be allowed such freedom, since, as one of the group's major members, Marquis de Mirabeau, declared, "The whole magic of a well-ordered society is that each man works for others, while believing that he works for himself" (1764, vol. 1, 117).

The Physiocrats were therefore harshly critical of the French government's attempts to manipulate the circulation of capital. They blamed high taxes, domestic tolls, import duties, and other barriers to trade for the poverty of the country's lower classes. Quesnay understood that his diagram was an abstraction, a model, but still saw it as a true discovery of natural order that showed only damage and stagnancy could result from the monarchy's meddling policies. This was especially true for those policies that impacted farmers, such as high duties on imported machinery that allowed French manufacturers to keep their own prices high. The purpose of a nation's economy is to grow; it could not do this if its natural processes were obstructed. "Laissez-faire, laissez-passer" ("Leave things alone, let them happen on their own") was the phrase that Quesnay apparently used in his discussions with others, a phrase whose ultimate origin remains unclear but which Quesnay made important.

The outlook that the Physiocrats opposed—and that Adam Smith would come to demolish—was mercantilism. Quesnay called it "Colbertism," since he saw its strongest proponent as France's former minister of finance under Louis XIV, Jean-Baptiste Colbert. This brand of economic philosophy and policy arose out of the circumstances of competitive protectionism, whereby the powerful nations of Europe each sought a high degree of self-sufficiency, based largely on control over political and economic activity. Monarchies saw trade as a zero-sum game; a state could best advance its condition only at the expense of others. This would happen if it hoarded its prime economic assets, gold and silver; if it exported more goods to other nations than it imported from them; and if it used its colonies as a private market, taking natural resources from them and selling back finished goods to them, with no allowance for a reverse flow by which the colonies could become more self-sufficient themselves. All capital was monetary and every government had to be protectionist; subsidies should be used to encourage domestic production and tariffs to reduce imports (Milgate and Stimson 2009).

It was a patchwork system in place for nearly two centuries when Adam Smith, influenced by Quesnay to some degree, and others still more, came to write *Wealth of Nations* in the 1760s. Smith found the strongest and most influential British proponent for mercantilism in Thomas Mun, a merchant of the early 1600s who, for a time, was director of the East India Company. Mun's posthumous *England's Treasure by Forraign Trade* (1664) argues the program very clearly. "The ordinary means . . . to encrease our wealth and treasure," he says, "is by *Forraign Trade*, wherein wee must ever observe this rule: to sell more to strangers yearly than wee consume of theirs in value" (McCulloch 1856, 125). Mun further proposed that all of England's fallow lands be turned to production in order to reduce or even eliminate whatever had to be imported for food. People should "soberly refrain from excessive consumption of forraign wares" so as to lessen all dependence on "strangers" (McCulloch 1856, 127). On the other hand, any English merchant would do well to take note of "our neighbors necessities," especially those in short supply, so he can find an opportunity to "sell them dear." All ships that transport English goods should be English ships; fishing "in his Majesties seas" should be by English fishermen; foreign wares "may be the more charged, which will . . . profit of the Kingdom in the *Balance of the Trade*" (McCulloch 1856, 133).

Mercantilism expressed an almost combative, fearful type of nationalism. "Beggar thy neighbor" was not quite the tenor of it; more accurate would be Mun's own phrase "sell them dear." But Thomas Mun was ahead of his time in one important area, and Adam Smith applauds him in this. Mun understands, Smith says, "that the exportation of gold and silver, in order to purchase foreign goods, did not always diminish the quantity of those metals in the kingdom; that, on the contrary, it might frequently increase the quantity" (Smith 1904, 398). The reason was that such goods, for example, spices and rugs from

India, could be resold to other nations at a high profit. Trade therefore, as Mun analogized it, could be compared to seeding and harvesting in agriculture. It was an image that Smith liked well enough to quote.

Adam Smith's Teachers

No great thinker conceives a program out of whole cloth. Smith had his predecessors and intellectual parents, as we've said, above all Francis Hutcheson and David Hume. He did not inhabit an era entirely before economics either. We know that he visited Quesnay himself in the 1760s, during his stay in France, and became friendly with a number of the Physiocrats, including Turgot and Mirabeau. We also know that this group was the very first to refer to themselves as "economists" (*économistes*). Smith spoke of Quesnay as a "very ingenious and profound author" and of the Physiocratic system, with its rejection of mercantilism, as full of imperfections yet "perhaps the nearest approximation to the truth that has yet been published upon the subject of political economy." Yet economics (or political economy), for which Smith is remembered, was not Smith's main concern. It was only meant to be an entry in the greater dream, albeit an important one.

Professionally speaking, by work and reputation, Adam Smith was a moral philosopher, like his mentor Francis Hutcheson. But by aspiration and achievement, he was a philosopher more generally, like his close friend David Hume. These two men, Hutcheson and Hume, who both wrote influential books with much discussion of ethics, social relations, and commercial society, impressed upon their younger colleague the need for philosophy to take a new turn. This venerable field, they said, should not merely theorize or pronounce upon its topics; nor should it waste time wading in the misty, heated waters of metaphysics. It should dive deeper, search for the underlying *principia* (the Newtonian word for natural laws) of human nature that direct everything else. True philosophy should be aimed at action—employing the lessons of science, its tools of observation and deduction, to discover the reasons why humans act, think, love, go to war, and build nations as they do, and how such discovery could be used to determine the ways by which a people might best grow in prosperity, liberty, and happiness. The intent, in short, was not merely intellectual or academic. Philosophy must aim at helping create a better Britain, a better Europe, and ultimately a better world.

Adam Smith was fortunate enough to be directly, indeed personally, influenced by these two great figures of Scotland's Enlightenment. Hutcheson, who held the Chair of Moral Philosophy at the University of Glasgow while Smith was a student there, had gained a considerable European reputation by the 1730s, both for his writings on man as a positive moral being (so designed by the Almighty) and for his unprecedented style of lecturing. Hutcheson was the first in his position to lecture in English, not Latin, and to do so with a species of enthusiasm, a mixing of drama and delight, that bewitched his students. He did this while delivering the message that human action is not sourced in primitive self-love, as Thomas Hobbes had claimed, or in jungles of vice, as Mandeville maintained, but instead in a natural inclination toward benevolence. Human beings had an innate "moral sense," given by God, that could be extended further by reason. In this, Hutcheson was himself influenced by Anthony Ashley Cooper, better known as Lord Shaftesbury (1671–1713), an erudite aristocrat who proposed that man tended toward virtue, being endowed with a conscience and reason to discern right from wrong. This kind of natural theology Shaftesbury saw as advancing the harmony of society in many aspects of life; his essays, therefore, took up art, politics, culture, and manners. Hutcheson, too, wrote and lectured on many subjects: ethics, aesthetics, logic, marriage, law, religion, literature, the history of societies, government, and trade. Such was the span of moral philosophy at the time. Its reach had grown in large part as a result of the challenges presented by the incessant wars over religion and the great brutality and insecurity they had brought in the previous century (Thirty Years' War, 1618–48). The writings of men like Hugo Grotius and Samuel von Pufendorf on the subject of ethics came to stress the concept of natural law, a complex idea that was sometimes tied to divine power but increasingly treated in more secular terms, as embedded in human nature and its rational aspects. These aspects were linked directly to ideas of fairness, trust, and systems of jurisprudence. Commerce, too, came into play, as an expression of fair exchange and as an agent of social cohesion. Under the impact of the Scientific Revolution, moral philosophy therefore sought its own rooting in the finality of nature (Broadie 2001).

Hutcheson blended these trends with two potent convictions that he pursued all his life and taught to all his students: first, that human nature was not innately corrupt, as Christian doctrine had long taught, but possessed "high dignity" and "great capacity for good"; second, that the most powerful and useful forms of knowledge were those that could employ observation and evidence toward some kind of demonstrable truth. It is no fortuity, therefore, that in his lectures, as collected in the posthumous *A System of Moral Philosophy* (1755), we find not only treatment of human perception and the nature of happiness but discussion of liberty and right to property, the conduct of commercial enterprise, and the types and roles of government. Describing Hutcheson's philosophy as "inclusive" would be an understatement.

As a teenager of fourteen when he entered the university, Adam Smith was among those deeply impressed by Hutcheson's munificent style. It seems he took his teacher's lecturing, with its mixture of performance and learnedness, as a model for building his own successful career. Hutcheson's expansive knowledge of classical authors (long passages from whom he could quote at will, with appropriate effect), his use of examples from common life, his emphasis on civil and religious liberty for social progress, and his demand for knowledge that was valuable and useful, that could be put toward some concrete form of betterment, all had a deep impact on Smith.

But if Hutcheson was crucial to Adam Smith's outlook, David Hume was essential. Hume's massive and restless intellect remained unparalleled by any philosopher of the time, except perhaps Jean-Jacques Rousseau and Immanuel Kant. Of all English and Scottish philosophers, Hume is perhaps second only to Smith in his influence on later thinkers. In his own day, however, he inspired a volatile mixture of admiration for his originality and denunciation for his questioning of accepted norms and religious piety. In fact, for placing imagination and the passions above reason, and for denying any role to theology in moral conceptions, he earned the eternal enmity of Hutcheson. Smith himself received a verbal thrashing at Oxford when he was discovered to have a copy in his rooms of Hume's *Treatise of Human Nature* (1739). The university had banned the book and immediately confiscated Smith's copy, an act of invasion that he never forgot or forgave.

Hume, like Smith, spent long hours as a youth following a rigorous, self-imposed program of reading and reflection, focused on classical authors. His own early books, especially the *Treatise*, established him as a notable skeptic and (to some, at least) an atheist. He was denied two academic posts that he much desired: the Chair of Pneumatics (mental workings) and Moral Philosophy at the University of Edinburgh and the Chair of Moral Philosophy at the University of Glasgow, which went to Smith. He was constantly under attack by the Church of Scotland and was even charged with heresy. Scotland, it appeared, could give birth to a diversity of great minds but remained unable to appreciate them (Mossner 2001).

Gregarious nonetheless, Hume traveled widely on the Continent and was on friendly terms with many eminent thinkers. Warm, outgoing, and interested in others, Hume attracted much esteem during this lifetime, and it is likely Smith appreciated his friendship most of all. Smith and Hume met in Edinburgh sometime during 1750, probably after one of Smith's public lectures. The two men soon became friends, though Hume was twelve years the senior and Smith had gained the post Hume desired at Glasgow. It was a relationship that would deepen with time. Yet even before their first handshake, Smith knew the older man's work intimately and was putting it to profitable use in his own thought (Phillipson 2010). Hume likely observed this in Smith's lecture and felt flattered and also amused. Here was a man spreading *his* ideas and getting paid for it. He was not one, however, to begrudge another gentleman of obvious intellect for using his work, especially one like Smith, who intrigued him. Hume, moreover, had already published several books and would go on to produce a fair number of others. Besides the *Treatise*, he had already produced *Essays, Moral and Political* in 1741–42 and *Philosophical Essays* in 1748, and he was about to bring out *Political Discourses* in 1752, a book that would prove pivotal to Adam Smith's thinking on commerce.

Hume spoke of the mind as a nexus of struggle, an unending roil of impressions and emotions. Experience, writ large, is all that we really have: "Let us chase our imagination to the heavens, or to the utmost limits of the universe; we never really advance a step beyond ourselves" (Hume 1826, vol. 1, 97). Morality is no different. It has no divine basis or foundation in rational thought. Human beings do have natural inclinations toward a number of passions—love, pride, hope, fear, and self-interest among them—but no wonderfully implanted "moral sense." People learn to be moral by observing the agreeable and beneficial consequences of their actions upon others and the actions of others on them. It is an empirical process expressed in the *Treatise*'s subtitle: *Being an Attempt to Introduce the Experimental Method of Reasoning into Moral Subjects.* Such a theory is therefore distinctly secular. It is also profoundly uncertain. It was too hard and cold for Scottish sensibilities at the time, and nearly so for England. But to Adam Smith, it was light and warmth. Both Hutcheson and Hume offered Smith the goal of a "Science of Man," but only Hume proposed a method.

The *Treatise* convinced Smith that he needed to pursue close and uncompromising inspection of the human mind and heart, what we would roughly call psychology today. This would provide the essential base from which to derive enduring *principia* about society and how it should be guided. In his Edinburgh lectures, he had advertised discussion of "rhetoric" and "jurisprudence," but he ranged far more widely than this, taking up topics in literature, language, systems of property, good and bad governance, concepts of justice, and "civil society" (a term he borrowed from Hutcheson). He touched upon commercial enterprise as well, but this appears not to have become a major preoccupation until he read Hume's *Political Discourses*, soon after accepting the position at the University of Glasgow. According to Dugald Stewart's biography, few books affected Smith's thought as this one did. Hume was no stranger to economic subjects, having dealt with these in his early *Essays, Moral and Political*. But in *Political Discourses*, he placed them front and center, taking up, in order: commerce, luxury, money, interest, balance of trade, taxes, public credit, and the idea of a Perfect Commonwealth. Hume proposed "The greatness of a state and the happiness of its subjects . . . are . . . inseparable with regard to commerce; and as private men receive greater security, in the possession of their trade and riches . . . so the public becomes powerful in proportion to the riches and extensive commerce of private men" (1826, vol. 3, 287).

The implications of such reasoning, for the link between economic freedom and "civil society," as well as the value of trade and a competitive merchant class, were not lost on Adam Smith. Nor was Hume's conclusion that money forms the real object of commercial exchange. Rather, money is "[not] the wheels of trade [but] the oil, which renders the motion of the wheels more smooth and easy" (Hume 1826, vol. 3, 317). When it increases, "labour and industry gain life; the merchant becomes more enterprising; the manufacturer more diligent and skillful; even the farmer follows his plough with greater alacrity and attention" (Hume 1826, vol. 3, 322). Hume understood that opening the economy to foreign trade, rather than being protectionist, was beneficial. Prohibitions and duties placed on the import and export of commodities will only weaken the entire system. Foreign trade, he says, "by its imports, furnishes materials for new manufactures; and by its exports, it produces labour in particular commodities, which could not be consumed at home. In short, a kingdom that has a large import and export, must abound more with industry . . . than a kingdom which rests contented with its native commodities" (Hume 1826, vol. 3, 296). The reason was simple. Workers and commodities were the true strength of any national economy, and restricting trade artificially to force surpluses only weakened it.

From Hume, Adam Smith learned many important things: the utility of self-interest (enlightened or not); the multiform, circulating nature of capital; the importance of labor; the relationship between wages and prices; and most of all the self-defeating character of protectionism as well as the futility of chasing after gold and silver, the bedrock of still popular mercantilism. Smith took all of these ideas, as he did those from Hutcheson, and made them his own. He chiseled and sanded them over the next eight years through his popular and much-anticipated lectures at Glasgow, polishing them further for *Theory of Moral Sentiments* (1759). It would be decades, however, before *Wealth of Nations* appeared. But that was fitting, and indeed necessary. Smith would go well beyond his two mentors in this work, mull over other writings in the meantime, like Richard Cantillon's book on the nature of commerce (*Essai sur la nature du commerce* published in 1755), and combine years of visits to merchants and their factories to produce his massively complex book.

As Emma Rothschild has written, Smith's philosophical outlook, like Hume's, was really one of deep uncertainty. This was also true of leading French Enlightenment philosophers like Condorcet. They rejected the certainty of religious faith and a divinely ordered world, accepting instead the insecurity of explanations that grappled with the reality of imperfectly informed and frequently illogical humans. For the Enlightenment, it was human beings who made the world. It was a frightening but also liberating idea, one that freed humanity from the belief that a higher, nonhuman fate controlled its destiny (Rothschild 2001, 38; Baker 1975). As Hume saw more clearly than most, this gave to human beings a fundamental responsibility: the world, after all, had to be unraveled by the mind alone, which, out of the unending anarchy of external phenomena and internal impressions, could perhaps discover the true underlying principles that gave order to everything. In 1734 Alexander Pope had written in *An Essay on Man* (Epistle I, part X) that "All Nature is but art, unknown to thee, All chance, direction, which thou canst not see; discord harmony not understood, all partial evil universal good." To Hume, as to a great deal of Enlightenment thought, this seemed like the voice of childish superstition. A philosopher of Smith's ambition, seeking the elements of a "science of man," rejected this claim that ultimate truth lay beyond sight and grasp, in the hands of the Almighty alone. Not so, said Smith and Hume, it is right here before us, in the workings of the daily world. The power of Smith's modernism, which rendered Pope and his ilk into quaint antiquities, consisted exactly in this view: the order of society, however much part of God's plan, is nonetheless knowable through close scrutiny and firm analysis, giving man a grasp of fundamental laws and therefore an ability and duty to improve what exists.

The World That Adam Smith Wanted to Build

Adam Smith's *Theory of Moral Sentiments* appeared in 1759, when Smith was thirty-six. It was followed by *Wealth of Nations* in 1776, when its author had reached the age of fifty-three. There is also a collection, *Essays on Philosophical Subjects* (1795), a small handful of reviews, roughly two hundred letters in all, and three collections of student notes from his lectures at Glasgow. The *Essays* were edited and brought to press five years after Smith's death by his literary executors, the chemist Joseph Black and geologist James Hutton. These were the same two friends who, attending to the bedridden author in his final days, were ordered to burn nearly all his unpublished writings right there on the spot. Many volumes of manuscript pages were apparently condemned to the flame. If this counts as a great loss to posterity (it does), we can at least find solace in Hutton's mention that the destruction did make Smith's mind "much relieved" and thus his end more bearable, even congenial (Buchan 2006).

Smith's two books had grand goals. They sought to explain how societies worked and how they could be made more civil and moral. Though their subjects appear entirely different, the two works were born from a consistent philosophical outlook, and to neglect the first, *The Theory of Moral Sentiments*, while nurturing attention only on *Wealth of Nations* is to miss fundamental parts of what Smith was trying to do.

Moral Sentiments

There is something a bit startling about *The Theory of Moral Sentiments*. Written at a time when daily life in Western society was structured in profoundly different ways than today, Smith's treatise still reads as highly credible psychology. In this work, Smith has put his own self under a microscope and probed it rigorously with honed instruments. He is no romantic, and yet he has clearly embarked on a voyage to the heart's interior. His interest is in the actual processes by which people learn to behave well, the feelings and mental experiences they use to evaluate their own actions and those of others. What does he say about this process? He expands on the idea of "sympathy" mentioned by Hume. Smithian sympathy means putting ourselves in another's position, projecting our emoting self into the circumstances of someone else, and, however imperfectly, going through what they go through. Then, by stepping back as an "Impartial Spectator," we evaluate whether the actions pursued by this other person are good ones, those we would have chosen. Smithian sympathy thus combines empathy with judgment.

Theory opens with a salvo against Mandeville as well as a clever rhetorical move: "How selfish soever man may be supposed, there are evidently some principles in his nature which interest him in the fortune of others, and render their happiness necessary to him, though he derives nothing from it except the pleasure of seeing it" (Smith 1984, 9). This seems a happy beginning; humans do have some innate goodness (a nod to Hutcheson). Only a few lines later, though, the author shifts focus: "Though our brother is upon the rack, as long as we ourselves are at our ease our senses will never inform us of what he suffers. . . . [I]t is by the imagination only that we can form any conception of what are his sensations . . . [that] we . . . enter as it were into his body and become in some measure him" (9). Smith calls up the image of a "mob, when they are gazing at a dancer on the slack rope," how they "naturally writhe and twist and balance their own bodies, as they see him do" (10). In the first two pages, then, we are taken from pleasure in another's pleasure to twitching at the end of the hangman's noose. Smith has our attention. We are gripped by these concrete examples and by a desire to know what is coming next.

Smith, however, doesn't always satisfy such desire. He seems to be searching himself and to stumble upon critical ideas. His writing has an eccentric quality, like the author himself on his long walks by the sea or through the fish market. We are drawn along through the irregular yet lush and sometimes weedy terrain of Smith's interior landscape, finding an isolated flower at many turns. Tucked away in a torturous paragraph on "selfish passions," we come across this: "the chief part of human happiness arises from the consciousness of being beloved" (1984, 41). It is an observation that makes us pause and one that is repeated in a number of places, where the author speaks about the deep need human beings have for "esteem and approbation." But Smith is interested in more than pithy maxims. In a chapter on "the origin of ambition," he says:

> It is because mankind are disposed to sympathise more entirely with our joy than with our sorrow, that we make parade of our riches, and conceal our poverty. . . . For to what purpose is all the toil and bustle of this world? What is the end of avarice and ambition, of the pursuit of wealth, of power, and preheminence? . . . To

be observed, to be attended to, to be taken notice of. . . . The rich man glories in his riches, because he feels they naturally draw upon him the attention of the world, and that mankind are disposed to go along with him in all those agreeable emotions with which the advantages of his situation so readily inspire him. (1984, 50)

We want to be wealthy to be admired and desired because this is how we feel about the wealthy ourselves. It is a conclusion with which even Freudians might agree.

Adam Smith, however, is no apologist for aristocracy. Indeed, he has cutting words for this stratum of society. The majestic bearing and solar gaze of a Louis XIV are "frivolous accomplishments" because before them, the genuine talents of ordinary people, including "knowledge, industry, valour, and beneficence . . . [lose] all dignity" (1984, 54). It is exactly these talents that are crucial for the "common man" who wishes to succeed. And here Smith gives us a pointed portrait of the "entrepreneur," who, "if ever he hopes to distinguish himself . . . must acquire superior knowledge in his profession, and superior industry in the exercise of it. He must be patient in labour, resolute in danger, and firm in distress." Moreover, "these talents he must bring into public view, by the difficulty, importance, and . . . good judgment of his undertakings, and by the severe and unrelenting application with which he pursues them" (1984, 55).

But the wealthy do have a productive role to play. Smith here sides with Mandeville: the rich consume little more than the poor in terms of essentials, but to satisfy their "natural selfishness and rapacity," they employ many thousands of people and thus divide the produce of a nation more broadly. "They are led," says Smith, "by an invisible hand to make nearly the same distribution of the necessaries of life, which would have been made, had the earth been divided into equal portions among all its inhabitants, and thus without intending it, without knowing it, advance the interest of the society, and afford means to the multiplication of the species" (1984, 184–85).

What makes all this possible is justice, the rule of law. Without it, everything "must in a moment crumble into atoms." But this does not mean that those who take the welfare of society in their hands, whether for the making of laws or not, should be seen as moral leaders in every case. Public benefactors, Smith says, may act less out of sympathy than out of a warped self-interest, a certain love of power. Their true interest may be in a desire to perfect a machine whose wheels must be freed of "any obstruction that can in the least disturb or incumber . . . its motions" (1984, 185). This is Smith again making comments almost in passing of enormous import. Those who take the public's trust in hand can become ideologues who promise an end to confusion and fear yet end up serving an inflexible, mechanized vision with violent possibilities. To those familiar with twentieth-century history, this will sound a certain chord.

The book's reception was strong and seems to have made Hume jealous. "I proceed to tell you the melancholy News," he wrote in a letter shortly after the book appeared, "For the Public seem disposed to applaud it extremely" (Mossner and Ross 1987, 35). Edmund Burke, meanwhile, felt inclined to be more explanatory in his appreciation: "I am not only pleased with the ingenuity of your Theory; I am convinced of its solidity and Truth . . . I own I am particularly pleased with those easy and happy illustrations from common Life and manners in which your work abounds more than any other that I know by far" (Mossner and Ross 1987, 38). Smith revised the book for five succeeding editions, the last one completed the year of his death, 1790. By the turn of the century, it had been translated three times into French and twice into German.

Theory developed out of the influences of Hume and Hutcheson, but Smith also drew upon a series of essays that he had begun in the 1750s, based on his university lectures, and that he continued to work on for decades. These were obviously precious to him, the only things he asked Black and Hutton, his executors, to keep from the flames. By any account, these essays are a curious lot. Three concern, as their titles proclaim, "The principles which lead and direct Philosophical Enquiries" for the histories of astronomy, ancient physics, and ancient logic and metaphysics. The other four take up imitation in the arts, the "affinity between music, dance, and poetry," "certain English and Italian verses," and the five "external senses." A polished style indicates they were likely intended for publication, perhaps as the nuclei for full-length volumes (they seem unfinished). Commentators have often noted their "remark-able" diversity of subject matter and depth of knowledge. But they were after much more than that. What Smith wanted to produce, particu-larly in the case of astronomy and physics, was not a history or popular-ization but an explanation of the intellectual and emotional urges that actually drive the human mind to do science. He finds this explanation in a single place: the mirror. Nearly all these essays, that is, aim at the same idea: the mind of a genius is the maker of systems. Science, phi-losophy, art, and the senses too are all engaged in a process of creating order, "connect[ing] together the otherwise disjointed and discordant phaenomena of nature," as Smith says in his essay on astronomy, which was his favorite (Smith 1976–87, 105).

Wealth of Nations

Smith had all this in mind during the writing of *Wealth of Nations*. This great monster of a book, with all of its wandering contents and sharp brilliance, its exasperating diversions and focused insights, was a work into which Smith poured many years of thought, never abandon-ing either his vision of intellectual power or his faith in the common man. Economics and morality cannot be found separated anywhere in this work. They are united by justice, rights, history, and nature. *The-ory of Moral Sentiments* hovers above nearly every page. (All quotations that follow are from the fifth edition of *Wealth of Nations*, first pub-lished in 1789, edited by Edwin Cannan in 1904, with citations given by book, chapter, paragraph.)

The wealth of any nation derives from two universal principles. One is the "propensity to truck, barter, and exchange one thing for another" (I.2.1). The second is "the desire of bettering our condition ... which ... comes with us from the womb, and never leaves us till we go into the grave" (II.3.28). To understand what makes a nation prosperous we need to begin with a degree of sympathy, of insight into ourselves and others. It is how ordinary people react to their surroundings, not the doings of the royal treasury or the pride of aristocrats, that is crucial. The primary role of any modern government, its most legitimate and continuous function, is to protect the freedom of exchange by upholding the rights that allow people to improve their state, especially the rights of owner-ship and contract responsibility, as well as their rights as citizens.

These are key ideas for understanding *Wealth of Nations*. The book went through multiple editions after its appearance in 1776, with the author making significant changes and additions, in part to keep it current. But the core of the book never altered. Smith sees society in the hands of the rich and powerful, who do not always have the public interest at heart and seek instead laws and policies that favor themselves and hold back progress. Society can improve, but only if there is general understanding of how "the mechanisms and wheels" actually work. This is where the philosopher enters; Smith takes on the task of delineating the principles on which society is based, showing where they have gone awry, and stating what should be done. So we return to the concept of "system."

From the beginning, this is a foundational concept. The realm of labor, capital, trade, and commerce comprises an endless circulation, a kind of natural engine without a true center, yet one whose operation can certainly be impeded. Good laws, based on knowledge of how the parts fit together and function toward balance, will make the whole more efficient, reliable, and beneficial for the entire community. Every member of society has a role to play, even the unemployed. Good laws will thus generate further "opulence," what we know as "economic growth." Smith is thus a reformist. He is no revolutionary democrat; much of his advice is reserved for the "sovereign" whom he hopes to enlighten. Yet a significant portion of *Wealth of Nations* is devoted to a harsh, in places even splenetic, attack on existing mercantile policies, with biting comments reserved in particular for those in the merchant class who try to restrict competition by self-serving protectionist laws.

Smith's great work is divided into five books, each of which can be discussed briefly to give an idea of the whole. Book I deals with the division of labor, money and its use, prices and wages, land rents, and markets. This may sound like rather technical material, but it isn't. Smith is writing for a broad audience that he hopes to instruct about the conditions in which they now find themselves. He demonstrates how the division of labor increases productivity manyfold and how wages, profit, and rents act to circulate the value of labor and how they rise and fall with expansions and contractions of an economy. There is such a thing as a "market price," determined by the ups and downs of supply and demand, and a "natural price," defined as "what is sufficient to pay the rent of the land, the wages of the labour, and the profits of the stock employed in raising, preparing, and bringing [a commodity] to market" (I.7.4). There exists, in other words, an ideal state of balance for any market. Smith's "market," we should note, is not like our contemporary abstraction (e.g., global markets) but much closer to the physical reality of a place where things are bought and sold. This helps us better understand his point when, taking a page from Hume, he says labor is the ultimate metric of value for any commodity. This value, however, cannot be easily measured; there may be more of it in an hour's work for a trade that took ten years to learn than in a month's toil at a low-skill job. The only way for value to be determined, finally, is "by the haggling and bargaining of the market."

Book II moves from labor to the nature of stock, its forms, and its uses as fixed and movable capital. Money, says Smith (channeling Hume again), can be considered a "general stock of the society," giving banks an important role in storing and making its circulation more efficient. Rates of interest and how they help accumulate capital are also addressed, Smith making the fundamental point that "whatever part of his stock a man employs as a capital, he always expects it to be replaced to him with a profit" (II.3.6). A key perception is that the stock of the poor is so small as to be sufficient only for short-term consumption, so the "advance of opulence" must come mainly from industry and trade. On the other hand, he calls it the "highest impertinence" for kings and ministers, and by implication others among the wealthy, "the greatest spendthrifts in the society," to preach restraint for the general populace.

Book III then moves the reader into economic history. Wealth has a natural evolution that begins with capital being directed to agriculture, then to manufactures (artisans), and finally to foreign trade. Smith states at the outset, "The great commerce of every civilized society is that carried on between the inhabitants of the town and those of the country" (III.1.1). He then proceeds to show how this involves a complex dynamic, with cities acting not only as markets but also as sites where new means of production, tools, and forms of exchange are invented. Smith says that the natural state of wealth has, unfortunately, been "entirely inverted" in Europe, where agriculture is still favored as the truest source of capital. This has resulted from feudalism and its long-term influence, which, in countries like France, created an impoverished peasant class without real property and an indolent and protected nobility that has found little incentive to improve its lands or the conditions of workers and that looks down on most forms of industry. Smith should be accorded no small accuracy in this observation, even if, as it happens, France was not really the worst possible case. Too much wealth in too few hands, particularly in the form of land held by a powerful elite, acted to prolong economic stagnation in much of the world throughout the nineteenth and twentieth centuries. Such elites, slow to innovate and often contemptuous of ordinary commercial enterprises, ruling over masses of impoverished, servile peasants kept largely uneducated and unable to innovate themselves, had to be pried loose from control for economic development to occur.

Book IV is what many economists today would likely consider the core of the work, as it argues in favor of free trade and against the "absurdities" of mercantilism. Smith is indeed angry in his attacks on those who support related ideas: "The capricious ambition of kings and ministers has not . . . been more fatal to the repose of Europe, than the impertinent jealousy of merchants and manufacturers," he writes, due to their "monopolizing spirit" (IV.3.38). Laws that prohibit imports of foreign goods create monopolies at home and impoverish the public by condemning the country to restricted abundance, high prices, and, in Britain's case, "the rude produce [of] its own soil." Any country that favors or punishes one type of industry, raising or reducing the capital it would "naturally" gain, "diminishes . . . the real value of the annual produce of its land and labour" (IV.9.50). From here, however, a key transition takes place. Smith has been placing before us the economic sins of society as it has come to be; now it is time for us to see what this same society *could* be, ideally speaking, were all these problems removed. We find, in fact, that much more than an increase in wealth would occur. For what happens is that "natural liberty establishes itself. . . . Every man, as long as he does not violate the laws of justice, is left perfectly free to pursue his own interest his own way and to reap the maximum reward for his industry and his capital" (IV.9.51). Smith is telling us, then, that there is a state of perfect civil society where personal liberty and personal industry and personal reward work together and reflect one another. The superior economy is the one that approaches this ideal condition, where each man becomes a noble atom of self-interest, and all atoms are in a state of righteous order and equilibrium.

Book V concludes *Wealth of Nations* with the economic responsibilities of the sovereign. This monarch has three obligations. First, national defense; second, domestic rule of law; and third, public works (e.g., roads, bridges, harbors, etc.) and institutions that no individual or group would undertake. Talking of the first two, Smith is a man of his time, as he suggests they can largely pay for themselves (that is, police and judges would be paid a fee by plaintiffs and defendants). For public works, he proposes usage fees, such as tolls assigned by vehicle weight so that the "indolence and vanity of the rich" is accounted for, with all such monies going strictly to maintaining the relevant infrastructure, not to other expenses, as this tempts the taxing authorities to increase tolls. A most important public institution is education. Here, too, Smith imagines that institutions of learning can generate some of their own revenue as students in his day paid fees directly to their teachers. The author has many criticisms of the university system, which he says works "not for the benefit of the students, but . . . for the ease [and] authority of the masters" (V.1.143). There is a strong suggestion that universal education should be made available by "establishing in every parish or district a little school [that] even a common labourer may afford" (V.1.183).

To sum up, *Wealth of Nations* gathers the insights Smith had acquired from Hume, Hutcheson, Mandeville, Quesnay, Montesquieu, and others, adds to them his own myriad perceptions and deductions, and employs the whole as Dante might, to lead us by the hand through the circles of modern society, beginning with the poorest laborer and ending with the sovereign in his castle. This journey has a logic to it: we begin with what the eye can see (labor, Book I) and then are shown what lies behind (capital, Book II), at which point, wondering how it came to be, history is revealed to us, bringing a fuller appreciation of the present and its imperfections (Book III). What can be done to amend these? Bad ideas and broken knowledge have injured the system, but this can be corrected so a proper awareness of the roles, duties, and responsibilities of the public and the sovereign are attained (Book IV). Finally, we find that the true aim of the whole is to match man's thoughts and actions to the natural principles that govern them, for this, in the end, is the way to true liberty and the only way a ruler can maintain a productive, advancing state (Book V).

Such an outline, however impressive, only begins to intimate the richness of Smith's actual text, filled as it is with all manner of clarity, complexity, and contradiction. A brief sampling of points and passages can hint at the many delights and challenges but also at the richness that allows for an array of very different interpretations, particularly if certain parts are seized upon and elevated above all others.

Division, or specialization, of labor is the basis for all of modern industry and the source of technological progress. Its origin is in self-interest:

> Give me that which I want, and you shall have this which you want . . . it is in this manner that we obtain from one another the far greater part of those good offices which we stand in need of. It is not from the benevolence of the butcher, the brewer, or the baker, that we expect our dinner, but from their regard to their own interest. (I.2.2)

An entire nation of such individuals, free to pursue their interests, will naturally raise the level of wealth. This is because as every individual strives to optimize the value he creates, he "necessarily labours to render the annual revenue of the society as great as he can. . . . [H]e intends only his own gain, and he is in this, as in many other cases, led by an invisible hand to promote an end which was no part of his intention . . . [and] more effectually than when he really intends to promote it" (IV.2.9).

On the other hand, to create a society of great inequality in wealth, with a large mass of the poor, is both a moral blight and a sign of a malfunctioning economy: "No society can surely be flourishing and happy, of which the far greater part of the members are poor and miserable. It is but equity, besides, that they who feed, clothe, and lodge the whole body of the people, should be themselves . . . tolerably well fed, clothed, and lodged" (I.8.35).

Monopolies are economic tyranny. Those able to manipulate a market, keeping it undersupplied in order to raise prices, do significant harm to their fellow citizens. Britain's own prohibitions on imports of cattle, salt, corn, and so forth give domestic manufacturers "a monopoly against their countrymen" and act to "direct private people in what manner they ought to employ their capitals, and must . . . be either a useless or a hurtful regulation. If the produce of domestic can be bought there as cheap as that of foreign industry, the regulation is evidently useless. If it cannot, it must generally be hurtful" (IV.2.11).

Being able to trade freely with other nations forms a basic principle of prosperity:

> It is the maxim of every prudent master of a family never to attempt to make at home what it will cost him more to make than to buy. The taylor does not attempt to make his own shoes, but buys them of the shoemaker. . . . If a foreign country can supply us with a commodity cheaper than we ourselves can make it, better buy it of them. . . . The general industry of the country . . . will not thereby be diminished . . . but only left to find out the way in which it can be employed with the greatest advantage. (IV.2.11, 12)

Government's role is not only to enforce rule of law but to prevent abuses. Such abuses are likely to come often from merchants and other "dealers." Merchants, after all, "seldom meet together, even for merriment . . . but the conversation ends in a conspiracy against the public . . . to raise prices." Their interest is "to widen the market and to narrow the competition." Expanding markets can be in the public interest, "but to narrow the competition . . . can serve only to [raise] profits above what they naturally would be" and thus to impose "an absurd tax upon the rest of their fellow-citizens." Therefore, "the proposal of any new law or regulation of commerce which comes from this order [of men], ought always to be listened to with great precaution. . . . It comes from [those] who have generally an interest to deceive and even to oppress the public" (I.11.264).

He was realistic about what governments really are about, and though he knew they were necessary to protect property, he also understood that they generally did not serve the interests of the masses. In modern society, "property" had come to mean capital in all its forms. In this sense, too, "Civil government . . . is in reality instituted for the defence of the rich against the poor, or of those who have some property against those who have none at all" (V.1.55).

Smith did not, however, want to endanger property, and however radical some of his ideas may have been in his time they are certainly not so today. He did want to raise the level of the common people to stabilize society and improve the economy. Properly educated, all classes would contribute to raising the general level of wealth and to making it clear why the defense of property was important. Education improves a society. An educated populace is less liable to hysteria and superstition: "An instructed and intelligent people . . . are always more decent and orderly than an ignorant and stupid one. They feel themselves . . . more respectable and more likely to obtain the respect of their lawful superiors. . . . They are more disposed to examine, and more capable of seeing through, the interested complaints of faction and sedition, and they are, upon that account, less apt to be misled into any wanton or unnecessary opposition to the measures of government" (V.1.189).

Wealth, Rhetoric, and the Common Man

Smith uses some of the same rhetorical techniques in this book as he did in *Theory of Moral Sentiments*. His skill in some places becomes inconsistent in others, shifting from well-cut phrases to slow and demanding narratives that meander through topics like a swollen river. But at his best, he is surely impressive. No better proof of this can be found than his remarkable opening chapter, where he begins with the making of a pin:

One man draws out the wire, another straights it, a third cuts it, a fourth points it, a fifth grinds it at the top for receiving the head; to make the head requires two or three distinct operations; to put it on, is a peculiar business, to whiten the pins is another; it is even a trade by itself to put them into the paper; and the important business of making a pin is, in this manner, divided into about eighteen distinct operations, which, in some manufactories, are all performed by distinct hands, though in others the same man will sometimes perform two or three of them. I have seen a small manufactory of this kind where ten men only were employed [and] though they were very poor, and but indifferently accommodated with the necessary machinery, they could, when they exerted themselves, make . . . upwards of forty-eight thousand pins in a day. . . . But if they had all wrought separately and independently, and without any of them having been educated to this peculiar business, they certainly could not each of them have made twenty. (I.1.3)

In this "very trifling manufacture," Smith reveals the enormous forces of productivity set loose by the division of labor. It is a famous and oft-quoted scene, as it should be. Yet at the end of this same chapter, the author delivers what must have been an even more striking conclusion, ushering the reader's mind into the full scale of a modern economy. He does this not by sketching the panorama of major businesses or the scale of capital in circulation.

He focuses, instead, on a pin-maker's overcoat. This mundane item, he says, embodies "the joint labour of a great multitude of workmen." It includes: "The shepherd, the sorter of the wool, the wool-comber or carder, the dyer, the scribbler, the spinner, the weaver, the fuller, the dresser, and many others." At a later stage, moreover, "how many merchants and carriers, besides, must have been employed in transporting the materials. . . . How much commerce and navigation in particular, how many ship-builders, sailors, sail-makers, rope-makers." What if we were to consider in this way *all* the possessions of this lowly pin-maker, every item of clothing, every stick of furniture, every towel and carpet, flask of liquor, bar of soap, and so on. Many thousands of workers are needed to provide even a poor person with daily necessities in a modern economy. We are presented with a stunning yet undeniable truth: "the accommodation of an European prince does not always so much exceed that of an industrious and frugal peasant, as the accommodation of the latter exceeds that of many an African king, the absolute master of the lives and liberties of ten thousand [souls]" (I.1.11).

All society is engaged in creating the rudest items of civilized life. If this is a machine, it is an organic machine. The poor benefit from this system as do the rich; though they are its gears and motions, they, too, command the labor of others. Little wonder if from this point on, the reader is prepared to accept what Smith has to say about the often invisible operations that comprise the political economy of a nation. Nor can we doubt, having read this first chapter, that Smith owns a great store of experience—visual erudition, we could say—and that he has visited many of the factories, offices, markets, and ports he talks about, shaken cold hands and traded warm conversation with workers, artisans, and merchants in their homes, places of business, and taverns, then meditated deeply on what he has found. He needs but a few pages to grip our attention with it all.

At the end of the book, the author returns to the dank floor of the factory where he began. This is where men with weathered hands and worn clothes repeat the same motions over and over, where they are paid at a level that serves the market well, which aids the production of general wealth but has other impacts too: "The man whose whole life is spent in performing a few simple operations . . . has no occasion to exert his understanding or to exercise his invention. . . . He naturally loses, therefore, the habit of such exertion, and generally becomes as stupid and ignorant as it is possible for a human creature to become." Smith calls this a form of "stationary life," and he says that for the worker it "naturally corrupts the courage of his mind [and] even the activity of his body." Yet in advanced societies, "this is the state into which the . . . great body of the people must necessarily fall, unless government takes some pains to prevent it" (V.1.178). Here is where Smith, the moral philosopher, returns to the stage. We can hardly doubt he has put himself in the place of such a worker, imagining the impact on his own capacious mind that putting heads on pins day after day in a dark and chill chamber would have had. Though he knew this would never have been the fate of someone like himself, given his social class and background, "sympathy" led him to a complicated and not altogether clear position about the factory system, in its larval stage. Hugely productive for the general economic welfare, it was deforming, even debasing, of the individual. Here, in short, are two sides of *Wealth of Nations*, one that came to be used in support of laissez-faire, the other to prefigure many of the nineteenth-century attacks on the dehumanization of industrial mass production.

Governments, as well as elites in industrializing countries, paid little attention to Smith's insight regarding workers. The searing truth of what he says was ignored, even as his name was waved like a banner on behalf of the "masters" (as he called the owners of firms) and against the rights, health, and education of labor. In this sense, it counts as a particularly bitter irony that "Adam Smith" came to be the single most important name attached to unfettered free market capitalism when his own writing was more complex and generous.

Finally, Smith's book appeared the same year that the American Revolution began. Given the economic powers the United States would come to command, what was his view of the colonies' desire for independence? In fact, during the early 1770s, Smith became quite preoccupied with related events, to the point that Hume complained he would never complete *Wealth of Nations* if he waited for "the fate of America" to be determined. In chapter 7 of Book IV ("Of Colonies"), Smith notes that Britain exploited America for political, military, and economic reasons. It used the colonies for securing strategic supplies and as a controlled market for exclusive sale of British manufactured goods. Even so, he notes that America had advanced economically far more rapidly and naturally than most of Europe. This was because it could employ modern tools to harvest untouched resources and vast tracts of good land. But it also came from the fact that the colonials had the "liberty to manage their own affairs their own way" (IV.7.38). Britain's policy to stymie American manufactures and to use the colonies as a cash cow for further empire-building was corrupt and inevitably led to trouble. It was a policy that offended Smith greatly, and he said so: "To prohibit a great people . . . from making all that they can of every part of their own produce . . . is a manifest violation of the most sacred rights of mankind" (IV.7.66). Such are lines that could easily have been written by one of America's Founding Fathers.

Early Impact of *Wealth of Nations*

Adam Smith was not by personal sentiment a revolutionary. As a Whig, he felt most comfortable in a constitutional monarchy, though preferably an enlightened one. As a moral philosopher, he wished to enlighten, not to stir rebellion. Such was what he hoped his Science of Man might finally do.

Wealth of Nations was a distinct success, though not yet a sensation, in its first few decades. While it sold quite well, and there is evidence for an impact on parliamentary debates in Britain, it was no instant authority among Britain's intelligentsia and did not take the political leadership by storm (Teichgraeber 1987; Ross 1998; Sher 2004). Such would have been asking too much, perhaps, of any single work. But in the 1780s it became a book of some repute in London and Edinburgh. It had a potent influence on William Pitt (the Younger), who became prime minister in 1783 and a key proponent of free trade. Pitt put forward new treaties liberalizing trade between England and France that reduced tariffs on many goods considerably, from roughly 75 percent to as low as 10–15 percent. This was a striking change that marked the beginning of a new economic era, one that was unfortunately postponed by the French Revolution and Napoleonic Wars but that thereafter gained momentum. Smith's book also had a deep influence on Alexander Hamilton, whose famous *Report on Manufactures* (1791) was in some ways a response to Smith's ideas and a successful plan for the early American economy. By the end of its author's life, *Wealth of Nations* was familiar throughout Britain, Ireland, and, to some degree, the United States, and it had gained attention in France, Holland, and Germany. Dugald Stewart, writing a few years afterward, said to the Royal Society of London that the fundamental ideas of Smith's book "are now so generally known" that it would be "tedious" to repeat them to a discerning audience.

But in the 1790s, reaction to the French Revolution spread a dense and miasmic fear throughout Britain, bringing a different kind of notice to *Wealth of Nations*. Many freedoms were suspended at this time in an attempt to keep at bay the so-called "French disease" of "mob rule."

A degree of hysteria grew and prevailed, making Adam Smith appear to some (e.g., because of his idea for a more universal education) a dangerous reformer. This attracted to him a part of Edinburgh's more liberal youth. But it turned many others against him, even those who had been his earlier supporters, while casting new readers into suspicion of his ideas (Rothschild 2001, 52–54). In short, the name Adam Smith and the title *Wealth of Nations* had both grown in reputation, but it was a fame from which they both had to be rescued.

Scholars of the period report that such rescue seems to have depended, to a significant degree, on Stewart's memoir read in 1793 before the Royal Society. "Account of the Life and Writings of Adam Smith" was printed in the society's famed journal (*Philosophical Transactions of the Royal Society*) and together with Smith's *Essays* two years later (Rothschild 2001, 57–64; Ross 1998). Stewart, interestingly enough, held the chair of moral philosophy at Edinburgh for a full generation and attracted many talented young men to his classes, including Walter Scott and James Mill (father of the great liberal philosopher John Stuart Mill). In the reactionary climate of the 1790s, he sought to recover Smith's reputation by giving a portrait of his life—the earliest and most significant in terms of its details—and a selective guide to his writings.

Stewart's picture of Smith is defensive, a pleading before judges. His subject, he says, was a lovable eccentric, humble and thrifty, prone to "enthusiasms," with a restless mind and a desire to know "the ways of humanity." He could be guilty of "thoughtlessness"; he could be swept away by "the flow of his spirits" or "the humour of the moment." But these were surely minor faults, particularly in a "giant" of Smith's true stature. It is Stewart's treatment of *Wealth of Nations* that strikes us most. After many pages devoted to *Theory of Moral Sentiments* (a politically harmless volume), Smith's masterpiece gets practically no depth analysis at all, merely a bit of paraphrase, careful description, and eloquent hedges. Stewart calls the book "speculative." He claims *Wealth of Nations* to be an "elementary treatise," not a major theoretical work with political implications. Still more, he boils it down to a single theme: "to demonstrate, that the most effectual plan for advancing a people to greatness [and wealth] is . . . by allowing every man, as long as he observes the rules of justice, to pursue his own interest in his own way, and to bring both his industry and his capital into the freest competition with those of his fellow-citizens" (Stewart 1980, 315). In another place, we are told more succinctly of "the unlimited freedom of trade, which it is the chief aim of his work to recommend" (1980, 318). But Stewart still feels another statement of such kind must be made, in order to render Smith unthreatening: "By the help of one [principle] alone, that of a perfect liberty of trade, he would govern the world, and would leave human affairs to arrange themselves at pleasure" (1980, 318).

No one familiar with *Wealth of Nations* could find such statements simple-minded. Certainly free trade is an important part of the book, but it is merely one part among many. Little or nothing is said about Smith's ideas regarding how markets work, the evil of monopolies, the indolence of the rich, the need for government support of the worker, and so forth. It seems, therefore, that Stewart helped rescue Adam Smith by making him thin enough to slip through the bars of suspicion and denouncement. Instead of a work of untold complexity, concerned with the morality of commerce and the corruptions of the wealthy, the role of individuals and government both, and the justice of American resistance, we are told Smith's magnum opus was really a brilliantly orthodox, moderately liberal book, with only a single idea at its core. That England's prime ministers at the time, Earl of Shelburne (1782–83) and William Pitt (1783–1801), both favored free trade themselves must have appeared to give some justice to Stewart's choices. Reading his memoir, we would have little idea that this could ever be considered a pathbreaking book with revolutionary as well as more moderately liberal ideas.

Today we are so used to a number of these ideas that we tend to forget how, for their time, they could be seen as intellectually radical even if they did not call for the violent overthrow of the established order. In *Wealth of Nations* Smith wrote about modern economics before there was a modern economy; indeed, his book proved a key source for the creation and legitimation of such an economy at a time when mercantilism was still widely accepted, when religious authorities bitterly resisted the notion of a secular world, and when any questioning of royal and aristocratic power was deemed dangerous. Such reactionary resistance remains in many parts of the world at present. Indeed, it may give us pause to consider that Adam Smith would be just as revolutionary in these regions today as he was in his own time.

The basic theory, meanwhile, has seemed to many readers over the past two centuries quite simple: a market economy in a modern state is built upon self-interest, the desire of individuals to "advance their station." Yet a sizable part of *Wealth of Nations* implies that this is not merely a rational impulse but an incurable condition. People, if they are at all enterprising, are never content and should never be so. It is really human nature and the source of enterprise, this unending urge and search and wish for something better, for "getting ahead." The more freedom it can safely be allowed, within monitored limits, the better, because it also propels the entire society forward. So has Adam Smith's thought often been cast.

But the removal of restrictions on domains of exchange has not given everyone more liberty in equal fashion. Indeed, as Smith himself pointed out with regard to the laborer who spends sixteen hours a day repeating the same simple movements, it can do the exact opposite. It cannot erase the idea of "natural inequity" or do away with slavery, make voting rights universal, or lead to greater freedom of the press and speech. Rather, free exchange unleashes the forces of productivity at full measure, providing space and reason for what John Maynard Keynes would later call "animal spirits." Such "spirits" will not remain content with the given rule of law that restricts freedom. As history has repeatedly revealed, they will prod those in power to try to change the law, bend it, go around it, or ignore it altogether in seeking their own advantage (Akerlof and Shiller 2009). Such is not in accord with Smith's own view, which argued on behalf of more freedom and opportunity, by peaceful and gradual reform, and for everyone. Nevertheless, from the text itself there does emerge the possibility that without such reform more drastic change can erupt.

One part of *Wealth of Nations*, in other words, unleashes society upon itself. Smith's desire to somehow balance all forces with the Stoic virtues of modesty and frugality must appear naïve in some regard. But again, the book's complexity provides other views as well. Here we might return to the worker, whose prolonged debasement under the heel of merchants and "dealers" would, Smith saw, eventually bring trouble to much of the Western world. Smith's recommendations for universal education, for workers' rights, for public health, and more remained revolutionary for many decades. With the benefit of more than two centuries' hindsight, we can perhaps imagine that Dugald Stewart's "rescue" was more in the way of an imprisonment. *Wealth of Nations*, properly understood, did more than lay the basis for understanding how market economies work and why they are beneficial. It provided distant warnings of the industrial transformation just around the corner and thus, in a sense, the *Communist Manifesto*. We should not be surprised, that is, to learn that two of Adam Smith's most ardent admirers were Friedrich Engels and Karl Marx.

AFTER ADAM SMITH: ECONOMIC THEORIES AND CONTROVERSIES

Paul Samuelson (1915–2009), who was the first American and the second recipient of the Nobel Prize in Economic Sciences in 1970, famously said that the three greatest economists ever were Adam Smith, Léon Walras, and John Maynard Keynes (Skidelski 2010, 31) and that it was Smith who founded modern economics. Samuelson is considered by many to have been the most influential economist of the second half of the twentieth century, though among conservative economists Milton Friedman (1912–2006) might be ranked above him. Certainly Samuelson's textbook, *Economics*, first published in 1948, has been the most widely used ever, and more than a mere textbook, it established what Samuelson called the "neoclassical synthesis" that ruled all economic thinking except that proposed by Marxists throughout the 1950s to the 1980s. It is still one of two dominant ways of conceptualizing economics, rivaled only by the conservative strain of what has commonly been called Chicago School conservative economics whose founding hero was Friedman and whose most prominent ideological exponent more recently has become Friedrich von Hayek (1899–1992). And in the long-running economic crises of the early 2000s Samuelson's synthesis of classical, neoclassical, and Keynesian economics has made significant inroads against the Chicago group's worship of completely free market, libertarian economic thinking.

It has to be emphasized, however, that what disagreements exist between the two "schools" is about macroeconomic state policy, not the microeconomic analysis of markets about which most economists fundamentally agree. Both groups agree about the importance of having relatively free markets and therefore about Smith's importance as the founder of modern economic thinking. In their most widely read nontechnical works, Friedman (1962/2002) and Hayek (1944/2007) abundantly praise Smith as someone who had shown that self-interest operating in a free market liberated from government control was the best way to assure prosperity and freedom. Smith may not have used the metaphor of the "invisible hand" often, but it has been repeatedly cited by others, and it does summarize what is seen as the most important aspect of his work. Samuelson's textbook agrees:

> Adam Smith, whose *Wealth of Nations* [1776] is the germinal book of modern economics or political economy, was thrilled by the recognition of an order in the economic system. Smith proclaimed the principle of the "invisible hand"; every individual, in pursuing only his own selfish good, was led, as if by an invisible hand, to achieve the best good for all, so that any interference with free competition by government was almost certain to be injurious. (1948/1967, 41)

But aside from the fact that Samuelson goes on to write immediately after this that modern economists need to recognize that real economies never work in a situation of perfectly competitive markets and that we now know more than Smith did about the proper role of government and the inevitability of the emergence of some quasi-monopolistic large corporations (1948/1967, 41–42), his later assertion that Walras and Keynes were the two other greatest modern economists points to the dual nature of the Smithian legacy.

Walras and Equilibrium Theory

Léon Walras (1834–1910) was a French economist whose academic career was in Lausanne, Switzerland. (The French never granted him an academic post because he lacked the proper degrees.) He was the

first major economist to turn that field into a largely quantitative enterprise by establishing the notion of an economy in perfect equilibrium
described by a set of simultaneous equations. He also was one of the
discoverers of marginal utility. His basic writings were published in the
1870s, a century after Adam Smith's great work, and were centered on
the theory that if left to function in a free market, economies tended
toward an equilibrium point that maximized prosperity. In order to explain this, however, it was necessary to invent the theory of marginal
utility.

There were others moving in the same direction in the 1870s, most
notably William Stanley Jevons (1835–82), and the notion of marginal
utility was fundamental to the work of Alfred Marshall (1842–1924),
who became the most influential economist of the early twentieth century (Milgate and Stimson 2009, 56–59).

In the German-speaking world Carl Menger (1840–1921), the
founder of the Austrian School of economics that would later produce
Friedrich von Hayek, applied marginal utility theory to try to explain
the social basis of demand and was equally influential. Despite some
efforts to make this Austrian school seem particularly unique, however,
it is also derived from the same basic ideas that shaped late nineteenth-
century and early twentieth-century "marginalist" economic theory.
Even as the successors of this Austrian School today remain the revered
founders of a conservative revision of Smith's theories, those insights
from *Wealth of Nations* about the importance of allowing free markets
to function without interference in order to maximize prosperity and
personal liberty are still at the heart conservative thinking (Caldwell,
Menger, and Barnett 1990).

What was Walras's innovation? Briefly, the notion that economies
tend toward equilibrium is based on the assumption that individuals
acting rationally will choose to purchase useful goods and services, driving up the price, so that firms will respond by producing more, thus
bringing supply and demand into equilibrium. Markets for land, labor,
and capital respond in the same way, so that if left to themselves free
markets stabilize, producing a balance between supply and demand.

To understand how this works over the many sets of markets in any
given economy we need to introduce the notion of marginal utility.
Purchasers of any goods or services gauge the utility they receive from

that purchase, which diminishes after a certain point because demand is partially satiated. In other words, price or value is set by how much the last bit of a particular product is in demand at that margin of utility, beyond which demand decreases as other goods and services become more attractive to purchasers. What works at the individual level works for entire economies. When every individual has two automobiles, demand will not rise at nearly the same rate as when there is a large unmet demand, and overall demand will tend to stagnate as only replacements for old cars will be sought.

The same holds for producers. In response to higher demand they will produce more, but to continue increasing production also increases the costs of each unit of the means of production that have to be purchased in a competitive market. Other producers are also hiring labor, looking for land and capital, and purchasing raw materials, so that increasing demand for these means of production raises unit prices beyond what can yield a profit. At a certain point the marginal cost of further production rises so steeply that increasing production is no longer profitable, and at that point supply will no longer increase unless purchasers are willing to pay a higher price.

Thus the point at which supply and demand meet and equilibrium is established is exactly where any increase in demand will raise the marginal price above what customers are willing to pay and any increase in supply will raise marginal costs beyond the point where a profit can be made so that producers will have no incentive to increase supply. This ensures general economic equilibrium but only if markets are free, that is, if bidding for products, services, and the means of production can be set by demand and supply and are free to respond to marginal utility and marginal costs. Equilibrium, in other words, is a natural condition, as in chemistry.

Artificially setting prices or restricting availability through government controls disturbs the markets and makes it impossible to obtain this equilibrium. Monopolistic control of markets will do the same thing. Thus both governments and monopolies, which ultimately have to be maintained by political power to prevent competitors from entering the market, distort supply and demand, causing the general economy to function less efficiently. Shortages of certain goods and services appear, production prices are distorted, and capital is used less efficiently. Unemployment will result unless it is artificially sustained in unproductive ways, but this greatly decreases the overall economy's productivity and thus the general standard of living. All this is now explained in great detail in standard economics textbooks, most of which essentially take off from Samuelson's original masterpiece, though subsequently more of the conservative, antigovernment side of economics has been included.

This explains why centrally controlled communist economies in the twentieth century were so inefficient. Prices as well as the supply of goods were determined by government policy, not by the decisions of consumers or the ability of firms to produce profitably, and while this did not make economic life impossible, it meant that communist economies performed at levels well below their potential. This was especially true in Europe where communist societies had knowledge of advanced modern technologies and possessed relatively well-educated labor forces such that they should have been able to be far more efficient. Even in more agrarian, less advanced economies government's direct control of agriculture and trade greatly reduced productivity (Kornai 1992).

All of this was inherent in Adam Smith's economics, and he would not have been surprised by the failure of socialist economics since he inveighed against political and protectionist regulations that were far less thorough than what communist regimes were able to impose in the twentieth century.

Though Smith did not possess the technical skills of Walras, he certainly would have approved of the way this economist formalized Smith's insights about the value of free markets. Until Walras and the other leading economists of a century after Smith came along, however, it was difficult to quantify or even to fully grasp the important fact that prices and production were set by marginal demand and supply, not by the absolute cost of producing goods and services. In other words in a booming period of demand for some products it is possible for supply to exceed marginal demand and for marginal costs of production to rise too steeply. This forces inefficient producers to fail, or cut back, and both supply and demand fall back to an equilibrium point that determines prices.

Karl Marx understood that overproduction was possible but failed to take into account that in a smoothly functioning market there could be a self-adjustment, with productive forces moving away from over-produced goods to those in greater demand and capital flowing to the most efficient enterprises. This remained the huge difference between what became in the late nineteenth and early twentieth centuries neo-classical (as opposed to the earlier classical) economics and the Marxist version that did not believe that markets could be self-correcting. To this day, as the large majority of economists would agree (whether followers of Samuelson and Keynes or of Friedman and Hayek), a form of the neoclassical approach dominates economic thinking, and that is based on the idea that markets are usually the best regulators of supply and demand.

So, despite his lack of the technical tools of more modern economics, his failure to foresee the Industrial Revolution, and his imperfect perception of marginal utility, Smith is indeed the father of that discipline, though of course Smith himself used many of the ideas of his eighteenth-century predecessors. That was, and remains, the reason why his legacy has been so influential.

Economics Abandons Adam Smith's Cautious Morality

That is not, however, the end of it because the development of the "marginalist" school of economics that emerged in the late nineteenth century and continues to predominate to this day was in some ways very unlike what Smith was trying to do. We do not need to get into the technicalities of the "marginal" and quantitative revolution in economics, whether through the influence of Walras, Jevons, Marshall, Menger, or all four of them and other economists of the late nineteenth century, to note that despite its basic acceptance of Smith's principles, it led to a very different kind of economics than the one in *Wealth of Nations*. Almost all modern economists (at least of the non-Marxist kind) certainly accept the notion that markets where self-interest, supply, and demand are best left to themselves to set prices promote greater prosperity and individual freedom. But under the influence of Walras and others like him, the field of economics claimed to abandon the philosophical speculation and concentration on politics and morality that had previously characterized economic thinking, particularly Adam Smith's.

Before Walras, John Stuart Mill had already made the distinction between the "scientific" nature of economics that explained how markets worked according to impersonal forces and the ideological nature of politics where personal morality and ideals played a large role (Milgate and Stimson 2009, 241). Smith, of course, made no such distinction because for him as for other Enlightenment thinkers of his time, scientific knowledge was supposed to reinforce good public policy and morality. He not only addressed his writing to those who might influence and reform policy but also had much to say about how to promote a better set of moral social values. Walras went further than Mill, dismissing the whole previous style of political economy and writing. He wrote, "Why should we persist in using everyday language to explain things in the most cumbersome way and incorrect way, as Ricardo has often done and as John Stuart Mill does repeatedly . . . when these things can be stated far more succinctly, precisely and clearly in the language of mathematics" (Walras in *Elements of Pure Economics*, quoted in Milgate and Stimson 2009, 258; see also Walker 2006). Turning economics into mathematics and producing models of a self-regulating set of markets were supposed to finally break economics free of philosophy and turn it into a science, like physics or chemistry, whose universal truths could be separated from moral and political preferences.

But that is very far from the reality of what happened to the study of economics because in claiming to be an objective science, it also established the basis for becoming a political force able to advise governments on policy. At the same time, by becoming increasingly mathematical and making the market an independent force supposedly answering to natural laws in the same way that physics described a universe governed by totally impersonal laws, economists laid claim to superior knowledge. But few political leaders, much less the general public, have been able over the years to master the increasingly intricate technical details of the mathematics used by trained professional economists. And yet hidden underneath the technical wizardry of the economists there lies a set of moral and ideological assumptions.

This tendency to make economics a political force that ultimately developed its own moral imperatives is certainly consistent with much that Smith wrote but not in a way that he would have welcomed. As far as Smith's influence is concerned, the invention of a new form of economics left him as an inspiring originator of an important idea but one who could not otherwise be used in the scientific pursuit of economic knowledge. His notion that economic markets can and should be self-regulating and that interference by the powerful, whether governments or monopolistic merchants, only decreased the general welfare was accepted, but the rest, including his insistence that excessive inequality was morally wrong and that powerful market actors were not necessarily beneficial for the general economy because their selfishness led to market distortions, was largely left aside in favor of a worship of self-regulating markets.

John Maynard Keynes and the Great Division in Economic Thought

This brings us back to the third of Samuelson's trio of great economists, John Maynard Keynes (1883–1946), who, far from being the socialist demonized by the political Right, was a truer follower of Adam Smith than the conventional economists of the early twentieth century. This is where the bifurcation of Adam Smith's influence became clear, with one side going from Keynes to Samuelson to such contemporary economic luminaries as Paul Krugman (1953–) and Joseph Stiglitz (1943–) and the other leading to Hayek, Friedman, and the late twentieth-century domination of conventional economists by Chicago School professors such as Robert Lucas (1937–) and Gary Becker (1930–2014), both also winners (along with Friedman, Hayek, Krugman, and Stiglitz) of the Nobel Prize.

We ought not be surprised by this bifurcation or by the fact that it is now the basis for a major controversy in policymaking, particularly since the advent of another economic crisis in the early 2000s that has in some ways paralleled, if not quite equaled, the catastrophe of the Great Depression of the 1930s. This is a controversy that will not go away as long as the world remains largely governed by capitalist economies, something that seems far more firmly established in the early twenty-first century than it did in the mid-twentieth. With the collapse of European communism and the conversion of the Chinese economy into something far closer to capitalism than to Marxist social-ism, albeit while still under the political control of the Chinese Com-munist Party, the analysis of markets and the questions raised by Adam Smith have once again become far more pertinent than they might have seemed in the early twentieth century. But what aspects of Smith to emphasize, what modern offshoots to believe, and how markets should be analyzed are as—or perhaps even more—open to dispute than ever.

Equilibrium theory, on which the entire structure of free market economics depends to legitimize itself, does not always work in the real world. Why not? Here is where the divergence between economists has taken place.

Keynes saw the Great Depression of the 1930s as the kind of mar-ket failure that should not have occurred. He had not anticipated it and had a deep, abiding faith in the power of markets to produce a vibrant economy; but obviously something had gone wrong. To sum-marize briefly, there had been overproduction of certain goods in the 1920s and continued financial instability in the aftermath of World War I. To this there was added the crash of stock markets in 1929 due to overly heated speculation, particularly in the United States in the late 1920s. This frightened investors, who pulled back, and combined with the sudden decline in aggregate demand this led to a downward spiral that produced the Depression. Then in 1931 a series of bank failures caused by the economic panic made everything worse. Gov-ernments in the advanced parts of the world, including the United States and in Europe, turned to orthodox conservative economic doctrine, trying to balance budgets as revenues fell and letting mar-kets reequilibrate on their own (Ahamed 2009). But this was exactly wrong, according to Keynes. The only way to rectify this and bring the economy back into a normal kind of equilibrium was for govern-ments to stimulate demand by their own spending (Skidelsky 2010, 68–69).

Already in 1926 in a lecture and essay titled "The End of Laissez-Faire" Keynes had written:

Let us clear from the ground the metaphysical . . . principles upon which, from time to time, *laissez-faire* has been founded. It is *not* true that individuals possess a prescriptive "natural liberty" in their economic activities. . . . The world is *not* so governed from above that private and social interest always coincide. . . . It is *not* a correct deduction from the Principles of Economics that enlightened self-interest always operates in the public interest. Nor is it true that self-interest generally *is* enlightened; more often individuals acting separately to promote their own ends are too ignorant or too weak to attain even these. Experience does *not* show that individuals, when they make up a social unit, are always less clear sighted than when they act separately. (1963, 312)

Later followers of Keynes also emphasized the high degree of income inequality that had existed in the 1920s, claiming that this depressed demand for all the new products that were being created in those times such as new electrical consumer goods, automobiles, and better housing (Galbraith 1955/1980).

Equally important was the fact that throughout the latter half of the nineteenth century and until World War I as the world economy grew and became more internationalized than ever, Great Britain had provided the world with a sound reserve currency and enough liquidity to stabilize world financial markets. After World War I, in Charles Kindleberger's famous words, by 1929 "the British couldn't and the United States wouldn't" (1973, 292). By then the United States had become by far the world's leading economy, but it refused to take up the challenge to stabilize the situation, retreating, instead, into protectionism and isolation. All this killed what Keynes called the "Animal Spirits," the propensity of capitalists to take risks and invest (Akerlof and Shiller 2009; Clarke 2009, 129–57). By this account, the American New Deal was a policy going in the right direction but was insufficient, and it was only the huge stimulus provided by deficit spending to arm America for World War II that ended the Depression in America.

It is not that Keynes or his recent followers reject market forces, the power of the "invisible hand," the fact that in normal times there is such a thing as an economic equilibrium, or that excessive government interference can be dangerous. Rather, they recognize that sometimes laissez-faire is not sufficient to stimulate a distressed economy back into normalcy.

Unfortunately for the world, Germany, the second largest economy in the 1930s, had adopted a highly interventionist solution when Hitler rose to power in 1933 and began a massive armaments and road-building campaign that put Germany back on its economic feet.

The recognition that government stimulus eventually if belatedly had saved the American economy so that it came out of World War II as the overwhelmingly dominant world economic power enhanced Keynes's reputation and helped make his advice a key part of the world capitalist system that emerged after the war, something called the Bretton Woods agreements (named after the New Hampshire hotel where the key conference setting up the rules for international trade and finance took place in 1944). This created the World Bank (more correctly, its predecessor) and the International Monetary Fund, institutions designed to prevent a recurrence of the "beggar thy neighbor" retrenchment and protectionism that had characterized the 1930s and that also made the United States the financial backbone of the international economy. Keynes's ideas, in other words, in a real sense rehabilitated Adam Smith's central idea that free markets were the best way to run economies but with the added perception that to operate well markets needed both international cooperation and a reliable financial base. When market failure loomed because of inadequate demand, financial instability, and a growing sense of panic, rather than retrenching governments needed to reequilibrate their economies with appropriate stimulation to get markets working again. At least until 1971 when the United States partially withdrew from the Bretton Woods System, but in most respects for some years afterward, that remained the new economic orthodoxy.

The Anti-Keynesian Reaction: Hayek, Friedman, and the Neoliberal Attack on Government

In the 1970s, however, a different version of Adam Smith became dominant once more, a reversion to the late nineteenth- and early twentieth-century theories of neoclassical economics. This was partly because of the economic crises of the 1970s but also because of the powerful rise of Friedman and his Chicago School and the acceptance of Hayek's antigovernment, libertarian theories. The tendency of markets, if left to themselves, to return to equilibrium and handle shifts in demand and supply without nonmarket interference regained respectability, and Keynesianism was rejected.

Smith understood perfectly well that all kinds of human foibles interfere with "the invisible hand," from the greed of certain economic interests who seek to protect themselves against market forces, to religious power that blocks the operation of markets, to self-seeking governments at every level enforcing or creating rules to benefit those in power. Indeed, that is exactly what determined defenders of free markets continue to claim, namely that when markets fail it is because of inappropriate government action. So the reversion to more doctrinaire free market theory was not a rejection of Smith's influence so much as it placed an emphasis on only one part of his thinking. The conservative reaction was not a naïve denial of the reality that human beings are imperfect and may individually be less than rational, or blindness to the fact that history has been full of major economic swings. It was, rather, the affirmation of a deep faith that on average and on the whole individual human actors do behave rationally and that markets are far better at determining prices, types of production, and means of finding a satisfactory equilibrium than any kind of planning. Furthermore, economists who believe this have plenty of evidence that errors by governments have produced economic catastrophes.

Probably the most important demonstration of the perversity of government action is the monumental work by Milton Friedman and Anna Schwartz that showed how the wrong policies of the American government and its Federal Reserve System in restricting the money supply created and perpetuated the Great Depression of the 1930s (Friedman and Schwartz 1963).

Going even further than his mentor Friedman, Robert E. Lucas later developed a whole theory of rational behavior that denied the utility of government actions to stimulate economic growth and blamed erratic government policies for the extreme swings such as those that led to the Great Depression and then perpetuated it for so long. With his colleague Gary Becker and prominent followers such as Finn Kydland and Edward Prescott, a whole theory of why market behavior is best left alone was elaborated (Kydland 1995; Lucas 1995, 2002). In something called "Real Business Cycle Theory" developed particularly by Kydland and Prescott (also winners of Nobel Prizes), conservative economists admitted that of course there were economic swings, but these were caused by the short-term effects of unexpected technological changes, and even if this might produce economic recessions, that was a rational market response that would quickly be overcome as long as no government interference occurred. Furthermore, as Becker argued, almost all human action could be explained by building rational choice models, so that trying to counteract markets by government action was futile at best and usually harmful (Becker 1992).

But as critics have pointed out with increasing vehemence since the seeming failure of deregulation and the subsequent severe economic crisis in the United States that began in 2008 and lasted for many years, this kind of reasoning goes far beyond what Adam Smith proposed about "the invisible hand." Furthermore, underneath the fancy mathematical apparatus deployed by these theorists lies a deeply conservative social philosophy that is no more scientific or dependent on natural and irrevocable laws than any other ideology (Karier 2010).

The intellectual godfather of this conservatism was Friedrich Hayek, who first became famous when he published *The Road to Serfdom* in 1944. Hayek wanted to warn the world about was what he saw as the fatal intellectual flaws that had led to German Nazism and Soviet communism. This flaw, as he saw it, was a rejection of the notion that free markets were not only the best guarantors of economic well-being but also, as Smith certainly would have agreed, of liberty itself. Wanting to improve the economy and make it more egalitarian by government planning and control, Hayek asserted, was impossibly complicated and could not be done. The millions of decisions by individuals and firms that make the market work could not possibly be efficiently replicated by any government or central planning, so in effect, to give too much power to government simply introduced inefficiencies and less than optimal economic performance. This much was conventional economics in the early twentieth century, but what Hayek added was the idea that once in power, socialist or central planning governments were bound to become increasingly dictatorial in order to force their inefficient policies to survive. In other words, the ideological framework that led political leaders to aspire to centrally controlled, more egalitarian principles also made them, once they were in power, increasingly likely to restrict freedom in order to carry out their fundamentally wrong ideas.

Nazism, as Hayek saw it, was the ultimate result of creeping socialist idealism that had infected Germany, combined with nationalist economic ideas that wanted to harness the German economy to make the nation stronger. The result was the destruction of liberty and of everything that the Enlightenment, including Adam Smith, had stood for. But on the Left the same thing had happened as the Soviet Union saw how impossible it was to maintain an entirely socialist economy without terror and the abolition of all liberty. Hayek had seen all this developing on the European Continent in the 1920s and 1930s, and he feared that the seemingly benign social democratic and mildly socialist direction of British politics could lead to the same fatal outcome. In *The Road to Serfdom* he wrote, in the midst of World War II, about the catastrophe Nazism had wrought and the danger of tyrannical Soviet communism:

> How sharp a break . . . with the whole evolution of Western civilisation the modern trend towards socialism means, becomes clear if we consider it not merely against the background of the nineteenth century, but in a longer historical perspective. We are rapidly abandoning not the views merely of Cobden . . . of Adam Smith . . . or even of Locke . . . but . . . the foundations laid by Christianity and the Greeks and Romans. Not merely nineteenth- and eighteenth-century liberalism, but the basic individualism inherited by us from Erasmus and Montaigne, from Cicero and Tacitus, Pericles and Thucydides is progressively relinquished. (1944/2007, 13–14)

Nevertheless, in his original formulation of the problems he foresaw, Hayek was not as hostile to government action as he would later become or as much as his latter-day followers have been. In a phrase noticed by less conservative economists but overlooked by his more dogmatic followers, and essentially later repudiated by Hayek himself, he wrote:

> Where, as in the case of sickness or accident, neither the desire to avoid such calamities nor the efforts to overcome their consequences are as a rule weakened by the provision of assistance . . . the case for the state's helping to organize a comprehensive system of social insurance is very strong. (1944/2007, 148)

Later, however, in *The Constitution of Liberty* (1960), Hayek inveighed against America's Social Security system and similar schemes in Europe, saying that they would have been better left to private insurance companies competing against each other (Hayek 1960/2011, 405–29). In the same work, Hayek also attacked the power of labor unions (anticompetitive monopolies), progressive taxation, public housing for the poor, and much else that had become accepted practice in advanced capitalist democracies by 1960.

Thus it should not have come as a surprise that the rightward turn in the United States and Great Britain in the 1980s was inspired by Hayek and his followers. Margaret Thatcher, the British leader of this attempt to implement more conservative policies, "tried once to end debate on Conservative Party policy by slamming a copy of Hayek's more dryly academic tome *The Constitution of Liberty* [1960] down on the table and exclaiming '*This* is what we believe!'" (Feser 2006, 1, emphasis in the original). Indeed, Hayek's ideas influenced Ronald Reagan, George W. Bush, and much of the intellectual support for the leaders of the American Republican Tea Party movement. This, too, is part of Adam Smith's legacy, or at least the part reduced to a fairly narrow view of the meaning of the "invisible hand" being best left alone to allow the magic of the market to work its wonders unfettered by government interference.

Hayek was certainly right in his condemnation of communism's inefficiencies and its inevitable tyranny because the system of total state control of the economy could only lead to unpopular outcomes;

repression became necessary in order to pursue the dream of socialism. His writing became particularly popular among dissident intellectuals in communist Eastern Europe who played a key role in bringing about the demise of communism (Kukathas 2006, 182).

Whether he was right about the infection of socialist ideas as being responsible for the rise of Nazism, and fascism in general, we will examine in a later chapter, but the thesis is not entirely fanciful. Whether the rise of a system of social welfare and insurance in advanced capitalist societies leads inevitably to tyranny is another matter, however, because there is no evidence that it does. Today, however, those ideas, complemented by the political writing of Milton Friedman and his followers, have a strong hold on conservative thinking in Europe and the United States.

The other most important intellectual beacon of conservative neoclassical economics (which, strange as it may now seem, used to be called classical liberalism and is sometimes still called neoliberalism for reasons to be explained later) has been Friedman. Friedman also called himself a follower of Adam Smith, concluding his most widely popular (and entirely nontechnical) book, *Capitalism and Freedom* (1962/2002), by writing that "Government measures have hampered not helped this development (greater prosperity). We have been able to afford and surmount these measures (government interference) only because of the extraordinary fecundity of the market. The invisible hand has been more potent for progress than the visible hand for retrogression" (200). And he begins the final paragraph of his book with, "As Adam Smith once said, 'There is much ruin in a nation'" (202).

In his 1962 book Friedman attacks almost every sacred cow of midtwentieth-century social democracy as it was practiced in Western Europe after World War II and by the New Deal and its followers in the United States: welfare and most of what has come to be called the social safety net, most public works, including national parks to conserve nature, a progressive income tax and any attempt at income redistribution, and many others. He agrees with Smith that monopolistic practices hurt the economy but claims that they only survive because of direct government support, and if markets were left to operate freely, they would quickly collapse because of competition. He is opposed to excessive spending for military purposes and is against the military draft except in case of extreme national emergency. He finds almost all unions and professional associations such as the American Medical Association that insist on licensing practitioners to be nothing more than monopolistic conspiracies designed to restrict competition and therefore harmful. He believes that the only task of central banks such as the Federal Reserve System of the United States is to maintain a non-inflationary, steady monetary policy that neither inflates nor deflates by sudden swings in policy. He is opposed to any government action to stimulate employment or economic growth, seeing those as purely counterproductive. He therefore calls for the dismantling of much that was, at that time and through the 1970s, commonly accepted public policy. Beyond this, Friedman follows Smith in extolling the virtue of private profit seeking, agreeing with Smith that it is the combined selfishness of enterprising people that brings about the greatest good.

Much more than Hayek it was Friedman who taught the next generation of conservative Smithian economists (or perhaps one should say "neo-Smithian") who came to dominate the profession in the 1980s and 1990s, and therefore to influence much of the policy that began to dismantle regulations in the leading capitalist economies, especially the United States and Great Britain, but that also set the tone throughout the world in the late twentieth century of how to conduct economic policy.

Believers in the Enlightenment, particularly its English version championed by John Locke, David Hume, and Adam Smith, could hardly foresee what the twentieth century might be like, but there is little doubt that one strand of their thinking could lead to Hayek and Friedman. As we have seen from Smith's own writing, and will examine in several of the following chapters, that is an issue that must be addressed because Smith's economics were in a real sense a culmination of the eighteenth-century Enlightenment's thinking about the importance of promoting personal liberty and using economic freedom to that end. Though there were of course different strands of the Enlightenment, even within the Scottish Enlightenment, there was general agreement with Montesquieu's point that trade and mercantile pursuits were more likely to bring about a more peaceful world than the pursuit of glory or honor, or particularly than striving for religious virtue, which had produced such terrible wars in sixteenth- and seventeenth-century Europe (Hirschman 1977). There was also, as Andrew Skinner has pointed out, the desire to emulate Newton's science and thus to explain economic outcomes as the result of natural laws. Adam Smith combined these with his conviction that free markets were the most efficient but also the most moral way to achieve the desired ends of the Enlightenment, and that it was possible to do so in a way that was based on observation and logic and was therefore scientific (Skinner 2003).

It is equally important to remember, as Jacob Viner's important 1926 article pointed out: "Adam Smith was not a doctrinaire of Laissez Faire. He saw a wide and elastic range of activity for government, and he was prepared to extend it even farther if government, by improving its standards of competence, honesty, and public spirit, showed itself entitled to wider responsibilities" (quoted in Skinner 2003, 200).

Despite Smith's moderation, the interpretation of his seminal economic work has a long history of tending toward the more dogmatic, absolutist interpretation of both Hayek and Friedman, that ultimately almost everything government did with respect to most forms of economic life, other than protecting the rule of law, defending private property, and maintaining a stable currency, was not only economically harmful but also infringed on personal liberties. And that extremism has roots in more than just Smith's economics; it goes back at least as far as John Locke's insistence on the rights of individuals over most communal ones, even to the point of claiming that individuals should make their own free choice about what nation they wanted to belong to (Locke 1690/1988).

A notorious policy position that resulted from this kind of thinking can be found in the English parliamentary debates about the Irish potato famine in the mid-nineteenth century, when the prevailing view was that the situation (a disease that destroyed potatoes, then Ireland's main food crop) did not call for help because allowing this calamity to follow its natural course would discipline the Irish and create a better economic situation. (Ireland was then an English colony.) About a million Irish died, out of a population of roughly eight million. *The Economist*, then a new magazine promoting (as it still does) free trade and free markets, strongly opposed government action because that would impede the functioning of free markets. This is what led to Horace Townsend's famous phrase that so many Irish had "died from an overdose of political economy administered by quacks" (Kinealy 1997, 66–70, 132–33).

An even more extreme, radically individualistic philosophy expounded by the novelist-philosopher Ayn Rand (1905–82) has spawned a virtual cult of free market idealists who not only hate government but also idealize selfishness and the heroic superior genius over the common collectivist herd. How an embittered, lonely Russian Jewish girl fleeing communism in the 1920s found refuge in the United States, became a successful movie screenwriter and novelist, and created a cult around herself is a whole story in itself that we need not repeat. What is worth noting is that one of her followers was Alan Greenspan, who headed the American Federal Reserve System from 1987 to 2006 (Heller 2009). It was Greenspan who, more than any other major central banker, pushed for deregulations and increasingly free markets and who in effect guided U.S. economic policy during the high point of America's political and economic domination of the world in the late twentieth century. And it was this that led ultimately to the crash of 2008 and the long period of subsequent economic misery in the United States and much of Europe.

It is also this particular strand of Smithian economics, buttressed by Chicago School distrust of government, Hayek's conflation of free markets with personal liberty, and Rand's celebration of radical individualism as the best way to personal freedom, that animates much the political Right in the United States today. This will be an important part of the discussion that will follow in some subsequent chapters, particularly the one that discusses the debates about the founding of the United States and the definition of liberty.

In the mid-nineteenth century, and until not so long ago in Europe, worship of the free market as the guiding light of a political economy that stemmed from an important (but not the only) strand in Smith's thinking and from the Enlightenment's promotion of liberty and freedom in general was called liberalism, in contrast to the conservatism of royalists and traditionalists, who bemoaned the rise of free market capitalism and wanted to return to an economic system governed by protective guilds and royal edicts. Conservatives in the nineteenth century, unlike liberals, distrusted markets, excessive individualism, and too much liberty. That today such classical "liberalism" is called "conservatism" by Americans, and increasingly elsewhere, shows how drastically opinions have shifted, at least in North American and European societies. The followers of Friedman and Hayek clearly are not calling for the return of religious intolerance, monarchy, or the repression of personal freedoms and free markets. There are such forces in the world, even in the West, but they are not prominently represented among economists as even the more "conservative" ones would have been called "liberals" in the nineteenth century. What was once a rather radical liberalism verging on what is still sometimes called "libertarianism" is now closely tied to "conservatism." We could say that this marks the ultimate triumph of Adam Smith, that so much of the debate about economics now lies within his own ideological boundaries, and is in some sense more a debate about how to interpret his ideas than any rejection of their basic thrust. This is also why many critics on the Left who decry the consensus about the importance of markets call "conservative" mainstream economics "neoliberal."

As we will see later, however, the older kind of conservatism that would reject everything that Adam Smith and the Enlightenment had to say remains alive. It threatened the entire world in the mid-twentieth century and seems to be, once again, a potent force. That will take us, however, beyond Adam Smith.

AGAINST ADAM SMITH: NEO-MERCANTILISM AND ANTILIBERALISM

To conclude, two discordant notes need to be added. One is about the survival of an anti-Enlightenment reaction that will be treated in later chapters. The cruelly antiliberal turn taken by Marxist regimes in the twentieth century will be the topic of one of these chapters. Though Karl Marx admired Smith and used his ideas, the Marxist-Leninist regimes that emerged from his theories abandoned Smith completely. They believed in neither free markets nor personal liberties. On the

Right, fascism as it came to be practiced in the 1920s to 1940s in important parts of Europe and Asia did the same, though it preserved the privileges of rich elites. That will be the subject of another chapter.

The other source of continuing opposition to the general Smithian consensus that continues to prevail among most if not all economists is the survival of, and even revival of, mercantilism, or what should properly be called neo-mercantilism.

Smith and almost all of the eighteenth-century Enlightenment thinkers condemned the then prevailing mercantilist theories that were held in high esteem by European governments (Heckscher 1934). The rather naïve idea that the accumulation of gold bullions should be the goal of government economic policy may no longer be particularly widespread, but the idea that protectionism to stimulate productivity and to foster exports is a good idea remains very much alive and has always been practiced by some states to try to catch up to the most advanced economies. As Great Britain was moving toward free trade and the acceptance of classically liberal economic ideas, the German economic theorist Friedrich List (1789–1846) was proposing that more backward economies needed protectionism to become industrialized. Most European economies and the United States remained protectionist as they industrialized. Much of the economic rationale behind the enormous spread of European colonization in the nineteenth century was based on the entirely mercantilist notion that colonies would create a market for manufactured goods from the metropole while they provided raw materials that could be cheaply obtained without paying other competing economic powers. Economic historians continue to debate the merits of this argument, as it is far from clear that the colonial powers by the late nineteenth century were actually making more from their colonies than they were spending, but there is little doubt that the leaders of the major Western powers and Japan believed that their economies benefited (Burbank and Cooper 2010, 287–380; Chirot 1986, 71–84; Hobsbawm 1987, 56–83). This was not a rejection of the utility of market forces in its entirety, of course, but an acceptance of certain aspects of mercantilism, something that would have outraged Smith, who decried colonial imperialism (Pitts 2005, 25–58).

In the twentieth century a new form of extreme protectionism and state-guided economic policies was proposed to help economically more backward countries catch up to the major industrial powers and to overcome the conflicts caused by free market capitalism. This came to be called corporatist or fascist economic theory. It was highly protectionist and almost classically mercantilistic as well as being dismissive of personal liberties. Strangely, this right-wing doctrine turned into a leftist argument for protectionism in the Third World after World War II. Communist economic policy, needless to say, tended toward autarkic self-sufficiency that had nothing to do with Smith's ideas on free trade and markets. In other words, the predominant economic thinking that stemmed from Smith was strongly challenged for much of the twentieth century from the Right as well as from the Left. There is an immense literature on these developments, some of which will come up in subsequent chapters. (See, for example, Irwin 1996; Love 1996; Packenham 1992.) Most Western economists, whether on the Keynesian side of Smithian economics or the more conservative Hayek-Friedman side, reject this kind of protectionist, autarkic policy. They may differ about the extent to which interference is justified in exceptionally difficult times and about the responsibility of governments to create a fairer society, but they still believe that sustaining relatively free markets and open economic systems are better ways of stimulating economic growth than are the kinds of neo-mercantilistic practices proposed by the far Right and far Left.

Nevertheless, in the early twenty-first century the most rapidly rising great economic power in the world is practicing a new kind of neo-mercantilism that is a significant rejection of Smithian macroeconomics and all of the various neoclassical syntheses that have come from it. China's government stimulates exports by subsidizing certain firms and trying to control the value of its currency, it is highly protectionist, and it is striving to construct a kind of new semicolonial empire to secure the raw materials it needs. China does not do this in traditional ways. It is protectionist by allowing in foreign companies in order to learn their technologies and then taking over their technologies to subsidize its own exporting industries. It does not hoard gold but has accumulated the world's largest foreign reserves. It does not conquer colonies but buys mines, lands, and investments in raw material–producing countries. On top of this, it is abundantly clear that the Communist Party of China, while it has encouraged free market behavior to stimulate internal production, has no intention of either moving toward democracy or ceasing to intervene forcefully to control the main parts of its economy. All of this is aimed not simply at enriching the Chinese but making it, as it was in preindustrial times, the premier power in the world (Jacques 2009; Callahan 2013).

Of course, today's *Economist* (if less callous about starvation in poor lands) is still wedded to classical Smithian liberalism and continues to predict that China will soon see the light and become more open and supportive of free trade. (See the special section in *The Economist* on the rise of East Asian economic power, "A Game of Catch Up," September 24–30, 2011. On the Chinese economy, see Lardy 2002, 2006, 2008, 2009.)

Earlier, South Korea also followed a heavily state interventionist and protectionist policy to turn itself into a major industrial power. Japan did the same thing and has continued to be a much more state-controlled economy than classically liberal economics would condone (Amsden 1989; Johnson 1982; Macpherson 1995, Streeck and Yamamura 2001).

In these Asian cases, it was not the power of the market at the microeconomic level that was rejected but the notion that at the macroeconomic, policymaking level, a kind of mercantilistic intervention was the best way. And the success of East Asian economies suggests that they may be right. Let firms compete, do not try to run all aspects of economic life as the communists did, but control and help the major producers, and, especially, use the government to stimulate and protect the most important kinds of economic activity. Nevertheless, in previous East Asian economic success stories, democratic reforms eventually accompanied economic progress and, with them, greater acceptance of Enlightenment liberalism. Will this ever happen in China? The answer is very far from being certain.

Adam Smith would have been shocked to see a modern form of autocratic mercantilism working so well, and neither the United States nor the Europeans have yet faced the full consequences of what is happening. Mainstream economics in the West, and especially the most drastically free market interpretations of Adam Smith's ideas, have not even admitted that this could be happening and that nondemocratic autocratic governments practicing a kind of neo-mercantilism could be such great successes. Yet that is what South Korea and Japan were doing during the height of their economic growth when they were catching up to the West and China still is. Nor are those who insist on emphasizing the need for perfectly free markets too careful in examining exactly how open the economies of now established Western powers really were during their periods of great expansion. In the nineteenth century Britain was a very open, liberal economy, but its European competitors and the United States were far more protectionist.

It will take many more decades before we find out whether Adam Smith's ideas remain as central to economic thinking as they have been, or whether, perhaps, he will be remembered as a major historical figure who changed the world, but only for a time, until events proved his theories too optimistic about human nature and the power of markets to solve our problems.

We should conclude this chapter, however, by saying that the world should hope that in the long run Adam Smith's ideas prevail, even if not in their more radically free market form, because the alternative could well be societies that have accepted the Enlightenment's view of scientific progress while rejecting its social philosophy of personal freedom. In the end, free and open markets in economic matters and free markets in the expression of political ideologies that are essential for democracy are tied together. Without them freedom of thought and personal liberty cannot be guaranteed. That idea, though never perfectly translated into policy, did set up an ideal that has contributed greatly to promoting both economic prosperity and individual freedom in large parts of the world. That is what Adam Smith and his eighteenth-century Enlightenment predecessors sought to promote. Ever since, however, it is an idea that has been contested and fought on both the Left and the Right by those hostile to the Enlightenment. That contest of ideas remains as important today as it ever was, and knowledge of Smith's work is still vital if we are to understand the conflict.

CHAPTER 2

Karl Marx

The Tragic Consequences of a Brilliant Theory

> Within the capitalist system all methods for raising the social produc-
> tiveness of labour are brought about at the cost of the individual labour-
> er; all means for the development of production transform themselves
> into means of domination over, and exploitation of, the producers; they
> mutilate the labourer into a fragment of a man, degrade him to the level
> of an appendage of a machine, destroy every remnant of charm in his
> work and turn it into a hated toil.
>
> KARL MARX, *CAPITAL*

> Without revolutionary theory there can be no revolutionary movement.
> VLADIMIR LENIN, *WHAT IS TO BE DONE?*

Karl Marx, born in 1818, was a difficult, irritable man who raged against
the world he lived in; yet he created a theory for how it would one
day become a near paradise. His anger was something we might understand, for his life was filled with tragedy and bitter ironies. He loved his
father, who died early, and hated his mother, who lived much longer
and kept him for a long time from his inheritance. His beloved wife,
to whom he was unfaithful, died of cancer. Most of his children died
very young. Painful carbuncles—pus-filled abscesses caused by bacterial infections—afflicted him for many of his adult years. Moreover, he
lived in near poverty, hounded by creditors, until his best friend and
coauthor, Friedrich Engels, a wealthy capitalist, was able to set him up
with an annuity.

Though some of his relatives were rich bourgeois, including a Dutch
uncle whose son founded the huge electrical (and today electronics)

firm of Philips, and some of them occasionally helped him financially, he loathed capitalists and the bourgeoisie. In his day, these were the people who formed an upper-middle class of businessmen and civil servants. He blamed them and the capitalist system they represented for the harsh misery and intractable inequality in the world at a time, he felt, when material progress had advanced to such a stage that these terrible ills should no longer exist.

It was while living in Paris exiled from his native Germany that he struck up a friendship with Engels in 1844. Engels was the son of a rich textile manufacturer with factories in both England and Germany. As the historian Frank Manuel has pointed out, it is doubtful whether Marx could have gotten by, much less managed to write so much, without the financial, emotional, and intellectual help he received from Engels. Compared to Marx, Engels knew more about some of the key topics his friend dwelled upon, notably science and technology, and yet he fell under Marx's spell and became his most devoted supporter (Manuel 1997, 55–87; Hunt 2009).

Marx's parents were Jewish, though his father converted to Lutheranism so he could retain a bureaucratic position in the Prussian civil service. The son was always considered Jewish nonetheless, but he hated this and wrote a tirade against Jews that sounded like the anti-Semitic vitriol spreading through Germany and the rest of Europe in the mid-nineteenth century. Marx, that is, blamed the Jews for being the archetypical greedy capitalists whose culture fed on nothing but the love of money. In 1843, at the age of twenty-five, he wrote, "Money is the jealous god of Israel before whom no other god may stand. . . . The God of the Jews has been secularized and has become the god of the world" ("On the Jewish Question," Marx 1977, 60). Revival and rapid growth of anti-Semitism during this time, not least among the working class, was based on the very same notion: that the Jews above all were responsible for the disruptions and inequities attending the new industrial age dominated by heartless capitalists.

Marx tried his hand at fomenting anticapitalist, socialist revolution. He failed, and his failure was a bitter pill. He could not have known— nor is it clear the news would have brightened his later days—that his ideas and his name would become the inspiration for the greatest revolutions in human history, beginning only a generation after his death in 1883 and in nations other than those he had himself targeted.

Put another way, this angry, often ill, and unfulfilled man, who abhorred so much of his own family, time, and Jewish identity, came to have more influence on the twentieth century than any other nineteenth-century intellectual, with the possible exception of Charles Darwin. The power of his writing, his vision of historical destiny, created a political movement, communism, that for a time came to rule a third of the world, while threatening to take over all of it. In fact, not only communism itself but many forms of socialism, including the political parties in the late nineteenth century that served as the precursors to large socialist parties around the world in the twentieth century, were inspired by Marx and considered themselves to be his followers. Even today's reformist and mildly socialist groups in Europe were once, and not so long ago, devoted followers of his ideas. When the European colonial empires collapsed in Africa and Asia after the mid-twentieth century, a large portion of the newly independent states also came to be guided for a time by various versions of Marxism, or at least claimed to be.

During the last decades of the twentieth century Marxism failed, not once but many times; yet it will not die. In its many versions it has killed many millions of people but somehow continues to arouse visions of a better world. Even after the fall of communism in the Soviet Union, after the discrediting of Marxist "Third Worldism," and after the transformation of China and Vietnam into mostly capitalist economies (though still autocratic and dominated by communist parties), the thoughts and writings of Marx and his diverse followers remain important sources of inspiration for reformers, revolutionaries, and anticapitalist, antiglobalization protesters. Marxism, that is, often has been consigned to oblivion as a dead cult or failed economic theory by its many critics, and this certainly seems to be closer to the truth today than it was, say, in 1970, when communism still appeared a permanent reality, even a growing world force. We may believe, in short, that Marxism has had its time. But the fact is that Marxism comprises a powerful set of ideas too firmly implanted in modernity itself to be dispensed with so easily. It may never regain the near religious power it once had, but it is most unlikely to expire and will again become the base for important political movements.

Understanding Marxism's power is not easy. Many thousands of books have been written about its ideas and its author, yet none could be called absolutely definitive. Part of the difficulty is that within Marxism there are innumerable sectarian divisions, making it hard to define its essence. Moreover, a great many of Marx's followers have transformed Marx himself into a godlike being, or at least a divinely inspired prophet, such that Marxism became itself a virtual religion (for some it remains so) and Marx's writings a kind of Gospel. Like any major faith blessed with a loyal following, it has spawned its own theological commentaries with conflicting interpretations of the original sacred texts. It has also produced even more simplified, practical guides and cruder handbooks of advice for the novitiate. Its multiple branches have accused one another of heresy, leading to deadly serious and even murderous rivalries. Under communist rule, as happened with Christianity, Islam, or Buddhism when in power, Marxism tended to be used as raw material, adapted by political elites to legitimize their own policies, thereby stirring up debates about whether such versions of Marx's thought were "correct," "heterodox," or "deviant" and deserving of suppression. From Lenin to Mao and many others, those who strayed from the official Marxist orthodoxy were all too often favored with imprisonment, execution, or exile.

No other thinker of the nineteenth century was ever the source of such transformative, life-and-death power. Herbert Spencer, who adapted Darwin's theory of evolution into a biosocial doctrine, had considerable influence for a time, as did the French sociologist Auguste Comte, whose positivism was widely adopted by intellectuals around the globe. But by the early twentieth century, such authors had been superseded by others such as Max Weber and Sigmund Freud, and they tended to be viewed as part of history, though some of the ideas they popularized continue to reverberate today. More purely analytical and balanced figures like John Stuart Mill and Alexis de Tocqueville actually had more political influence and were more successful in their day than was Marx. But after 1900, they were read more as social and political commentators than as creators of systems for transforming the world.

Such is not to say that Marx was wholly without competitors. Max Weber, the great German sociologist and economic historian, provided very different explanations of society than Marx did, explanations that continue to be relevant. Léon Walras and other late nineteenth-century economists (discussed in our chapter on Adam Smith), meanwhile, produced a theory that laid the foundation for modern mathematical economics that treats Marx's ideas largely as an irrelevant sideshow. The writings of these men, which issued from the last decades of the nineteenth century, were significantly more advanced, and certainly more balanced, than Marx's, but no political movements emerged from them, much less quasi-religious adoration.

To be sure, some political leaders, business tycoons, scientists, inventors, and others who labored to turn the wheels of power have in the past one hundred years hugely impacted humanity. What is so astonishing about Marx, however, is that his influence led to the wholesale restructuring of societies, with unparalleled consequences, achieved purely through the ideas he expressed in his writing. He never wielded the scepter of authority like a Napoleon Bonaparte or Otto von Bismarck, much less the tyrannical hammer of his twentieth-century disciples Joseph Stalin and Mao Zedong. He amassed no fortune to give away to the public and built no new institutions of finance or education or social rescue. Neither did he alter our understanding of the material universe, like an Albert Einstein or Ernest Rutherford, or introduce into daily life material innovations that would change forever the character of modern society, like a Thomas Edison or Henry Ford. Everything Marx produced is contained in his writings, many of them still in fragmentary form when he died, left to be edited by Friedrich Engels and others. Some of what were to become his most cited texts were not even published until the 1920s and 1930s, a half century after his death.

Marx did have one very big idea that bound together all of his writing. It was a complex idea but one that could be boiled down into a comprehensible, tremendously attractive theory capable of being turned into a cohesive guide to action. By this idea, he was able to explain the past and predict the future with enough accuracy that, to a great number of readers, it appeared he had discovered nothing less than a form of eternal truth. In that sense, he was the nineteenth century's greatest prophet.

No amount of criticism, however valid and articulate, has been capable of causing his most devoted followers to abandon the faith.

It took some time for Marx to work out the big idea that would bind together his economic and philosophical thinking with his quest for a more just and egalitarian world because in his youth he had saturated his mind with denouncement and complaints about everything he found to be wrong with the industrializing western European society he lived in. He inveighed against its celebration of individualism and deprecated its fledgling democracies. These, he said, were nothing but a bourgeois fraud, designed to solidify the power of an emerging capitalist class. Nor did he spare the older forces trying to hold back change, some of which also attacked democracy and industrialism but from the opposite, reactionary viewpoint. Aristocrats, monarchs, and all forms of religion were reviled unremittingly. They constituted barriers to the social revolutions that Marx believed were wholly necessary to emancipate the impoverished masses forced to live inhuman lives of endless and unrewarding toil that alienated these millions from any fulfillment and meaning that should be everyone's right.

As a university student in the 1830s he was gregarious and an eager joiner of philosophical clubs. He translated several Latin classics, wrote love poems, and even completed a satirical novel called *Scorpion and Felix*. But even more, and above all in his letters home to his father, to whom he was emotionally close, we see a young man eager to devote himself to a higher cause, especially one that he himself would designate. "If we have chosen the position in life in which we can most of all work for mankind," he said in an 1835 letter (written in Latin) when he was only seventeen, "If we have chosen the position in life in which we can most of all work for mankind, no burdens can bow us down, because they are sacrifices for the benefit of all; then we shall experience no petty, limited, selfish joy, but our happiness will belong to millions, our deeds will live on quietly but perpetually at work, and over our ashes will be shed the hot tears of noble people" (Marx 1835). Given the anger that would come to weigh down his work and the enormous brutalities practiced in his name later on in communist regimes, this glimpse into the mind of a still naïve and optimistic young man reminds us of the idealism that moved him and shaped his ambition.

Even as a young man he was frequently outraged by the stuffy, reactionary, and autocratic Prussian government under which he lived. His high school, run by liberal humanists in Trier, had been raided by police agents and forced to fire a number of staff and alter its curriculum. After obtaining his doctorate he went to work for Cologne's new, leftist newspaper, *Rheinische Zeitung*, established in 1842. Recognized for his talented writing, he became its editor later in the same year, when he was only twenty-four. Isaiah Berlin, the noted twentieth-century British liberal philosopher, has written about Marx's first venture into journalism, "he conducted his paper with immense vigour and intolerance: his dictatorial nature asserted itself early in the venture, and his subordinates were only too glad to let him do entirely as he pleased. . . . From a mildly liberal paper it rapidly became a vehemently radical one. . . . It published long and scurrilous attacks on the Prussian censorship, on the Federal Diet, on the landowning class in general." The paper gained more readers, and for a time Marx was able to outwit the censors, who were, as Berlin put it, "men of limited intelligence" and not all that rigorous. It all ended when Marx attacked much more oppressive and reactionary Russia, and its emperor, Tsar Nicholas I, happened to see that article. Nicholas's envoy to Prussia demanded that the newspaper be shut down, and the Prussian government complied (Berlin 1963, 60–62).

By the 1840s, Marx's thought had swung strongly toward a mixture of philosophy and economics, convinced that the only way to understand all the suffering he saw and the evil that resulted was through an analysis of the forces that had created man's material existence and how they had developed over time. Gradually he worked out the one big idea that would make him such a powerful theorist.

Marx's Big Idea: Dialectical Materialism as the Theory of History

Marx understood that merely ranting about the inequities he saw would not do. Nor would setting out the kind of fanciful remedies that had been offered by the popular French utopian thinkers Henri de Saint-Simon and Charles Fourier or by the anarchist Pierre-Joseph

Proudhon. Something more powerful and substantive was needed. He had to ground his critique of capitalism in a theory of history and economics, one that took into account the material progress achieved by humanity. He proposed that history has been divided into progressively more complex "modes of production." Marx's concept was far larger, more encompassing, than simply the output of goods in a particular era. Rather, a mode of production constituted the entire economic structure of society, the real foundation, on which rises a legal and political superstructure and to which correspond definite forms of social consciousness. The mode of production of material life conditions the social, political, and intellectual life process in general. It is not the consciousness of men that determines their being, but, on the contrary, their social being that determines their consciousness. (Marx 1977, 389) For any given society Marx held that there is a particular economic system that determines all else: its political and legal institutions, its cultural values, the very forms of daily life. His theory depended on a purely materialistic interpretation of history, one that saw economic reality as shaping every aspect of human existence from its organization, its varieties of action, its intellectual trends, and the very way in which people give meaning to their lives and understand the world around them.

It is more than a little ironic that a man whose ideas did so much to alter social and economic systems, and who spent his life so completely alienated from his own class and ethnic origins, should have insisted to the contrary that ideas were merely the product of economic forces. The very success of his ideas derived from his reading of philosophy and from his original theories about history suggests quite the contrary.

What were the main points of this theory of history? Humanity's first stage was idyllic. Drawing directly on Enlightenment thought, which had frequently proposed that human existence began in an uncorrupted condition, Marx stated that primitive life had been free and fulfilling. What people produced, in however rudimentary a manner and with little division of labor, was theirs and theirs alone. No one took it from them or lorded over them. Land on which they hunted and gathered was plentiful, and it was owned by the community. There was no state with its governing apparatus of soldiers, priestly mediators, and other legitimizers of system, no officials, aristocrats, or kings. And, finally, there were no rich or poor. Marx called this the tribal or communal mode of production. Later Engels would do more work on this stage of history; it was really he who became the father of Marxist anthropology. But it was important for Marx to first conceive this phase of human existence, as it set the scene for everything to follow. Indeed, Marx needed a kind of Garden of Eden, as yet unspoiled by the inequalities and brutalities of man's exploitation of man, to highlight the deeper meaning and direction of history.

The next stage begins with the notion of private property. This arose as some tribes came together, gained power, and built the first towns. Now it became possible for some—the strongest and cleverest—to accumulate wealth and hire others to enforce their will. This was the forbidden fruit that destroyed the idyll of communal life. States with rulers and a ruling class were formed, and a new mode of production began. Marx's ideas here were informed by his own education as a nineteenth-century west European intellectual, with the classical Mediterranean world serving as his model. In the Greek city-states and especially in early Rome, the new ruling classes used their power to engage in wars, seizing territory and wealth and taking prisoners, who were turned into slaves. These were then forced to work on the lands owned by the elite, which had mostly expropriated them from formerly free peasant agriculturalists. Thus was installed the "slave mode of production," whose key resource was not land or the food it produced but the landless, propertyless, subjugated source of labor.

Here, something new came into play. Each mode of production, according to Marx, has built-in contradictions. Some aspect in the economic and political mechanism of the system generates a form of resistance, an internal instability whose presence grows over time, impeding any further advances. The kind of contradiction Marx had in mind was that of new social classes, whose power and importance develop to such an extent that they challenge the old ruling class. Productive forces of the existing mode then stagnate, so that those who were once dominant lose their ability to control and contain the threat. Eventually the prevailing mode of production fails altogether, to be replaced by a new one, with its own ruling class, as well as the seeds of its own contradictions that will one day bring it down. Pieces of past modes can live on in cases where they support the new ruling class—slavery was one such institution, Marx noted. But overall, the structure of authority and all that depended upon it, economically and culturally, would be changed with each new era.

This cyclical vision was based originally on the German philosopher Georg Friedrich Hegel's theory that the progress of history, as an unfolding of a unifying "spirit" or principle, generates contradictions that challenge it and ultimately go on to produce a new and more advanced version. This was called a "dialectical" process of change. Marx accepted this, but in the place of ideas as the primary agents of change he put economic forces. To Hegel's "dialectical" view of history, he added modes of production. This is what is meant by "dialectical materialism," the cornerstone of Marxist historical theorizing, the heart of his big idea.

Rome built an empire that encompassed the entire Mediterranean and extended from Britain to Mesopotamia, from the fringes of the Sahara Desert to what were then the dark, cold forests of Germany and to the edge of the Eurasian steppe. In Marx's analysis, the slave mode of production that the empire installed gradually eliminated the free peasantry on which Rome's military strength had been built. Moreover, it brought population decline because slaves were so badly treated. Roman armies came to rely on mercenaries, increasingly from barbarian tribes on the empire's borders. Conquest beyond these borders became impossible because of geographic barriers, so no new sources of slaves were made available. Cities, trade, and the urban-based, slave-owning ruling class all declined. The latter were eventually replaced by local landowners, who mixed with the barbarian invaders who soon stormed and destroyed a weakened empire.

This landowning class was a rural elite that became the aristocracy of the European Middle Ages and the ruling class of the next historical stage—the "feudal mode of production." Land was the key resource: it was owned and controlled by the lords, who purposely restricted the mobility of serf peasants in order to maintain the labor force and prevent shortages of workers. Still, peasants had some limited property rights and could not be bought and sold or moved about at will. Though exploited, they were not as hopelessly alienated from their

communities and their own labor as slaves had been or as later industrial workers would be. The contradiction that developed during this
historical phase was more complex than in previous eras but also more
interesting. It came, basically, from the growth of urban life. At first
there were only scattered, small towns, since Rome's collapse had destroyed trade and reduced the regional economy to mostly rural, subsistence agriculture. But as the political situation in Europe stabilized,
urban life and commerce revived. The producing artisans in these towns
were craftsmen, not alienated wage laborers, and with their apprentices
formed a new community. However, although this constituted a new
social class as well, it did not immediately produce instability in the
feudal mode of production. This rose from the ranks of a unique class of
merchants who accumulated a new key resource, capital. As towns and
trade grew, so did their capital and power. This was the rising bourgeoisie (so named after the French term for town dwellers), signaling that
a different era dominated by the capitalist mode of production would
soon begin. (For a fuller explanation of the early stages, see Marx and
Hobsbawm 1965.)

Marx was far more interested in the transition from feudalism to
capitalism than anything that had come before. His real focus was the
rise to dominance and ultimate fate of the capitalist mode of production, but it was also essential to show the historical background and
how it had led up to the present stage. We have simplified the theory
here, to be sure. But even in its full form, as worked out by Marx, it
left many gaps and thus questions about how closely it corresponded
to historical reality. Endless debates have occurred ever since between
Marxist and non-Marxist historians about whether Marx got it right.
The point, however, is that the theory was taken as a convincing account that made sense of a vast body of knowledge about the past and
how human society had developed, even if many details needed to be
worked out. Marx hoped to fill in the material about capitalism, in particular, to prove his major argument and dedicated his most productive
decades to doing just that.

Capitalists, it turned out, were highly inventive. In more urban settings, they fostered technological change and initiated the transformation that led western Europe into a new age. But as the bourgeoisie grew

in power and the economy advanced, the full flowering of this new age was hindered by old feudal laws, restrictions on personal freedom of movement, aristocratic pretensions and privileges, and outdated cultural values. These resulted in antifeudal revolutions, the most important of which was the French Revolution of 1789, which overthrew the monarchy and ended feudal barriers to trade and industry, or so claimed Marx and the many succeeding generations of historians influenced by Marx. There emerged a new mode of production, a new set of cultural values, and a whole new form of governance based not on democracy or constitutional monarchy but on the domination of the new capitalist bourgeois class. This, for Marx, was the great event that also revealed what the future would hold. Modes of production developed contradictions, namely classes increasingly hostile to the old ways, and these new classes over time accumulated enough power to overthrow the existing order and replace it with a more advanced mode of production. The transition, or overthrow of the old system, was never smooth or simple. Elites were never willing to just give up power and privilege, but these things were exactly what the new class strove toward. Thus each transition occurred in a violently revolutionary way, and it took some time for the old to be forcefully swept aside in order for the new to be installed in its place. The bloody nature of the French Revolution showed this clearly enough. (Much of this is scattered throughout his writings but has been elegantly explained and updated in Hobsbawm 1962. See also references to Marx's writings in what follows.)

Marx and subsequent Marxist historians, it should be noted, did not include the American Revolution as an important part of this transition. It did not qualify, as it was far less violent and did not bring a new class to power. Plantation-owning southerners and northeastern merchants retained control. American colonial elites already consisted of market-oriented capitalists. For Marxists, the American Revolution was more of a local event whose repercussions are best treated as a footnote to the majestic unfolding of the dialectic in which the world-changing French Revolution played the central role (Hobsbawm 1962, 76).

Many historians today do not see it this way. Indeed, the French Revolution itself is far from being so clear-cut in terms of its historical role. It may have actually done more to impede than to advance French economic development, while the American Revolution was more of a precursor of the future than Marxists have recognized. Furthermore, it was in England that the Industrial Revolution began, not France.

Subsequent Marxist historians "fixed" this problem by saying that the seventeenth-century English revolution against the monarchy that ended with the beheading of Charles I in 1649 was actually the first bourgeois revolution, and the landowners who dominated much of England's political life into the nineteenth century were, according to this historiography, really landowning capitalists who furthered trade, industry, and urban life (see Moore's 1966 version). Such is one of the beauties of Marxism. The theory is broad and seemingly robust enough to be flexibly adapted without throwing out its essence. As contrary evidence has piled up over many decades, its supporters have always been able to bob, weave, and come up with reinterpretations that seem to validate Marx's original insights.

Capitalism and Its Discontents

There is no doubt that capitalism and a new class of entrepreneurial bourgeois came to dominate western Europe. Nor can it be questioned that this accompanied industrialization and a huge change in how people lived and that this took place in western Europe and North America in the nineteenth century as Marx was observing it. Capitalism certainly had its own contradictions, quite brutal ones, and this is what fascinated Marx.

Indeed, life was dismal for the new industrial class of workers laboring in the mines and factories of the early nineteenth century. Whether things had been any better for the rural peasants and artisans who had populated most of the world before the Industrial Revolution is a matter of debate. It would be naïve, at best, to romanticize the "natural" existence of feudal agrarian life. But in the teeming, smoke-laden, and polluted industrial cities there was plenty of misery to go around—as there also was in a countryside where technological advances in agriculture were starting to make most peasant workers redundant, while local artisans were being driven to ruin by more efficiently produced manufactured goods. Marx and Engels were not the only ones to perceive such changes and to feel outrage at them. On the contrary, there was growing awareness in the most advanced parts of western Europe that much inequity existed, that the powers unleashed by technology and science needed to be harnessed for the betterment of the poor majority, not merely for the benefit of a bourgeois minority and the great wealth of a tiny few. Marx's aim was to go beyond utopian dreams and lay an actual "scientific" basis for what he saw as the future collapse of capitalism and the rise of a new and better system. Use of the word "scientific" was not just a ploy. By the mid-nineteenth century, science had gained enormous prestige as the realm of final, materialistic truth. Marx claimed to be part of this domain for reasons that were partly legitimate at the time, namely his purported "discovery" of the fixed, natural laws governing human history and social development. Such, after all, had been a distinct goal of Enlightenment thought, a goal to which thinkers from John Locke to Adam Smith felt themselves committed. Marx's own theory, meanwhile, had to compete with the "scientific" concept of organic evolution applied to history by Herbert Spencer, Marx's contemporary and a strong proponent of Darwin.

As Marx saw it, the laws of historical development he had "discovered" could not be fundamentally altered. Replacement of feudalism by capitalism was as inevitable as the tides, and so was capitalism's coming demise. Reactionary forces could delay but not stop this, and heroic revolutionaries could make it happen sooner. "Men make their own history, but they do not make it under circumstances chosen by themselves," Marx wrote (1967, 300).

Analyzing capitalism therefore meant, to a great extent, finding its contradictions. In studying the economic problems that beset western Europe from the 1820s to the 1840s, Marx found plenty of evidence that all was not well. The Industrial Revolution had originally taken off in England in the late eighteenth century through the combination of waterpower, machinery, and semiskilled labor, allowing inventers like Richard Arkwright to mass-produce cotton yarn and cloth. Over the next half century, there appeared the widespread introduction of steam power, improved mining technologies to extract coal and iron, more powerful machines with exchangeable parts to accelerate productivity, better ships to extend trade, and superior weapons to allow the major

European states to conquer far-off lands from which to extract raw materials. Within a few brief decades—but what decades they were—many parts of Britain and increasingly some of the rest of western Europe were utterly transformed. Rural, agricultural, and provincial in 1780, these areas had become a realm of factories, railroads, steamships, and teeming cities by 1840, a place Voltaire and Adam Smith would have barely recognized. England was particularly successful at developing the new forms of industrial power, not least the steam engine and railroad. But it was cotton cloth that first placed the British in the lead of the new age.

By the 1820s and 1830s, cloth-making technology had begun to spread widely across western and into central Europe, with still more investment pouring into the industry, swelling its productive capacity and labor force. But as a consequence a series of major crises struck, culminating in great popular unrest and revolutionary movements, which came to a head in 1848. (For a recent, excellent overview of all this, see Berend 2013.)

The problem, Marx believed, was overproduction. Too much cloth, mass-produced, flooded markets and caused prices to plummet everywhere, thus making many manufacturers and suppliers to go bankrupt. Huge numbers of both urban and rural workers attached to the textile industry lost their jobs. With little prospect of new employment, masses of men and women, thus families as well, sank into misery. Marx concluded that this was the unending fate of capitalism: huge increases in productivity, efficiency, and wealth (unevenly distributed) contributed to greater prosperity overall but were followed by a calamity of overproduction and speculation, leading to financial panics, unemployment, and what we now call recessions or depressions. It was a cycle in which wealth and poverty, economic progress and great wretchedness, were intimately linked. But it was a cycle whose essence was self-destruction. Like previous modes of production, capitalism was doomed.

Such was the contradiction that emerged. The ruling class, now made up of capitalists, stood upon the backs of exploited workers, the "industrial proletariat" in Marx's memorable terminology. These were the true basis for the entire system and the ones who would also bear the burdens of periodic economic crises. Each crisis, moreover, would be more severe than the last. Each time, the least efficient firms would fail, leaving a handful of the most efficient and large-scale companies in charge of the economy. But there was always a darker side. To remain competitive, these firms had to keep driving wages down, even to bare subsistence level. Eventually a few rich capitalists would come to hold all wealth in their hands, while the middle classes shrank and were progressively reduced to the same poverty as the proletariat. The system would then enter its final phase of instability.

For Marx, the key to all this was the relentless, ironclad logic that led to the exploitation of workers. Because of the need to stay ahead of, or keep up with, their competitors and earn profits, capitalists had to extract the maximum amount of what Marx called "surplus value" from the workers. He defined this as the difference between the value of what they produced and the price at which it could be sold. Workers' wages had to be as low as possible, at a bare minimum, because competition among different companies kept prices as low as the most efficient producers charged. We could look at the fate of a number of American industries and their workers in the late twentieth and early twenty-first centuries and see something exactly like this going on, even if the wage cuts (or at best slow decline) imposed have not reduced those who have kept their jobs to bare subsistence. Marx proposed that technological improvements, which would increase efficiency and thus profitability, could only help avoid downward pressure on wages temporarily. Other companies, after all, would quickly take up such improvements.

Ultimately as efficiency continued to improve and prices declined, Marx supposed that wages would drop to a bare subsistence level for firms struggling to stay alive. Only if the competitive, unregulated, and chaotic pattern of boom and bust were eliminated could the full advantages of progress be equitably distributed. But for that to happen, the capitalist bourgeois system had to be overthrown. There was no other way for things to end.

A few other aspects of Marx's analysis deserve mention. Unlike slaves and serfs of the agrarian past, workers in industrial cities were concentrated, increasingly literate, and far better able to organize. This provided a special opportunity. If properly educated by Marx's ideas, workers could create revolutionary organizations that would become ever more active and eventually revolt and thus bring a new system to life, namely communism.

The Marxist vision of this revolution was nothing less than apocalyptic. The *Communist Manifesto* of 1848 predicted that once the industrial proletariat was organized, it would sweep away the existing order by means of revolution and make itself the ruling class. Thus:

> In place of the old bourgeois society, with its classes and class antagonism, we shall have an association, in which the free development of each is the condition for the free development of all. . . . Let the ruling classes tremble at a Communistic Revolution. The proletarians have nothing to lose but their chains. They have a world to win. (*Manifesto* in Marx 1977, 233, 237–38, 246)

For Marx, the invention of private property had made all of history an endless, violent conflict between classes over the control of key resources. The crucial example was how the French Revolution, whose effects swept across Europe and as far as Latin America, had overthrown feudalism, monarchy, and aristocratic rule. Capitalism, beset by economic crises, inequality, and inferior use of the great technologies and science it had created, was going to collapse in violent revolution, too.

All this was to be worked out in his magnum opus, *Das Kapital*, on which he worked so hard that he lamented that he had "sacrificed health, happiness, and family." He never actually finished. Volume 1 was published in 1867, but even that was not entirely completed, and volumes 2 and 3 were put together from Marx's notes by Engels after Marx's death. A projected further five volumes were never begun, and even the first volume was reedited by Engels to make it more complete and readable (McLellan 1995, xv; this book is a more readable, abridged version prepared by McLellan). The British Marxist scholar David McLellan has written about this immense, turgid, complex work, "For a book which has a reputation for length and difficulty, *Capital* is an unlikely best seller. But best seller it is: translated (in its massive entirety) into more than fifty languages, it has proved one of the most widely quoted books of the last hundred years" (1995, xiii).

It is not surprising that with every capitalist crisis, from the "panics" of the late nineteenth century to the Great Depression of the 1930s, as well as the recent world financial collapse of 2008, Marxists have taken heart. Finally, it has seemed to them, the words of the prophet will be vindicated; revolution is just around the corner. Nor should we be astonished—given what is presumably at stake—that every communist revolution of the twentieth century has been violent and that once in power communist regimes have launched bloody purges of those they considered to be class enemies. That is what Marx had predicted when, as early as 1848, in the *Communist Manifesto*, he had written:

> The history of all hitherto existing society is the history of class struggles. Freeman and slave, patrician and plebeian, lord and serf, guild-master and journeyman, in a word, oppressor and oppressed, stood in constant opposition to one another, carried on an uninterrupted, now hidden, now open fight, a fight that each time ended, either in a revolutionary reconstitution of society at large, or in the common ruin of the contending classes.

And:

> Our epoch, the epoch of the bourgeoisie, possesses, however, this distinct feature: it has simplified class antagonisms. Society as a whole is more and more splitting up into two great hostile camps, into two great classes directly facing each other—Bourgeoisie and Proletariat. (Marx 1977, 222)

No wonder that twentieth-century communists were nourished on the fundamental idea that the bourgeoisie, their class enemy, was so deeply hostile that its survival could only mean the destruction of their own grand ideals.

What, in fact, was supposed to come at this stage, right after the proletariat revolution? Marx and his earlier followers were a bit vague on this point, though the broad outlines could be seen. Because the new ruling proletariat class would at last comprise the majority, there would be no exploitation. Private property would vanish, and with it, inequality. The marvelous inventions of the industrial age would be put at the disposal of all, allowing everyone to develop his or her full potential as a human being. Humanity would return to its original condition, with communal sharing of the means of production—except that this would be at a tremendously higher technological and scientific level so that there would be general prosperity. Once this had happened, there would be no need for state power to enforce unequal property rights. Competition between states, responsible for the wars of the past, would vanish, and there would be universal peace. The future would therefore be a golden return of an idyllic past but at an unheard-of level of material prosperity.

In other words, Marx was no less a utopian than any of the contemporary thinkers he mocked for unscientific idealism. But he succeeded where these other thinkers did not, in part because he couched his vision in a rigorous economic analysis. Moreover, as we have noted, his ideas were convincing to many because they contained a whole theory of history, indeed of human existence. Marx's observations about the flaws of capitalism, its tendencies to fall into crisis, to provoke competitive wars for resources and markets, and to increasingly concentrate power into a few big firms—all phenomena that could be seen throughout the nineteenth and early twentieth centuries—seemed to confirm his view with no small force. Indeed, we can look at the history of any industry, whether steel, oil, railroads, automobiles, airplane production, banks, computers, or now pharmaceuticals and information technology, and see exactly the kind of concentration Marx predicted. At first, as each industry comes on line, there are many firms. Most fail, and eventually a few giants come to dominate.

Despite this, the prediction of capitalism's apocalyptic collapse leading to an idyllic communism has hardly come to pass, and we explore why in a later part of this chapter. But enough of Marx's theory rang true in the second half of the nineteenth century, and continued to do so for much of the twentieth, to make it believable. Even today, parts of the theory can still be dragged out of the closet to explain certain kinds of economic and political failure in the capitalist system, and even very sophisticated analysis suggests that in the long run capitalism may well tend toward ever greater inequality (Piketty 2014).

That is not, however, a sufficient explanation for why Marxism became and remained so powerful for so long. After all, despite his numerous insights, much of Marx's analysis and historical understanding was obsolete by the end of World War I. Had he been merely a brilliant social analyst, generations of subsequent followers would not have tried so hard to explain away his errors, update his theories, or continue to present them as useful guides to the future. It was the attempt to use his ideas as the basis for constructing entire societies, the political success of his thought, that turned him into such a powerful force. This was a function of the strength of his analysis, combined with and amplified by his prophetic vision and language.

Marx the Prophet

It has struck many analysts that even though he loathed all organized religions, including those he knew best, Judaism and Christianity, Marx's was a fundamentally Christian view of the world. It was a view, moreover, that drew heavily from the Jewish prophetic tradition as well. In 1951 Raymond Aron, the liberal French political analyst, wrote, "Marxism is a Christian heresy. As a modern form of millenarianism, it places the kingdom of God on earth following an apocalyptic revolution in which the Old World will be swallowed up" (Aron 2002, 203, and more generally, 203–23).

The parallels, in fact, are easy enough to draw. The history of the world unfolds as a preordained plan. In the beginning, there was communal paradise, soon despoiled by the fruits of private property, bringing mankind's descent into sorrow. One day, however, a prophet was sent to redeem the world with the Gospel, but he was rejected and persecuted and the future was left to his followers. Eventually the great battle between good and evil, the revolution to end all revolutions, would arrive, bringing a violent triumph for the prophet's words. Those who fought on the side of evil would be damned, as spelled out at the end of the Revelation of John: "the cowardly, the faithless, the polluted, [the] murderers, fornicators, sorcerers, idolaters, all liars, their lot shall be in the lake that burns with fire and brimstone, which is the second death" (Rev. 21:5). Indeed, such would be the fate of those deemed too bourgeois in the communist regimes of the twentieth century: in case after case, from Russia to Cambodia, such murderous verdicts were handed out to those proclaimed to be dangerous "sinners." Marxism, like Christianity, promised not only salvation but also revenge for the humiliated who would see their enemies burned in hell, except that for the antireligious followers of Marx, it would be a man-made hell while those saved would be in an equally man-made heaven.

The world Marx inhabited was a deeply religious one, not least for the working class. Part of Marx's brilliance was to understand this at an intuitive level and to fashion a rhetoric that suited it excellently, especially in the *Manifesto* but also in some other parts of his writing that can read like an almost poetic spoken sermon. This was truer of some of his earlier writings, before he engaged in the difficult task of analyzing economies. In early 1844 in a journalistic essay meant to be an introduction to an unfinished manuscript, "Toward a Critique of Hegel's *Philosophy of Right*," he wrote:

> Religious suffering is at one and the same time an expression of real suffering and a protest against real suffering. Religion is the sigh of the oppressed creature, the feeling of a heartless world, and the soul of soulless circumstances. It is the opium of the people. The abolition of religion as the illusory happiness of the people is the demand for their real happiness. . . . The criticism of religion is therefore the germ of the criticism of the valley of tears whose halo is religion. (Marx 1977, 64)

It is to his early writing that Marxists more inclined to admire his humanistic philosophy rather than his strictly economic side have turned. Eager to separate this from the harshness of subsequent communist regimes, they have claimed that this was the true Marx (see Bottomore 2002; Jay 1986). There is little evidence, however, that the more benign interpretation of Marx had all that much effect on his politically powerful followers. On the other hand, his contempt for religion, his hatred of the bourgeoisie, and his prophetic vision of a classless future utopia were deeply ingrained into the thinking of those who actually used his ideas to reshape the societies they controlled. Writing about the Marxist intellectuals who saw only the utopian side of communism and excused the harshness of Stalinism and Maoism, Raymond Aron turned around Marx's phrase about religion in 1955 in a revealing book titled *The Opium of the Intellectuals* in which he accused those intellectuals of having substituted a despotic faith for old-fashioned religion (1962; see also Judt 1992).

As early as a decade before Marx's death in 1883, the term "Marxism" had been born in debates about the future of capitalism. After his death and into the early twentieth century, as his ideas spread across Europe and North America, they had to confront traditional religion, whose representatives saw Marxism as inimical to forms of Christian belief and outlook. But for those who did want reform and who saw established religion as a support for the existing order, in league with the privileged class, it was not enough to find a doctrine that merely explained the economics and politics of inequality and exploitation. There had to be more. A spiritual dimension was needed that provided the promise of ultimate redemption—a new faith in search of a following. Moreover, this faith could not reject Western science and technology, acknowledged source of material truth and power and the road to greater prosperity. Marx considered himself to be an objective, "scientific" follower of the Enlightenment's admiration of knowledge and progress. His ideas therefore fit the bill perfectly. They offered a distinct prophecy, wrapped in the voice of redemption, employing the vocabulary of Western science and Enlightenment.

Equally beguiling in areas where European imperialism had power during this same time period, Marxism appealed to intellectuals in the colonies looking for a way to free themselves of foreign domination without rejecting Western progress and modern science. Marxism could be turned against the West itself. It explained that the evil lay with European capitalism, not modernity. The true enemy was the Western bourgeoisie, not science and material progress.

Marxism thus offered a model for freedom and prosperity that could utilize Western thought without accepting Western domination in the colonies or bourgeois rule in the advanced West. Indeed, it served as an attractive addition to the existing belief that fixed laws directed the biological evolution of society, except that Marx's laws determined social evolution. Moreover, it received two great boosts from early twentieth-century developments. The success of the Bolshevik Revolution in 1917 and the survival of the new regime thereafter seemed to prove that Marxism could be the basis for building a modern progressive society even in relatively backward Russia. Merely a decade later, there came disaster throughout the capitalist world, as Marx had predicted, with the Great Depression of the 1930s.

It seemed, indeed, that Marxism was all that it had promised to be. No modern prophet ever pledged so much, in so logical a way, with so much support from actual events. Whatever the long-term failures of Marxism (and they are many), to minimize its attraction and intellectual power would be a grave error.

THE RISE OF MARXIST PARTIES AND THE FAILURE OF MARXIST PROPHECY IN THE WEST

Even if there had been no Karl Marx, the growing industrial working classes would have organized themselves and made demands for reform. But with a potent set of principles and even a higher purpose in hand, they were able to do this more rapidly, assertively, internationally. The power of Marx's analysis and prophecy was already by the time of his death starting to be widely accepted by working-class organizers in Europe. By the time Engels died in 1895, Marx had become the leading theoretical inspiration for the growing European social democratic parties (as socialist parties called themselves) throughout western and central Europe, particularly in France and Germany.

The number of those in the industrial working class, those we would today call blue-collar workers in factories, expanded greatly in the advanced parts of Europe and the United States in the last part of the nineteenth century. It was to this group that the new socialist parties most appealed—even for those unable to grasp the complexities of Marx's *Capital*. The promise of liberation from poorly paid, dull work and the promise that they would inherit the Earth once the revolution took place had undeniable appeal. Others who were also poor and dependent came to see and hear in socialist parties the promise of hope for betterment and a measure of revenge against those who had oppressed them. Agriculture was a declining, though still important, part of advanced economies. There continued to be poor farm workers, especially in southern Europe, who began to lean toward revolutionary socialist ideas. And in the cities, there were many service workers and artisans with small businesses who were anything but rich and in no sense what we might today call middle class. At the same time, the growth of the bourgeoisie and its struggle against older, aristocratic elites forced the most advanced Western countries to become more democratic. Elites still ran these societies, including the United States. But demands for voting rights had expanded the electorate to include large portions of the male industrial working class and others who might sympathize with the cause of reform. As a result, by about 1910 socialist parties using various forms of Marxism were powerful enough to gain large numbers of representatives in the parliaments of Europe. This was truest in Germany and Scandinavia, but it was on the horizon elsewhere, too (Hobsbawm 1987, chapter 5).

The German Social Democratic Party gained 34.8 percent of the vote in 1912 and became the largest single party in parliament. Though it was split into three sects—a relatively moderate wing, a somewhat more radical section, and a small, uncompromisingly revolutionary faction— all of them were united on being inspired by Marxism (Holborn 1981, 349–61). The French SFIO (French Section of the Workers' International, a part of the so-called Second International named after the much smaller First International in which Marx and Engels had played a leading role), an explicitly Marxist party, gained over 1,400,000 votes in the last election before World War I, almost 17 percent of the national total (Judt 1986, 105). By that time, socialist parliamentarians were important players in various left-wing coalition governments in France. The Labour Party of Great Britain, originally socialist but rather less Marxist than its relatives on the Continent, went from 2 out of 672 parliamentary seats in 1900 to 40 in 1910. But only a decade later, in 1922, it had displaced the British Liberal Party as the main leftist opposition to the Conservatives (Butler and Butler 2000).

Among advanced nations, the United States was the exception for many reasons. First, without an entrenched aristocracy, it never experienced a bourgeois struggle against an old order. It was also the first to achieve widespread male suffrage (with the major exception of the South). The American Revolution creating the United States had not threatened the existing social structure as it was led by the moderately liberal elite, particularly in economic matters, but it also recognized the virtues of democracy from the beginning so that its bourgeoisie did not have to fight to gain this. Again, as we will see in a later chapter, it was only in the South that a landowning elite increasingly turned against liberal Enlightenment ideals in order to defend slavery (Wood 2009). The ideas of the Revolution embodied in the Declaration of Independence always held out the promise of reforms through nonrevolutionary means. The closest thing to violent, radical action was the abolitionist movement. This did begin a social transformation, but it was one that took place through a civil war whose victors fought to preserve the Union and extend citizen rights and liberties, not to install a whole new system of authority and economic influence.

Second, even though the European industrial cities had attracted a heterogeneous population from the countryside, most people in each nation still saw themselves as ethnically related. In the United States, however, the divergent groups of immigrants who made up the working classes—Irish, Italian, Jewish, German, Scandinavian, eastern European, and eventually African American—were in many ways too diverse to come together in a single socialist party. The combination of expanding access to the vote, a tradition of reform, and the varied nature of the working classes led to a labor movement that was, by and large, far less impressed by Marxism or united than were the European working classes (Lipset and Marks 2000).

Nevertheless, even in western Europe where socialist parties seemed most loyal to Marxism and grew rapidly, their very success did much to nullify Marx's predictions. This was evident by 1914, but World War I made it entirely clear: the grand promise of international working-class solidarity would not be fulfilled. Marx's analysis and predictions, perceptive and farsighted as they may have been, erred in several important ways, though it would take most of the twentieth century to make this clearer, and most of these errors continue to be denied or explained away even today by Marxists.

Neither Marx nor Engels understood the growing pull of ethnic nationalism. They certainly knew it existed. Theirs was an age of intensifying national consciousness and chauvinism, as well as increasing anti-Semitism and protests by minority ethnic groups in the multiethnic empires of their day. Irish demands for independence from England and Polish and Finnish claims for freedom from Russia were a staple of politics by the last several decades of the nineteenth century. Romanians, Czechs, Slovaks, Serbians, and Italians in the Austro-Hungarian Empire made similar claims, helping render the empire an ever-more fragile entity. In the Balkans, meanwhile, the various Christian ethnic groups, aided and abetted by the European powers, were engaged in a confusing and bloody set of protests and wars against the Ottoman Empire that had ruled for centuries. After 1870, the major powers themselves fell into an arms race, stoking nationalist fears among their citizens. But Marxist theory held that all this heat of nationalist fervor was really an artifact, a matter of bourgeois provocation intended to conceal from the toiling masses the reality of their exploitation. Once the working classes were organized and made properly conscious of their real interests, they would recognize their real enemies and then would unite across borders to form an international socialist workers' movement. It was Marx and Engel's unshakable prediction that in the event of a major war among the European powers, workers everywhere would refuse to fight, turn against their governments, and bring a halt to hostilities. By the early twentieth century, such was the line taken by all major Marxist parties. It was not long before they were proven wrong.

When the Great War broke in August 1914, only small minorities of the social democratic parties in France and Germany tried to vote against financing it. The greatest disappointment to Marxist theory was the most successful Marxist party of all in Germany. Party leaders quickly fell in line with the workers' ardent patriotism and voted to support the war. Indeed, in doing so they found comfort and confidence in words written by Marx and Engels, namely that it was legitimate to defend Germany against a backward, autocratic Russia and that such a war would actually free that country from its primitive state (Holborn 1981, 428). In France the socialist leader who was considered most opposed to the war, Jean Jaurès, was assassinated by a right-wing nationalist who feared that Jaurès would lead his party to prevent war. But this proved wholly unnecessary, as French workers and a majority of socialists joined in the effort to defend against the German threat (Agulhon 1995, 143–45). In the heat of the times, nationalism trumped Marxism. Solidarity of the international working class proved a frail dream.

That Karl Marx did not understand the strength of ethnic and nationalist feelings was not surprising. He was, after all, a true world citizen who belonged nowhere. Born in Prussian-held western Germany but living mainly in England, fluent in French and English, from a family that was Jewish but rejected identification with Jews, hostile to the governments of every place he lived, Marx could hardly imagine the lure and power of identifying with tribe, "race," and nation. It was a blind spot, to be sure. Keenly aware of so much in his day, he missed one of its key forces. During his time in England, he benefited greatly from that country's liberal toleration of free thought and from London's great public library. But he felt no attachment or even gratitude for the freedoms he had. The ultimate irony was that he was the epitome of what later came to be called the "rootless cosmopolitan" in Joseph Stalin's Soviet Union, where he was officially lionized as the founder of communism. But Stalin used the attack against "cosmopolitans" as part of an anti-Semitic campaign he conducted in the last years of his tyrannical rule (Weiner 2001, 191–235). It is easy to imagine that, had he been living in the Soviet Union of Stalin's time and not so famous, Marx would have been exiled to a prison labor camp, or worse.

Marx's second and equally serious error was to think that ruthless competition among capitalists would make it impossible for working-class wages to ever rise. It was true that there were periodic crises due to overproduction of certain key goods, declining profit, and the resulting speculative asset bubbles. Capitalism has remained prone to these, as was made obvious by the Great Depression of the 1930s and more recently the financial panic of 2008 that initiated a deep, worldwide recession. But each time, new technologies and new products increased productivity; higher demand for newly available goods and services then restabilized capitalist economies. (We will discuss how Marxists have explained this in order to preserve the theory a bit later in this chapter.) The textile industrial revolution of the late eighteenth and early nineteenth centuries was followed by an age of railroad construction, then by a whole new set of technologies in steel production, organic chemistry, and electrical machinery, so that by 1914 the advanced industrial countries of the West were far better-off than before. Contrary to what Marx predicted, elites in these countries, including the owners of companies, grasped that if workers were kept at near subsistence levels they would indeed have much motive to organize and resist, bringing the system down. Indeed, the growing number of strikes, their level of violence, and the rise of socialist parties, many inspired by Marxist leaders, began to succeed in winning important concessions. The problem was understood by Marx's staunchest defenders, one of whom, Vladimir Ilyich Lenin, in a highly influential 1902 essay (*What Is to Be Done?*), identified such "trade unionism" as a danger to the Marxist vision. If the workers acquired even slightly better wages and working conditions, they would be weakened in their resolve to achieve the true revolutionary goal, that of overthrowing the system. Here, indeed, was a perverse logic: to attain Marx's promised utopia, workers had to be kept in miserable, starving conditions.

In 1899 one of German socialism's most prominent intellectuals, Eduard Bernstein, published a book declaring that Marx had been wrong. Socialist parties, said Bernstein, should be reformist because the capitalist system did *not* inevitably impoverish the proletariat (1993). Bernstein had lived in England for a time and was impressed by the moderation of its Fabian socialists and the improvements in the standard of living of the British working class. He was, of course, immediately denounced by orthodox Marxists and by the leaders of the German Social Democratic Party, even though in fact they were themselves moving in the same direction. Reformism was also the direction that the American labor movement took, despite the considerable violence its strikes and demonstrations generated.

The third problem that Marx overlooked was subtler. Indeed it was denied entirely by Marxists who adhered to a materialist interpretation of history. This is because it had to do with ideas and morality. In nations guided by Enlightenment ideals—the United States early on, but then most of western Europe, and even Germany up until the 1930s—there were moral imperatives against reversing the democratizing trends of the nineteenth century. When these imperatives were violated by such things as slavery, genocidal violence against colonized peoples, and brutal repression of labor protests, there would arise active protests and dissent in home populations. Moreover, this was fairly widespread, occurring among the growing middle classes, among religious reformers, and even among elites who overcame their class prejudices to campaign for greater democracy. Such is a key subject taken up elsewhere in this book, but it is important to point out here that wherever Enlightenment traditions persisted, moderate reformers saw both reason and opportunity for improving the lot of the common man and woman. Violent revolution was an unnecessary evil, rejected entirely. Why risk destroying everything, with all the terror and harm that would result, when society could be productively reformed? This, of course, is why orthodox Marxists have always reserved their greatest hatred for what they considered to be hypocritical and corrupt "bourgeois" democracy. However one interprets the legacy of the Western Enlightenment, Marxists and other revolutionaries have been perfectly right to see its democratic aspects as inimical to revolution.

This was not something Karl Marx could ever grasp. Instead he saw exploitation as the inevitable, central fact of all human relations, even in democracies. He felt that the failures of liberal Enlightenment values were not exceptions or impediments that could be successfully fought over time but inherent sins of bourgeois rule. Again, the irony drips from his own life story: even as he found a safe home in democratic Great Britain, the most tolerant of dissent and radicalism among the great European powers, he refused to see how such openness might challenge his most cherished theories. Instead it was in the parts of the world that had no similar liberal tradition that Marxism scored its most successful, violent revolutions. It was in those places that the promise of gradual, democratic reform was weakest.

MARXISM ASCENDANT: THE BOLSHEVIK REVOLUTION AND THE LENINIST-STALINIST VERSION

By 1914 the analytic flaws of Marxist theory were quite evident to those who were not among the faithful. By then the leading socialist parties and labor movements in western Europe and the United States had moved distinctly toward peaceful political action and what Lenin had called "unionism," practical demands for reform rather than revolution. As already noted, the outbreak of World War I in that year blew apart the cherished notion of international working-class solidarity. However, Marxist theory did not weaken or die. Instead of being disgraced, it was reinvigorated by new interpretations and adaptations. Even the war itself was recast as "proof" of Marxism's validity.

In 1917 Lenin proposed a particularly convincing explanation in one of his classic works, *Imperialism, the Highest Stage of Capitalism* (1939). This pamphlet took nothing away from the dream of world revolution. It was an idea that other Marxists, such as Rosa Luxemburg, had proposed a year before World War I. Capitalism's survival depended on imperial expansion and thus increasingly militarized competition between capitalist powers (Luxemburg 2003). Lenin, witnessing the war, used data and analysis first put forward by the liberal Englishman John Hobson (1902) to explain why it had broken out. The key perception here was that expansion of Western control over vast colonial empires in Africa and Asia in the late nineteenth century had been driven by capitalist greed and desire to control resources and markets. For Hobson, this was unnecessary, wrong, and immoral. For Lenin, it was inevitable. Marx had been right that profits were being continually squeezed by capitalist competition, and this *should* have reduced proletarian wages to bare subsistence levels, bringing revolution. Why had this not happened? Because capitalist empires established monopoly power over their colonies (thus reducing competition), and they could exploit colonial people enough to be able to afford to pay their own domestic labor forces somewhat better. But this only postponed the final crisis as long as there were new colonies to exploit. Eventually these would be fully exploited, and new colonies would no longer be available. Then competition between capitalist powers for territories would lead to war. Such was World War I.

By the end of the conflict in 1918, over fifteen million had been killed and four big power empires, the Russian, German, Austro-Hungarian, and Ottoman, had collapsed. It was difficult to find a clear explanation for such a colossal, destructive event. Ascribing it to the irrationality of a few elites, foolish as they may have been, was unsatisfactory; still less sufficient was the killing of an Austrian crown prince in the distant Balkan city of Sarajevo by an obscure Serbian nationalist fanatic. The revised Marxist explanation provided by Lenin, one of the most careful readers of Marx and Engels's work, made the whole thing seem quite rational and part of the normal unfolding of the dialectic. Monopoly capitalism had brought about the war as part of its own quest for further profits, which, exactly as Marx had predicted, would lead it to self-destruction. The existence of colonies, and, more recently, of exploited "third world" countries, has since remained a staple Marxist explanation of why capitalism still survives. But it also shows why, one day, according to the theory, when these exploited regions free themselves from capitalism's grasp, revolution will come to the most advanced economies (Wallerstein et al. 2013).

As Eric Hobsbawm, the most prominent Marxist historian of the late twentieth century, has written, the debate about whether or not World War I was indeed the inevitable result of capitalism's desperate reach for imperial possessions has long become an argument about the validity of Marxist-Leninist theories of history (1987, 60–63). Hobsbawm concludes that this is somewhat beside the point, since at the time imperial competition certainly seemed to be a main cause of war. Capitalists, as well as political and military leaders, may have had other than pure economic motives for both imperialism and war, but aside from fervent nationalism, imperialism and colonial expansion at the time were considered both necessary and useful. Germany's ambition to overtake Great Britain as the world's leading imperial power certainly played a major role, as did its sense that it was being squeezed between France and Russia and therefore in danger of losing its growing economic and political power (Kennedy 1980; Kennan 1979). But we do not need to plumb the complexities of what happened to understand how Lenin's little book could be convincing and could reassure Marxists everywhere that the theory was sound.

It was, however, more than his theoretical insights that turned Lenin into the key Marxist figure of the early twentieth century. The disintegration of the Russian Empire under the stress of war in 1917 provided an opening for seizure of power by Lenin's "Bolsheviks" (Russian for "majority," expressing how Lenin's faction had won a majority of the Russian Social Democratic Labor Party in 1903). It was his Bolshevik wing of the Russian socialist movement that became the Communist Party, and it was Lenin who led his party in the October 1917 revolution that ultimately created the Union of Soviet Socialist Republics (USSR) after the fall of Tsar Nicholas II.

Russia was the most economically backward of Europe's great powers in 1914 and the least democratic. But its industrial growth rate for the two decades preceding the war had been extremely rapid, so that it already had a modern economic sector with a large urban working class. Russia's autocratic regime—the tsar's power was almost entirely unchecked by parliament—made a reformist path far less promising than in more advanced, democratic Western societies.

Russia had followed a unique path to modernity. Tsar Peter the Great (ruled 1682–1725), who made Russia a major European power, relied on its vast area and population, brutally coerced serf labor, and domination by a small, partly Westernized bureaucratic elite led by an absolute, autocratic tyrant. It worked, but at the cost of tremendous human suffering. Tsarina Catherine the Great (ruled 1762–96) corresponded with French Enlightenment philosophers but made serfdom even more onerous, expanded the powers of the small class of landowning nobles, ruthlessly put down a major peasant revolt, and helped enforce the religious power of the Russian Orthodox Church while expanding Russian territory (Avrich 1972). The nineteenth-century tsars prevented any kind of meaningful democratic reform, except for Alexander II (ruled 1855–81), who freed the serfs without, however, providing them enough land of their own. He was assassinated by revolutionaries. His successor, Alexander III (ruled 1881–94), was a pitiless reactionary who survived assassination attempts, one of which involved Lenin's older brother, who was hanged for his efforts in 1887. Nicholas II (1894–1917) followed his father's intolerant and anti-Semitic policies and was quite unable to grasp the implications of the changing historical situation in Russia at the turn of the twentieth century (Hosking 1997).

Frustrated, educated Russian youths who wanted their country reformed and modernized turned to violent revolutionary ideas. For decade after decade, from the first attempted coup led by progressive military officers in 1825 through various assassinations, plots, and schemes to mobilize the vast number of oppressed peasants, efforts at change had come to naught. In the 1880s, however, Russian intellectuals who had assiduously been reading German and French social philosophy were introduced to Marxism, which quickly caught on among the more radical members. Marxism seemed to be scientific, based on empirical analysis, wholly modern like the best of Western knowledge they so admired. Marx's ideas also satisfied a deep longing for redemption among these partly Westernized Russians, who otherwise despised the stultifying dogma of the Russian Orthodox Church as well as its complete submission to the tsars. Marxism also rejected the corruption and hypocrisy of the advanced capitalist Western nations. It spoke to the nationalist feelings of these young Russians that their homeland, despite its many flaws, was still morally superior to the immoral, wealthy West.

A particularly intolerant, nationalistic version of Marxism proposed that Russia had the ability to leapfrog the stages Marx had delineated for the West. It could establish socialism by force if it created an elite revolutionary party led by brilliant theoreticians who would bring about a miraculous transformation. Russia would become modern without going through the degeneration of bourgeois rule. This was Lenin's vision, and as Tim McDaniel has pointed out, it resonated deeply with many Russians, from members of the elite to the peasantry, who were not, strictly speaking, believers in socialism but still sought to escape the backwardness, inequality, humiliation, and hopelessness of their condition (McDaniel 1996, 80–85).

Lenin's careful reading of Marx gave him two clear ideas. First, a tightly controlled intelligentsia (as Russian intellectuals were called) could, indeed should, lead the revolution in Russia. Second, it was vital to embrace the industrial working class, who were likely to understand the need for revolution better than the peasantry. Marx had believed that despite the inevitability of revolution, only the select few, chiefly himself, Friedrich Engels, and those who were their loyal disciples, really understood dialectical materialism and how to use it. Lenin's contempt for those who dissented, his ability to write profoundly analytical and historically informed books, his anger against the prevailing conditions of his society, and his desire to dominate all revolutionary forces fully matched Marx's outlook. But Lenin was a far shrewder political tactician, and he had better material to work with. By 1914, a significant portion of the Russian urban working class was indeed sympathetic to his plans, partly because industrial working conditions were so brutal and also because moderate unionism was so harshly repressed (Pipes 1990; Bonnell 1986; McDaniel 1988).

Even before this, the tsarist regime had lost a great deal of its legitimacy. In 1904 Russia entered a disastrous, losing war with Japan that exposed the corruption and incapacity of its rulers. A revolution then broke out in 1905 and came close to overthrowing the tsar's government. It failed, but it provided Lenin and his Bolsheviks with valuable lessons on how to channel discontent through workers' councils (called "soviets" in Russian). After that war, Tsar Nicholas II and his closest advisors refused to face the enormous shame and discontent Japan's victory had caused. They continued to block any and all attempts at needed reform. Then, in 1914, the tsar led his country into the calamity of World War I. Defeat after defeat, starvation, and disease increased the growing disgust among ordinary soldiers. The nobility, meanwhile, watched as Nicholas II, seemingly befuddled by his German wife and the dissolute monk Rasputin who was her close confidant, stumbled from one bad decision to the next. It all contributed to the regime's complete loss of legitimacy (Ferro 1993).

In February 1917 (March by the Western calendar), the tsar's government collapsed and was replaced by a reformist, liberal regime. Intending to remain moderate and avoid radical changes, the new administration made the fatal mistake of staying in the war and suffering more losses. In October (November by the Western calendar), the Bolsheviks finally struck. Backed by dissident sailors and the workers' soviets, they were able to take power. The Bolsheviks did not have a majority of the various revolutionary parties that claimed to be socialist, much less anything close to a majority of all reformists, but they were the most organized and the most ready to ruthlessly manipulate others in order to gain and hold onto power. Once Lenin was in control and realized that he could never win a free election, all prospects of having one vanished.

There followed a long and deadly civil war. The Bolsheviks and their supporters were opposed by a loose confederation of landowners, conservatives, reactionaries, monarchists, liberals, and other socialists, as well as democratic reformists. Lenin managed to rally peasants who were afraid that a counterrevolution would take away the land they had seized. He also brought to his side workers and soldiers who hated tsarism, as well as a significant number of Russian nationalists who feared that the counterrevolutionaries would be pawns of foreign powers ready to dismantle Russia. Many of Russia's minorities, including Poles, Finns, Baltic peoples, various ethnic groups from the Caucasus, and its Jews had been no lovers of tsarism and felt it was worth seeing what the liberating movement might bring. Many of the leading Bolsheviks were themselves members of some of these minorities, including, most famously, Leon (Lev) Davidovich Trotsky, a Jew who became the chief of the new Red Army, and Joseph (Iosif) Vissarionovich Stalin, a Georgian from the Caucasus who eventually became general secretary of the Communist Party. Lenin was a good judge of human abilities and put together an array of highly capable leaders. By 1923, the Communists had vanquished their main enemies and solidified their rule (Von Hagen 2006; Smith 2006; Raleigh 2006).

After the victory in 1921 of the Bolsheviks in the civil war, they relaxed their socialist program to allow economic recovery from the ravages of war. Lenin died in early 1924, and Stalin gradually solidified his hold on the Communist Party of the new Soviet Union. By 1928 he had outmaneuvered his rivals within the party, including Trotsky, and had put in place the whole repressive security police apparatus designed to keep control. Then Stalin launched a series of increasingly stringent steps to create a Marxist socialist economy and society. Rapid, heavy industrialization was pushed to the front of economic development, both to advance arms production and to create an industrial working class considered an essential source of support for socialism. Steel, heavy machinery, petroleum, and electrification were developed over the production of consumer goods. To pay for this, agriculture was collectivized, and food was taken from the peasants. There was significant peasant resistance, but Stalin crushed it, using a series of ruthless measures. The combination of direct killings, forced deportation to harsh labor camps in desolate parts of Soviet Union, and deliberate starvation tactics killed millions of peasants (Snyder 2010, 21–154).

This was only the beginning, however. Stalin next proceeded to purge the party of any conceivable enemies, to imprison and kill vast numbers of ordinary workers and officials blamed for the repeated shortcomings of the system. As a result, from 1928 to 1938, another two million people were murdered (Fitzpatrick 2008). Stalin then turned to the ranks of his own military, eliminating most of its higher officer class, identified as potential threats. And as World War II approached, "troublesome" ethnic minorities in sensitive border regions were deported en masse to areas in Central Asia and Siberia. It was a tactic that continued both during and after the war (Germany's invasion of the Soviet Union led to a peak in deportation). Purges, killings, torture, and imprisonment on a mass scale continued as late as 1953, until the total number of dead reached at least twenty million, making Stalin one of the greatest mass murderers in all of history (Courtois and Kramer 1999, part 1). This does not include the three million or so who had died during the earlier civil war and repression or the fifteen million who perished in World War II (Fitzpatrick 2008).

In a sense, it all worked. Stalin combined Marx with Lenin, the vision of a better world with the brutal practicality that would force it into existence. In more detailed terms, he sought to unite the theory of materialist history and a socialist future with the necessity of terror to destroy internal enemies and lead the masses into that future, no matter what the cost. Stalin, carrying Lenin's work further, created the world's first modern totalitarian state. Rapid industrialization proved to be effective, as it allowed the Soviets to withstand a German invasion in 1941 and then equip a vast Red Army that played a key role in defeating Germany and winning World War II (Barber and Harrison 2006). To go over the details of how this happened would take us too far afield. The important point is that to much of the outside world, this all seemed like an astonishing success, particularly in light of what happened elsewhere in the 1930s. That it came at such an incalculable cost, and was actually on the verge of disintegration because of its grotesque inefficiencies, massive killings, economic weaknesses, fear and distrust, and general paralysis by the time Stalin died in 1953, was not well-known or understood.

Even at the end of his life, Stalin was planning a whole new set of purges, starting with the deportation of Jews to Siberia. Given the staggering loss of life during the 1940s and the advent of the Cold War and a powerful new enemy (the United States), a fresh round of massive interior expulsions might well have brought down the system, causing millions more to perish. But in 1953, the man who killed more Russians than Hitler died of a stroke, and his successors quickly began to relax the terror to keep the Soviet Union operational (Knight 1993, 146–86).

Would Marx have approved of Lenin and Stalin? He certainly would have given his approval to the early stages of the Communist revolution, even if he might have been surprised that it took place in backward Russia rather than advanced Germany. Lenin, after all, was clearly a devoted Marxist and, once in power, set up an institute that translated, edited, and published all of Marx's work in many languages. Given the violent tenor of Marx's writing, his hatred of the bourgeoisie and of capitalism, his contempt for other socialist theoreticians who disagreed with him, and his delusions about the possibility of creating a utopia dominated by a morally superior proletariat, he would have sanctioned Lenin's brutality. The threat of violence had already been expressed in the *Communist Manifesto*, where Marx and Engels had written, "The abolition of bourgeois individuality, bourgeois independence, and bourgeois freedom is undoubtedly aimed at" (*Manifesto* in Marx 1977, 233). Lenin and later communists, not only Stalin, once in power, interpreted this as a need to physically destroy their countries' middle and upper classes.

Lenin's own scorn for all who opposed him, his conviction that only a knowledgeable elite was fit to lead the revolution on behalf of the proletariat, and his disinclination to let his revolution be threatened by democratic elections would not have disturbed Marx at all. On the other hand, the extraordinary and relentless brutality of Stalin's garrison state, as well as its autocratic concentration of power in one man, might have made even Marx somewhat disillusioned. It is hard to imagine the Karl Marx who spoke so often about "emancipation," especially of those who labored in factories and fields, finding it justified the murder, deportation, and imprisonment of these very people in such enormous numbers. But who can say? In one of his most widely cited works published in 1852, *The Eighteenth Brumaire of Louis Bonaparte*, Marx called the coup and seizure of power by Napoleon III in France in 1851 a farce. But he also explained that the coup had succeeded because of support from an ignorant peasantry that did not understand what kind of progress was needed, an observation that led Lenin and Trotsky to be tremendously suspicious of this class (Marx 1967). When Stalin destroyed Russia's peasantry, he was carrying out something other Marxists had already decided might be as necessary as eliminating the bourgeoisie (Shanin 1972).

What about bureaucratic authority, a crucial aspect of the modern state that Marx himself had identified as such? He did not trust it. Large bureaucracies, he said, were there to support and maintain the centralized power of the capitalist state. In his analysis of the radically revolutionary Paris Commune of 1871, he claimed, however, that professional bureaucrats could be replaced with ordinary workers, whose fundamental honesty and idealism could do a much better job of building an egalitarian society (Marx 1977, 539–58).

Stalin was always torn between both conceptions of bureaucracy. He certainly built up a vast bureaucratic apparatus, but he also remained suspicious of his own creation, feeling that it could threaten the revolution since the need for technical competence opened it to bourgeois ideas and counterrevolutionary sentiments. In fact, throughout his rule, Stalin veered between a "leftist" orientation that privileged anti-bureaucratic, mass mobilization and a "rightist" view that supported bureaucratic competence and control. He could never resolve the contradiction. He instituted material incentives for good work, but he also periodically wanted to purge the bureaucracy to stop it from subverting his socialist ideals, and he never gave up on the idea of somehow transforming his people's consciousness to make them better communists. This was why he would periodically return to the theme that the class struggle continued, even after the aristocracy, bourgeoisie, and independent peasantry had vanished. Though these social classes were gone, treacherous bourgeois ideas kept creeping back in through the professional bureaucracy (Davies and Harris 2005, 193–98).

It was a concept born of the contradictions in Marxism itself, one that led to terrible purges and many executions. That it was indeed endemic to Marx's own ideas is shown by the fact that the very same veering back and forth, with equally disastrous consequences, characterized the later rule of China's first communist leader, Mao Zedong.

The most gifted and eloquent Russian Communist theoretician and historian after Lenin was Leon Trotsky, who was exiled by Stalin and eventually murdered in Mexico on his orders in 1940. Trotsky himself never renounced violence and terror. As military chief of Lenin's regime, he set a pattern for extreme repression, most notably in putting down a revolt of formerly Bolshevik sailors against Lenin's government at Kronstadt in 1921 (Avrich 1970). When he subsequently criticized Stalin, it was purely on the grounds that the latter had a "petty bourgeois" and bureaucratic mentality. He never claimed it was illegitimate to use force at any level in order to preserve the revolution. But to call someone a petty bourgeois had an ad hominem violence all its own. It was one of Marx's own favorite insults, as he had deep contempt for the middle classes. To see Stalin the professional revolutionary, the mass murderer, and the builder of the world's second most powerful state as a "petty bourgeois" stretches the imagination, but it was clearly Trotsky's way of saying that Stalin was not a real Marxist, only a contemptible pretender (Trotsky 1937).

This proved to be something of a problem, since Stalin was the one in power. But Trotsky was not easily disposed of or eliminated. A gifted writer who won many admirers around the world, he was a favorite of Marxists who tried to find a way of accepting the successes of the Soviet Union while rejecting the murderous means necessary to keep the Communist Party in power and to force rapid industrialization. For a long time Trotsky's interpretation of Stalin as a boorish opportunist was accepted by those who wished to hold onto their dreams of a Marxist Russia but recoiled at what had to be done to impose it (Deutscher 1963).

Stalin, however, knew how to explain Marxism-Leninism to the many new Communist Party members in the 1920s who lacked Trotsky's and other leading Bolsheviks' cosmopolitan background and now resented Trotsky's intellectual arrogance. This helped Stalin win popularity within the party. It did not hurt, either, that Trotsky was a Jew, and many of the new joiners shared widespread Russian anti-Semitism. Once in full power Stalin systematized his interpretation of what the theory and history of Marxism-Leninism meant and this remained the official theoretical and historical textbook of Soviet communism until 1956 (Stalin 1939).

Did Stalin betray Lenin's vision, as some have claimed (Medvedev in Tucker 1977, 204–5)? To think so is to miss the point. Later communist regimes all tried in one way or another to impose the same policies of land confiscation and forced collectivization. All purged their supposed class enemies. All conducted intraparty purges of those who questioned such policies or in some way opposed the leader.

Stalin was undoubtedly a careful student of Marx, but even more than Lenin, he charged himself with creating a new social structure. He had to weather one crisis after another, and, as a very clever politician, he knew how to get his party's backing against his enemies and also when to back away. He could not just follow Marx's blueprint because none existed for his task. Even Lenin hadn't provided enough details in his writings. The vision remained Marx's and Lenin's, but the means fell to Stalin, in terms of action and policy. It was he who designed and carried out the brutal measures we have described, who imposed the terrible suffering. We cannot say that Marx would have agreed with everything Stalin did or that everything that happened was inherent in the original Marxist texts. But we can certainly say that Marx's theories, in part filtered through Lenin, continued to inspire Stalin to the end (Davies and Harris 2005, chapters 9–10).

Did Stalin have moments of doubt? At one of the worst points in his career, shortly after Hitler invaded the Soviet Union on June 21, 1941, and was advancing rapidly toward Moscow, Stalin blurted out, in a rare moment of despair, "Everything's lost. I give up. Lenin founded our state and we've fucked it up. . . . Lenin left us a great heritage and we his successors have shitted it all up." His secret police chief, Lavrenti

Beria, who was present, later told Nikita Khrushchev that Stalin had said, "Lenin left us a proletarian state and now we've been caught with our pants down and let the whole thing go to shit" (Montefiore 2004, 374; these quotes come from the reminiscences of men from his inner circle, Anastas Mikoyan, Vyacheslav Molotov, Lavrenti Beria, and Nikita Khrushchev). Stalin's reference to Lenin in this moment of greatest stress, when his own life and political system were threatened with annihilation, is telling; it suggests he really believed he had been carrying on Lenin's work as the voice of true Marxism.

The Soviet Union's success has been cited by some latter-day Marxists as a tragedy that ultimately failed because of Russia's own backwardness (Hobsbawm 1996, 372–94). Yet Marx's vision had failed no less because of the power of democratic reform to take the place of revolution in wealthy capitalist societies. In semimodern countries like Russia that were industrializing rapidly but were still ruled by uncompromising autocrats and small elites, unwilling to countenance major reforms, movements for change were forced into the arms of revolutionaries. Marx's vision, in a sense, was caught in a historical irony—rendered more and more improbable in the nations it was originally predicted for, yet incapable of bringing the idyll of peace and equality in less developed countries where it was embraced.

Despite this, the Soviet Union's seeming success was appealing in war-torn, chaotic conditions or in colonial societies whose intellectuals wanted progress without rule by the capitalist West. Revolutionary Marxism offered a solution, and the Soviet Union quickly became a model for many other Marxist revolutionaries in less industrialized, poorer parts of the world. Marx's influence spread far more broadly than even he would have anticipated, to nations he would have thought were not ready for his ideas. When World War II created chaos across much of Eurasia, as World War I had done in Russia, and divided the world into U.S.-dominated capitalism and Soviet-dominated communism, the way was open for more Marxist revolutions.

Rather than trying to claim either that Marx was responsible for everything that Stalin did or the opposite, that Stalin betrayed the Marxist ideal, we can say that Marx inspired the Bolshevik Revolution, provided some historical guidelines, and offered a convincing utopian vision. But in trying to carry it out, to transform theory into practice, first Lenin and then Stalin created their own model of how to achieve these goals. That, in turn, changed Marxism and how it was viewed by the world, both by its supporters who took heart from Stalin's successes and by anti-Marxists who understandably interpreted the horrors of Stalinism as the product of Marx's thoughts.

Thirty-six years after Stalin's death in 1953, when Mikhail Serge-yevich Gorbachev decided to loosen the bindings of the police state and allow freedom of expression, hopeful that his people would vol-untarily accept socialism, the whole system began to collapse. In states and territories that had been part of the Russian and Soviet empires movements for independence were no longer crushed or sabotaged as they had been under Soviet rule. Piece by piece, the Soviet Union broke apart, while Russia itself turned toward limited, though short-lived, democratic reform. In a brief two-year period, the world saw one of the greatest political entities of modern times self-destruct in a spectacular creation of fifteen new countries. The final end of the USSR came in 1991, proving that Lenin and Stalin had been right all along. Had Lenin practiced real democracy he would have lost power. Had a gentler form of communism been instituted in the late 1920s and early 1930s, as Nikolai Bukharin, a leading Bolshevik theoretician, had wanted (see Cohen 1973), the system would not have survived. The only conclusion we can come to is that Lenin and Stalin took the only course that could have made Marxism work in Russia. There was bound to be resistance, of course, and we now know that confiscating the means of production and imposing total state control can only be carried out by extreme force. All communist regimes have followed the same path. That does not mean Lenin or Stalin gave up on theoretical Marxism. On the contrary, they were its true and most successful dis-ciples, though after them, Marxism became something different than what it had been when it was merely the writing of a brilliant and angry nineteenth-century visionary. What they did was to abandon Marx's deepest hope for a more equitable, humanitarian, communal type of so-ciety. What they embraced was Marx's anger, his contempt and hatred of class enemies, and his approval of force to carry out his dreams. In the vortex of twentieth-century history—a history of massive conflict that they themselves helped create—and in the oceans of blood and death they themselves pursued, the utopian dream for a better, more peaceful and just world proved to be unreachable.

Marx's Theories Confirmed: Depression, War, and New Revolutions

The misery and disillusionment that followed World War I saw an enormous rise in labor activism, strikes, and a number of attempted communist revolutions in Central Europe, all of which failed. Despite these failures, the fear of communism remained deep and widespread and brought forward a powerful reaction from the far Right. By this time, the basic principles of Marxism were vaguely known by a great number of educated people. Marx's prediction and communism's proclamation of coming destruction for all of society, including the traditional family, religion, education, and the nation-state itself, created much resistance in otherwise disparate quarters. Conservative reaction came from capitalist interests, important remnants of aristocracies, and fearful middle classes. Such reaction became one of the key elements in the rise of conservative anticommunist and fascist movements. This is a subject we will treat in a later chapter.

Of more immediate concern for us now is that it was during these same decades, too, that Marxist ideas and communist parties spread widely beyond Europe. Russia showed that communism could win power outside the advanced West by combining what seemed to be a Western science of revolutionary progress and a rejection of the capitalist system that underlay colonialism. To spread communism and advance the cause of the world revolution he hoped for, Lenin set up the Third International, usually called the Communist International, or Comintern, in 1919. The First International had been Marx and Engels's creation, and the Second had included the pre–World War I socialist parties that were now, in Lenin's eyes, disgraced by not having resisted going to war in 1914. The Second International survived as an alliance of moderate social democrats, and it was the Comintern, dominated by Moscow, that now became the leading edge of revolutionary Marxism as it began sending out agents around the world to help organize communist parties (Lazitch and Drachkovitch 1972; Courtois and Panné in Courtois and Kramer 1999, 271–322).

The Communist Party of China (CPC) was founded in 1921, a mere four years after the successful Russian Revolution. Its creators were intellectuals who had been studying Marx and who had received financial help and advice from Comintern agents sent by Lenin. The CPC's first meetings took place in the French-controlled part of Shanghai. Ho Chi Minh, the later leader of the Vietnamese Communist Party, was living in France when the French Communist Party was founded in 1920 and he was one of the original members. He later went to work for the Comintern, lived in Moscow, and then moved to China where the Vietnamese Communist Party was founded in 1930 in British-held Hong Kong. These two major parties were founded with Comintern help by intellectuals well versed in Marxist and Leninist theory. Both were heavily influenced by men who had studied or lived in France such as Deng Xiaoping, China's leader after Mao Zedong, and Zhou Enlai, Mao's longtime foreign and prime minister. This tells us a great deal about the way in which Marxism's influence spread from the West around the world (Woodside 1976; Spence 1990, 305–25).

What came next was a stunning turn of events. Seemingly without warning, the entire capitalist world was struck by the Great Depression. By the end of 1930, it looked as if Marx's predictions were about to come true. Even as the capitalist nations sank further into economic failure, Stalin's Soviet Union appeared to be rising on a path to rapid industrialization and modernization because it was following a Marxist path. As for Stalin's brutality, most of the growing number of faithful denied its actual scale and level of violence. Moreover, they could justify what cruelty took place as necessary to combat socialism's enemies in order to eventually reach the salvation of Marx's promised utopia.

The Great Depression did not just see an economic decline. Like communism, it was a key influence on the proliferation of fascism—a counterideology that had arisen out of capitalism itself. As some capitalist democracies became fascist this appeared to be one more confirmation of the Leninist version of Marxism that said that militaristic nationalism and aggression were the last desperate attempt by the capitalists to save themselves. Germany was the most obvious case as it voted Adolf Hitler's Nazi Party into power in 1933. Japan, which had invaded Manchuria in 1931, fell into the hands of a fascist-like military government. Civil war broke out in Spain, where a fascist government gained power in 1939. But it was not only Marxists who came to believe that capitalism and democracy were facing extinction. Faith in liberalism generally declined in the great capitalist democracies, France, Great Britain, and the United States (Hobsbawm 1996, 102–69; Polanyi 2001, 245–68). All this made Marxism appear an ever more viable, not to say prescient, alternative.

Finally when World War II broke out, communists in both the German-occupied parts of Europe and the Japanese-occupied parts of East Asia, notably in China, proved to be highly effective in mounting armed guerrilla opposition. This was partly because, being accustomed to secret organizations willing to use violence, they were better prepared for underground work; but also their coherent ideology could accommodate both socialist revolutionaries and nationalists who saw them as the best-suited movement to defeat fascism. All of this combined with the massive Soviet sacrifices and Stalin's triumphant defeat of Hitler helped make the world that emerged after the war even more prepared for the expansion of Marxism than after World War I (Johnson 1962; Judt 1992, 15–44; Judt 2005).

MARXISM TRIUMPHANT: THE SPREAD OF COMMUNISM IN EUROPE AND ASIA

This expansion began on a large scale in Eastern Europe, where the Soviet Army remained an occupying force. Between 1945 and 1948, Poland, Czechoslovakia, East Germany, Hungary, Romania, and Bulgaria were all transformed into Stalinist dictatorships, with former Comintern agents in charge, backed by Soviet troops. Soon thereafter, each nation began to have its own purge trials similar to those that had taken place in the Soviet Union during the 1930s, with the same ritual confessions and executions and with hundreds of thousands sent to labor camps as former bourgeois, fascists, or members of any other category deemed a threat to Soviet hegemony (Applebaum 2013). Yugoslavia and

Albania, with homegrown communist movements that had helped liberate their countries from German occupation, were for a time Soviet allies but then broke away and became independent Marxist states.

Soviet occupation plus pure opportunism among local officials certainly played the major role in establishing communist regimes in most of Eastern Europe, but without the thousands of Marxist believers in all these countries to carry out his wishes, Stalin would never have been able to control his new satellites to the degree he did. All of these places embarked on plans to develop heavy industries, cut back on consumer goods, collectivize agriculture, and build the machinery of secret police and security forces to maintain control (Janos 2000, 125–256).

In France and Italy, meanwhile, the communists emerged from World War II as heroic fighters against fascism. They became the largest political movements of the day, though in neither case were they able to take power democratically. Without Soviet troops, whatever electoral victories the communists gained were insufficient. Instead, moderate conservatives and moderate social democrats led Western European reconstruction with economic reforms and the expansion of the welfare state that stabilized democratic capitalism and gradually diminished the appeal of radical Marxism and communist parties (Judt 2005).

This did not happen in East and Southeast Asia. While American occupation of Japan and South Korea kept these nations from becoming communist, other parts of the region moved in a different direction. The cruelty of Japanese colonization, which had affected large portions of the region, as well as Western colonialism, created a widespread desire for independence and for new political ideas. In China, Mao Zedong had used the war against Japan to strengthen his army and increase popular support for communism. Like Lenin, Mao was himself an intellectual who adapted Marxist theory to his own purposes and to China's situation. After Japan's surrender in 1945, he waged a successful war against anticommunist Chinese Nationalists and defeated them in 1949 (Westad 2003).

Vietnam offers a different example. In 1945, as Japan's Asian empire collapsed, Ho Chi Minh declared his country's independence from France, starting a bloody war with the French that ended with Ho's victory in 1954 and the creation of a Marxist North Vietnam. Twenty-one years later, after an even more deadly war with the United States that was also won by the communists, all of Vietnam was united under their rule (Lawrence and Logevall 2007; Logevall 2000). By this time, moreover, the other portions of what had once been called "Indochina" (the area under French colonial occupation), including Laos and Cambodia, had also been taken over by their communist parties.

China and Vietnam were not the only places where Marxism triumphed. The Soviet Union used an established Korean Marxist movement, which had fought with the Chinese against Japanese colonialism, to establish a North Korean communist state. Its attempt to unite all of Korea under communism led to the devastating Korean War of 1950–53, which ended in a stalemate (Cumings 2010). Strong communist parties emerged in much of Southeast and South Asia, as well as the Middle East. In Africa, meanwhile, Marxism helped inspire a number of anticolonial movements during the 1950s and 1960s, leading to independence. Communist parties also grew in influence in Latin America.

What was Marxism's appeal in all these places during the postwar era? We have spoken of the Soviet Union's success as a world power, its key role in the victory over fascism, and its purported economic rise as the globe's second biggest power. These facts had potent influence in the first decade after the war, as did the fact that capitalist democracy championed by the Western Europeans and Americans was tainted by its association with Western colonialism. Marxism, on the other hand, appealed to intellectuals behind independence movements because its ideas were still able to explain a great deal of the world, not least the enormous, demoralizing disparities between wealth and poverty that capitalism had brought and that, in the postwar era, seemed more apparent in colonial and newly independent areas than ever. Marxism, that is, continued to offer a mixture of scientific certainty and idealism. However brutal it may have been in practice, the theory never lost the Christian ethic of redemption at its core, putting forward the cause of the downtrodden against riches and privilege and promising a more moral and equitable society. Independence leaders inspired by Marxist ideals could see themselves as father figures who, like Lenin, Stalin, and Mao, would lead their people out of colonialism and its shadows to independence, unity, and economic success.

The perception that Marxism was now sweeping the world was re-inforced by the conversion of many intellectuals in the Western world to Marxist ideas. All these successes shaped at least three decades of in-ternational affairs after World War II, making Marx the world's most influential political prophet a full century after his major writings. Not only was the Soviet Union the world's second most powerful state and one of only two global superpowers, along with the United States, but the world's most populous country, China, had also become commu-nist. Inspired by Marx, Engels, Lenin, Stalin, and, more recently, Mao, revolutionary thinkers, movements, and parties throughout the world were on the ascendant.

MAOISM: MARXISM'S APOGEE AND TRANSFORMATION

China's history in the nineteenth and early twentieth centuries was marked by disaster and failure even more than Russia's before the Bol-shevik Revolution. From a position of great strength and stability in Asia before 1800, China thereafter crumbled into a failing, subservient state. Western powers, most of all Britain, bullied and occupied parts of it, acting contemptuously toward the region's oldest and, for many cen-turies, most dominant and influential culture. China's failure to mod-ernize and create a thriving industrial base cost it dearly. In two "opium wars" (1839–42 and 1856–60), the British easily defeated China, forc-ing it to accept opium imports that made British merchants rich and extracting major concessions, such as the right to establish the British colony of Hong Kong as a key port to capture massive amounts of trade away from China itself. Following this humiliation, other European countries, and then Japan, forced similar demands on China, putting a series of treaty ports and parts of major cities, particularly Shanghai, under their control.

As if this were not enough, the mid-nineteenth century saw China deeply shaken by a series of terrible civil wars, notably the Nien (1851–68) conflict in the north and the Taiping Rebellion (1851–64) in the east. The Taiping Rebellion alone caused thirty million deaths, prob-ably the bloodiest war in human history until World War I. In its reli-gious fanaticism—the rebellion's leader, Hong Xiuquan, claimed to be the second son of the Christian God, able to converse with his older brother, Jesus Christ, and their father—its emphasis on forced communal living, and a puritanical devotion to the cause (while the leader lived in self-indulgent luxury), the Taiping set a precedent. We should be less than shocked to learn that Mao Zedong greatly praised both sets of rebels as true revolutionaries (Perry 1980; Spence 1997).

Most humiliating of all, however, was the rapid, successful, and ultimately threatening rise of Japan. Indeed, in a single generation after the Meiji Restoration of 1868, Japan was able to become a true industrial power, greatly expanding its factories and trade, strengthening its workforce, and fulfilling a primary goal of building a modern, Western-style army and navy. In 1894–95, Japan's military utterly crushed China in a brief conflict over control of Korea. The Chinese were forced to cede both some coastal ports and the island of Taiwan to Japan. Though it was clear after all this that China needed to modernize, its antiquated imperial system held on, blocking meaningful reform, until it collapsed in the revolution of 1911 (Wakeman 1975).

A series of unstable governments then tried to hold China together as various provinces fell under the sway of local warlords. After its foundation in 1921, the Communist Party of China in 1923 allied itself with the much larger, noncommunist modernizing party, the Guomindang (the Chinese Nationalist Party), which was also being helped by Comintern agents who were reshaping it into a Leninist organization controlled by a small elite. The Guomindang was soon taken over by General Chiang Kai-shek, who had spent some months in Moscow in 1923 learning how to organize such a party. The Soviet Union got the CPC to make common cause with the Nationalists because China was deemed too unready, too backward to undergo a communist revolution. But in 1927, Chiang turned on the communists, nearly obliterating them. Mao Zedong and those of the CPC who shared his concept of a peasant-based Marxist revolution performed a series of strategic retreats called the "Long March," withdrawing to a remote area in northern China. Recent scholarship has shown that during this period the CPC was saved by funds from Stalin. The money was used to buy food and to bribe local warlords for passage through their lands. Nonetheless, great hardships were endured. At most, only nine thousand out of an original twenty-five thousand survived the Long March to set up a new base camp and regroup closer to the Soviet Union (Taylor 2009, 110–14).

In 1931 Japan invaded and colonized Manchuria. In 1937 it invaded the rest of China. The Nationalist and Communist parties nominally became allies fighting against Japan, but the Nationalists, who were more based in urban areas, were badly weakened by the Japanese, who seized the main cities and richest Chinese territories. It was also the Nationalists who bore the brunt of the fighting against the better-armed Japanese. The Communists, on the other hand, were more successful in building up their armies by relying on peasant soldiers and the enthusiasm of a whole generation of educated young Chinese idealists who saw in Marxism the possibility of salvation from a century of humiliation and devastation (Johnson 1962; Mitter 2013).

World War II had an immense impact. The Japanese proved to be as brutal on the mainland as the Nazis were in Europe; they were also imbued with the same kind of intense racism. Like German intellectuals, who brought forward the idea of an Aryan-Teutonic race destined to rule the West, Japanese ultranationalist thinkers reached back into the mists of mythology to claim the sole divinity of their emperor and the chosen nature of their people, whose calling was to enslave the rest of Asia. (See chapter 5 on the Counter-Enlightenment and fascism.) A rough estimate holds that between 1937 and 1945, twenty million Chinese died as a result of the war with Japan, with about a hundred million more, a quarter of the population, turned into internal refugees (Lary and MacKinnon 2001, 3–15). Then, as soon as Japan surrendered, Mao's Communists resumed their war against Chiang's Guomindang, bringing still more death and displacement to this broken, bloodied nation. By 1949, however, the CPC had won a complete victory (Taylor 2009, 378–408).

But peace remained far-off. Almost immediately, the Chinese Communists initiated the same kind of purge of "class enemies" as those by Lenin and Stalin. Nearly a million former landlords and well-off peasants who had not backed the communists were executed (Spence 1990, 517). Even as this was taking place, moreover, Mao decided on intervention in the Korean War against the Americans, which continued from

1950 to 1953. Then copying the Soviet path, China turned to massive industrialization (Lardy 1983). In 1958, Mao decided on a new path. The Soviets, it seemed to him, had abandoned revolutionary Marxism after Stalin's death. To understand what followed over the next eighteen years, up to the time of Mao's own demise, requires that we return to debates within Marxism and how Mao interpreted these.

Mao was a well-read intellectual. We see this, for example, in the interviews he gave to the American journalist Edgar Snow. Speaking of his own thought before 1936, the point when, during the Long March, he took over the leadership of the CPC's refuge in northwestern China, he portrayed himself as a youth who had embarked on a rigorous program of self-education, reading Chinese translations of classical Western works.

> I read Adam Smith's *The Wealth of Nations*, and Darwin's *Origin of Species*, and a book on ethics by John Stuart Mill. I read the works of Rousseau, Spencer's *Logic*, and a book on law by Montesquieu. I mixed poetry and romances, and the tales of ancient Greece, with serious study of history and geography of Russia, America, England, France, and other countries. (Snow 1961, 144)

He also immersed himself in Chinese philosophy and the works of Chinese intellectuals who had studied in Europe. These intellectuals had brought back not only Darwin but also Herbert Spencer and his version of Social Darwinism. Spencer's enormously influential views on the progress of society, adopted by large parts of educated society in East Asia, raised for Mao the problem of why China had become so weak. He could not accept the notion popular in Europe during the early twentieth century (a distortion of Darwin) that this had to do with race. Such, after all, would consign China to perpetual backwardness. Instead he found an answer in the work of Friedrich Paulsen, a German philosopher and educational reformer, who emphasized the importance of will and military spirit in a nation's progress. As Paulsen died in 1908, his ideas were mainly intended to help strengthen Germany (Thilly 1909). Ignoring the result of World War I, Mao heard in Paulsen a call for physical vigor and strengthened spirit as a way to reenergize China (Wakeman 1975, 201–4).

In Beijing (then called Peking), Mao had seen the student movement that led to the modernizing and nationalist protests of May 4, 1919, utterly fail (Schwarcz 1986). As an assistant librarian at Peking University, he worked for Li Dazhao, who was promoting the view that the Bolshevik Revolution in Russia should be a model for China. Li was a strong nationalist who saw Lenin's revolution as a way to transform and revive China. He also urged his young followers to go out into the countryside and work with the peasants to create a larger movement (Spence 1990, 305–19). These early influences remained with Mao his whole life. He read more of Marx and Engels later on, particularly in the 1930s, when many Marxist works were newly translated into Chinese. But by then he had already combined revolutionary theory with his belief in the need to restore China to its rightful glory (Schram 1969, 30).

Mao's early reading and his experience as a leader in the civil war between the CPC and the Nationalist Party from 1927 to 1949, as well as against the Japanese from 1937 to 1945, convinced him that the voluntary, populist, most violent side of Marxism was appropriate for his country. It was a view undoubtedly solidified by the Chinese army's success in beating back the Americans in Korea, then holding them to a draw, despite their huge material advantage. China thus had the internal capability to place itself once again among the most powerful of nations. To achieve this, however, Marxist struggle was necessary. The great historian of China, Frederic Wakeman, went so far as to say that Mao's version of Marxism was really Social Darwinism. But it was a peculiar form of Social Darwinism in which classes, not species or races, competed against each other, and only the historically fittest would triumph. This had to be the proletariat, meaning, in China, the peasants. And that could only be achieved by ceaseless class struggle, as Marx and Lenin had specified even though they had spoken of the industrial working class as the leading one, not peasants, who were not considered by them to be revolutionary. As China was so overwhelmingly rural, Mao just transformed his idealized peasantry into a Marxist revolutionary class (Wakeman 1973, 236–37).

Though Stalin had held similar ideas about the need for continuing class struggle, as we saw earlier, he never went as far as Mao in promoting eternal class war. Mao combined his sense that willpower and energy were such a great force that anything was possible with Marx's thinking about the Paris Commune of 1871 suggesting that revolutionary enthusiasm could overcome any administrative obstacles. This way of thinking, however, discredited expertise in favor of spontaneous, raw daring and trust in the fundamental capacity of less well-educated working classes and peasants to shape a new society. Appealing as the concept was to many Western intellectuals seeking a recipe for a pure, Marxist egalitarianism, and attractive as it was throughout much of what came to be called the "Third World," it proved to be hugely destructive. From the very beginning, as an intellectual concept, it suffered from a threatening irony—intellectuals, at base, could not be trusted, since the future would be formed by those who worked with their hands, not their minds. That Mao was himself an intellectual shaped by his reading of classical Western texts was, as far as he was concerned, no longer relevant.

Seeking to put his own version of Marx's theory to work, Mao prodded China to abandon the Soviet model for even more breakneck industrialization and total collectivization of agriculture. This was the so-called Great Leap Forward. Peasants were ordered to produce steel in every new village, as they were herded into communal living arrangements designed to break up traditional ("bourgeois") family solidarity. The immediate objective was to force more work out of people and give birth to a new socialist human being. Mao told his colleagues that new agricultural techniques he had invented would so increase productivity that much of the land could be turned into parks. In his economic analysis, Marx had stated that technological progress alone could not save capitalism because it could only temporarily delay the destructive competition that caused crises. But in Mao's version of Marxism, this came to mean that human will could trump technology. This also came through in Mao's view of nature, which, in effect, was similar to the Western view in the nineteenth century, namely, that humankind could reengineer nature at will for the sake of progress. It was an outlook, however, that Mao took to a destructive extreme. He decreed a campaign to eliminate all sparrows, as they fed on grains, only to see the insects also eaten by the birds, especially locusts, proliferate and destroy the major portion of rice harvests. Other such campaigns involved heavy deforestation, filling in of wetlands, massive building of dams, and poorly designed irrigation projects, all of which together resulted in enormous devastation to river ecology, healthy microclimates, water purity, and other vital services that natural landscapes had previously provided. The ultimate result was that many millions of Chinese were forced to abandon other work and engage in these "improvements," which ended up destroying, not expanding, much of China's capability to produce food (Shapiro 2001).

Peasants, furthermore, were ordered to melt down their tools in backyard furnaces to produce useless pig iron, while agriculture languished. Mao also insisted on exporting more food to pay off China's debts to the Soviet Union. All of this, in conjunction with the devastation wreaked upon the country's natural systems, led to terrible, widespread famine, possibly the most extensive in human history. Estimates of the number of people who perished between 1958 and 1961 range from fifteen to forty-six million. Two recent estimates of deaths, both from starvation and from the violence that accompanied it, have been provided by a longtime journalist from the People's Republic itself, Yang Jisheng, and by the historian Mark Dikötter. Yang, whose book was originally published in Hong Kong in 2008, suggests that thirty-six million died (Yang 2012). This book remains banned on the mainland. Dikötter estimates it was closer to forty-five million (Dikötter 2010). Such estimates, moreover, do not include the tens of millions who survived but suffered the lifelong (or life-shortening) effects of severe malnutrition. All agree the destruction was on the same scale as that of the Taiping Rebellion or the Sino-Japanese War of 1937–45 (Chan 2001; Thaxton 2008).

Horrified by these happenings, members of the CPC's inner circle moved gradually to wrest away control of the economy. They sought to sideline Mao as they returned to more orthodox Marxist, or perhaps one should say Stalinist, strategies. But Mao was not to be marginalized so easily. As the true apostle of Marxist vision, he plotted his return and managed in 1966 to unleash the "Great Proletarian Cultural

Revolution." He called on all who were dissatisfied, particularly the young, to turn against the bureaucracy and the Communist Party itself, both of which had been penetrated by what he called "bourgeois" thinking and habits. His prestige remained a considerable source of power, giving him the ability to purge, imprison, and kill those of his associates who had tried to reason with him during the Great Leap Forward (White 1989; Dittmer 1974). Violent gangs of youths, the Red Guards, stormed the countryside, humiliating and often killing officials. Millions of urban youth, students, and intellectuals were exiled to rural places for "reeducation." Memoirs from the period paint a horrible picture that included not only political stasis and economic regression but also the stripping from China of its educated class—its "human capital." An entire generation received little or no higher learning, as schools and universities were severely disrupted (Cheng 1987; Heng and Shapiro 1984). According to historian Jonathan Spence, "Embedded within this frenzied activism was a political agenda of great significance, what might be called a 'purist egalitarianism,' that echoed the values of the Paris Commune of 1871 so vividly evoked for China by Mao Zedong" (Spence 1990, 607). In other words, Mao continued to draw direct inspiration from Marx's own writings, in this case his analysis of the Paris Commune. Marx's ideas, that is, though warped to a context far beyond their origin, continued as a source of Mao's own visions and ambitions.

The number who died as a result of the Cultural Revolution is not known. Of eighteen million or so "cadres"—officials in the government and Communist Party—three to four million were arrested. By 1969, it was clear that Mao had set loose a maelstrom. Things were so out of control that Mao himself had the army try to restore order, leading to hundreds of thousands more being imprisoned and killed. As many as twelve to twenty million, including one million from Shanghai alone, were forced into the hinterlands. Purges and counterpurges continued as near civil war raged between various factions. By the end of 1973 the situation quieted somewhat, but the terror and chaos continued locally until Mao died in 1976 (Courtois and Kramer 1999, 513–38; MacFarquhar and Schoenhals 2006).

One consequence of all this was a deep rejection of Maoist ideas. The surviving members of the ruling CPC had been traumatized; Mao's successors, led by the old revolutionary Deng Xiaoping, began a careful move toward reform, beginning in 1978. Over the next twenty years, after three decades of Communist revolutionary turmoil, China made an amazing about-face. It accepted the legitimacy of many capitalist concepts, at least in part: much privatized commerce and business, extensive though somewhat limited private property rights, extensive trade with noncommunist states, the importance of advanced, specialized education in science and technology, and the need for true expertise. By 2000, China was well on its way to becoming a substantially capitalist economy, though with both a large sector of the economy controlled by state-owned enterprises and complete control of politics by an autocratic Communist Party.

The CPC, meanwhile, had itself abandoned most of Marxism as a guiding philosophy. Indeed, it had traded Marx for a version of Adam Smith. "Social harmony" was to be bought through economic development. The CPC, that is, transformed itself into a guarantor of national order as its civilian and military elite learned to profit from the rapid privatization. Dissent, in the form of pro-democracy movements, continued to be crushed, often violently. But in every other domain, the China of the twenty-first century appears in many ways to be the exact opposite of what Marx and Mao had wanted and hoped for. But in order to maintain some continuity, ironically, Mao continues to be celebrated as a great patriot even today (Baum 1994; Vogel 1989; Shirk 2007; Lardy 2002; Callahan 2013).

The Spread and Decline of Marxism in the Third World

From the 1950s to the 1970s, much of what was going on in China remained poorly understood in the outside world. It seemed to many that Mao's ideological model had become an active competitor to the Soviet precedent, as the two communist giants became increasingly hostile to one other. The Soviets had more technology, money, and military hardware to offer as aid, but the Chinese claimed that their version of Marxism, depending more on the rural population, was more egalitarian, less bureaucratic, and better suited to the poorest parts of the world, especially in southern Asia and in Africa.

In 1952 a distinguished French economist and demographer, Alfred Sauvy, coined the term "Third World." Sauvy was a man of the moderate Left who believed in capitalism, with controls. He was no Marxist, yet his phrase, and the idea behind it, played a central role in a major ideological movement over the next forty or so years: "Third World-ism." How did Sauvy express his idea? In *L'Observateur* on August 14, 1952, he wrote:

> We speak freely of two existing worlds [he meant capitalist and communist], of their possible confrontation, of their coexistence, etc., forgetting all too often that a third one exists, the most important and indeed the first in chronological order. . . . For this Third World, ignored, exploited, scorned, like the Third Estate, also wants to be something. (quoted in Malley 1996, 78)

"Third World" referred to nations neither among the advanced capitalist societies led by the United States—the "First World"—nor part of the communist ones dominated by the Soviet Union—the "Second." The reference to the Third Estate was meaningful, too, in that this had included neither the nobles nor the clergy but the rising bourgeoisie who had benefited from the French Revolution of 1789 against the monarchy, aristocracy (the "First Estate"), and Catholic Church (the "Second"). Thus, for Sauvy, it was the Third World that held the real revolutionary potential, just like the Third Estate of the 1780s. If taken seriously, this analysis called for a revision of Marxist predictions about where anticapitalist revolutions would take place.

Indeed, in the early 1950s the world was beginning to agree with Sauvy. Ho Chi Minh was leading an anticolonial war against the French, one he would win in 1954 when communist North Vietnam was established. India and Pakistan won their independence from Great Britain in 1947, with the new Indian government under Jawaharlal Nehru established as a democracy but leaning in socialist directions. The Dutch, meantime, had been forced to give up the East Indies (Indonesia) in 1949, which, under its first president, Sukarno, looked for economic support from the Soviet Union and Mao's China. The Egyptian monarchy, beholden to and dominated by Britain, had been overthrown in 1952, and the country's new leader, Gamal Abdel Nasser, also made overtures of friendship to the Soviets. (See also chapter 7 on Islam.) At the same time, anticolonial movements were growing in Africa, and within the next decade most of the European colonies on that continent would be replaced by independent states, many of them, as already mentioned, with sizable communist parties or Marxist-inspired leaders.

Some of these movements and leaders claimed to be overtly Marxist, some not. But all were touched by Marxism in some way. They accepted that the major parts of their economies should be controlled by the state, something that seemed more equitable and more able to resist domination by the West. At a meeting of African and Asian leaders in Bandung, Indonesia, in 1955, Zhou Enlai came from China and succeeded in inserting his country into the greater movement as an example of how to promote economic growth for all people while keeping out foreign control. Over the next few years, Third Worldism coalesced into an openly socialist, anti-Western movement. At its height in the 1970s, it included leaders as different as Yasser Arafat of the Palestine Liberation Organization, Kenneth Kaunda of Zambia, Fidel Castro of Cuba, and the heads of various Latin American guerrilla movements. In the West itself, moreover, Third Worldism as a concept of liberation became a common cause among students and radicals, particularly during the tumultuous 1960s and early 1970s. Marxism, in whole or in part, was the underlying ideological thread that bound all these phenomena together. By this time, however, it was a thread of changed composition and color. No longer did it talk of proletarian internationalism but increasingly of the heroic, romantic worship of violent anti-Westernism. Indeed, while Marx was the acknowledged founder of communist "historical science" and Lenin was recognized for his practical contributions, the new heroes were Mao, Ho Chi Minh, Che Guevara, Fidel Castro, Yasser Arafat, and the great intellectual apostle of violent anticolonialism, Frantz Fanon, a French-educated doctor from Martinique who had joined with the Algerian rebels during their 1956–62 war of liberation against France (Malley 1996, 77–114).

Marx and Engels would have been astonished. How had the twentieth century gone so far astray from their prophecy for advanced capitalist economies? Russia in 1917 at least had an industrial base, though a weak one, and its workers had a hand in the Bolshevik Revolution. But China's revolution took place in an agrarian society with few industrial centers, while Vietnam had essentially none. Neither nation had anything like a proletariat or bourgeoisie in the classical Marxist sense. And what of North Korea and the other localized versions of communism and socialism pursued in Africa, such as Julius Nyerere's program of Ujamaa (literally "familyhood" in Swahili but meaning a plan to collectivize village lands to create socialist communes in the countryside) in Tanzania? What brought Marxism to victory in such places was hardly the historical unfolding of capitalism. Indeed, it rose from an intense desire for national unity that would use the Soviet—and even more the Chinese—example of rejecting capitalism from the start and moving directly to socialism without waiting to pass through the fully developed capitalist stage.

Such is what Third Worldism was largely about: a wish to restore or, in many cases, to create national pride, as well as a faith that state-centered, self-sufficient economic development, imitating some of what the Soviets and Chinese had done, offered a better way to achieve this than market-oriented policies. Instead of classical working and bourgeois classes, these countries had an educated, partially Westernized, young and idealistic set of leaders eager to use Western knowledge to liberate and advance their nations. Marxism appealed to them because it classified the major European states, in their imperial phase, as enemies of liberation and equality, while still holding out such liberation as a historical necessity. These leaders understood that Marx's original program was the inspiration, but Leninist, Stalinist, and, even more, the Maoist versions were more practical.

The economic policies they followed, however, turned out to be far less workable than imagined. By the time the Soviet Union and Eastern European communism collapsed between 1989 and 1991 and China turned away from socialism, Third Worldism had also largely failed, leaving only a sprinkle of feeble survivors, most prominently Cuba. By then, the Third World was no longer really part of the story of Marxism.

Inequality, injustice, humiliation, anger, and the revolutionary ideals meant to address these ills did not disappear. But to understand them requires looking at sources other than Karl Marx. We will return to ideas that have influenced such movements in later chapters.

MARXISM'S DECLINE AND FAILURE

Communist movements inspired by Marxist ideas proved skillful at mobilizing popular discontent, nationalist grievances, and the idealism of intellectuals. Where Marxists actually gained power, they were almost always aided by anarchic, wartime conditions that fatally weakened existing governments, including colonial ones long perceived as unjust and corrupt.

There were things that communist regimes did well. Once in control, they were adept at mobilizing their people to prepare for and fight wars. They created the basis for mass education and literacy, as well as basic medical care. To a significant degree, they launched their societies on the road to further modernization. But the costs were immense and horrific. The murder of millions of "class enemies" and the suffering of many millions more by forced migration, agricultural collectivization, and the takeover of the means of production by inefficient, increasingly corrupt bureaucracies were repeated again and again. Communism succeeded, temporarily, only through human sacrifice on a monstrous scale. Indeed, it advanced by a constant call for ever more revolution and therefore ever more victims, thus leaving behind a bitter, disillusioning legacy (Chirot 1996; Courtois and Kramer 1999).

Even before 1991, when the Soviet Union disintegrated, much of the communist world had turned away from Marxism. In Yugoslavia, for example, Josip Broz Tito, who had led the communists to power through guerilla resistance to invading fascists, turned gradually away from the Soviet Union after Stalin in 1948 tried to gain dominance over the country. Tito became a kind of alternative model for many Third Worldist regimes, particularly in Algeria, because of his independence and his tolerance for partial market reform. But by the time of his death in 1980, Yugoslavia was on its way to dissolution. What resulted in the early 1990s was the unleashing of a phenomenon that Marx and Engels had utterly ignored: ethnic conflict, which in this case led to a series of terrible civil wars (Glenny 2000).

Examples in Asia also show a turn away from Marxism. For Vietnam, the 1975 victory in the "American War" left the country in deep poverty. In 1986 the Communist Party, drawing on the reforms in China by Deng Xiaoping, implemented a movement called Doi Moi ("renovation") that gave peasants control over their own production and allowed an increasing number of capitalist enterprises. Vietnam entered the world economy, became a major exporter of rice and coffee, and started on the road toward greater prosperity and industrialization, even as the Communist Party kept its control over politics (Murray 1997; Boothroyd and Pham 2000). North Korea, by contrast, remained a client state of the Soviet Union but in the Stalinist mode—cruel, oppressive, totalitarian, and absolute in cultish devotion to its leader, Kim Il Sung. It sealed itself off from the outside world, developed its own philosophy of self-reliance, known as *juche*, and, after the Soviet Union collapsed, fell into dire poverty. In the early 1990s the country was struck by major famines that killed over a million people and crippled or incapacitated millions more. In a first for any presumed Marxist state, its leadership has involved a royal family; Kim Il Sung's death in 1994 brought to power his son, Kim Jong Il, whose subsequent demise, in 2011, gave the scepter to his own son, Kim Jong Un (Lankov 2013). By then it was not Marxism that remained as the main ideology but worship of the deified Kim family.

Still more grotesque was the case of Cambodia, briefly and brutally ruled by its communist party, the Khmer Rouge, from 1975 to 1979. During this time, they murdered and starved to death roughly a quarter of the entire population, launched a war against their communist neighbor, Vietnam, and were overthrown when Vietnam invaded. The ideas propelling this monstrous episode were not Marxist but instead an extreme form of Maoism. The Khmer Rouge pursued a form of total social engineering, turning their back on modern industry, emptying their cities, eliminating the intelligentsia, and engaging in an orgy of killing that proportionally exceeded anything done even by Stalin or Mao. The reality is that their ideology was really a combination of warped history (originally put into their minds by French historians), racist eugenics as extreme as the Nazi version, and admiration for a kind of primitive communal living in which family life was eliminated and everyone toiled in the fields like slaves (Kiernan 2008). We might guess that Marx and Engels, or for that matter Lenin and Stalin as well, would have considered obscene a genocidal system that claimed to be communist but rejected urban life, industry, modern science, literacy, and all intellectual endeavors.

What of the twenty-first century? In a few places—in Nepal, in some of the most impoverished parts of northeast India, in the mountains of Peru where remnants of the Shining Path group still exist, and in some other similar, desperately backward places—violent movements that claim to be communist still exist. Almost necessarily, however, they are Maoist, not Marxist. There are also a number of regimes that call themselves socialist in Latin America and elsewhere. These tend to be populist, however, with state-centered economies, hostile to the world capitalist system, but owing little to Marxism.

Does all this mean that Marxism is finally moribund? No, it doesn't. Marx's ideas continue to evoke not merely discussion and debate but devotion and belief. This is particularly true among intellectuals.

THE CONTINUING INTELLECTUAL LEGACY OF MARXISM

To this point, we have been concerned with Marx's ideas and their impact in the political, social, and economic realms. A focus here is easily justified: these realms are where such ideas were brought to bear directly upon the lives of hundreds of millions of people, altering the nature of entire societies and the political character of the modern world. The massive, wholesale transformation of some of the largest and most autocratic nations into a Marxist heartland must surely count among the most spectacular and devastating experiments of the entire modern era. Its ultimate collapse and failure take nothing away from the necessity to understand how a purely intellectual construct won over so many followers and had such a dramatic impact.

Raymond Aron, the French political philosopher cited earlier, tried to explain why so many intellectuals were attracted to Marxism, why, in his clever phrase, it had become "the opium of the intellectuals." There was what we have mentioned: the Christian theme of just revenge for the humiliated, who will be saved while the unworthy are cast into hell; the promise of material bounty as the productive forces of modernity are properly harnessed for the good of all instead of being monopolized by a small, greedy elite; and the attraction of what seemed to be a rational science, so that those who understand it qualify as "experts," the ones who should rightfully be placed at the head of the transformation that will lead humanity toward its golden era. This last particularly appeals to intellectuals who want to become the saviors of their societies (Aron 2002, 203–4).

Aron's perceptions of Marxism's religious aspects, however, help render it understandable that a wide range of people, from poor peasants and exploited workers to idealistic bourgeois and scholarly thinkers, should be attracted to Marx's doctrine. In prerevolutionary Russia, China, Vietnam, Cuba, and the Third World, as well as among underground movements fighting against fascism or to liberate themselves from foreign occupation, it all made sense. Marxism provided the promise that oppression, either domestic or foreign, would not prevail. It could be, and would be, overthrown. And as we pointed out earlier, the Marxist perspective has also offered a way to be anti-Western while at the same time justifying the adoption of Western science and technology.

For Aron and other, particularly liberal, critics of Marxism who remain committed to Enlightenment values, the big question is not so much why it appealed in poor countries whose intellectuals were desperately looking for a way to overcome backwardness and colonial dependency. Rather, the mystery is why so many learned Western intellectuals, in comfortable positions, by the 1950s, knowing about the horrors of Stalinism, remained in the ranks of believers? Ultimately the continuing attraction of Marxism has something to do with the fact that like Nazism (which we will examine in a later chapter), it was a kind of godless religious faith that fed the hope for a better future during a time when much of the world, including the advanced nations, were shattered with conflict, hatred, violence, and, not least, uncertainty. Intellectuals, or at least many of them, need to have a faith, a hope in an unrealizable glorious future, in other words, a religion even if they no longer believe in God.

In communist societies, Marxism was turned into a rigid, formulaic catechism and over time became an anti-Marxist vehicle for glorifying the political leaders of these regimes. But in the freer countries of the West, paradoxically, it entered a flourishing period of intellectual creativity from the 1930s well into the 1970s and 1980s, while never gaining much political power. To a significant degree, the legacy of Marxism entered a new phase, one that came to be centered in Western academia. In Britain, for example, great historians such as Eric Hobsbawm, E. P. Thompson, and Christopher Hill enriched Marxist analyses of the past while finding ways of excusing communism's crimes and failures even when admitting that they occurred (Hobsbawm 2002). Not just in Britain but all over Western Europe and in the United States, Marxist social science, philosophy, and literary scholarship gained an expanded following, even as the terrible consequences of Stalinist and Maoist repression became widely known. Stalin's crimes were not much discussed by the new Marxist movements. Instead, deep worries over the inequities created by capitalism, its failures exposed by the Great Depression, the gigantic destructive power and dehumanizing effects of modern technology, and the sense of injustice raised by fading colonialism all contributed to a profound dissatisfaction with progress as defined in Western terms and a longing for alternatives. Even in Eastern Europe young, mostly student protestors against communism in the 1960s and 1970s used Marxism and the promise presumably held out by Maoism to demand revolutionary changes.

More important in the West were the social upheavals of the 1960s. Nearly every advanced nation, from France to the United States to Japan, underwent a paroxysm of student defiance aimed against governments, corporate power, imperialism, consumerism, and institutional religions that were deemed to be spiritually corrupt. Condemnation of the United States for its war in Vietnam from the early 1960s to 1975 and for its culture of racism was also a major factor. Student movements throughout the West, Japan, and many Third World countries became enthusiastic critics of arrogant American foreign policy, military power, and corporate wealth.

These movements helped revive Marxism in the West, but not the Marxism of communist regimes or political parties. Rather, it was a more intellectualized form, to some degree in line with Marx's early humanistic background and outlook. The new Marxism drew inspiration from the writings of French existentialism and the German Frankfurt School, a loose grouping of philosophers and social theorists who rejected traditional communist adherence to "proletariat revolution" and instead turned toward analyses of social reality, mass consciousness, and the individual. This neo-Marxism, focused on a multidisciplinary indictment of Western society, grew rapidly through the 1960s and into the 1970s and 1980s. At this point, it became further expanded and intellectualized by French Marxist philosophy, particularly that of Louis Althusser and Michel Foucault, and by rediscovery of the work by the Italian communist Antonio Gramsci. All of these thinkers tended to return to Marx and Engels's writings to gain insights from close interpretive readings. For neo-Marxists, forms of oppression operate everywhere in the social environment, just as Marx implied, even in the most subtle ways. They are constantly being regenerated in education, media, popular culture, advertising, and so on. Marx's concept regarding "modes of production" is therefore amended such that its materialism is expanded to include all forms of discourse (language, images, art, knowledge), as well as the daily actions of citizens (Bottomore 2002; Jay 1986).

Such views found easy commerce with other movements that emerged from the counterculture, such as feminism and environmentalism, as well as the social sciences and, above all, the humanities. The new Marxism had a particularly long-lasting effect on universities, as the students and young scholars who found themselves persuaded by its outlook in the 1960s and 1970s came to dominate many academic fields for the next generation (Fink, Gassert, and Junker 1998). Out of this was born the larger part of postmodernism, whose varied intellectual currents became established in universities around the world, including the United States (Manuel 1995, 203–4). No part of all this—what some have called the neo-Marxist turn—admits any connection with the brutalities of Soviet and Maoist communism.

But the waters here are a bit muddy, historically speaking. Tony Judt, analyzing the strong favor Marxism had among French intellectuals after World War II, indicated how major writers like Jean-Paul Sartre were drawn to revolutionary violence as a way to reject capitalist culture and find a solution to inequality and oppression. When disillusionment with the Soviet Union began after Stalin's crimes were denounced by Khrushchev in 1956 and after the Soviets crushed reformist movements in Hungary (1956) and, especially, Czechoslovakia (1968), Sartre and others turned to Maoism and violent Third Worldism. By the early 1970s, after the failure of the spontaneous, youth-led "revolution" of May 1968, calls for violence decreased. French Marxist intellectuals moved away from street revolutionary action into literary theory and the analysis of culture (Judt 1992, 275–319). That is where Marxism mostly resides today.

What of the future? We should divide the question into two distinct but related parts: the political side, which calls up Stalin, Mao, Pol Pot, and Castro; and the theoretical side, which includes neo-Marxism with its many faces.

Marxist political systems, like orthodox Marxist doctrine, do not recommend themselves to the future in the first decades of the twenty-first century. Yet to write off all possibility of further recurrence would be shortsighted. The dark episodes of the last century suggest a message of warning: Marxist ideas remain appealing to some who need a model for the construction of a better, fairer, more utopian future society. Particularly for those who seek to meld their faith in science with a quasi-religious yearning for personal salvation, Marxism offers an eschatological promise of redemption. In times of great social and economic stress, and what seems to be looming chaos, the extremes of both Right and Left gain ground. For the latter, Marxism will remain the theory of choice, or at least in some modified form. It attacks the inequities of excessive laissez-faire capitalism, it explains periodic economic crises, it promises solutions, and it claims a measure of ultimate historical inevitability.

Finally, too, there is the reality that as the tragic and traumatic outcomes of communism gradually recede into historical memory, into a bygone century, their edges are rounded off and their horror lessens. There is evidence that untempered capitalism leads to growing inequality when countervailing union and government power is absent. That would seem to be happening within the United States and very possibly other advanced capitalist societies as well (Piketty 2014). The temptation to turn again to Marx's promise could well find fertile soil before long.

Karl Marx's theories encompassed much of what was both good and dangerous about the Enlightenment. He sought scientific rigor, idealized progress, and wanted to liberate mankind. But his rage about injustice combined with his utopian vision resulted in a whole series of nightmarish, ultimately failed political systems. He articulated a set of ideas about domination, revolution, and secular salvation that have since become integral to the modern imagination. These ideas are to be found wherever there is angry indictment of exploitation of one or more classes of people and where it is felt that radical changes to society must be made in order to establish a more equal order and to set things on a more just path. Ideas that link together revolution and liberation have a distinct Marxist cast to them even today, whether they involve workers or not. Misuse of people for profit—economic, political, aesthetic, cultural, sexual—calls upon the Marxist sensibility of rage against unrighteous conditions. Rage, however, is every bit as much the point as exploitation. We cannot, now or in the future, separate the Marxist sensibility from the fury that gave it birth. Let us not, therefore, assume too quickly that the Marxism being held today in reserve by supposedly irrelevant intellectuals has no political future. It does.

CHAPTER 3

Charles Darwin

Struggle and Selection in the Realm of Ideas

> Owing to this struggle for life, any variation, however slight and from
> whatever cause proceeding, if it be in any degree profitable to an indi-
> vidual of any species, in its infinitely complex relations to other organic
> beings and to external nature, will tend to the preservation of that
> individual, and will generally be inherited by its offspring.
>
> CHARLES DARWIN, *ORIGIN OF SPECIES*

Charles Robert Darwin did not live as he thought. Born in 1809, this
conventional and kindly Victorian gentleman, often ill and confined
to bed, married his own cousin and retired at an early age to a country
home near London, where he lived with his family and worked with
the most unthreatening of creatures imaginable: pigeons and barnacles,
earthworms and bees. Yet from his hands emerged a theory of the living
world as an endless process of change and death, a theory that finally
pulled down centuries of belief in a fixed, divinely ordained universe
built by a benevolent God. Still more, the book that gained Darwin
fame, *Origin of Species*, set the terms for a modern conflict over the
meaning of existence that may never be resolved, while it also released
into the world a set of ideas adapted by others to redefine the very aims
of human society and the institutions that power it.

Darwin had no desire to do this. He was a modest person who lived
quietly, attended the occasional scientific meeting, and shunned public debate, leaving the defense of his ideas to others, above all the vitu-
perative Thomas Henry Huxley. Darwin was the furthest thing from a
limelight scholar. For twenty years he held back writing and publishing
Origin, his masterwork, harried it seems by a perfectionist streak and by

worries over the impact such a book would bring, not least to his pious wife, Emma. Friends like the geologist Charles Lyell had to persuade him to finally produce his work when news of a nearly identical theory by a younger researcher, Alfred Russell Wallace, arrived at his doorstep from Malaysia. Darwin's gentility, that is, could have given away all priority of discovery. On July 11, 1858, the day that his and Wallace's ideas were made public before the scientific Linnaean Society in London, Darwin himself was absent, mourning the death of his two-year-old son, Charles Jr., from scarlet fever (Browne 1996).

That day, many have said, marked the beginning of a new era in our understanding of life. While this may exaggerate the reality, it is true to the perception: Darwin's book has been understood for over a century to have brought a turning point in history. What was so powerful in his discovery? Why has evolution by means of natural selection been called "the single greatest idea ever"? In concise terms, Darwin altered "nature" and the "human." He did so, moreover, in ways that can only be called sweeping, indeed, as some still feel, even violent. He was not the true originator of all that he wrote about, far from it. Evolution and adaptation, even the hypothesis that man and apes are biologically related, had been proposed before (Bowler 2009). Yet he knitted these ideas into a tapestry of grand, explanatory logic and added to them the new concepts of natural selection and common descent. Most of all, he gave these ideas, and evolution itself, an ultimate authority through the imprimatur of science, a domain that commanded untold respect in Victorian times.

Before the mid-nineteenth century, the era of Darwin, species were fixed entities in a wondrously static world, human beings were a specially privileged form of life, and society unfolded to a divine plan. Before Darwin, the primary vision of life was the Great Chain of Being, a glorious hierarchy where everything had its ordained place and no gaps were to be found. Above all, before Darwin, nature revealed the hand of an active, loving God who had made Creation as a realm of infinite beauty and order for the pleasure and instruction of humankind. After Darwin, none of this held sway any longer. The links of the Great Chain lay shattered on the ground. Species were ever-changing, dynamic entities and humans merely one among them. Nature was no glorious final assembly of forms and meanings but instead a realm of struggle and, for science, discovery. Religious faith remained, as it remains today, but it was not the same faith. To speak of a "Darwinian revolution," therefore, is fully justified (Ruse 1999). Its victory was not sudden and not due to Darwin alone, but its impact was not the less because of this.

Darwin was necessary for this revolution but was not its only source. There had been, as we pointed out in the previous chapter, serious questions raised by the Enlightenment about the role of God in human affairs. Cracks in Creation, as an unchanging and benevolent cosmos, had already been opened by the significance of fossils and notions about the depth of geologic time. Between the early eighteenth and mid-nineteenth centuries, conclusions by naturalists required that the concept of divine order make room for the reality of change and rendered it more difficult to view the Bible as literally true. Darwin's ideas, however, dealt the holy plan a final, magisterial blow. Nature, in all its glory, lost the quality of a sacred edifice and became instead an unending conflict for survival and reproduction. Life was now a material process without any clear and final purpose, a "design without a designer" (Dennett 1995). For Darwin himself, whose religious faith dimmed in view of his own thought and the death of two of his children, these ideas actually took nothing away from the splendor of life. Rather, it freed nature, he once said, from "supernatural meanings." But for many others, the new universe was a difficult, frightening, and unacceptable place. It was a realm that had turned hostile to traditional belief. In no uncertain terms, Darwin's ideas changed the meaning of the world.

More even than Adam Smith or Karl Marx, therefore, Darwin has been taken by some to mark a clear and sharp boundary between the premodern and the modern (Himmelfarb 1959). In truth this is a bit hyperbolic, but it does not strike too far from the mark. Like the thought of these other men, Darwin's ideas came to have an influence that spiraled ever outward, vastly beyond anything he himself could have imagined. To the new Darwinian world, nearly every discipline of human knowledge eventually had to respond, in substantive ways. Even before 1900, every major world language had allotted a shelf to versions of Darwin's writings that were as often adaptations as real translations, works that were rendered by words intended to inform, shock, sway, and even convert distant cultural-historical settings. If the world was changed by these writings over time, it often changed them in turn. Those who found them useful included not only scientists but politicians, economists, authors, ideologues, and revolutionaries. However, if evolution, especially, found wide and varied acceptance, such was not the case for natural selection, which had a difficult time at first, not least within science. Since the 1930s, when it finally became central to biology, there have been fierce debates about how important it really is and how far it can be taken as a method of explanation in the realm of human behavior.

Biological determinism was widespread in the nineteenth and early twentieth centuries. It existed well before Darwin, in concepts of race for example. Many thinkers used Darwin to claim support for the "science" of eugenics and for the belief that "struggle" between groups of people, social classes, ethnic groups, and even nations was natural and inevitable (Alexander and Numbers 2010; Ruse 1999). Hadn't Darwin, after all, in the very subtitle of his famed work, put it as "The Preservation of *Favoured* Races in the Struggle for Life"? Hadn't he provided the basis for identifying those who were "fit" and "unfit" and thus, by extension, those who were superior and those inferior; those who should be encouraged to breed and those who should not; those who would "ennoble the race" and those who would pollute it? It was a long and twisted series of roads that led from the garden at Down House to the gas chambers at Auschwitz.

Two years before *Origin* appeared, Darwin commented to a friend: "You ask me whether I shall discuss man. I think I shall avoid the whole subject, as so surrounded by prejudice" (Darwin 1887, vol. 2, 109). These, indeed, were words both prescient and ironic. Prescient, because of how his work would be used in a thousand ways to further an equal number of biases, institutions, laws, and acts. Ironic, then, because of this same fact—it was humanity that Darwin's ideas most deeply affected. Try as he might, he could not escape "man." And he soon gave up trying. After the tumultuous debates over *Origin*, Darwin wrote in rapid succession *The Descent of Man* (1871) and *The Expression of Emotions in Man and Animals* (1872), two works that linked human beings and organic nature directly. Neither had the impact of *Origin*, nor could they. The crucial shift had already occurred. Today readers return to *Origin* hoping to find something essential. Like no other work of science, it continues to be read for its graceful voice and for signs of how it all began.

VICTORIAN SCIENCE: THE CONTEXT FOR *ORIGIN OF SPECIES*

Darwin's success depended deeply on ideas he adopted from other thinkers, both scientists and nonscientists. We can't really understand the force of Darwinian thought, in fact, without looking at this context, for it tells us why science and society were ready to seize upon certain portions of this thought, mold it to other ambitions, and apply it in so many different ways. A number of the debates that began in Victorian times, in fact, continue today. It makes sense, therefore, to start with England in the first half of the nineteenth century, when Darwin grew up.

In that time and place, the rapidity of social change was unprecedented. In a single generation, between roughly 1800 and 1830, the spread of industrialization had brought into existence a vast working class confined to the factories, mills, mines, and streets, and to poverty and unrest. It brought forth an expanding middle class, desiring security and the signs of advancement, threatened by the chaos of the French Revolution and the Napoleonic Wars that followed. The young Alexis de Tocqueville spoke of England as a land of "two rival nations," the rich and the poor, an image taken by Benjamin Disraeli, future prime minister, in his own novel *Sybil, or The Two Nations*, which appeared in 1845, the very year Friedrich Engels's *Condition of the Working Class in England* came out. Material progress did not slow or cease but continued to accelerate, bringing even more change in the next generation, dislodging any sense of peace or refuge. When Darwin was born, most people still lived in towns and hamlets, worked in fields, cooked over open fireplaces, and did not travel. A half century later, by 1859 when *Origin* appeared, British cities were teeming, mills were working day and night, coal ovens were common, and trips through the countryside in comfortable trains were common fare for those with means. Thousands of miles of railroads now crossed the country, knitting it together as never before, circulating its goods, its influences, and its citizens (Mitchell 1996).

Responses to the new age were complex. While many beliefs from the Enlightenment held firm, others fell into uncertainty. Notions of a need for greater political liberty were tempered, in part, by surging prosperity: British manufactured goods dominated trade in Europe, while industrial production created a new abundance at home that brought prices down, urging the first mass markets into existence. Wages and income, however, did not rise in tandem among workers. While the middle and upper classes advanced, poverty did not abate for labor and dissatisfaction grew. The degree of overall confusion can be summed up by observing that at the very time laissez-faire economics found widespread favor, so did the novels of Charles Dickens, with their brutish portraits of English society. What linked these together was faith in the power of progress to make conditions better, to bring society more in line with the natural laws that dictated both individual and national advancement.

"Progress," a fundamental concept of the age, found embodiment in many domains, from politics and economics to social theory and the arts. It drew no small inspiration from Enlightenment notions regarding the natural development of society from barbarism to civilization and that of the human mind from superstition to reason. The idea that nature was at work in this great unfolding made it inevitable that concepts of organic evolution would come to play their part. Progress became both a philosophical idea and a reflection for the British of their own rising state and hopes for their progeny and country (Hoppen 1998). The concept was not wholly secure, however. Religious belief in an ordained world persisted for portions of the public and for scholars and even some scientists, while a wave of religious revival in the form of evangelism opposed all ideas of change or evolution. The Romantic Movement, meanwhile, extending into the late 1830s, tended to trouble the issue by opposing the ideals of industrialism with calls to private feeling and mysticism, while at the same time celebrating the individual and the superior natural setting of Britain. The educated classes mostly avoided religious fervor but absorbed the Romantic nostalgia for rural simplicity, even as they indulged a taste for art, books, and the most advanced ideas—most of all, those from science. In the wake of Newton's achievement and the technological marvels that poured forth from "the workshop of the world" (as England was known), science had gained, and was continuing to gain, an immense authority. As the expanding realm of truth about physical reality, it could be applied to the Earth, life, human beings, and society. Widely used phrases such as "the economy of nature," which Darwin himself employed, make this interpenetration between socioeconomic and scientific domains clear. At the Great London Exhibition of 1851, with its fabled Crystal Palace filled by myriad inventions and its open park with the first life-sized models of dinosaurs, over six million visitors from every European capital came to see what wonders human ingenuity had made and what terrible and sublime things nature had produced (Auerbach 1999).

The Victorian period was a pivotal era for science in professional terms as well. The year Darwin sailed out of Plymouth Harbor aboard the *Beagle*, 1831, the word "scientist" did not exist. It was there waiting for him when he returned, five years later, having been invented in 1833 by the polymath William Whewell. At this time, researchers were still mostly gentlemen investigators. They worked out of their homes or in small university quarters, bought or built their own equipment, and analyzed specimens often in makeshift and inventive ways. A large majority of them, especially in natural history, were ordained ministers. But they were materialists, too, up to a point. They greatly approved of experimentation, the use of microscopes, and the value of precise observation. Mere descriptions and classification were no longer enough. Study of structure and function, the determination of process and cause, were now core goals. Above all, it was the search for "laws" governing the natural world that were the true prize, an aim articulated by astronomer John Herschel's *A Preliminary Discourse on the Study of Natural Philosophy* (1830; 1987 copy), a book that deeply influenced Darwin (Lightman 1997; Browne 1996).

Over the span of the next few decades, science had great successes in the area of discovery. A veritable parade of brilliant individuals, such as William Buckland, Humphrey Davy, Michael Faraday, and William Thomson, became famous for their work, many of them acting as public intellectuals to promote the importance of science. By the time of

Darwin's death in 1882 many of the aspects associated with professional science today were appearing on the horizon. Researchers had created scientific societies, journals, and symposia and were often engaged in service projects for the government. Though rather thinly scattered within the larger intelligentsia, they were nonetheless given university posts, labs with equipment, funds to pursue their work, and opportunities to lecture in popular settings. During Darwin's lifetime, the fields of "natural philosophy" (study of the physical universe) and "natural history" (description of phenomena) began to dissolve. In their place would soon stand the "natural sciences": physics, chemistry, biology, geology (Porter 1978). Still, a crucial legacy existed and proved pivotal. Those, like Darwin, who studied natural history in its twilight years moved in and out of what soon became geology, paleontology, botany, and zoology—their research covered both the living and nonliving domains of the Earth. Thus it was inescapable that they ask questions about the relationship between these two domains and whether it was fixed or dynamic.

Darwin matured at a time when scientists were still loyal to the past in one other area: writing. Though technical journals had existed for some time, Victorian scientists made their major contribution through books. They were authors. This meant appealing to both colleagues and the expanding readership created by industrial prosperity. Volumes on geology and natural history often sold as well or better than popular novels (Lightman 1997). John Murray, Darwin's publisher, saw *Origin*'s main competition in 1859 as Dickens's *A Tale of Two Cities* (Browne 1996). Moreover, the borders between science and educated discourse were fluid. Authors like Whewell and Herschel wove ingredients into their books from philosophy, religion, and the Latin classics without any sense of trespass. Such broadness was reflected in the style of writing, too. The most articulate scientists produced extended lines of reasoning with many complex rhetorical elements, ranging from novelistic anecdotes and poetic phrasing to dramatic metaphor and satirical commentary. Unlike the gray voice of today's science, Victorian researchers had a full palette of literary technique to draw upon. Darwin was among the best of them, to be sure, but in this he was neither original nor originator (Beer 2000).

Views of Life and Evolution in Darwin's Day

When it appeared, Darwinian evolution had to vie with several reigning ideas about organic existence (Bowler 2009; Ruse 1999; Hodge 2008). These contained what we would identify today as obvious religious elements that were accepted parts of science in the early nineteenth century. The primary example was called "natural theology." This sought to prove the existence of a Creator and a divine order through the use of reason and observations of nature. In England, the theory was best articulated by William Paley's *Natural Theology* (1809), a hugely popular work first published in 1802 that was required reading for educated people during the first half of the century. By 1809 it had already gone through twelve editions. Its influence on Darwin was due to fine-textured and accurate descriptions, its lucid prose, and, not least, the "long line of argument" (Darwin's phrase) that began this way:

> In crossing a heath, suppose I pitched my foot against a *stone*, and were asked how the stone came to be there; I might possibly answer, that, for any thing I knew to the contrary, it had lain there for ever. . . . But suppose I had found a *watch* . . . I should hardly think of the answer which I had before given. . . . [The reason is] that, when we come to inspect the watch, we perceive . . . that its several parts are framed and put together for a purpose. . . . [T]he inference, we think, is inevitable, that the watch must have had a maker, an artificer. (Paley 1809, 1, 4)

Paley's metaphor of God as divine watchmaker offered a world built with precise care for a reading audience already tuned to the mechanical miracles of industrialism. Given the watch as a regulator of daily life, Paley implied that society also had orderly, God-given rules—a view attractive for political reasons, as it argued for stable hierarchy over civil unrest or revolution.

Among professional men of science natural theology was accepted by some, but for others it had problems. It suggested that nature was static, with forms of life either immutable or changeable only by the Creator's hand. Such notions ruled the mind of Carl Linnaeus, the Swedish botanist and zoologist who conceived the modern system of biological naming (*Systema Naturae*, 1758), but they were rejected by influential naturalists who came after: Buffon, Cuvier, and Lamarck. Even before 1800, fossils were widely accepted as the remains of ancient life. Cuvier was the unmatched innovator here. Though Buffon had speculated on the possibility of extinction (and rejected it), Cuvier, with a thorough knowledge of animal anatomy, was the one to actually identify fossilized teeth and bones of mammals that no longer walked the Earth, that had therefore died out perhaps by some catastrophe (he supposed this to be the biblical flood). It was a radical idea, and it forced a change. Once established, by the first decade after 1800, extinction became a required element in any theory about species and their origin. A fateful turn in scientific thinking had occurred: nature could not be fixed since it had a history. Study of the Earth's rock layers also indicated change over time. While Cuvier believed that all of this change came from divine intervention, Buffon proposed an entirely materialistic history (no godly elements) in his influential *Histoire naturelle* (1749–89), stating that species could even "improve" and "degrade" over time (Rudwick 2007).

The theory of Jean-Baptiste Lamarck (1744–1829), however, was the first to claim that all living creatures developed from earlier forms. Coming only a decade after Cuvier's discovery of extinction, *Philosophie Zoologique* (1809) was itself a radical leap even beyond Buffon's materialism. Lamarck held that species made up a progressive scale of complexity, worms and other "simple" creatures at the bottom, humans at the top, and that organisms have moved up this scale through "transmutation" ("evolution" was not yet used). This involved animals and plants passing on to their immediate progeny any changes acquired by adapting to their environment, such as the neck of a giraffe presumably stretched by continual effort to reach food in tall trees. Environment was the primary agent, and change was rapid: move an animal to a new setting, it would be modified and would pass its newly acquired characteristics to its offspring. Such ideas were viewed by Cuvier as either atheistic or ridiculous. But by the 1830s they had given rise to further endorsements of changing organic forms over time, such as those of the prominent physician and naturalist Geoffroy Saint-Hilaire, a colleague and defender of Lamarck, who wrote, "My view is that there is but one system of creations incessantly reworked, progressively improved, and merged with previous changes under the all-powerful influence of the surrounding environment" (Saint-Hilaire 1835, xi).

All of these authors, from Herschel and Paley to Lamarck and St. Hilaire, were early influences on Darwin, but they were far from the only ones. No less important was the great naturalist and explorer Alexander von Humboldt (1769–1859), whose journeys through Central and South America between 1799 and 1804 and multivolume publication of his experiences, *Le voyage aux regions equinoxiales du Nouveau Continent* (translated as "Personal Narrative," 1805–34), provided immediate models for Darwin's own voyage on the *Beagle*. Darwin was also deeply indebted to the geologists Adam Sedgwick and Charles Lyell. Sedgwick taught Darwin at Cambridge and nurtured him in techniques of mapping and observation. But it was Lyell's monumental *Principles of Geology* (1830–33) that Darwin read, along with Humboldt's work, on his five-year *Beagle* journey that had the deepest impact of all. *Principles* served as the founding text of modern geology. Its central theory was "uniformitarianism," proposing that gradual processes on the Earth today have operated in the past to create the world as it is. The idea retains a place in Earth science even today. But for Darwin, it was Lyell's questions about species that had an electric effect, and we can see why. Lyell felt it essential to inquire:

> first, whether species have a real and permanent existence in nature; or whether they are capable . . . of being indefinitely modified in the course of a long series of generations? Secondly, whether . . . [they] have been derived originally from many similar stocks, or each from one only . . . ? Thirdly, how far the duration of each species . . . is limited by its dependence on . . . conditions in the state of the animate and inanimate world? Fourthly, whether there be proofs of the successive extermination of species in the ordinary course of nature, and whether . . . new animals and plants are created from time to time . . . ? (Lyell 1830/1990, vol. 1, 1–2)

Here, in brief, are the main issues Darwin himself was to pursue in *Origin*: were species real; did they evolve; if so, did they have a common ancestor; what was the role of the environment? Lyell spent a fair number of pages attacking Lamarck's theory and other ideas of evolution. Though he had no use for Genesis as science and saw geologic time as vast, he remained a theist: the Earth needed a Creator. But his idea that small changes could have vast effects over eons of time was critical to Darwin's thought.

Also pivotal was a concept Darwin acquired from a very different kind of thinker, writing on a wholly different subject. Thomas Malthus first published *An Essay on the Principle of Population* in 1798, setting off a fiery debate (Malthus 1807). A scholarly clergyman who rejected Enlightenment portrayals of society as orderly and benevolent, Malthus claimed that population growth had led throughout history not to advancement but to suffering and death. The reason: increase in people follows a geometric pattern, doubling every so many years, outstripping food supply that can only grow arithmetically, by a fixed annual amount. All forms of life "if they could freely [reproduce], would fill millions of worlds" and thus quickly exhaust every resource. It was the "struggle for existence" (Malthus's phrase) that this created, forcing competition among individuals for survival, that was key for Darwin. Malthus, however, was a moralist who saw death and suffering as required for improvement. Human population could be "checked" only by famine, war, disease, birth control, celibacy, and poverty—the poor, who were largely to blame for their plight because they were unwilling to control their appetite for progeny, should not be aided by wage increases or charity else their profligacy be fed and their numbers grow still further. Some discussion of these views appeared in Darwin's later writings on human beings but not endorsement. Malthus was not a scientist, and his book was not viewed as a scientific book. But it nonetheless postulated laws of nature, above all the "struggle for existence," that required consideration because they were backed by quantified evidence. Malthus's conclusions about the nature of society, resource constraints, and the correct path of ethics have been controversial down to the present (Nekola 2013).

Finally, there was Herbert Spencer (1820–1903), who introduced "evolution" to considerations of society even before *Origin of Species* appeared. Darwin, in fact, is perhaps best known for a phrase that Spencer actually coined: "survival of the fittest." A civil engineer turned journalist and polymath, a libertarian who hated aristocratic privilege and socialism, Spencer in the early 1850s applied a version of Lamarck to the human enterprise. While working for *The Economist* he published *Social Statics* (1851) and then, from the late 1850s to the 1890s, an extended series of works meant to popularize biology and psychology, to create a science of sociology, and to summarize all basic knowledge of the natural sciences. Spencer's ambitions were not modest; he was an indefatigable author who built a mammoth reputation. It is essential to point out, however, that his idea of evolution was entirely different from Darwin's, though it later came to include some Darwinian elements. It was a process of continual "integration" that underlay everything in the universe, an unfolding of inorganic and organic forms via processes of "concentration" and "dissolution." Animals and plants followed a linear pattern from the simple to the complex or, as Spencer put it, from "the homogeneous to the heterogeneous."

Society was a part of nature. "It was all of a one with the development of the embryo or the unfolding of a flower" (Spencer 1851, 65), thus an integrated organism that obeyed the same laws. Progress, meanwhile, was the social form of evolution. It, too, advanced from homogeneity to heterogeneity, from a despotic "militant" stage to a more individualistic "industrial" state. Such progress, Spencer claimed, "is not an accident, but a necessity" (1851, 65). And when nations did achieve the "industrial stage," as Europe and America had (but not the rest of the world), humans must be allowed near absolute freedom—with elites dissolved, all class-bound laws erased, all government help for the poor obliterated, and any hints of "legislative meddling" in any domain abolished—so that so that immutable principles of nature could flourish and direct the adaptation of human beings to this new state of existence. Over time, "as surely as there is any efficacy in educational culture . . . so surely must the human faculties be molded into complete fitness for the social state" (Spencer 1851, 65). These words were not lost on Darwin. Each new generation was capable of passing its improvements to its offspring, in Lamarckian fashion, and thus could diversify ability and expand happiness—a comforting philosophy for those Victorians unsure of what the future might hold. If there was a dark side, it was the state interfering with society's natural direction.

Spencer's ideas, because associated with evolution, came to be incorrectly but effectively merged with Darwin's name in the decades after *Origin* appeared. This was understandable, no doubt. The confusion was aided by Darwin's own adoption of Spencer's "survival of the fittest" into later editions of *Origin*. Spencer was wrongly called a "Darwinian" before the century was out, another error that remains unchanged today, though the partial convergence of the two men's ideas increased the tendency to adopt Spencer's political pronouncements as if they stemmed from Darwin's scientific observations, which they certainly did not. In truth, Spencer's ideas gained enormous impact and were used to argue for minimal government in everything from the economy to what we would call "social services" (Taylor 1992). No less, his view of human societies as lying along a linear plane of development gave much justice to colonial beliefs in policy that would help "backward" peoples advance toward the European standard.

In the last quarter of the nineteenth century, Spencer came to sway the entire English-speaking world, much of Europe, and nations as distant as Japan. Nowhere was his impact more forceful, however, than in America, where he was revered as a voice of the age (Werth 2009). In *The Education*, Henry Adams wrote of the year 1870: "Never had the sun of progress shone so fair. Evolution from lower to higher raged like an epidemic. Darwin was the greatest of prophets in the most evolutionary of worlds" (1918, 284). Adams erred: it was not "Darwin" but his presumed emissary, Herbert Spencer, who so grandly brought evolution to American society.

Who Was Charles Robert Darwin and What Did He *Really* Say?

Charles Darwin was born in 1809 into a prosperous family in the early years of the Industrial Revolution and grew up a happy and much-loved child. His father, Robert Waring Darwin, was a successful doctor, and his mother, Susannah Wedgwood, was the fortunate granddaughter of Josiah Wedgwood, famous for his pottery and china business. Robert's own father was the freethinker, physician, and evolutionist Erasmus Darwin, who died before Charles was born. Science, as Darwin says in his *Autobiography*, was never far away at any time. His early years were spent in Shrewsbury, a leafy country town twenty miles south of London, where fishing, hunting, and exploring were common pursuits for those of his class. Darwin the boy lustily explored the nearby fields and woods, becoming a compulsive collector of specimens and a hungry reader of nature books (Browne 1996). His childhood, however, was not a complete idyll. When only eight, he lost his mother to an illness or condition that remains mysterious. In truth, there was a dark side to the Darwin family: the grandfather, Erasmus, saw his first wife perish from cirrhosis of the liver and his eldest son, Erasmus II, commit suicide. Charles's own father was man of rude temper and huge dimensions—six feet two inches tall and 336 pounds. Yet none of this seems to have deeply perturbed the waking hours of the future geologist-biologist. After his mother's passing he was raised with considerable care by his three older sisters. Spiritually, however, he was likely adrift, pulled between his sisters' respectable belief in Anglican Christianity and the freethinking atheism of his father.

Darwin was not a brilliant student. Greek and Latin bored him, medicine frightened him, and theology struck him as irrelevant. He was, however, an exceptional learner of geology, botany, zoology, and natural history, which he studied often on his own. After returning from his journey around the world (1831–36), he married his first cousin Emma Wedgwood in 1839 and three years later moved with her to the village of Down, in Kent, about sixteen miles from London. Here, in a country setting similar to that of his childhood, Darwin lived and worked until his final year, 1882. He was deeply devoted to his wife and eight children (two others died in infancy) and to his own gardens, where he often took walks to ponder his work. Out of deference to his wife, a devout Protestant, he did not begin calling himself an "agnostic" (a term coined by his friend Thomas Huxley) until well after the crushing death of his favored child, Annie, in 1851. "We have lost the joy of the household, and the solace of our old age," he wrote at the time. It was a terrible blow from which he never fully recovered. He stopped all churchgoing and religious participation after the funeral.

Darwin's father hoped his son would choose a medical career, like the previous two generations of Darwin men, and sent him to the University of Edinburgh. But at sixteen Charles witnessed two very bad operations, one on a child, and was turned from medicine thereafter. Nonetheless, his time at Edinburgh, among the great universities of Europe, exposed him to advanced physical science and to opportunities for pursuing natural history in an area rich in geologic exposures and nearby marine life. At eighteen, Darwin left Scotland to enter Cambridge, backed by his father's resolve that he study for the clergy, a dignified position offering ample time for forays into nature. Darwin was at Cambridge three years. It was where his interest in biology and geology bloomed, where he tasted elite intellectual society and was befriended by a number of professors. One of these was the botanist John Henslow, who provided Darwin the greatest opportunity of his life, a voyage circumventing the globe on Her Majesty's 10-gun sloop, the *Beagle*.

Darwin's gifts as a scientist and as a writer matured on this voyage, which began when he was only twenty-two. Planned by the Admiralty as a two-year mission to complete a survey of southern South America, it turned into a scientific expedition lasting half a decade, with Darwin given great leeway and time for exploration. He was twice blessed, in fact. Beyond the confines of the ship's cabin, he was free to wander the lands before him, to observe and collect as he saw fit. Onboard, he could roam a library of over 240 books, including Humboldt's *Personal Narrative* and Lyell's *Principles of Geology*, which the author had personally sent to him. In his own hugely readable travelogue, *Journal of Researches* (1839), today known as *The Voyage of the Beagle*, Darwin used Humboldt's book as his clear model. In all that he did on this journey, his tramping into forests and over mountain passes, his slow shoreline strolls and poking into insect mounds, his innumerable inspections of living and geologic forms, and, not least, his theorizing, Darwin can seem as indefatigable as the great German naturalist. But he was not made of such sturdy stuff. Even as the *Beagle* left England under a soft December rain, Darwin felt seasick and began to have second thoughts. Seasickness plagued him throughout the voyage. After returning, he never again left his homeland. Much of his adulthood was spent suffering from bouts of unexplained headaches, fevers, and nausea that left him disabled for weeks. His explorations were confined to his garden and the fields near Down House. A boundless excitement, evident on every page of his *Journal of Researches*, kept him vigorous and robust on the *Beagle*'s voyage. But he seems to have contracted something that plagued his physical being. Thereafter, he probed nature's workings with his microscope, his vast correspondence, and, most of all, his pen.

Darwin wrote dozens of papers and twenty books, including *Geological Observations of Volcanic Islands* (1844) and *Insectivorous Plants* (1875), encompassing worms, barnacles, orchids, domesticated animals, and plant fertilization, as well as the origin of species and the descent of man. His notebooks and diary from the *Beagle* voyage gave him rich material for a number of volumes, especially on geology, which he largely abandoned afterward in favor of biology. These works established Darwin's scientific credentials beyond all doubt. They won him election to the Royal Society, the most admired scientific organization of the time. They also solidified his style as an author and made him a voice of authority. What type of style was this? An example from *Journal of Researches* helps reveal it:

> One day, at Bahia [Brazil], my attention was drawn by observing many spiders, cockroaches, and other insects, and some lizards, rushing in the greatest agitation across a bare piece of ground. A little way behind, every stalk and leaf was blackened by a small ant. The swarm having crossed the bare space, divided itself, and descended an old wall. By this means many insects were fairly enclosed; and the efforts which the poor little creatures made to extricate themselves from such a death were wonderful. (1845, 35)

Darwin could therefore paint a picture in a few lines, turning the reader into a witness of events filled with drama and a Romantic intensity of emotion. He borrows from the genre of the English travel narrative, brought to a peak in the late eighteenth century by such examples as James Cook's *Voyages to the Pacific Ocean* (1784–1814). But Darwin shifts the lens: his focus is less on exotic sights than on the ordinary "inhabitants" (as he calls the animals and plants). On the other hand, when he wrote specifically for scientists, as in *Geological Observations on South America* (1846), his pen could dry a bit: "The several [fossil mammals] embedded in the Pampean formation, which mostly belong to extinct genera, and some even to extinct families or orders . . . having existed contemporaneously with mollusca, all still inhabiting the adjoining sea, is certainly a most striking fact" (104).

Thus he had more than one voice at his command. Nature is intricate; it cannot be embraced by only one discourse. An army of ants devouring other insects is one thing, great mammals that went extinct while simple mollusks survived unscathed are something else. Species were *not* created as "perfect" entities. But to try to convince his age of this, Darwin would need a new strategy, one that combined both popular and scientific registers.

Darwin's Masterwork: *On the Origin of Species by Means of Natural Selection*

Origin has its own fascinating story (Browne 2006). As early as 1838, not too long after returning on the *Beagle*, Darwin conceived natural selection as a primary basis for evolution. He recorded the very moment in his notebooks (September 28) as an effect of reading Malthus and being struck by the image of unending struggle in nature, with too many individuals born of every species so that the great majority perished and only the better adapted survived and reproduced. Nature, in short, did over eons what breeders and gardeners do every year: select and multiply the superior variations. Simple as it may seem to us today, this was a moment of colossal insight that both followed certain forms of scientific logic of the period (Lyell's concept of small but constant changes over great periods of time) and rejected widespread beliefs about Creation. As much as it required vision, it depended on denial as well.

Darwin knew this only too well. His *Autobiography* says: "Here then I had at last got a theory by which to work; but I was so anxious to avoid prejudice, that I determined not for some time to write the briefest sketch of it" (1958, 120). He was true to his word. Jotting a brief outline of his theory in 1842, he attempted a longer version two years later after a hugely controversial and widely read book, *Vestiges of the Natural History of Creation*, had brought the idea of "organic development" into the awareness of most literate Europeans. This book, published anonymously by the Scottish journalist Robert Chambers, was an eloquent patchwork of facts, half-truths, and speculations, describing all of creation from the making of stars to the birth of species. The popularity of *Vestiges* revealed the hunger that the British public had developed for news about a dynamic, evolving world. Nonetheless, the book was ridiculed by most scientists, not only for its factual errors but also for its proposal that humans were descended from animals. None of this was lost on Darwin; the scorn that *Vestiges* earned from the professional scientific community kept Darwin from publishing his own ideas. Twelve years went by (1856) before Lyell could stand it no longer and begged him repeatedly, urgently, to finally do so. Darwin relented and sketched out, then began, a multivolume work. But in 1858 he received an essay from Wallace ("On the Tendency of Varieties to Depart Indefinitely from the Original Type") proposing a nearly identical theory of selection. Darwin was persuaded to abandon the large work and write a shorter "abstract" for quick publication. In a mere nine months, after so many years of meditating on his plans, he poured out *Origin* complete—one of the greatest works of modern science—in a fever of unrelieved and obsessive work.

What kind of a book is it? Its author famously described it as "one long argument." Unlike other natural history texts, *Origin* is not illustrated; it has only one image, the "tree of life" that shows branching descent. It has no drawings of plants or animals, no tables or charts, no maps, stratigraphic sections, cross sections, or anything similar. It does have a glossary, showing an aim to reach a nonscientific audience. Yet it is a book about all of nature without any visual traces of nature in it. This is remarkable enough. But as we have seen, Darwin could draw images with words well enough, and so he does. We do, indeed, find a great part of the living world between these covers. He begins with domesticated species, from pigeons to horses, then moves on to large mammals in the wild, alive and extinct. He writes about marine invertebrates from nearly every ocean; about dozens of insects and birds, from every continent; about moles and rabbits and worms and fish; and about dozens of species of plants, both flowering and non, sexual and asexual. His narrative moves from the temperate woods of England to the tropical forests of Brazil, from the plains of North America to the peaks of South America, from the deserts of Africa to the tundra of Asia. Wherever he goes, Darwin draws from his own experience and, bountifully, from the work of other scientists whom he gratefully acknowledges. *Origin of Species* is nothing if not a "who's who" of Western natural history to 1859. It is as if scientists from a dozen nations had endorsed and contributed to the work.

Darwin does not follow established scientific custom. Instead of presenting his evidence first, then his conclusions, he leaps right in with theory. His first chapter takes up "variation under domestication" or "artificial selection," a familiar reality to everyone. Chapter 2 follows with "variation under nature," or nature differences among individuals of a given species in the wild, while chapter 3 adds the essential element of the "struggle for existence." This sets the stage for chapter 4 to propose the idea of "natural selection" itself. This is succeeded by "laws of variation" in chapter 5, explaining details of the theory, and then a striking innovation: an entire chapter devoted to "difficulties of the theory," a clever treatment of objections that other scientists might have. In just the first six chapters, then, less than half the book, Darwin presents the reader with not only his entire theory but also the most probable attacks upon it and why they are mistaken. In style, it is gentle, guiding, firm in places, but full of qualifications: "I believe," "It is reasonable to conclude," and "An argument of great weight would be," and the like.

What of the actual scientific message? A concise way of describing it is to outline the different hypotheses it contained (Mayr 1993). They include:

1. *Evolution itself:* The living world is constantly changing, with organisms undergoing transformation over time.
2. *The principle of variation:* Some individuals in a species are randomly born different from others in certain traits. These varieties may develop new species.

3. *Gradualism*: Evolution takes place by long-term change in populations, not the abrupt appearance of brand-new individual types.
4. *Inheritance*: Many traits of organisms are passed down from parent to offspring; offspring resemble their parents more than any other individuals.
5. *Common descent*: Groups of similar or related organisms evolved from a single ancestor, with all forms of life going back to some single, original source.
6. *Natural selection*: Each generation brings forth variations that nature then "selects" through competition, giving those with some adaptive advantage in their environment a better chance of survival and thus reproduction. "Fitness" does *not* necessarily mean an organism is stronger, faster, or more intelligent than others of its species. It could apply to a variety that is smaller, weaker, and slower but had some other, more effective, survival advantage, like coloration, beak shape, skin toxin, and so on.
7. *Humans are like other animals*: By implication, owing to their close similarity to apes, humans have a common ancestor with them and are thus part of nature. (This hypothesis is not stated in *Origin* but strongly implied.)

It took enormous brilliance to knit these diverse ideas into a whole. Darwin was drawn to do this, however, by his own unique desire for fathoming the actual mechanisms of evolution. The first four of these concepts, as we have seen, already existed and were debated in Darwin's day. Together, they describe the appearance of new varieties with inheritable characteristics. The next two were original to Darwin (and Wallace) and are now thought to be his most profound contribution. Finally, the idea of a human-ape connection had been floated in the eighteenth century, for example by Rousseau, but was rejected by natural historians like Linnaeus and Buffon (Niekerk 2004). It appeared again in *Vestiges of the Natural History of Creation*, but, as noted, this book was rejected by the scientific community. It was Darwin, and only Darwin, who provided the elegant and refractory logic of explanation that was needed.

Nature, acting over eons, could create extremely complex and precisely adapted life forms from a small set of less adapted ancestors. No divine fingerprints or footsteps were needed. No sacred interventions were permitted. *Origin* thus recalls the reply Pierre-Simon Laplace gave to Napoleon when asked what place the Creator had in his theories: "I have no need of that hypothesis," the great mathematician said. But Darwin went further than the idea that all nature could be described in elegant equations. He reconceived life on Earth as a ceaseless mill of grinding activity, blind to final purpose. Even the word "selection" was entirely metaphorical; there was no entity to do the choosing. As Darwin himself expressed it, there was both beauty and brutality in this:

> Nothing is easier than to admit in words the truth of the universal struggle for life, or more difficult—at least I have found it so— than constantly to bear this conclusion in mind. Yet unless it be thoroughly engrained in the mind . . . [it] will be dimly seen or quite misunderstood. We behold the face of nature bright with gladness, we often see superabundance of food; we do not see, or we forget, that the birds which are idly singing round us mostly live on insects or seeds, and are thus constantly destroying life; or we forget how largely these songsters, or their eggs, or their nestlings, are destroyed by birds and beasts of prey. (1859, 62)

The book was thus bound to upset many, and it did. Darwin took away any anchor for the traditional belief in a divine presence living in nature, as well as a universal moral code inscribed upon existence by a loving, wise God. Indeed, read carefully, *Origin* even denied that any form of biological "progress" took place. True, it does say that "natural selection works solely by and for the good of each being" and that its success can produce "corporeal and mental endowments [which] will tend to progress toward perfection" (1859, 489). But in what does "perfection" consist? Increased adaptation and reproductive success; such are the ultimate "goals" in the Darwinian world. There is no advance to a higher plane of existence and no escape from the struggle for survival ("perfect" adaptation cannot free a species from becoming prey). Nature really cannot be used as a model for society (Spencer was wrong). There were other troubling implications as well. How, in this world of embattled life, are we to comprehend our own purpose on Earth or discern whether we have an immortal soul, if "all the living forms of life are the lineal descendants of those which lived long before the Silurian epoch," that is, if humans are not special and separate? What faith can be accorded any longer to biblical Genesis if, as the author maintains, it is natural selection that has the prerogative to promise "Light will be thrown on the origin of man and his history" (1859, 488)? Darwin, in the end, did not treat man as a subject, as he said he would not, and yet it is exactly this same subject that haunts the shadows of this brilliant text after all.

Darwin, however, did not abandon his era entirely. *Origin* claimed that creation and extinction of animal forms "accords better with what we know of the laws impressed on matter by the Creator" (1859, 489). In fact, the Creator appears as many as seven times in the book's first edition, rising to eight and nine times in subsequent versions (there were six editions in all). But again, these appearances are less than they appear. Most invoke the Creator for the sake of criticism aimed at traditional religious ideas about nature, for example, regarding the divine creation of each being: "we can only say that so it is;—that it has so pleased the Creator to construct each animal and plant" (1859, 435). As an explanation, Darwin says, "nothing can be more hopeless." It is no explanation at all, he implies, only a plea for ignorance. Still, the author seems to have regretted his concession in making so much use of God (Browne 1996). But it hardly mattered. *Origin of Species* ends with a meditative song in which the divine has no place:

> Thus, from the war of nature, from famine and death, the most exalted object . . . namely, the production of the higher animals, directly follows. There is grandeur in this view of life, with its several powers, having been originally breathed into a few forms or into one; and that, whilst this planet has gone cycling on according to the fixed law of gravity, from so simple a beginning endless forms most beautiful and most wonderful have been, and are being, evolved. (1860, 491)

Darwin did not claim that natural selection explained all of evolution and the myriad forms of life; there must be other mechanisms, he said. If this seems forgotten in more recent times, it is perhaps because of the enormous influence natural selection has had since the mid-twentieth century.

This was not always the case, however. Within ten years of its publication, *Origin*'s version of evolution was established science—*except* for natural selection. Continued advances in biological and geological work, as well as the success of Darwin's intellectual lieutenants in defending his other ideas, had done much to make evolution a household word and to weaken any shock at the idea that human beings had themselves evolved and might have a shared ancestor with apes (an idea proposed not in *Origin* but in Darwin's subsequent works of the early 1870s). Selection, however, as the primary mechanism for evolution was rejected, even by Lyell and Huxley. For reasons we will discuss later in the chapter, selection, with its dependence on chance and random change, was ignored in favor of Lamarckism.

By the late 1860s, Darwin felt he needed to catch up to the fame of *Origin*, particularly the discussions it had raised about humans in new writings by his friends Lyell and Huxley. Lyell's *Geological Evidences of the Antiquity of Man* (1863) firmly set down in elegant style the evidence for "co-existence in ancient times of Man with certain species of mammalia long since extinct." For a good portion of the educated public, this book nailed the coffin shut on the dating of Creation to 4004 B.C., published in 1652 by Bishop James Ussher based on biblical genealogy. Then, just as Lyell's volume was gaining attention, Huxley's work on human evolution, *Evidence as to Man's Place in Nature* (1863), appeared. This short book, the very first devoted to its subject, brought its own sensation and controversy. But Huxley, too, was a master of exposition and presented his evidence as a series of quotations from earlier works, including religious ones, stories of discovery and anatomical observation of "man-like apes," and descriptions of behavior. It was soon after these two works that Darwin began to conceive *Descent of Man* (1871) and *Expression of Emotions in Man and Animals* (1872). Scientifically speaking, these later books were largely added chapters to *Origin*. They broke little new theoretical ground and, despite originality in some areas, did not excite attention as *Origin* had. The exception was Darwin's straightforward and forceful statement that humans and apes had descended from a common ancestor. As with other things

Darwinian, this was mistakenly understood—as it still is today, in some part—to mean that humans came from apes, a concept that unsurprisingly raised some offense and was exploited by Darwin's opponents.

Descent of Man takes up several subjects: similar forms between humans and mammals, especially apes (but many others, too); evidence for mental powers in animals (they show fear, courage, affection, even humor); the origin of social and moral attributes (due, in savage races, to peer pressure, self-sacrifice, and the "instinct of sympathy"); and more. Darwin used his conclusions to try to answer questions about whether the human mind is unique and beyond analogy with animals (he said it wasn't); how to explain forms of beauty, like plumage, that had no clear survival utility and thus implied divine design (their purpose was sexual selection); and whether natural selection applies to society. Regarding the last, he had something very interesting to say. A section titled "Natural Selection as Affecting Civilized Nations" tells us that while "savages" allow the weak to die so the more vigorous will survive, "civilized men do our utmost to check th[is] process." We take care of the sick, maimed, and poor, build asylums for the insane, make laws to help the unfortunate, all of which allow "the weak [to] propagate their kind" with a result that "must be highly injurious to the race of man" (1871, vol. 1, 168). A reader who stops at this point will be shaken by such pitiless logic. But Darwin has not led us here merely to face the ax. Helping the helpless, he says, comes from "the instinct of sympathy"—an instinct that primitive society suppresses but that civilized society releases and trains through education and reflection. "Nor could we check our sympathy," says Darwin, "even at the urging of hard reason, without deterioration in the noblest part of our nature" (1871, vol. 1, 168).

It would seem a key moment in the unfolding of Darwin's thought and work. Moreover, it could well have been aided by a reading of Adam Smith's *Theory of Moral Sentiments* (1759), which proposes "sympathy" as a defining trait of human nature essential to a successful, advanced society. Like Smith, Darwin feels that human beings are not instinctively, hopelessly selfish. Morality, however, as a set of behavioral codes and judgments, is not an instinct; it comes from upbringing, education, and culture. Civilized man is not a container for thoughtless forces. "[I]f we were intentionally to neglect the weak and helpless," he says in *Descent*, "it could only be for a contingent benefit, with a certain and great present evil. Hence we must bear without complaining the undoubtedly bad effects of the weak surviving and propagating their kind" (1871, vol. 1, 169). In the end, then, Darwin leaves us a little unsure about the depths of his own "sympathy." Politically he was a Whig (liberal), who voted for the Reform Acts of 1832 and 1867, extending voting rights to millions, but was never especially outspoken publicly except for his fierce opposition to slavery.

Unlike Spencer and so many other thinkers of the time, Darwin shows both acceptance of *and* restraint to biologizing human reality. He clearly does not embrace ceding to biology all territory in this domain. But in the wake of Darwin's achievement, the scientizing of society acquired new and more far-reaching dimensions. Indeed, without ever intending the result, Darwin's scientific and popular success gave no small support to Herbert Spencer's theories in a public mind where the swirl of new ideas about the Earth, evolution, and the human were bound to bring confusion as to "details." Victorian Britain, moreover, as well as the United States and large parts of Europe, showed an eagerness to find in science the answers to many questions about the state and direction of civilization (Numbers 2006; Gould 1981; Hawkins 1997; Young 1985). Such eagerness did not die with Queen Victoria. A century later, we find a similar impulse employing natural selection, Darwin's most original idea. The philosopher Daniel Dennett (1995) expresses, perhaps, the late twentieth-century mixture of hubris and anxiety toward such uses by calling natural selection a "universal acid" whose ability to turn human phenomena into the result of competition and adaptation eats into everything, from stem cells to economics. How ironic then that it proved the most difficult idea of all for science to accept.

DARWIN'S IDEAS: THE FIRST ONE HUNDRED YEARS

Darwin's ideas entered Western culture at a time when revolutionary ideas and conservative reaction, with free market liberalism somewhere in the middle and assailed by both extremes, were in major conflict. Institutional religion was no longer able to give secure meaning to a world in the midst of such change. Standard Christian explanations of man's place in the sacred order were inadequate to deal with the new scientific discoveries, with the realities and impacts of industrialization, the squalor, disease, unrest, and inequality of the new society, its spectacular wealth and new machines, and the sense shared by many that everything was hurtling toward some definite yet unknown end. In this milieu, evolution became a discourse that people could use to put order back into the direction of society. The public may have been shocked by *Origin* but not entirely and not for long. It had been made ready by such events as the debate over *Vestiges* (1844), the discovery of what were called "giant, extinct reptiles" by Richard Owen (1840s), and the finding of primitive humanoid remains in the Neander Valley near Düsseldorf.

The impact of *Origin* was like a series of waves, both geographic and intellectual. England was affected first, then America, Europe, Russia, and by the 1870s and 1880s the Middle East and Asia. In a kind of parallel fashion, natural history and religion were first affected, then the "sciences of man," ethnology and anthropology, then social science, economics, politics, philosophy, and literature. The progression was neither orderly nor predictable, but once underway it proved unstoppable. Darwin's ideas gained influence because they were "science," the abode of truth, and not just any science but the science of life, its history, origin, future, and meaning. As accepted by the public, "evolution" was often leavened with Lamarck's concept about the inheritance of acquired characteristics—each generation providing the possibility for improvement of the next, thus the required conditions for biological progress. Darwinian gradualism obviously could not work for society; human history was far too short and change, at least by the nineteenth century, too rapid. Still, during the heated controversies of the 1860s, Darwin's name became interchangeable with "evolution." Precisely what *kind* of evolution didn't matter: "Darwin" and "Darwinian" became shorthand for evolving phenomena in any and all contexts.

Applied to society, evolution meant the success of some groups with certain characteristics, who thus proved themselves more "fit," while others simply carried on, stagnated, or died out. Of course, this was not the end of things. Evolution was also twisted to "prove" that progress had a distinct path to follow and anything "unfit" that interfered with that path had to be minimized or eliminated. This was more an adaptation of Spencer than Darwin; but again, it didn't seem to matter. Darwin's name had to be evoked in order that the authority of science obtain. His name appealed equally to Karl Marx, Andrew Carnegie, Sun Yat-sen, and Sigmund Freud.

Origin did not ignite a battle between science and religion. There was no lining up of biologists on one side and clerics on the other. The fight, rather, was between those who felt Darwin could be reconciled to Christianity and those who did not (Himmelfarb 1959). This was especially true in England, America, and Germany, where attacks tended to come from the older generation, wedded to natural theology, while Darwin's most avid supporters were generally young, rising stars in science, journalism, politics, and even the clergy. Charles Kingsley, a famous minister, found in the book a "noble conception" of God, while the journalist Walter Bagehot, in his popular *Politics and Physics* (1867), enlisted Darwin in a theory of social advancement based on a complete misreading of *Origin* in Lamarckian terms (each generation inheriting the advances of its predecessor). The eminent naturalist Sir Richard Owen (coiner of the word "dinosaur") saw the book as a denial of Creation and loaded with radicalism and disorder (Glick 1988).

Despite much bitter attack early on, Darwin had clearly won the day by 1870. Not Darwin alone, moreover, but those who fought and argued in his favor and who attached their burgeoning careers to his success. From this point forward Darwin's name carried well beyond the bounds of science. In realms both bright and dark, brilliant and terrible, those who called upon his ideas set many patterns of Western intellectual life. From a blind and mindless process, dependent on random variations in animals and plants, "evolution" came to justify the most planned and purposeful ambitions of social change.

Reception and Aftermath: The Sciences

Acceptance of *Origin* depended on the tireless efforts of Thomas Huxley, Joseph Hooker, and Charles Lyell in England, Asa Gray in America, and Ernst Haeckel in Germany. Organized, committed, eloquent, and savvy, these men understood the nature of the opposition and what was at stake. They employed to good effect the new media of newspapers, popular magazines, and public lectures, as well as scientific journals and book publication. They wrote hundreds of reviews and commentaries and engaged in constant debates—Asa Gray fought repeatedly with Louis Agassiz in the United States, just as Huxley did with opponents in Britain, and Haeckel in Germany. They taught courses, spoke to Parliament, and carried out a forceful series of counterattacks on Darwin's critics (Browne 2002). Their objective was to gain approval for Darwinian evolution, not natural selection (most of them rejected it), and so their arguments ended up largely against natural theology. For these men, and for the growing number of ambitious young researchers, traditional faith greatly restricted what science could do. Huxley wanted to evict organized religion from any role whatsoever in the sciences. He was convinced, and worked to convince others, of its anti-intellectualism rooted in supernatural explanations.

What is perhaps most difficult for us to comprehend today is how natural selection was largely and purposely left out of the scientific discussion. Indeed, it would not be accepted by the biological community for another seventy-five years. There are several reasons for this. Unlike Huxley, a fair portion of the scientific community remained religious to some degree and continued to believe in special creation (by God) for human beings. This was certainly the case for Alfred Wallace himself, who published *Contributions to the Theory of Natural Selection* in 1871, which included what became a well-known essay, "Limits of Natural Selection as Applied to Man." There he argued that selection could not explain many human characteristics, including brain size, and that civilization itself could not have progressed as it had unless the mind had been created by a "superior intelligence." This essay, given its source, was apparently a delight to Darwin's enemies. More generally, however, natural selection was viewed by biologists as highly speculative. Without a precise theory of heredity, it remained merely one hypothesis among others, unable to serve as a final mechanism. Preferred instead was some version of Lamarckism or orthogenesis by which life has an innate tendency to evolve in a linear fashion. Natural selection was not intuitive and could not be seen, whereas a progression from simple to complex forms was everywhere in evidence in the natural world and, seemingly, in the fossil record (Bowler 2009).

Biologists, that is, were members of society too. Their science, like all sciences, was impacted by certain core ideas. They were unwilling to give up the notion that evolution meant not only change but some form of progress. In biological terms, this meant *development*, that is, some kind of improvement in structure, adaptation, and survival potential. They found it difficult to accept the haphazard, groping version that was natural selection.

Genetics was needed to bring natural selection into the picture. By 1900, new evidence from detailed studies of multiple plant species, combined with the rediscovery of Gregor Mendel's work on inheritance of traits in pea plants, strongly suggested that heredity worked in a specific way, with individual traits having their own carriers. That is, inheritance did not "blend" characteristics of single traits—the offspring of a tall plant and a short plant of the same species, for example, would not be a medium-sized plant but either a tall or short one. Heritability had to be carried by "particles" of some kind. The term "pangenes" was coined for these particles, later shortened to "genes." The word "mutation" for new traits that might appear in a generation was also introduced. Mutations were thus changes to the genetic material itself, a conclusion soon confirmed by early studies of the fruit fly, *Drosophila melanogaster* (whose chromosomes are large and visible). In the 1920s, mathematical techniques began to be used for analyzing population changes. It turned out that certain groups with shared traits statistically out-reproduced others and that this greater rate of survival could be tied to "fitness criteria." At this point, natural selection began to enter the realm of consideration. But it was the final combining of lab and field studies, showing the high level of genetic diversity and survival potential in nature, that turned the tables (Bowler 2009; Mayr 1985). Probably no single work did more to establish a new view of the genetic role in evolution than Theodosius Dobzhansky's book *Genetics and the Origin of Species* (1937), whose title aptly gives homage to Darwin's text. *Genetics and the Origin of Species* has been often called the most influential single work on evolution in the twentieth century. If so, it is a confirmation of the fame that is due to Darwin himself, given how often it refers to natural selection and its implications for the diversity of life.

So by the 1940s, a "Neo-Darwinian Synthesis" had emerged, with natural selection given a secure place in biology (Mayr 1985). It is a place that has been further solidified by a vast and growing body of observations and studies, including DNA research and detailed work on bacterial evolution. Some of this work has highlighted the role of other processes in evolution, such as massive extinctions caused by volcanic events or meteor and asteroid impacts. As an element of nature, however, natural selection is today beyond scientific doubt, no less certain than gravity, once a hypothesis too.

Darwin's core idea, then, faced struggles within science at the same time it did in society generally. For a brief period, these realms of resistance overlapped: nature could not be conceived apart from some kind of design, whether involving a teleology that drove life toward improvement or, more simply, that came from the Creator. Given what it truly meant—the final secularization of the living world—natural selection faced a higher degree of challenge than any other foundational concept of modern science. And this remains as true today as ever.

Darwin in Europe

When we turn to the sociopolitical realm beyond England, we find that Darwin's ideas engendered both fervent acceptance and hostile opposition. Indeed, the waves of influence from *Origin of Species* broke upon continental Europe with gathering force from the 1860s to the 1880s, shaped by the landscape of each nation's intellectual and political culture. No less was this true in places as distant as China and Japan. Each setting tended to draw from the Darwinian corpus what suited its purposes—scientists, philosophers, politicians, reformers, social critics, and novelists all found in "Darwin" and "evolution" a source of argument for intellectual battles already in progress. But it is too simple to say that each nation and decade shaped Darwin to its own needs. There were consistent and meaningful patterns, some of which have continued to the present. A fair number of the early public spokesmen did not actually read Darwin but gained their notions of him via other writers, especially Herbert Spencer, Ernst Haeckel, and Ludwig Büchner, who all claimed to be inspired by Darwin yet whose books were far more philosophy and social theory than actual science. "Darwinism," that is, became a set of diverse, often contradictory, and pseudoscientific claims, ranging from the utopian to the pragmatic. The range of misunderstanding applied to "evolution" was crucial to its impact.

In the case of the Dutch, for example, *Origin* arrived soon after the liberal bourgeoisie had taken over many positions of authority and gained dominance in the universities. Combined with the sophisticated technical culture grounded, like England's, in the seventeenth-century Scientific Revolution, this individualistic and socially conservative class provided a welcoming home for Darwinian biology, which they saw as both deistic (God removed from direct intervention but still the great planner) and supporting their more guarded ideas of slow social advancement (Bulhof 1988). Skeptics of religion, however, accepted Darwin because of his seeming atheism and because evolution could be used to argue for a social order more open and progressive than what the bourgeoisie preferred. Rejection of Darwin's ideas certainly existed among Catholics and evangelical Protestants. But the role of the scientist as a beacon of progress made Charles Darwin too much of a multifaceted hero to Dutch modernists to be suppressed.

In France, by contrast, there was no warm welcome. The French pretty much rejected *Origin* outright. The book was not translated for several years, and when it appeared it was criticized for its denial of divine causes and its lack of proper empiricism—there were not enough facts presented. The spell of Cuvier, who had denounced Lamarck thirty years earlier for the same reasons, continued to hang over French natural history. Darwin, in fact, was viewed by many French naturalists as a second-rate Lamarck (Stebbens 1988).

Spain, meanwhile, presented yet another type of response. *Origin* remained practically unknown until well after the country's Glorious Revolution of 1868, when the monarchy of Isabella II was overthrown. Intellectuals encountered Darwin a few years later through a French translation of *Descent of Man*, which drew almost universal attack. But the appearance of *Origin* and Haeckel's writings very soon after helped change this. Republican fervor for democracy created a great interest in evolution. Both Haeckel and Darwin, at least in name, were adopted by Left-leaning intellectuals in anthropology, sociology, and political economy to argue that a new era was at hand and that Spain's stilted, self-absorbed past was over. Even restoration of the monarchy in 1875 did little to change this. "Darwin" as icon of new ideas from England and Germany became a badge of the Left, anti-Darwin sentiment an orthodoxy for the Right (Glick 1988; Glick, Puig-Samper, and Ruiz 2001).

Origin appeared in Germany, meanwhile, only a few months after its publication in England. Though biologists and geologists debated its contents for nearly a decade, the rising influence of the zoologist and physician Ernst Haeckel helped turn the tide in Darwin's favor. German science at this stage was already the envy of Europe, highly advanced, especially in the physical sciences, and strongly state supported. Many of Darwin's allies, like Haeckel, were materialists through and through and had already abandoned religion. Contributing to this was the renown of the physicist Hermann von Helmholtz, who, along with other members of the Berlin Physical Society, set a formidable standard for scientific professionalism. Already in 1847, the group had declared a "materialist manifesto" that all life could be reduced to chemistry and physics. A number of these men also held left-wing political views as "freethinkers" and socialists, and Darwinian theory appealed to them for this reason, too. Haeckel leaned this way in the beginning, becoming a powerful public speaker, author of widely read illustrated books, all in favor of Darwinism, not only as science but as part of a program for educational and social reform to advance German society. Haeckel did make many important contributions to biology; the terms "phylum," "ecology," and "phylogeny" are his. He is most widely known for his "ontogeny recapitulates phylogeny" hypothesis, proposing that embryos undergo in the womb the evolutionary stages of their species, an idea later proven false but that generated much productive debate. Haeckel was not a total Darwinian. Like so many others, he rejected natural selection in favor of Lamarckian inheritance of acquired characteristics. Politically, too, he found himself moving toward the Right after Bismarck's success in creating a unified Reich, which encouraged strong nationalistic feelings in a large part of the German intelligentsia from the 1880s on (Montgomery 1988). But Haeckel held true to most of Darwin and never moved in fascist directions; his theories were rejected and his books burned by the Nazis (Richards 2008).

Karl Marx read *Origin* in 1860 and again in 1862. Unlike Haeckel and many of his countrymen, Marx had command of English and thus read the original. This was significant since the German translator, Heinrich Georg Bronn, made alterations to Darwin's terminology, rendering "favored" (as in "favored races") as *vervolkommenet*—"perfected"—and the "struggle for existence" as *Kampf ums Dasein*—"battle/fight for existence." He also added a final chapter of explanations and criticisms. When Marx read the original, he had no such artificiality to deal with. He wrote to Engels on December 19, 1860, to say, "this is the book that contains the basis in natural science for our view" (Colp 1974, 330). Engels had read the book, too (he had bought one of the initial 1,250 copies), and commented in a letter dated June 18, 1862, "It is remarkable how Darwin rediscovers among the beasts and plants, the society of England with its division of labour, competition, opening up of new markets" (cited in Hunt 2009, 280). Engels's more subtle perception, however, was lost on many later socialist thinkers who projected Darwin onto society to suit their own purposes. Marx, however, did not do this, at least not overtly. He did, however, include direct references to Darwin in footnotes to *Kapital*. One of these seems particularly interesting: "Darwin has interested us in the history of Nature's Technology, i.e., in the formation of the organs of plants and animals, which organs serve as instruments of production for sustaining life. Does not the history of the productive organs of man, of organs that are the material basis of all social organization, deserve equal attention?" (Colp 1974, 331). It is a powerful suggestion—Marx nearly falls prey to the lure of a Darwinian view of society. But he pulls back. In the very next line, he says that the evolution of technology would be far easier to construct than that of nature, since "human history differs from natural history in this, that we have made the former, but not the latter" (Colp 1974, 331).

Marx held his own ideas separate from those of biological determinism and was highly critical of anyone who ignored his own "scientific" theories of human history. There are hints that he may at one time have envisioned himself writing a parallel to *Origin* with regard to the evolution of human society. He did send Darwin a copy of *Kapital* in 1873, to which Darwin replied: "Though our studies have been so different, I believe that we both earnestly desire the extension of knowledge, & this . . . is sure to add to the happiness of Mankind" (Colp 1974, 334). It was a polite enough rejection and reflected Darwin's graciousness. In truth, he never read Marx's book, the pages of his copy remaining uncut. Darwin thought that a connection "between Socialism and Evolution through the natural sciences [was] a foolish idea" (Hunt 2009, 280).

Russian intellectual society, meanwhile, responded to Darwin in a positive way, though less so in the sciences than in politics. After Russia's defeat in the Crimean War (1853–56), the intelligentsia wanted an end to stagnant and oppressive autocracy and sought a new positivist basis for a truly modern, national culture (Vucinich 1988). *Origin* added energy to this nationalistic perspective in several ways. Many Russian thinkers found in the book's materialistic view of nature an argument against the divine order believed to give the Church and tsar the absolute quality of authority. But there were aspects to *Origin* that Russian scientists found disturbing. Many refused to abide the "struggle for existence" metaphor, which, in echo of Engels's comment, struck them as too reflective of Britain's combative, individualistic culture, too denying of more harmonious aspects in nature (Todes 2009). Anti-tsarist intellectuals declared the function of science was both to elucidate nature and to help create a freer, more cooperative society, and they did not see natural selection as useful in this regard. Instead, "struggle" was rejected in favor of another concept. In a highly influential book, *Mutual Aid: A Factor of Evolution* (1903), the geographer, zoologist, and anarchist Peter Kropotkin condensed this view: "Under any circumstance, sociability is the greatest advantage in the struggle of life" (1910, 57). Kropotkin's book mixed scientific discussion of animal societies with cultural anthropology and historical analysis of human communities, emphasizing the central role of collaboration. His view, in fact, found its way into evolutionary theory in the late twentieth century through observed examples of evolutionary cooperation both within and between species. Though Kropotkin was denounced by socialist-Marxist thinkers, the opening lines of his book are revealing for what they say about the uptake of Darwin by such thinkers:

> The conception of struggle for existence as a factor of evolution, introduced into science by Darwin and Wallace, has permitted us to embrace an immensely-wide range of phenomena in one single generalization, which soon became the very basis of our philosophical, biological, and sociological speculations. An immense variety of facts: adaptations of function and structure of organic beings to their surroundings; physiological and anatomical evolution; intellectual progress, and moral development itself . . . were embodied by Darwin in one general conception. We understood them as continued endeavours—as a struggle against adverse circumstances—for such a development of individuals, races, species and societies, as would result in the greatest possible fullness, variety, and intensity of life. (1910, 1)

In these few lines we see how easy it was for even the most sophisticated thinkers to transport Darwin's ideas out of their biological context and into other realms, how fluidly they could move from "adaptations of function" to "moral development," from "species" to "societies" without any sense that boundaries were being crossed. At this point, that is, such boundaries had come to exist in professional research and academic study (geologists and biologists in 1900 were no longer being asked about the nature of society), but they were less known and obeyed in popular discourse. As Kropotkin makes clear, what legitimizes this leap, and keeps it therefore unseen, is not so much the idea of competition, as Engels thought. More central are the ideas of struggle, the perception that one is facing "adverse circumstances," and triumph, whose arrival will bring a new stage or era of advancement.

Russian Marxists, in fact, seized the moment to proclaim that "Marxism is Darwinism in its application to social science," as put by Georgi Plekhanov (Rogers 1988, 266). This was a statement Darwin would not have endorsed. Nor would he have enjoyed Engels's statement in his oration on the occasion of Marx's death: "Just as Darwin discovered the law of development of organic nature, so Marx discovered the law of development of human history" (Hunt 2009, 275). Lenin, however, greatly admired Engels and considered Plekhanov the best philosopher of Marxism alive at the time. He himself, in his important essay *What Is to Be Done?* (1902), used natural selection to describe the political process in an open democracy, where "every activist finds his appropriate place." But in tsarist Russia, Lenin said, such adaptation was impossible. Tyranny and the secret police could be overcome only if secrecy and conspiracy were used.

Stalin claimed that he had been inspired by Darwin as a youth and that after reading *Origin of Species* he had become a convinced atheist (Tucker 1974, 78). But he later rejected Darwin, specifically the Neo-Darwinian Synthesis, which he called capitalist pseudoscience. Indeed, partly motivated by fascist use of eugenics, he declared Western genetics a fraud and sent to the gulag, or to execution, many of the Soviet Union's best geneticists. He endorsed a neo-Lamarckian view that agreed with communist faith in the Soviet state as a new stage in human existence. Stalin's handpicked director of the Soviet agricultural sciences, Trofim Lysenko, promised to feed the nation by increasing wheat yields through Lamarckian methods. Improvements he was going to make would be inherited by the new seeds. His utter failure turned "Lysenkoism" into an eponym for the infection of science with political ideology (Mayr 1985). It was, in any case, far removed from anything resembling Darwin's work or the scientific spirit and set back Soviet biology for decades.

Darwin in the Middle East and East Asia

By the end of the century, ideas of evolution, the struggle for existence, and "survival of the fittest" had spread to the Islamic part of the world, to Japan, and to China. In these regions, modern biology did not yet exist. Philosophy, religion, and theories about morality and the cosmos were all inseparable. As Western scientific truth about organic nature, evolution was likely to attract great interest when brought into ongoing debates about modernity and the future. But in contrast to Europe, Darwin's books were not the sources involved. It was instead translations of Huxley, Haeckel, and above all Spencer that mattered.

Islam was an interesting case. After defeat in the Russo-Turkish War (1877–78), the Ottoman Empire was forced into a series of territorial and economic concessions. Much agitation for reform ensued among Muslim students and intellectuals, who saw traditional religious authority and the sultan as backward, weak, and unable to protect Islam from imperialism. By the 1880s and 1890s, the prestige of Western science underlay a movement to modernize and thereby strengthen Muslim society, and Spencer-Darwin became part of this. Their first proponent was the Syrian Christian physician Shibi Shumayyil, who, in a number of well-circulated articles, preached a philosophy of radical secularism and universal progress based on evolution. Despotism was unnatural (no tyrannical "nations" in nature); needed instead was a secular state where Muslims and Christians were equal and intellectual work focused on natural science (Hourani 1983; Bezirgan 1988).

Predictable denunciation came from the clergy. However, the most influential polemic was written not by a cleric but by the philosopher Sayyid Jamal al-Din al-Afghani (1839–97), whose *Refutation of the Materialists* (1882) contended angrily against all nonreligious views of nature, particularly Darwin, who he said wanted to remake Islam into a pale copy of Europe. Al-Afghani aimed at a pan-Islamic unity based on Muslim principles and acceptance of Western technology (Keddie 1968). (We have much more to say about how al-Afghani sought to modernize Islam in chapter 7.) His writings show some curious misreadings of Darwin: "He [Darwin] reports that one society used to cut off the tails of their dogs, and after . . . several centuries their dogs began to be born by nature without tails. He apparently is saying that since there is no longer need for a tail, nature refrained from giving it. Is this wretch deaf to the fact that the Arabs and Jews for several thousand years have practiced circumcision, and despite this . . . not one of them has been born circumcised?" (Keddie 1968, 136). Al-Afghani may have actually never read *Origin* or *Descent*, though during the time he lived in Paris in the early 1880s Darwin's work was certainly being widely discussed.

Japan and China, meanwhile, welcomed Darwinian thought—or what they called "Darwinian"—in unabashed fashion. Both nations first encountered this thought in translations of Spencer and Huxley. As in Islam, the shape of influence reflected sociohistorical circumstances. This meant Japan's successful but troubled rise as an industrial-military power, China's parallel failures along these same lines, and both countries' growing nationalism and fear of Western imperialism. In Japan's case, the Meiji Restoration of 1868 that brought accelerated modernization began a phase of avid institution building, industrial development, and discussion on the proper role of government. The new oligarchy in power had much interest in Westernizing Japan's infrastructure and military but little concern for modernizing the social order. It brought experts and teachers from the West to act as advisors to the state and sent promising students abroad, while encouraging traditional forms of obedience among the populace. The flow of personnel, however, brought a surge of foreign books into Japan, with immediate impacts. Works on political economy, government, and natural rights were widely read, starting in the 1870s. Because of their enormous popularity in the West, Spencer's works were included, and by 1890 nearly his entire oeuvre, over thirty volumes, had been translated. During the crucial period of the 1880s and early 1890s, nothing less than a "Spencer boom" developed in Japan. His organic view of progress as adaptation to new social conditions, and these conditions as evolving from a savage to an advanced industrial stage, proved hugely attractive to Japanese intellectuals of every stripe. It found use both by conservatives in government and by reformers who advocated broader rights and democracy (Howland 2000).

Debate over Spencer helped introduce concepts for which no words yet existed, like "society" and "the state." Authoritarians, such as Kato Hiroyuki, first president of Tokyo University, could portray the autocratic state as a needed creation from "survival of the fittest" conflict, while opponents argued that real progress could only evolve toward liberalism and freedom. In the 1890s, the aging Spencer was asked for advice by the government itself. In reply, he said it was "impossible that the Japanese, hitherto accustomed to despotic rule, should, all at once, become capable of constitutional government." Power in Japan, indeed, remained autocratic, aided by victorious wars against China (1894–95) and then Russia (1904–5), establishing the country as a new and unexpected world power with imperial ambitions.

Lacking disciplines like geology and paleontology, Japanese science was wholly unready to absorb evolutionary biology. It came via translations of two books: Huxley's *Lectures on the Origin of Species* (translated 1879) and the American zoologist Edward Morse's *Evolutionary Theory of Animal* (1882). *Origin* itself did not appear until 1896 and was not widely available until after 1900. The public, meanwhile, knew little of Darwin until 1904, when biologist Oka Asajiro published *Shinkaron Kowa* ("Lectures on the Theory of Evolution"), a popularization. Oka's book was extremely popular and like so many other popularizations of Darwin did not refrain from venturing into nonscientific domains. Oka had studied zoology in Germany and was subject to Haeckel's influence in applying Darwin to every aspect of organic and social existence. In all this writing, both translation and popularization, certain aspects of Spencer remained prominent. It is evident even in the term coined for "evolution" itself: *shinka*, combining the ideograms for "advancement" and "change," thus embodying the notion of progress. On the other side, Kato Hiroyuki's translation of "survival of the fittest" into *yushoh reppai*, "victory of the superior over the inferior," reflects an authoritarian version of Spencer's emphasis on unrelieved competition, one that was retained into the era of ultramilitarism. By that time, Darwinism had also helped inspire socialist interpretations of collective struggle, similar to those then current in Russia. The history of evolution's impact is nearly parallel to the development of political debates over Japanese modernism (Bartholomew 1989; Watanabe and Benfrey 1990).

A similar pattern, with alternate details, can be seen in the case of China. Here, Darwin had no significant presence until the late 1890s, when he was introduced in the wake of the country's humiliating defeat during the Sino-Japanese War (1894–95). Coming thirty-five years after the launch of its "self-strengthening movement" that was meant to modernize China, this defeat caused shock and widespread self-recrimination. It was into this setting that the scholar Yan Fu (1854–1921) injected an adapted version of Darwin to explain China's weakness. Yan was an important translator, bringing into Chinese such works as Adam Smith's *Wealth of Nations*, Mill's *On Liberty*, and Spencer's *Study of Sociology*. But it was his volume *Heavenly Evolution* (1898), a paraphrase of Huxley's *Evolution and Ethics* (1893) written in elegant classical Chinese, that had a major effect over the next two decades. Yan had been sent to England in 1877–79 to study naval science, and in the wake of the loss to Japan, taking blame upon himself, he came to a conclusion. Technology and training were not enough; building a strong, modern nation required a transformation of the mind and an understanding of evolutionary laws. China had to abandon its age-old beliefs and adopt a doctrine of "struggle, dynamism, and energy" (Xiao 1995, 85; Pusey 1983). But it could not do this all at once. Evolution was gradual; revolution was sudden, destructive.

In his version of Huxley's book, Yan practiced a form of strategic adaptation, inserting traditional philosophical terms, such as *tao* (way), *sheng* (life-producing), and *tian* (heaven), and altering "natural selection" into "heaven's choice," "evolution" into "the theory of progressive change," and even adopting Kato Hiroyuki's "victory of the superior over the inferior" (Huang 2008; Pusey 1983, 2009). Yan claimed there was a need to modify existing institutions and begin liberal reforms, not to indulge in radicalism. It was a viewpoint partly echoed by another influential reformer and widely read author, Liang Qichao, who also desired both ideological and institutional changes as well the elimination of corruption. Liang's use of Darwin was also an adaptation: "Western evolutionists say that the world progresses through competition. . . . To survive one must seek strength and intelligence . . . [which come from] pooling the strength . . . and pooling the intelligence of the people" (Pusey 1983, 187). Autocracy therefore represented an earlier evolutionary form; next comes an "age of civilized freedom"—freedom not for the individual, however, but for "the whole people" to whom individuals must be loyal.

Uses of Darwin, however, also gave aid to revolutionaries (Pusey 2009). If Yan and Liang argued for a step-wise ascent to democracy as a triumph of "the group," Sun Yat-sen claimed that evolutionary law demanded sudden, drastic change, the extinction of outmoded and "unfit" political forms. Rebellion was a natural law, an inevitability produced by social evolution. So, apparently, was racism. Western ideas along these lines, with a dash of Darwin mixed in, were targeted at the Manchus who had ruled China since the beginning of the Qing Dynasty in 1644 and were now called "unfit" (Pusey 1983). But it was the image of "struggle" and a biologically sanctified socialism that drew the imagination of the Chinese Communist Party from the 1930s onward. In 1957, Mao Zedong was to close the circle in claiming that socialism was set to triumph because it was fittest.

It has been said that Darwin's ideas did much to create the conditions for radicalism, both by destroying traditional forms of belief and by providing the rationale for violence. As the examples of Russia, Islam, and East Asia make clear, this view is far too simplistic. Darwin's ideas were part of a larger movement in Western thought, one that grew directly out of advances in knowledge, the rise of nationalism, the spread of and then resistance to colonialism, and failures of authority in monarchical systems supported by traditional religious institutions. As the French and American revolutions, as well as those of 1848 in Europe, showed, Darwin was not needed for radicalism. But it is essential to realize, too, that while Darwin's ideas were not final causes, they were potent raw material and were repeatedly used as such to change minds and help inspire many schools of thought, some that Darwin himself would never have supported. His intent was never to destroy religion or kill God, yet men as different as Spencer, Huxley, Nietzsche, and Stalin all derived such meaning from his work. The issue of responsibility is therefore complex. Great, powerful ideas gain a life separate from their originators; yet they require such originators to exist in the first place. As we mentioned earlier, Stalin once claimed that while at a Georgian seminary as a teenager it was his reading of Darwin that awoke him to the fact that there was no God.

The Problem of Social Darwinism

All of this raises the issue of "Social Darwinism." Though variably defined (Hawkins 1997), the phrase is usually aimed at conservatives who claim that those at the top of society are more "fit" and "best adapted" and that redistributing resources to the rest of society, especially the less fit, violates the natural order (Hofstadter 1955). Social Darwinists are said to be against all liberal reforms and in favor of laissez-faire economics. Corporate titans are counted among its best examples, justifying their wealth by Darwinian rhetoric, such as the railroad magnate

James J. Hill ("The fortunes of railroad companies are determined by the law of the survival of the fittest"), the steel baron Andrew Carnegie ("While the law of competition may be sometimes hard for the individual, it is best for the race, because it ensures the survival of the fittest in every department"), and the founder of Standard Oil, John D. Rockefeller ("The growth of a large business is merely a survival of the fittest. . . . The American beauty rose can be produced . . . only by sacrificing the early buds which grow up around it" (Hawkins 1997, 118, 120).

There are problems with all this, however. Social Darwinism is common in historical discussions and will not go away, while Spencer is routinely considered its archdeacon (or demon). But as we have noted repeatedly, Spencer was not a Darwinian. He much preferred Lamarck, and though he did incorporate some of Darwin's ideas, he often argued with other points, making positive references instead to other scientists like Carl Friedrich Wolff and Karl von Baer, founder of embryology. Conservatives, moreover, were hardly the only ones to take up evolution in their causes or to biologize social realities. On the contrary, this was also done by the Left, even the radical Left in Russia, China, and Japan. Between roughly 1880 and 1920, Spencer, Darwin, Haeckel, and others were often combined in an ideological stew to nourish positions that ranged from authoritarianism to revolution. Threads of biodeterminism run through many tapestries.

Was Darwin himself a Social Darwinist? Did he believe that natural selection could be applied to society? The answer seems a pretty clear "no" in *Origin of Species* but a definitive "yes" in *Descent of Man*. By the time of the latter work, however, he was a late arrival to such notions. Thinkers in France and the United States, along with Bagehot, Wallace, Spencer, and Galton in England, Haeckel and his followers in Germany, as well as others elsewhere in Europe, had already weighed in with biosocial theories. Darwin's lateness on the scene is apparent in that he himself had to cite a number of these authors in *Descent*.

So forceful and commonplace did the use of social evolutionary rhetoric become that even the greatest thinkers on society and history felt forced to employ it. In the 1890s, Émile Durkheim in his first major book, *Division of Labor in Society* (1893), relies on *Origin* and "the struggle for existence" to help explain how specialization of labor develops under conditions of growing resource scarcity. Max Weber in his own early work *The National State and Economic Policy* (1895) attempted to show how racial differences in appearance and thought played a part in the "economic struggle for existence" between nations. Both these thinkers, however, soon turned away from Darwinian explanatory schemes. Durkheim argued directly against Spencer, proposing that society generated some of its own internal forces rather than acting as an organic sum of free individuals. Weber, meanwhile, soon abandoned biological interpretations altogether and became highly critical of all such biosociology (Hawkins 1997). But as young men in the first stages of their careers, Durkheim and Weber both felt compelled to adopt what had become, in essence, a new type of supposedly "scientific" orthodoxy.

Eugenics: The Evil That Ideas Can Do

Natural selection was ignored by much of biology before the 1930s, but portions of it were adopted and applied elsewhere, with potent effect. Eugenics, as a type of derivative pseudoscience, took pieces and methods from Darwinian thought, biomeasurement, statistics, racial studies, and early genetics to support an idea that was sociopolitical in nature (Kevles 1985). As originally conceived, it involved selective breeding applied to humans. The primary goal was to improve the national gene pool by promoting reproduction among those deemed more fit and discouraging or preventing births among the unfit. In its initial phase, the 1880s to the 1930s, it created a major global movement that contributed directly to terrible abuses of human beings, not only in authoritarian states but also in democracies. The movement remains a testament to how bad ideas, backed by the presumed authority of science and supported by institutional programs, can lead even well-meaning individuals (as well as corrupt demagogues) to support heinous acts in the name of "progress." It is also a lesson about how powerful ideas, even those that have advanced human knowledge and inspired worthwhile enterprises, can also be used to inspire beliefs and actions that would have been firmly rejected by their original authors.

The Victorian explorer, thinker, and first cousin of Darwin, Francis Galton (1822–1911), was the originator of eugenics. He coined the word in 1883 from the Greek *eu*, meaning "good" or "well," and *genes* for "born." Galton was no ordinary intellectual. He was a polymath who made contributions to geography, statistics, meteorology, and forensics, and he was among the relatively few who accepted Darwin's hypothesis of natural selection early on. He received many honors in his lifetime, including knighthood and election to the Royal Society. Above all else, he was a man of numbers whose motto was "whenever you can, count." Quantification, especially using statistics, was the tool he wielded to give his work the heft of real science. Galton's idea for eugenics came soon after he read *Origin*. He wrote to Darwin saying that the book "drove away the constraint of my old [religious] superstition." It also seems to have implanted concepts that Galton then expanded into the human realm, especially the notion that higher fitness levels, in terms of "mind capacity," could be purposely selected and passed down (Bulmer 2003).

In 1869, Galton published his theory in the book *Hereditary Genius*. His basic method was to use obituaries and lists of famous people to find statistical evidence supporting the concept that "natural ability" tended to run in families. Matters of social privilege and education, as well as questions of whether reputation alone was a valid measure of "genius," he briefly considered, then rejected. Lack of fame for Galton meant lack of talent. Sentimentality had no place in science, he declared. Humanity, however, could be elevated with rational planning and purpose. Galton, that is, claimed to show that a man's natural abilities are derived by inheritance, under exactly the same limitations as . . . the whole organic world. Consequently, as it is easy . . . to obtain by careful selection a permanent breed of dogs or horses gifted with peculiar powers of running, or of doing anything else, so it would be quite practicable to produce a highly-gifted race of men by judicious marriages during several consecutive generations. I shall show that social agencies of an ordinary character, whose influences are little suspected, are at this moment working towards the degradation of human nature, and that others are working towards its improvement. I conclude that each generation has enormous power over the natural gifts of those that follow, and maintain that it is a duty we owe to humanity to investigate the range of that power, and to exercise it in a way that, without being unwise towards ourselves, shall be most advantageous to future inhabitants of the earth. (1869, 1)

Galton did not feel, as Darwin did, that sympathy toward the weak was ennobling. He argued for "the best form of civilization in respect to the improvement of the race," and this meant encouraging the "highly gifted" to marry earlier and have more children, the weak to marry later or "find a . . . refuge in celibate monasteries," and inviting only the "better sort of emigrants and refugees from other lands" (1869, 362). That Galton saw himself as one of the gifted may not surprise us (he could not produce offspring, however). The link made with *Origin*, however, was definitive: "what Nature does blindly, slowly, and ruthlessly, man may do providently, quickly, and kindly" (Kevles 1985, 12). He thought this could be done in a "kindly" way, perhaps not quite grasping the implications of what he was proposing.

These implications were not difficult to see. Indeed, Galton made some of them clear enough by invoking the specter of Malthus: reforms to help the poor, the less intelligent, the mentally disabled, and so on were bound to make things worse. At the same time, every nation did need a fair and equal public education system so that gifted individuals had a chance to reveal themselves and their abilities. Still, the way to improve the human prospect was artificial selection, based on measuring intelligence and engineering aspects of marriage and childbearing. This did not sit well with Catholics, who saw man taking over God's role. It also ran somewhat afoul of Spencer's own social evolutionism, which taught that generations could advance irrespective of birth considerations.

The new century, however, showed itself to be fertile ground for Galton's ideas. His most important followers, Karl Pearson in England and Charles Davenport in the United States, acted as successful disciples of the gospel. Pearson was a disciple, continuing his mentor's work in statistics. But he also shifted toward a more blatant and defensive nationalism, reflecting the tensions leading up to World War I. History proved that a high state of civilization had been produced by a struggle of races against each other, with only the physically and mentally fitter race winning (Halsall 1998). Davenport, a mathematically oriented biologist, agreed but went further. Appointed director of the new research station for evolution studies at Cold Spring Harbor in 1904, he sought evidence that patterns of inheritance were responsible for insanity, alcoholism, pauperism, prostitution, criminality, and more. This was helpful to those who promoted intelligence testing in order to identify the "feebleminded," the presumed source of all sociopathology. Good human "stock" existed in the middle class, according to these theorists; the "melting pot" was a dangerous fable. Davenport reasoned that if government could impose capital punishment, it certainly could intervene in reproduction (Davenport 1911).

By the 1910s, eugenics had taken hold in much of the English-speaking world. It gained the most institutional, financial, and legal force in the United States, where immigration was a trenchant issue and books like *The Passing of the Great Race* (1916) by Madison Grant found wide readership. Grant, a tireless outdoorsman, conservationist, and lawyer known to several presidents, wrote in the tradition of threats to the "Nordic race," which meant Britain, northern France, Germany, and Scandinavia—thus early settlers of America, in contrast to those from eastern and southern Europe after 1880. Darwinian rhetoric was applied freely to the effect of arguing for "the elimination of . . . social failures" and "defective infants." The book went through multiple printings, losing favor only in the Great Depression. By this time, however, it was a favorite reference for a rising political star, Adolf Hitler, who wrote Grant a brief fan letter before becoming chancellor of Germany in 1933 (Black 2008).

Eugenics, in fact, collected many anxieties in early twentieth-century America—those about rising crime, "failing" education, labor unrest, women's rights, temperance, and economic uncertainty that came with the many recessions and depressions (then called "panics") during this period. All political persuasions were involved. Believers could be progressives or reactionaries, socialists or capitalists. They included ordinary individuals, social reformers, journalists, and American presidents. Teddy Roosevelt and Woodrow Wilson were believers, as were the radically minded H. G. Wells, Emma Goldman, and Harold Laski. So was Margaret Sanger, founder of Planned Parenthood, whose dedication to women's sexual freedom stemmed from her maxim: "more children from the fit, less from the unfit—that is the chief aim of birth control" (Gordon 1976, 72–85). Eugenics demonstrated how an idea could create a social movement built from conflicting perspectives, seeded by a range of worries and hopes and nurtured by the promise of a more "pure" future. Pursued by some with missionary zeal, for innumerable others it simply became part of everyday belief, as ordinary an idea as "health food" today. Major universities, as well as corporate philanthropies like the Rockefeller Foundation and Carnegie Institution, fully endorsed the movement. And if the Protestant middle class proved the main support, their faith was justified by writings and speeches of prominent intellectuals. A most influential example was *Blood of the Nation: A Study in the Decay of Races by the Survival of the Unfit* (1903) by David Starr Jordan, biologist, and president of Stanford University. Here is a sample of Jordan's racial science:

> *The blood of a nation determines its history*. This is the first proposition. The second is, *The history of a nation determines its blood* .... Those who are alive today are the resultants of the stream of heredity as modified by the vicissitudes through which the nation has passed. ... The blood which is "thicker than water" is the symbol of race unity. ... For example, wherever an Englishman goes, he carries with him the elements of English history. It is a British deed which he does, British history that he makes. Thus, too, a Jew is a Jew in all ages and climes. ... A Greek is a Greek; a Chinaman remains a Chinaman. (1903, 7, 9)

It seems shocking today to see such words emerge from so elevated a source. The author was not merely a well-known evolutionary biologist, promoter of science, and university president but a peace activist, director of the Sierra Club, and an expert witness on behalf of the defense in the famous Scopes Trial. Named after him are schools, parks, lakes, roads, species of fish (many), and a research prize for young scientists in evolutionary studies, established in 1986. It gives us pause, perhaps, to see memorials in the employ of amnesia.

"Race" was a messy concept, associated not only with skin color but with national origin. The United States was an especially complex mixture, where ideas of "fitness" were multiple. To those who favored "Nordic" races (as Jordan did), it suggested policies to limit immigration from southern and eastern Europe, as well as Asia. To many in the South, it continued to be used to define blacks as innately inferior. For the white urban middle class, "fitness" meant specific things: good grades and behavior, school honors, professional jobs, and other forms of official recognition, a fact that helped give rise to intelligence testing (Kevles 1985). This was appropriated from Alfred Binet's method for measuring "mental age" in French children who needed help in school. The Stanford eugenicist Lewis Terman revised Binet's test into the famous Stanford-Binet exam, adapted to assess over 1.7 million recruits during World War I. The basic concept, using a onetime written exam to gauge lifetime mental capability, was extended to design standardized tests for American schools. Princeton psychologist Carl Brigham adapted the Stanford-Binet in the late 1920s to form the Scholastic Aptitude Test, or SAT. Though he soon rejected its use—scores, he said, reflect schooling, family background, and English ability too much—Brigham could not stop others from implementing the SAT as a college-entrance aptitude measure that was only partly reformed in the 1980s.

But the darkest side to the eugenics story came in the form of political and legal action. This began in the 1890s, with marriage laws passed against those with mental "infirmities." In 1907, Indiana became the first of thirty-three states to begin forced sterilization, specifically for convicted criminals, "idiots," and rapists. Declared unconstitutional by the state Supreme Court, the original statute was carefully rewritten into a "model eugenics law" by Harry Laughlin, director of the Eugenics Record Office at Cold Spring Harbor, and then used successfully by dozens of states. In 1924, Virginia enacted sterilization for the mentally retarded, and when this was challenged, the case went to the U.S. Supreme Court where, in *Buck v. Bell* (1927), the Court upheld Virginia's statute by an 8–1 vote. The ruling by Justice Oliver Wendell Holmes Jr. argued that the interests of the state in lessening public burdens overrode an individual's right to his or her own body. The decision led directly to more systematic use of the "technique." In all, 60,000–70,000 Americans had their reproductive capability destroyed between the 1920s and 1980s, by which time all such laws had been finally repealed (Kevles 1985).

Such actions, backed as they were by educated and influential people across the country, as well as newspapers and popular weeklies, show why the impact of the famous 1925 Scopes Trial in Dayton, Tennessee, was inevitable. Tennessee had passed a law that year (Butler Act) prohibiting public schools from teaching Darwinian evolution and denying the truth of the Bible. In response, the American Civil Liberties Union convinced high school teacher John Scopes to defy the law, leading to his arrest and trial. Scopes was found guilty and fined $100, but the verdict was overturned on a technicality. The result, however, was national humiliation for the state, the South, and fundamentalist Christianity in particular. The American media, responding to national opinion, wedded to evolution *and* eugenics, heaped ridicule upon the South and fundamentalism as backwaters yet to find their way into the twentieth century (Larson 1997).

Meanwhile, eugenic measures in America became a model for what was soon to follow in Germany. By the early 1930s, the fascists had essentially stolen Darwinian discourse out of the mouths of democrats and social reformers. It is striking to read Hitler's own *Second Book* and find it riddled with platitudes of eugenic and evolutionary speech, for example: "While nature, out of the multitude of creatures that are born, spares the few healthiest and most robust in the struggle for survival, man reduces the number of births but then tries to preserve the lives of all those who are born, regardless of their true value and inner quality" (Hitler 2003, 19). Hitler believed Germany had become weak as a result of inferior and degenerate elements; German "blood" needed to be cleansed. He saw "struggle" everywhere—struggle for life, living space (*Lebensraum*), nationhood, destiny. Indeed, no word in his writing is more abundant—the German *kampf*, with connotations not only of competition but of violence, appears in the title of his *Mein Kampf.* In 1933, after coming to power, Hitler's regime implemented the Law for the Prevention of Defective Progeny, instituting mass sterilization. Over the next three years, more than four hundred thousand people, most living in asylums, were sterilized by doctors, an effort that Davenport's Cold Spring Harbor publication, *Eugenic News*, said brought "substantial advances" (Black 2008, 300). More laws came in 1935, identifying Jews as "racially unfit" and criminalizing all marriage and sexual contact with them. By the late 1930s, legal action had turned to "euthanasia." The infamous Aktion T-4 program authorized certain doctors and officials to execute those identified as "unworthy of life." The program began with infants and young children but soon expanded to adults and was run as a pilot for concentration camps. T-4 succeeded with cooperation from the German medical establishment, much of which had accepted eugenics and received generous support from Hitler's regime (Proctor 1988; Lifton 1986; see also chapter 5 on the Counter-Enlightenment). If Nazism claimed to be "applied biology," as Rudolph Hess said—a statement showing how exploited Darwin had become—it was not biology at all but the logical extreme of a naïve vision, translated into political murder.

That eugenics died by 1940 as a social movement had to do with genetic science properly understood but far more with the monstrous events perpetrated in its name. Nazism both revealed eugenics for what it truly was and killed it as an acceptable idea. Layer by layer, all gleaming pretensions of social betterment were stripped away by sterilization and slaughter. Eugenics was always about selective death; Galton makes this plain in his deformation of Darwin's theory by the idea that only the strongest seeds should be sown. Ultimately, it supported institutional genocide. Doubtless the most striking and disturbing reality of the whole eugenics era is that intelligence, education, and a progressive, democratic outlook were no protection whatsoever against belief in the central idea—on the contrary, desire for "progress" and "social improvement," even for "a better world," led many of the most accomplished people of early twentieth-century America, including authors, reformers, politicians, and scientists, to fall before the concept of social breeding.

The shadow this era casts is therefore long and sharp, not to be forgotten. Advances in genetic science that enable the identification of possible birth defects render life-and-death decisions related to heredity wholly contemporary. The imperatives to perfect society may be gone (or may not be), but the issues they raise continue. Needless to say, Darwin would have been filled with horror to see what could be made of his work. That his ideas remain crucial to our understanding of evolution and basic biology will forever make him one of the great founders of our modern era. That they could also be turned or twisted into something so sinister, however, should not be brushed aside. The eugenics era, lasting more than sixty years, was brought to an end only by the most destructive, murderous war in history. This truth puts in bold letters the need to assess and interpret important ideas not merely to bolster our own predilections (e.g., Darwin, hero of modern science) but to comprehend their detailed contents, implications, and historical uses.

BEYOND BIOLOGY AND POLITICS: DARWIN AND THE HUMANITIES

Darwinian concepts, selectively used in combination with ideas from Spencer, penetrated into many other intellectual endeavors that had their own institutional effects in daily life. In more than a few cases, these effects were taken to a point where Darwin's specific influence is no longer clearly in sight, as it is the source of so much that is today commonplace. The secular worldview that sought models, lessons, and insight from science, biology in particular, entered the twentieth century like a reactive fluid, spreading through a permeable medium. As it seeped into the imagination of the time, it interacted with its environment in ways that obscured its origins.

Philosophy and Literature

Darwin's impact on philosophy was extremely wide-ranging and is difficult to summarize easily. From the 1870s, Spencer's social and political philosophy, along with that of Huxley and Haeckel, had incorporated Darwinian ideas and been debated, accepted, studied, and institutionalized in nations from England to Japan. The evolutionary worldview was forceful in helping drive religion to the periphery of politics and most forms of social organization, even before 1900. Marx had been touched by *Origin*, and so was later Marxist philosophy, as already noted, which used the ideas of struggle, fitness, and adaptation to strengthen the sense of communism as the natural destiny of humanity, as Marx had declared.

One of the most influential philosophers of the past 150 years, Friedrich Nietzsche, also felt it necessary to come to intellectual terms with Darwin. Nietzsche's response to Darwinian thought, in fact, was complex and multilayered. Moreover, it was focused on Darwin's writings specifically. On the one hand, Nietzsche seems to have embraced the Darwinian divorce between God and nature and the implication that human morality has no grounding in transcendent, divine purpose but is largely contingent and shaped mostly by history. Moreover, the concepts of struggle and superior fitness merged well with Nietzsche's idea of the *übermensch* ("superhuman"). At the same time, however, Nietzsche attacked Darwin in a number of his works. One of his main objections was that natural selection and adaptation emptied all life forms of any complexity, spontaneity, "will to power," turning them into mere obedient mechanisms. Overall, the subject of Nietzsche pro et contra Darwin continues to define a domain of research in the history of Western philosophy.

Nietzsche died in 1900. By 1910, it was possible for the American intellectual John Dewey to write an essay titled "The Influence of Darwin on Philosophy," stating that "*Origin of Species* introduced a mode of thinking that in the end was bound to transform the logic of knowledge, and hence the treatment of morals, politics, and religion," and further, that Darwin's ultimate influence "resides in his having conquered the phenomena of life . . . and thereby freed the new logic for application to mind and morals and life" (Dewey 1910, 19, 25–26). Of course, this newly liberated logic, as redefined by Galton and his followers, was precisely what underlay eugenics. Dewey was writing at a time too soon to realize where such logic, released into the minds of new interpreters, might eventually lead. Thus it is interesting to see that he himself came late to the philosophical debate over Darwin. His older contemporary, William James, belonged to a discussion group, the Metaphysical Club, that took up matters pertaining to evolution as early as the 1870s. The group also included later Supreme Court Justice Oliver Wendell

Holmes Jr., who would one day write the majority opinion supporting eugenic sterilization. James's essay, "Great Men and Their Environment" (1880), came out of those early debates, arguing as it did that Spencer's emphasis on environmental factors as the cause of social evolution was wrong. Darwinian concepts, James said, implied that society develops through individual geniuses, whose acts and ideas are "selected" on the basis of the benefit they bring. Holmes, who came to serve on the U.S. Supreme Court for thirty years (1902–32) and has remained influential on common law issues ever since, differed with James on such points yet fully agreed that "encounters with reality" were vital and that, in jurisprudence, legal interpretations should themselves change along with the society they serve (Menand 2002).

Switching from philosophy to literature, we find similar trends of thought but differences, too. Novelists from the 1860s to the 1920s understood that the new biological world demanded new ways of interpreting human experience. It set loose great uncertainties but also ineluctable laws that the individual had to face (Beer 2000; Levine 1988; Dawson 2010). Often this led to styles of literary pessimism, as in the writings of Thomas Hardy, Émile Zola, and Joseph Conrad, whose characters find themselves at the mercy of factors and forces they can barely comprehend. Evolutionary thought urged writers to focus on the material conditions of existence, to hold a mirror up to life in its immediate environment, not merely for the sake of "realism" and reader engagement but to depict how the individual must strive against massive powers extending from the natural into the social, creating not only success but misery, injustice, and unfulfilled hope. The first lines of George Eliot's 1874 novel *Middlemarch*, considered the high-water mark of realist Victorian fiction, could nearly have come from one of the more eloquent passages in *Descent*: "Who that cares to know the history of man, and how the mysterious mixture heaves under the varying experiments of Time." Eliot was indeed an avid reader of Darwin's work and well understood its greater significance. In America, too, Darwin and Spencer entered deeply into the literary imagination (Levine 1988). Their ideas, at times blended with those of Marx, helped bring forth a concern with the lower classes and the "struggle for existence," as expressed in Upton Sinclair's *The Jungle* (1906), for example. But pessimism was far from the only response.

These comments merely suggest the breadth of influence Darwin's thought had in the aesthetic domain. Fiction was but one entry—poetry and drama, the visual arts, and music were all touched by Darwin's ideas (Larson and Brauer 2009). The arts acted not merely to echo the attention these ideas received but to teach and demonstrate their meaning and implications to millions who might never have read a scientific book. In this way, these ideas gained a status nearly as respected in cultural circles as in science. High art, moreover, was only the beginning. There were innumerable "low" forms as well: cartoons and caricatures of Darwin and apes; humorous and satiric songs; chinaware adorned with *Origin*'s tree of life image; statuettes of a monkey contemplating a human skull (Lenin is said to have owned one); and many other objects for ordinary consumption (Browne 2002; Milner 2009).

Psychology and Education: Institutions of the Mind

Toward the end of *Origin*, Darwin wrote: "In the distant future I see open fields for far more important researches. Psychology will be based on a new foundation, that of the necessary acquirement of each mental power and capacity by gradation" (1859, 488). It is not surprising that his contributions here began with the question of human beings' uniqueness in the natural order. Both *Descent* and *Expression of Emotions* held that there are connections between animals and humans at many levels of mentality, including use of language, tools, instinct, even feeling. Animal and man, said Darwin, share the expression of a wide range of mental states, from fear and anger to curiosity and humor. In a remarkable statement for its time, *Descent* said the "difference in mind between man and the higher animals great as it is, certainly is one of degree and not of kind" (1871, vol. 1, 105). This marked a major break from existing theory. Such theory held, for example, that the mind was divided into faculties of "reason" and the "passions," with the former a solely human capacity (divinely provided) whose purpose was to control and direct the animalistic passions. In proposing complete continuity between man and beast, Darwinian thought helped move the human mind, and thus learning, into new realms.

In education, the Darwinian paradigm found its way into the thinking of highly influential voices of the early twentieth century. One of these was the French developmental psychologist Jean Piaget, whose child-centered theories have had an enormous and lasting impact on teaching methods and classroom organization. In truth, his theories were revised over a span of more than forty-five years, extending from the 1920s to the 1960s, but they held true to a program combining biological, sociological, and psychological perspectives to define how the mind structures new information as it evolves through several distinct, unified stages of development. Piaget was interested in younger children, who he showed could solve certain problems only at certain ages. By a process he called "adaptation," the child's mind creates schemas that organize information and adjust themselves over time through interaction with the environment (school, home, peers), seeking "better forms of equilibrium." Piaget thus adopted language from the hard sciences and from Darwinian rhetoric to help legitimize his concepts. Though he was not a Darwinian—like many thinkers before him, Piaget rejected natural selection as too dependent on chance and on a view of organisms as passive entities—he nonetheless drew fully on the evolutionary paradigm (Vidal, Buscaglia, and Vonèche 1983). His ideas of education, meanwhile, led to near universal reform in Western schools, replacing an older view of children as empty vessels with the child as active explorer and builder of knowledge.

No less important was Darwin's influence on Sigmund Freud. Freud's realm was the self and personality, the relation between child and adult, dreams and sexuality, and the hidden world of the unconscious. That his theory of the mind is no longer accepted makes no difference as to its enormous impact on twentieth-century culture, particularly in the humanities and the arts. Freud's writings impacted the entire domain of human subjectivity—how modern society conceives of the self, the importance of childhood, and the psychological forces that shape personality. What, then, was his debt to Darwin? Freud grew up in a freethinking, middle-class Jewish family in Austria and enrolled in medical school at the University of Vienna in 1873, when Darwin's fame in biological circles was near its peak. At that time, he says in his

Autobiographical Study (1925), "the theories of Darwin . . . strongly attracted me, for they held out hopes of an extraordinary advance in our understanding of the world" (Freud 1952, 7). For the first ten years of his career, in fact, Freud worked as a biological researcher in animal physiology. By the 1880s he had switched focus to the study of hysteria, but in writing up his patients, he treated Darwin as a close colleague, referring to him more often than any other authority.

Freud built an evolutionary theory of personality based on psychosexual stages. Each stage involved conflicts whose resolution required adapting to external demands. There are Lamarckian as well as Darwinian elements in this theory, but at its conceptual base it reveals Darwin's greater impact (Ritvo 1990). Freud adopted from Darwinian biology the idea that humans retain primitive instincts from the evolutionary past and that such instincts are both held in check and re-formed, or channeled, by the influences of civilization. Calling Freud a "biologist of the mind," as some have done, may well exaggerate the case. But applying the evolutionary paradigm to the individual mind, complete with notions of struggle and adaptation, did a great deal to alter the very conception of the "person." Through Freud and psychoanalysis, some piece of Darwin has had an untold effect on modern concepts of self and identity, on the idea of "personality," and on the origins of creativity and art.

Ultimately, then, the first century after *Origin* appeared saw Darwin's influence spreading into an enormous variety of domains, throughout the world. If we have sampled but a small part of this influence, it is because entire volumes would be needed to adequately treat the topic, even at an introductory level. Darwinian ideas and language entered the speech and imagination of politicians, economists, philosophers, educators, novelists, artists, social critics, and more. It shaped policies and movements, therapies and institutions, to such an extent that its presence is part of the very fabric of contemporary culture. In science, Darwin's ideas have become the basis for modern biology, as well as aspects of medical and agricultural research. The metaphor therefore seems fair: Darwin was key to the genetic makeup of the modern era. But has this remained the case into our new century?

DARWIN TODAY: NO SIGN OF AN END

There seems little doubt that Darwin's ideas in the first decades after 2000 are more alive, controversial, and capable of inspiring emotion than ever. Within the life sciences, Darwin continues to be immediately relevant, tested and reconfirmed and also modified. His fundamental theory that evolution proceeds mainly by the mechanism of natural selection, acting upon varieties that emerge in populations, is more solid than ever. But his ideas continue their force beyond the sciences as well. We can recognize two major areas where this is true.

First, Darwinian evolution continues to be a target of attack from religious sources. This has come from diverse groups: conservative evangelicals, Christian fundamentalists, large parts of Islam, creationists, and intelligent design proponents, to name only the most well-known. Such opposition is not trivial. Nor is it new or alien to advanced societies. As other chapters in this book show, the rejection of evolution and other parts of modern science has been present since the Enlightenment and constitutes a central element of the rejection of modernity among various reactionary groups. Many of these have held fast to one or another type of natural theology. Darwinian evolution forced such ideas out of the mainstream in most advanced nations, but they have remained very much alive in conservative religious communities. Rejection of Darwin tends to depend on literal readings of sacred, monotheistic books, the Bible and the Qu'ran (the Catholic Church does not condemn Darwin). Fundamentalist Protestants in Africa, South America, and the United States include many millions of people and have impacted discussions over education. Dismissal of Darwin in Islamic societies may be tied to renewed distrust of Western society in general but also stems from traditional adherence to the Qu'ran, which states that humans are a special creation of God. Anti-Darwinism, in other words, comes from the conservative side of mainstream Muslim culture, not simply from more extreme believers. Creationism and its offshoot "intelligent design" (the idea that life is too complex to be without a Creator), when not overt about their religious underpinnings, seek to invoke William Paley's "no design without a designer." Religious fundamentalists tend to view Darwin as a destroyer. His ideas are felt to deny all higher, spiritual meanings and, in some cases, to be responsible for the greatest evils of the twentieth century, including fascism and totalitarianism.

A second area where Darwin is in the foreground of discussion travels an opposite track, finding in Darwin ultimate explanations for all human phenomena. Since the 1970s, an expanding and diverse community of scientists, economists, humanist scholars, and others has taken up the mantle of biologizing social, cultural, and psychological phenomena, using natural selection (not evolution) as a universal explanatory model with few, if any, limitations. These "Darwinian fundamentalists" (Gould 1997) are a vocal contingent within biology and philosophy that has been criticized as a revival of Social Darwinism. Human sociobiology, or evolutionary psychology (its new title), forms one core of this program and has inspired thinkers in many fields to use Darwin's key idea to elucidate phenomena as diverse as art and infanticide.

These two realms, then, one intensely pro-Darwin, the other fervently against, continue to battle for important portions of the public mind. The ultra-Darwinians in general can be said to have done better, professionally speaking. Creationism and biblical literalism are denied by the entire weight of contemporary science and its immense institutional apparatus, including government support. Creationists now yield to science by adopting its language and trying to argue points of weakness in evolutionary biology (Numbers 2006). But because it begins from a fixed premise of final causes, has no research program, cannot be tested by experiment, and develops no new hypotheses, Creationism does not speak the discourse of science and cannot be reconciled with it. Yet the battle for public opinion defines a complex affair; many people in the United States, for example, who are not strongly religious but do believe in a Creator and a spiritual dimension to the natural world find Darwinian evolution troubling, barren of important meaning. Creationism indeed has had some success with local school boards, though mostly temporarily. Scientists vigorously oppose each new case, perceiving it as a crack in the edifice of a modern, progressive society and a reversion to ways of thinking that deny value to science itself.

To an unfortunate degree, they are correct. Opponents of Darwin and evolution have also rejected embryonic stem cell research, fetal research in general, human responsibility for climate change, the chemical beginnings of life, and the scientifically determined age and origin of the Earth, planets, galaxies, and universe. The emphasis on biology reflects an immediate association with an organic dimension that directly involves human beings. But in fact, if pressed only slightly (or not at all), the deniers of Darwin would readily resist a great many other facts and concepts of modern science, including nearly all of geology, astronomy, cosmology, subatomic physics, biochemistry, radiometric dating, physical anthropology, and so on. Darwin, in short, forms merely the prow of a great ship that must be sunk. It is the scientific worldview itself, therefore—materialist, de-spiritualized, insouciant to demands of faith—that is at issue.

In this sense, the attempt to overturn Darwin defines an impossible goal. For all the reasons given thus far, Darwin cannot be deleted, diminished, or otherwise removed from the modern world. Evolution can certainly be condemned, even forbidden as a subject of teaching and study. It can be demonized as a threat of terrible proportion but not without dire effects, like severe intellectual isolation. Such deprivation does not seek escape in medievalism, as the history of religious fundamentalism shows (see chapter 6). Desired instead is the remaking of the world into an alternative modernism, one based on immobile religious principles, denying of science, yet accepting most modern technologies. Such a modernism is barely possible and would soon fail; as fields like medicine and biotechnology make clear, no clear boundaries between scientific and technological domains exist today (prohibiting all stem cell research destroys an area of future medical therapy). None of this, however, matters to anti-Darwinians. The battle for influence will not be resolved under existing terms.

Evolutionary Psychology and the Reach of Natural Selection

Evolution has never stood still. Within the precincts of science, it has continued to develop and to be debated. Part of this development has involved advances in fields like genetics and paleontology, particularly those regarding genetic process and the history of life. But evolutionary science has also grown into new disciplines, like evolutionary medicine. Founded in response to the discovery that some pathogenic bacteria have over time become resistant to antibiotics and other treatments, this new area of research looks at the adaptive evolution of pathogens, both in the external environment and inside an affected (usually human) body. Such research requires new interdisciplinary work. There are complex aspects to consider, like the interplay between bacteria and the immune system, changes in virulence over time, and the role of diet and the intestinal environment, all serving to create new subfields: evolutionary physiology, evolutionary neuropathology, evolutionary microbiology. New applications and modifications of Darwin's ideas that expand our understanding of the dynamism in organic life are ongoing.

But there are other, more controversial, extensions of Darwin beyond biology. One of these is human sociobiology, inaugurated in 1975 by Edward O. Wilson, an entomologist, in his book *Sociobiology: The New Synthesis*. Wilson's primary subject was animals, his realm of expertise being ants. He defined sociobiology as "the systematic study of the biological basis of all social behavior," thus, in effect, promising to include humans at some point. By the twenty-first century, the new field along with its cognate "behavioral ecology" was an established and highly productive area of zoology. But Wilson and his followers, as pledged, did not stop with zoology. In the last chapter of his book, Wilson proposed that culture itself is a biological product, and he characterized as "extreme" the view that it is learned, not inherited.

"Scientists and humanists," he wrote, "should consider together the possibility that the time has come for ethics to be removed temporarily from the hands of the philosophers and biologized" (Wilson 1975, 563). Wilson's aim was to place all of the humanities and social sciences under the auspices of biology, a goal he pursued more assertively in a later work, *Consilience* (1998), where he wrote: "culture and hence the unique qualities of the human species will make complete sense only when linked in causal explanation to the natural sciences. Biology in particular is the most proximate and hence relevant of the scientific disciplines" (1998, 292). The author's choice of examples, however, gets him into trouble, revealing both naïve and dangerous aspects. Treating the Rwandan genocide, he bypasses ethnic problems to don the robes of Malthus and declare overpopulation as the "deeper cause," so that "The teenage soldiers of the Hutu and Tutsi then set out to solve the population problem in the most direct possible way" (1998, 315). This turn away from colonial history and ideas of identity becomes a way of saying that explanations using social science and the humanities are largely a waste of time.

Biologist Richard Dawkins, another leader of the Darwinian fundamentalists, agrees with Wilson but takes a different approach. In *The Selfish Gene* (1976), he offered the idea of the "meme," a "self-replicating unit of culture" analogous to the gene. Memes are supposed to include any type of cultural element—a form of technology, a type of furniture, a melody, and so forth—but their real utility was to call upon natural selection as the process by which human culture developed and advanced. Dawkins's idea blossomed into the theory of "memetics," which seeks to build Darwinian models of cultural evolution, encompassing everything from road signs to religions. However fanciful and indiscriminate this may sound, it has a less imaginative side: people become mere vessels for the process of cultural replication. The humanities again become irrelevant, their work itself a kind of meme. Why spend time studying literature or art if all they do is recirculate characters, stories, forms, and so forth whose deeper meaning comes not from human beings, gifted with powers of expression, but from the same blind, amoral process responsible for the creation and destruction of species?

Evolutionary psychology (EP), meanwhile, takes Darwin in yet another direction. It views the mind as a "set of information-processing machines that were designed by natural selection to solve adaptive problems faced by our hunter-gatherer ancestors" (Cosmides and Tooby 1997). In contrast to Darwin's own day, when evolution seemed to argue for progress, EP depicts people as rooted in the Paleolithic past: our contemporary skulls are home to "a stone age mind." From this premise, everything becomes a simple search for explanations of fitness. We are back to debating yet again the nineteenth-century idea that organic evolution and cultural evolution are homologous. Claiming that "genes hold culture on a leash," as Wilson repeatedly did, leads logically to a search for deterministic elucidations of behavior and institutions. By any other name, this smells of Social Darwinism. EP loyalists go so far as to propose rape as "an evolved mating tactic" for low-status males. Indeed, there have been many such "just so stories" (as the paleontologist Stephen J. Gould called them). Take a behavior, and then come up with an evolutionary story that fits it "just so." They have been conceived, in fact, to explain phenomena as diverse as ethnocentrism, homosexuality, drug addiction, sexual preferences (why women are attracted to men with "resources"), infanticide, depression, and so on. If this jogs our familiarity with eugenic thinking, it is no accident. But the danger here is not stigmatizing people and preventing them from breeding; it is close to the opposite, stating that their behaviors are natural and therefore inalterable and in some way inevitable. Everything humans do, in other words, can be apprehended as a type of adaptation, genes seeking ways to promote their own survival.

Thus the cruder side of EP. More sophisticated thinking recognizes that the analogy between biological and cultural evolution is flawed and unable to offer many useful insights. How helpful can it be to "discover" that killing one's children might be an adaptation to a glacial era of limited resources? Still, it is said, *some* part of human mentality must have a biological component; we are not born empty headed but come equipped with certain inclinations. It makes sense, the softer side of EP maintains, to focus on a limited set of behaviors that might actually have some evolutionary significance—language, for example, or cooperation.

But the central question remains: how far can natural selection be applied as a legitimate framework for interpreting human beings *beyond* their own evolution as a species? Certainly the basic idea of struggle or competition leading to selective success can be used to simplistically describe a huge number of situations. But what is actually happening when we extend the Darwinian paradigm into the mind (versus the brain, as an organ) or society, or culture? The past is our guide. The temptation to do this, after all, has never really weakened or waned. Where in the 1860s, laissez-faire was viewed by its proponents as a policy in accord with natural competition among individuals and companies, in the 2000s we have "evolutionary economics" to reinterpret the Industrial Revolution as a result of "increased selection pressure" brought on by natural resource factors. If Darwin/Spencer were invoked to justify imperialism, a gentler "Darwinian politics" today claims that human evolution creates our political preferences, including a drive toward freedom and democracy or, in a harsher interpretation, that the reason democracy has not become ubiquitous is that "evolution has endowed our species . . . with a predisposition for hierarchically structured social and political systems" (Somit and Peterson, 1997, 27). Darwinian literary theory, on the other hand, has scholars discovering evidence of natural selection working behind the scenes in poems and novels, such as adaptionist male bonding in *Beowulf* or evolutionary constraints on mate selection in *Pride and Prejudice* (Gottschall and Wilson 2005). Darwinian psychopathology finds that mood disorders like depression are evolutionary defense strategies (inward oriented) in the face of same-species aggression (Sloman and Gilbert 2000).

Such examples (and there are many others) answer our question of "how far" by suggesting a "universal Darwinism," natural selection as a cosmic algorithm independent of any context. This might recall how Marxist and Freudian concepts were once wielded with happy abandon to illuminate realities of history, politics, culture, and much more. But the reach of Darwinism in recent decades has gone still further, embracing the totality of human life, thought, and experience. Darwin himself, no doubt, would view all this as a kind of grand historical irony: natural selection has become the Creator.

Such is remarkable not only for its enthusiastic lack of limits but because it utterly ignores what has happened in biology. To what degree, after all, does natural selection speak for all of evolution? Darwin himself called it only one among several or more processes that might account for the history of life. In fact, since the Neo-Darwinian Synthesis of the 1940s, new mechanisms for evolution have indeed been discovered in the field and lab. One such mechanism involves the migration of species into new environments, which then impact survival directly. Geologic work on the last several million years expanded this to include major climatic changes (no migration required) and even smaller-scale variations, such as wet and dry periods, causing marked shifts in the abundance of plants, mammals, reptiles, insects, and inevitably (and consequentially) bacteria. Another evolutionary mechanism is "genetic drift," by which specific genes are multiplied or lost in a population because some individuals randomly produce more or less offspring than others. Darwin, meanwhile, was heavily influenced by his friend Lyell in believing profound change depends upon great stretches of time, but since the 1980s, evidence for catastrophic events, including mass extinctions, has become overwhelming and accepted in geology and biology. One hypothesis, "punctuated equilibrium," proposes that species can remain stable for long periods, then undergo fairly rapid modification in response to alterations in the environment. Another position stresses the impacts wrought by comet/asteroid impacts, gigantic volcanic episodes, and large-scale glacial periods that wiped landscapes clean. All of this poses a challenge to the universal primacy of natural selection. The Earth, as understood today, is not the Earth of Victorian times. Its spectacular (and more interesting) dynamism has come to be matched by an understanding of how diverse and unpredictable evolution has been.

Ideas, not just data, continue to lie at the heart of biology. Evolution is far from a settled matter. There are debates about natural selection itself. To many, it targets the single organism for improved survival; to others, a population. For the strong Darwinian program, however, it is the gene that rules: natural selection involves certain genes gaining higher representation in later generations at the same chromosome positions. In the end, Darwin's "dangerous idea" can be called the *summa theological* only for those who believe it has all the answers.

The Ideas That Conquered All Life?

What, then, is Charles Darwin's ultimate legacy? It would be impossible in the span of a dozen volumes to offer a full answer. The metaphor of waves breaking upon near and distant shores is apt; at great distances, it is no longer evident where the original movement began.

But the real answer is that we cannot yet say what Darwin's legacy might be. The year 2009, bicentennial of his birth, saw the largest celebration ever thrown for a single historical figure, extending to over forty-five countries and including hundreds of events, publications, films, exhibits, and much more. The journal *Nature* devoted a series of excellent articles to the topic of "Global Darwin," a look at his influence around the world. Perhaps predictably, such revelry bid forward an outpouring of complaint, rejection, and Creationist fervor, in negative echo.

Darwin, it would appear, has never left. The modern world will not let him go. But it is not really Darwin, the man, we are speaking of here. The true protagonist is his thought, his ideas, both on their own and, still more, as adapted and translated in the thinking of so many others. These ideas, after all, have been applied, exaggerated, and deformed in ways that will undoubtedly continue well into the future. The worldview Darwin's ideas helped inaugurate, organic, materialistic, vigorous, changeable, uncertain, with "human" and "animal" inhabiting a godless continuum, is still very much in progress.

Rejection is a form of influence, too. If the power of Marxism is embodied in the vast literature written to refute it, this is just as true for the denial of Darwinian evolution by many millions of the faithful in several of the world's major religions. Such rejection, in fact, has not faded or calmed but has grown, and not a little. Such is the power of foundational ideas: they motivate hate, fear, and insecurity, as well as conviction and loyalty, on a mass scale. And while it is common enough to bemoan the ingrained resistance to Darwinian thought, it seems important to also recognize why it exists and what it signifies. For those who find meaning and purpose in religious certainties, the Darwinian worldview can be enraging, frightening, even terrifying. It recognizes nothing that can be called "sacred." It poses an inexorable universe, full of beauty and death but emptied of spiritual content, a universe drained of sin, redemption, grace. Rejecting the Darwinian worldview has always been a secondary theme in the larger legacy that *Origin of Species* has created. It could not be otherwise.

By such reckoning, Darwin's ideas are bigger than life. The other end of the spectrum from religious denial is the attempt to re-create the world as the embodiment of a single concept, natural selection. Over the past century, we have seen Darwinian thought extended into ever new realms, in ways that can release important new insights but that can also flirt with scientific arrogance, blindness, and determinism. There is much worry in the twenty-first century about what would happen if fundamentalist religion gained significant control over political and legal institutions. But what are the implications of conceiving the human mind as a "stone age" product, and human behavior, including such acts as rape and infanticide, as natural and inevitable? What kinds of policies, legal decisions, or social programs might emerge from such a view? History, in the case of eugenics for example, shows that forms of more extreme or unlimited Darwinism can have all too practical effects. Intelligence is no protection against such excess. On the contrary, it has proven an essential element for it.

Invoking Darwin, whether today or a hundred years ago, means much more than bringing the vast authority of science to bear. Part of the legacy of *Origin*, too, has been its unquenchable powers of implication and suggestion, its untold diversity of possible meanings. Whether we read this great work with a literal eye or with one eager for explanatory metaphors, it tempts us with more ways to elucidate the world than we might ever anticipate. If we consider only a handful of the terms it employs, terms charged with heated signification in Darwin's own day—struggle, competition, survival, existence, instinct, colonization, descent, succession, and extinction—it becomes clear in how many untamed directions the understanding and the use of this single work would have inevitably gone. The story of Darwin's influence is this same story of magnificent and disconcerting plurality. It is fitting, then, that *Origin* approaches its end by drawing this conclusion (Darwin 1859, 489): "Judging from the past, we may safely infer that not one living species will transmit its unaltered likeness to a distant futurity."

CHAPTER 4

Making Democracy

The Jefferson-Hamilton Debates

> I never expect to see a perfect work from imperfect man. The result of
> the deliberations of all collective bodies must necessarily be a com-
> pound, as well of the errors and prejudices, as of the good sense and
> wisdom, of the individuals of whom they are composed. The compacts
> which are to embrace thirteen distinct States in a common bond of
> amity and union, must as necessarily be a compromise of as many dis-
> similar interests and inclinations. How can perfection spring from such
> materials?
>
> ALEXANDER HAMILTON, *THE FEDERALIST* #85

The word "democracy" was coined in ancient Athens. Its two parts,
demos and *kratos*, directly signified "the common people" and "rule."
In actual practice, forms of popular governance could almost certainly
be found in various parts of the world long before the rise of Classical
Greece. Indeed, Athens in the sixth century B.C. may have given us the
name for this political system, but it did not really supply the model. By
our terms, Athenian democracy was not very democratic. The *demos* of
voting citizens included men over twenty years old, a mere fraction of
the population that left out all women, foreign-born immigrants, and
slaves, whose numbers were greatest of all. The "people" was a small
minority.

If we turn to the successful rebirth of democracy for the modern
world, we find that it took place not in a major urban center, like Athens, but along a colonial frontier distant from Europe. This was no mere
fortuity. As observed by the French aristocrat and author Alexis de Tocqueville, only in an embryonic nation, full of political "amateurs" living

far from the monarchical capitals of the Old World, could an idea as old as democracy be rendered so vitally new.

Democracy's rebirth, however, was not so sudden. Over the two millennia between the fall of Athens to Philip II of Macedon and the American Revolution, various aspects of democratic government appeared intermittently, for example in the elected medieval councils of Scandinavia and Parliament in England. Without any doubt, the vast majority of people continued to live in mainly agrarian societies everywhere under monarchy, oligarchy, and tyranny. Ideas regarding limits to monarchical power began to grow a century before the American Revolution, arriving in the early part of the Enlightenment, with such supporting concepts as individual rights and self-determination. We have seen some of this in our discussions of Adam Smith and the importance of John Locke's philosophy. Many historians, in fact, feel that a critical moment came with England's Glorious Revolution of 1688, when a hereditary king, James II, was deposed and forced to leave the country after having tried to weaken and manipulate Parliament. The resulting English Bill of Rights imposed new restrictions on kingly authority while expanding the independence of Parliament as a partly elected body. At the same time, the Glorious Revolution was very much a religious affair as well (James II, a Roman Catholic, had enraged Protestant England by his favoritism toward Catholics and, still worse, by producing a male heir who would be given the crown instead of his Protestant sister, Mary). It was not entirely an Enlightenment victory.

Tocqueville recognized that democracy's chances of flowering were always weaker in the ancient landscape of Europe, with its authoritarian traditions. America had no hereditary aristocracy at its beginning, no taste for oligarchy. There could be problems in the South, where an agrarian culture rooted in slavery had formed. But at America's founding, its leaders had lofty ideas about the nation they wanted to build. Backed by the Enlightenment's liberal philosophy, some of the new nation's most important leaders had come from the South, including George Washington, James Madison, and, of course, Thomas Jefferson. Each of these men, as well as their contemporaries from the North, such as John Adams and Alexander Hamilton, had wished to create a state that would set new standards for freedom, a state that would begin and remain imperfect but that would strive to improve itself in liberty over time.

Enlightenment thinkers of the eighteenth century and liberals of the nineteenth century believed the values of democracy would bring a universal civilization. This has not happened. On the contrary, we see today many different types of governments, even varieties of democracy, and we see different styles of life in each of them; however, the growth of democracy overall, especially in the twentieth century, has been striking. In 1900, there were about fifteen democratic states in the world (though for the most part they still excluded women and some of their minorities) representing a slow increase during the previous fifty years. This number grew rapidly after World War I but then fell dramatically. By the late 1930s, there were fewer than twenty, none outside western Europe, North America, and Britain's former colonies in Oceania. Democracy itself faced an uncertain future as a result of the apparent collapse of liberal capitalism in the Great Depression and the confident rise of fascist and communist tyrannies. But after World War II, growth in the number of electoral democratic systems resumed. If, following the system used by Freedom House (a respected independent organization that has existed since 1941), we divide countries into those that are "fully free," "partly free," and "not free," the count in 2014 of genuinely democratic, partly democratic, and not at all democratic countries is as follows: eighty-eight countries containing 40 percent of the world's population are fully free and democratic, fifty-nine containing 25 percent of the world's population are partly so, and only forty-eight containing 35 percent of the world's population are not at all freely democratic (Freedom House 2014). Even among the undemocratic and unfree countries of the world, the vast majority nevertheless hold fraudulent elections because their rulers recognize that some sort of general popular support is necessary to claim legitimacy. Their elections may not be genuine, but they claim to be.

This is an astonishing reversal of the situation a century earlier. It makes it all the more important to examine how the first modern democracy was established and why the controversies that attended its birth remain to this day both divisive and unresolved.

Democracy's ascent can be tied overall to three factors. First was the historical success and power of Great Britain, including its parliamentary system and its assertive turn away from monarchical power. Second was the Enlightenment, which filled Europe and the North American colonies with ideas of liberty and established the connection between future progress and individual freedom. Third and probably most important was the example and influence of the United States, the world's oldest surviving constitutional democracy, though that would not have been possible without the first two factors. The ideas that forged America's Revolutionary era, those set out in raw form by England's Declaration (or Bill) of Rights in 1689 (Pincus 2009, 292–93) but then extended, broadened, and refined by American thinkers, spread over the next two hundred years among intellectuals and reformers not only in Europe but also in Latin America, the Ottoman Empire, China, and Japan and around the whole world. Such were ideas that promised new realms of freedom and prosperity and seemed borne out (though with major limits, too) by America's own successes. It is this set of democratic ideas, then, that continues to inspire so much hope despite all of its imperfections.

Crucial among these ideas were the primary concepts of individual rights, freedom of the press, assembly, and religion, and of legal protection of self and property, as well as the crucial idea of representational government. Most of these principles were not native to the United States but were articulated in Europe during the seventeenth and eighteenth centuries, partly to defeat the theory of Divine Right. But only in America did they find full embodiment in democratic institutions, becoming the living basis for a new nation that would soon vie with the great powers across the Atlantic. Such institutions, however, were ever incomplete. Slavery held its place for eighty years after the Revolution; blacks, Indians, and women had no vote into the twentieth century. It took nearly two hundred years for the United States to even approach the fulfillment of its own principles. And yet all of Europe understood that America was a profound creation. It proved that democracy could work in a modern state and could lay out the codes of liberty by which it would itself be measured and judged (Wood 1992; Tilly 2007).

Two Visions of Enlightenment Democracy

For this, the visions of Hamilton and Jefferson, the most encompassing of their day, were required. Bluntly put, they were visions of two different Americas, not friendly to one another. Derived from similar starting material—above all, British philosophical and polemical writings, French and Scottish Enlightenment thinkers, and classical Greek and Roman authors—each conceived a plan and a doctrine for the new nation that was radical for the time and radically different. Hamilton saw a strong central authority, a large military, a federally driven industrial economy, and an active foreign policy. Jefferson wanted a weak center, local militias, a nation of yeoman farmers, and "entangling alliances with none." One vision was urban and expansive, the other rural and more parochial. And though they could not coexist easily, coexist they soon did and have ever since. Federal and libertarian beliefs, hopes, and hallucinations have been part of the "American prospect" into the twenty-first century. From government bailouts and federally funded research to antitax fervor and deregulation, Hamilton and Jefferson doth bestride the present as invisible yet living colossi. America has always been at odds with itself in the realm of the mind, tossed between the guideposts of these two brilliant individuals.

Hamilton and Jefferson were bitter political enemies. This, however, made them typical of their time (Ellis 2002). The Founders were anything but a fraternity of backslapping colleagues, united in mind and spirit. If hope for a new nation joined them, notions for how to build it tore them apart. Hamilton and Jefferson knew each other as foes, but so did they both battle with John Adams. Hostility between Adams and Benjamin Franklin, meanwhile, was legendary. Washington and Jefferson may share immortal granite on the face of Mount Rushmore today, but in life the general sided far more often with his secretary of the treasury (Hamilton) than with his secretary of state. Madison, America's fourth president, began as a Jeffersonian but then wrote *The Federalist* with Hamilton. John Jay, America's first Chief Justice, was so roundly hated by Jefferson's Republican Party that he once said he could find his way at night by the light of his burning effigies (Wood 2007). It is not by chance that the national conversation about U.S. democracy has always been more of a street brawl than a debate over brandy.

Both Hamilton and Jefferson knew well that their visions extended beyond politics. Building a new nation meant building a new society. Building a new society meant restructuring the political, economic, educational, and religious aspects of life. And doing all this involved creating new possibilities for human welfare. How could it be, then, that the primary concepts of modern freedom, which have spread around the globe to overturn so many powerful monarchs and tyrants, ideas that have also been key to the advance of capitalism and social progress, came together at a single pivotal moment, in the incompatible minds of two men?

No doubt some will feel this treats the truth with undue leniency. Shouldn't we focus on the long tradition of limiting kingly power in England, the Glorious Revolution of 1688, and the ensuing English Bill of Rights? What of the Swiss cantons, some of them self-governing since the Middle Ages, or the Corsican Republic founded in 1755, a democracy with universal suffrage (Boswell 1769; Steinberg 1996)? What of the *Declaration of the Rights of Man* approved by the French National Assembly in 1789? Surely these are worthy examples. Indeed they are, but not as final models. England in 1800 could hardly be called democratic in flesh or fiber: an aristocracy of four hundred families held actual power for another full century, such that less than 10 percent of adults could vote even in 1860. The Swiss cantons, to be sure, were a wonderful success, but as test tube experiments—small in land, tiny in population—they were "proof" that such a system could never work in a full-sized state. The Corsican Republic of Pasquale Paoli, meantime, barely survived a decade before being crushed by the invading French, whose own Revolution led to the Terror and then Napoleon. As a true democratic state, America had no real precedent (Tilly 2007; Dahl 2000).

There will be objections to the choice of Hamilton and Jefferson. How can we overlook James Madison, dominant author of the U.S. Constitution and the Bill of Rights? What of John Adams, whose *Thoughts on Government* (1776) laid out the concepts for a bicameral structure and a separation of powers? John Dickinson's *Letters from a*

Farmer in Pennsylvania (1768), with its claim that the colonies were self-governing by right, did much to unify anti-British sentiment early on. And can there be any justice in ignoring the most accomplished individual in the New World, Benjamin Franklin, or the most outspoken radical of the day, Tom Paine? There is no discounting the necessity of all these men. And yet none of them, it is fair to say, assembled a philosophy of society to steer the new nation through an inevitably turbulent future. Hamilton and Jefferson were the ones who best understood the desperate need for such a philosophy. Like the country they hoped for, they were ambitious, pragmatic, idealistic, impetuous, self-chosen.

They were also fearful. Reading letters written by the Founders, what surprises us most is not their boldness but their disquiet. These men worried greatly, interminably, about whether America would survive (Bailyn 2003). Why such dread? Because everything in their learning and experience told them that power was dangerous, tyranny omnipresent, freedom a trembling leaf in the storm. When one looked at Africa, Asia, and even Europe, despotism was the condition of mankind. George Washington, in his farewell address of 1796 (drafted by Hamilton), spoke at length about threats to the Union: "from different causes and from different quarters, much pains will be taken, many artifices employed, to weaken in your minds the conviction of [our need for Union]; this is the point in your political fortress against which the batteries of internal and external enemies will be most constantly and actively directed" (Washington 1997, 964). Doubtless he had in mind, among other things, the vicious party politics of the day but also specific events, such as the armed march on Philadelphia by unpaid, half-drunken soldiers of the Revolutionary Army in 1783, threatening violence on an assembled Congress. Standing armies, Washington knew—and here he fully agreed with Jefferson—were able, at any moment, to crush civilian authority, a truth that has been repeatedly proven in the modern period from Latin America to Africa and the Middle East.

Optimism and certainty were not the states of mind indulged by the Founders when they thought of the future. True, they often spoke publicly in buoyant tones, knowing the need for positive theater. "The spirit of our citizens . . . rising with a strength and majesty . . . will make this government in practice what it is in principle, a model for the protection of man," wrote Jefferson on February 21, 1799, to Thaddeus Kosciusko, the famous Polish engineer who had helped build fortifications during the Revolutionary War (Jefferson and Randolph 1829, vol. 3, 430). Yet why, we might ask, employ the word "protection"? Why not "liberation" or "progress"? But security was never assured. America would remain defined by struggle more than stability, crisis more than confidence. Only two weeks after he wrote these lines, Jefferson penned a letter to his friend Thomas Lomax bemoaning the actual state of the Union: "The body of the American people is substantially republican. [Yet] they have been the dupes of artful maneuvers, and made . . . willing instruments in forging chains for themselves" (1829, vol. 3, 432). He was speaking, of course, about the "artful" Hamilton and his Federalist followers.

The United States defined a very large concept. Jefferson, Hamilton, Adams, Franklin, and Washington all referred to it as an "empire." Otherwise, they spoke of it in the plural. In its earliest years, it was bound by weak forces, each state tending to hold itself apart as a separate realm. But the United States was a powerful concept nonetheless. Its intellectual makers, with no real models before them, worked with uncertain, sometimes shaky hands on the wet clay of possibility. The project was not merely bold. To most educated Europeans, it was spectacular, outrageous (Bailyn 2003). Who were these provincials, living at the edges of civilization, to think they could ignore a millennium of royal tradition and improve even on antiquity, source of eternal wisdom? What political experience did they have? What firsthand knowledge of government and law? Were they not like children, wandering in the wilderness?

From Whence They Came

In a very real way, the rebellion against England arose out of the consequences of the Seven Years' War (1754–63), the world's first global conflict (Wood 1998). Fought by every major power in Europe, the war had fronts on five continents, involving the far-flung colonial domains of England, France, and Spain. Major battles took place in the Ohio

Valley, off the coast of Portugal, near the cities of Bengal, on the islands of the Philippines.

For Britain, it was the fourth major conflict in a century and by far the most costly, not only in money but in men, materiel, and goodwill. Britain went into heavy debt, lost many ships, and acted arrogantly toward its colonies. It had its victories, to be sure, most notably in North America, where the conflict was known as the French and Indian War. Britain gained the greater part of New France, a huge area in eastern Canada, and in India, too, it drove out the French. But the war began with a national debt already at £75 million, and by the end, this had soared to £133 million. There was now the immediate need to administer and defend vast new territories. The American colonies? They had benefited greatly from the conflict. Direct subsidies and contracts for supplying British forces helped the colonists prosper, even as the home country sank deeper into debt. More than a few in Parliament were incensed by the colonials' refusal to supply troops against the French while carrying on illegal trade with French plantations in the West Indies instead of obeying a British monopoly (Wood 1998; Armitage 2000; Bayly 2003).

Parliament saw no alternative but to alter policy. Previously, under the hand of Robert Walpole, England's first de facto prime minister (1721–42), the colonies had been loosely administered based on voluntary cooperation, low taxes, and self-governance. Edmund Burke famously termed the policy "salutary neglect," since it resulted in successful trade for American merchants and thus duties paid to Britain. The colonies, therefore, became used to governing themselves. But with Walpole gone (he died in 1745) and the attitudinal insurgence of America too obvious to ignore, Parliament abruptly changed course. The colonies would now be ruled, not indulged. More direct control, higher taxation, legal instruments demanding obedience, and other authoritarian measures would be put in place (Foster 2014; McCusker and Menard 1991).

There came a relentless march of new laws: the Writs of Assistance (1761), allowing British customs officials to search homes and warehouses for contraband; the Proclamation of 1763, forbidding any settlement west of the Appalachians; the Sugar Act (1764), placing new taxes on sugar, wine, coffee, and indigo; the Quartering Act (1765), ordering colonial governments to provide housing and board for British soldiers; the Stamp Act (1765, repealed 1766), a tax on all newspapers, legal papers, even playing cards, by demanding they bear an official stamp; the Declaratory Act (1767), giving Parliament the power to enact whatever laws it deemed necessary; and the Townshend duties (1767), adding taxes on all imported paper, glass, paint, and tea. Each year brought new burdens. There were no negotiations, few warnings. America was an economic province; for too long it had enjoyed more liberty than had the home country itself. Now it was time for colonials to understand their place. Relations soured and did not improve following the Boston Massacre (1770), when taunted redcoats fired into an unarmed crowd, killing five. To appease the anger, most of the Townshend duties were repealed, but in 1773 came the Tea Act, intended to kill American "smuggling" of cheap tea from Holland and to create a monopoly for the British East India Company. The resulting "vandalism" of the Boston Tea Party appalled the British, who retaliated through a series of punitive Intolerable Acts (1774), reducing colonial freedoms and bringing the first Continental Congress to Philadelphia that same year. Within eight months, the Revolution had begun (Wood 1998; Foster 2014).

The crucial period leading up to war was thus blunt and brief: barely a decade divided the end of the Seven Years' conflict from the shots fired at Lexington and Concord. Another six years brought Cornwallis's surrender to Washington (1781) and thus a new nation. There was little time to find, conceive, and gather together a set of principles that might justify such independence—let alone design and implement a brand-new kind of state that abandoned nearly all previous models of governance. Jefferson was a highly educated man of thirty-three, with a family and a career, when revolution broke, Hamilton a flushed youth of eighteen. Rapidity of events and the intellectual demands they brought made these two men into contemporaries.

Indeed, this deserves a moment of focus. Despite their fears and worries, Jefferson and Hamilton and the Founders in general proved themselves both committed intellectuals and true radicals. They did not wish merely to restore the era of "salutary neglect"—far from it. Their sense of injustice and opportunity drove them to work for something truly new, to transform a loose scatter of colonies into a nation able to fend for itself, prosper economically, and set an example of freedom for the world. These were all conscious goals (Peterson 1975; Ellis 2002; Wood 1992). To be sure, cases of an imperial power imposing stricter laws and punishments on a territory are rife in history. What made the American colonists unique was how their anger and sense of injustice sought legitimacy in the realm of ideas. With a few strokes of the pen, they crossed out rules that had stood for a thousand years—rules about the nature of sovereignty, the proper goals of government, and the need for religious legitimation. Specialists of the period, like Bernard Bailyn, emphasize "the creative reorganization of the world of power" that took place (2003, 3). Scholars also point to the unique faith that a written constitution, when "upheld by judicial bodies, can effectively constrain the tyrannies of both executive force and populist majorities" (Bailyn 2003, 4). Where, then, did such conceptions come from?

Texts of the Times: What Did Americans Read and Know?

Since the 1730s, colonial thinkers had built a curriculum of authors that served, beyond the sparkle of ornament, as intellectual fuel and light for American political ideas (Bailyn 1967/1992; McDonald 1978; Lutz 1992). We can divide these works into several main categories.

First are political writings, beginning with the English Bill of Rights itself. This was a list of complaints against King James II, who had suspended Parliament and begun installing a Catholic elite, plus a series of demanded protections from arbitrary royal intrusion. Equally indispensable was John Locke, father of classical liberalism, whose *Second Treatise of Civil Government* (1689) was required reading, developing as it did the idea of "unalienable rights" (including the right to private property), the necessity for the rule of law (without which there could be no real freedom), and the need for limited constitutional government. Locke's ideas were given verve by the most popular of all British authors and the most biting, sardonic wits of Whig journalism, Thomas Gordon and John Trenchard, whose *Cato's Letters* had a place on the shelf of nearly every educated colonist (Bailyn 1967/1992). Another

category of favor consisted of Roman authors, particularly Cicero and
Tacitus, who mourned the decline and fall of the republic (McDonald
1978). These were greatly admired as the bearers of wisdom—the classical world at this time remained a fundamental point of reference for
all discussions concerning government. Also crucial were works dealing
with the venerable concept of natural law (a system of jurisprudence
meant to accord with humanity's basic nature) such as those by Hugo
Grotius and Samuel Pufendorf. For those trained in the law, as Hamilton and Jefferson both were, William Blackstone's four-volume commentary on English law (1766) served as a universal textbook and had
a potent influence on the writing of the Constitution (Lutz 1992). Also
hugely popular was a selection of French authors, above all Montesquieu, who discussed ideas of liberty, freedom, and the nature of political systems (Bailyn 1967/1992; McDonald 1978).

From this it is clear that the Founders were anything but rude fron-
tiersmen. They were men of the Enlightenment; Europe was their home
territory of mind. They stayed in perennial contact with it through a
commerce of books, tracts, periodicals, and letters. Few British thinkers were as widely read as Jefferson or as serious about their reading as
Hamilton. If they lived on the edges of civilized life, in eighteenth-
century terms, they were still in touch with its inner circles of thought.
They had the advantage of the Enlightenment without being subject to
its confining social structures. The idea of America emerged out of the
forge, not the ashes, of the Old World.

Three entries in the Founders' library require more attention. Locke's
Second Treatise provided a nimble counter to Divine Right theories and
to Hobbes's conclusion in *Leviathan* that an all-powerful sovereign was
needed for an orderly society. Locke spoke to much that was on the
colonists' minds: the nature of power, the role of government, individual rights, legitimate and illegitimate leadership. One specially admired
passage occurs in the chapter "Of Slavery":

> The *natural liberty* of man is to be free from any superior power
> on earth, and not to be under the will or legislative authority of
> man, but to have only the law of nature for his rule. The *liberty of
> man*, in society, is to be under no other legislative power, but that

established, by consent, in the common-wealth; nor under the dominion of any will, or restraint of any law, but what that legislative
shall enact, according to the trust put in it. (Locke 1764, 212)

Rulers deserve their place only insofar as their actions reflect the consent of the governed—an idea that Hobbes had put forward. When
they cease to do so, seeking "arbitrary power" over a people, they set up,
Locke says, a "state of war." Rebellion then becomes just, even necessary.

Such basic tenets were music to colonial ears. By the 1760s, the colonists had enjoyed decades of watching financial scandal and corruption unfold in the mother country. First came the disastrous South Sea
Company debacle in 1720–21, a failed, government-sponsored trading
venture with massive public investment, bringing penury when it collapsed to a great many and involving bribery and payoffs in Parliament.
Then came the favor-thy-friend patronage system under the administration of Robert Walpole (1721–42), which appeared to many as a second
monarchy in parliamentary stockings. Locke was a rich source for every
critic that took this to task (Foster 2014). But Tacitus and Cicero were
seen as no less relevant to Britain's corruptions, writing as they did of
the seductions held out by dictatorship.

For Jefferson, Tacitus was "first among writers," yet a deeper devotion went to Cicero (Ellis 1998). Jefferson owned more than forty volumes by him and felt Cicero's life of study, duty, and rural contemplation (minus, perhaps, exile and murder) an ideal for his own. Hamilton,
too, found a compatriot mind in the prime defender and orator of the
republic, whom, along with Plutarch and Sallust, he called upon repeatedly in *The Federalist* (e.g., No. 8). Adams, Madison, and Marshall
were all admirers of Ciceronian thought and expression. They tended
to ignore the great orator's skepticism toward democracy and focus
on other points. Especially respected were Cicero's words in Book I of
De Officiis (*On Duty*), which speak of a divine and rational order to
the world, with men given reason and a moral sense to live according
to this order, recognizing the bond that exists between them. Reason
and order require the creation of just communities, institutions, and
states. Cicero, that is, spoke of "natural law" and the idea of legitimate
government long before Pufendorf or Locke. He also, in Book III of

De Re Publicia (On the State), says that liberty is something that must be guaranteed "in fact as well as in profession." By "fact," he meant a strong and uncorrupted judiciary, something essential if "written rules" for social order and liberty were to be maintained (Bailyn 1967/1992). These concepts of Cicero were well-known to English intellectuals, too. But to the colonists, Britain had proven itself little better than Rome in bringing them to life.

Most admired among the colonists was *Cato's Letters*. This series of 144 essays by Gordon and his colleague John Trenchard first appeared during the 1720s in the *London Journal* and *British Journal* under the pseudonym "Cato" (invoking the lithic integrity of Cato the Younger, foe of Caesar). Gathered into four volumes, the series went through numerous editions in London and America. They began with outrage at the South Sea Company fiasco and other forms of corruption but went on to treat topics related to liberty, natural rights, freedom of speech and the press, and government power. No other work had as much influence on political ideas in colonial America (Bailyn 1967/1992; Wood 1992; Lutz 1992). It is not difficult to see why. Style-wise, these brief pieces strike with sharpness and a driving logic, borne by a tone of combative rectitude: "Without freedom of thought, there can be no such thing as wisdom; and no such thing as publick liberty. . . . This sacred privilege is so essential to free government, that the security of property and the freedom of speech always go together; and in those wretched countries where a man cannot call his tongue his own, he can scarce call any thing else his own" (Trenchard and Gordon 1737, vol. 1, 96). But it is in attacking tyranny that these essays rise to oratory:

> Nothing that is good or desirable can subsist under tyrants, nor within their reach . . . [for] they measure their own happiness, and security, and strength, by the misery and weakness of their people; . . . That wealth, which dispersed amongst their subjects, and circulated in trade and commerce, would employ, increase, and enrich them, and return often again with interest into their coffers, is barbarously robbed from the people, and engrossed by these their oppressors, and generally laid out by them to adorn their palaces, to cover their horses or elephants, or to embellish

their own persons. . . . Such is the pestilent, savage, and unsatiable nature of this sort of monster, whose figure, throne and authority is established upon the ruins of reason, humanity, and nature: He takes all that his subjects have, and destroys them to get more. (1737, vol. 3, 56, 59)

Cato's Letters brought the language of liberty to the everyday speech of the inn or coffeehouse. For patriot colonials, it was a discourse of "the people," both in sound and sense. With these two writers, as with Locke, England birthed the ideas that would come to defeat its armies.

HAMILTON: THE NECESSITY OF STRENGTH

Alexander Hamilton was born on the island of Nevis in the British West Indies. Nevis was basically a slave colony for the production of sugar, with a tiny, landed aristocracy, a large number of black slaves, and a minority of mostly poor whites. Hamilton's mother, Rachel Fawcett, belonged to this last category. Well before his birth, she suffered a lifetime of ill fortune—a bad marriage, an abusive husband, accusations of indecency that put her in jail, and flight from Nevis, only to land in poverty and desperation. She then encountered James Hamilton, prodigal son of a well-off Scottish family, and within five years had given birth to two boys out of wedlock, James Jr. and Alexander. James Sr. failed at one business venture after another, finally abandoning the family. Rachel then ran a small store on St. Kitts island, but in 1768, when Alexander was barely eleven, she came down with fever and died. Her first husband, from whom she had never legally divorced, swooped in to seize and auction off everything, with only a collection of books by classical authors saved by a family friend for Alexander. The brothers were then briefly adopted by a melancholic cousin, who took his own life, leaving the pair homeless again. It was at this low point that Hamilton's fortunes began to turn (Chernow 2005).

Having seen and known little beyond poverty, abandonment, and death, the child Hamilton was now adopted by a Nevis merchant and given work in a local trading company, where he acquired direct experience of commerce. Within a few years, he was trying his hand at literature as well. Several efforts found publication in early 1772 with the *Royal Danish American Gazette*, a newspaper in St. Croix. These included a purplish account of a Caribbean hurricane, followed by clever poems, gaining the teenager much notice. Friends of his adoptive family, taking pride in a local prodigy, decided to send him to America to further his education. Hamilton was seventeen when he landed in the colonies and enrolled in a New Jersey academy. Yet even at so early a stage, we see the signs of an indomitable confidence: he applies to the College of New Jersey (later Princeton), asking to complete his degree in half the normal time. When refused, he simply repeats the request at King's College (now Columbia), where he is accepted (Chernow 2005).

Hamilton's entry into New York Harbor in early 1773 came at a time of high political heat. The Boston Massacre (1770) still seethed in public memory. The Tea Act and Boston Tea Party both exploded on the scene soon after Hamilton's arrival, bringing the Intolerable Acts several months later and, in response, the First Continental Congress in early 1774. This rush of events provided the teenager, who had only just begun college, with a chance to propel himself headlong into the action. The summer of 1774 saw him make a sensational, unrehearsed speech to a mass rally held in New York, then publish several forceful letters in the *New York Journal* (a popular patriot voice) arguing the colonists' side. But it was when clergyman Samuel Seabury released a pamphlet ridiculing the new Congress that Hamilton struck with real brilliance. His retort, "Full Vindication of the Measures of Congress," showed not only a firm grasp of political events but solid knowledge of America's trade relations, rules of commerce, and theory of natural law, all of which he wrapped in the assertive, sometimes overwrought prose of the pamphlet style. He will, he says, defend Congress "from the calumnies of their enemies" and show, regarding Seabury, "his *sophistry* . . . exposed, his *cavils* confuted, his *artifices* detected, and his *wit* ridiculed" (Hamilton 2001, 10).

Hamilton wrote like a longtime countryman: "What, then, is the subject of our controversy with the mother country? It is this: whether we shall preserve that security to our lives and properties, which the law of nature . . . and our charters, afford us; or whether we shall resign them into the hands of the British House of Commons" (2001, 10). To call this presumptive for a youth not yet twenty, with the dust and salt of an immigrant journey still thick upon his shoulders, would be understandable. What we hear, however, is the voice of one who is finding his place in the historical moment and intends to make his mark. It seems fair to say, as many have, that Hamilton took America's time of trial as his own. To this young man bursting with talent and energy, America offered the prospect of liberty as an intellectual challenge and a chance to rise well above a troubled and perhaps even shameful past. The task of Alexander Hamilton, we might say, was to find his own future in the future of America.

The Challenges of War and a Weak Congress

At the outbreak of the Revolution, Hamilton gained a commission as artillery captain and quickly distinguished himself in battle and in person. In 1777 Washington appointed him his aide-de-camp, with the rank of lieutenant colonel. Hamilton had been in America for five years; today, he would still need another two years to become a citizen.

He wrote nearly all of Washington's correspondence during the war, both to officers and to Congress, and was sent on important, sometimes secret missions. His fluency in French, acquired from his Huguenot mother, made him a liaison between Washington and French military representatives. Still, Hamilton yearned to lead in open battle, not to serve in the general's tent. After four years on staff, during which he pleaded repeatedly for a command (Washington valued him too highly to say yes), he used the occasion of a small reprimand from the general to leave the staff. Washington regretted the separation, but he nonetheless later gave Hamilton command of an entire battalion, which led a major assault at Yorktown. While on Washington's staff, Hamilton was a spectacularly quick study, teaching himself military tactics, engineering, wartime finance, and the British tax system. He began a correspondence of his own with members of Congress, notably John Jay and Robert Morris, superintendent of finance.

In 1775, Hamilton wrote to Jay about an incident where the Sons of Liberty (who had carried out the Boston Tea Party) looted the office of James Rivington, a libelous loyalist publisher. It is a revealing letter. Hamilton confirms the "detestable" character of Rivington yet disapproves of the action taken against him, for a particular reason: "In times of such commotion as the present, while the passions of men are worked up to an uncommon pitch, there is great danger of fatal extremes" (Hamilton 2001, 44). He goes on: "it requires the greatest skill in the political pilots to keep men steady and within proper bounds . . . I am always more or less alarmed at everything which is done of mere will and pleasure, without any proper authority" (2001, 44). Hamilton, we find, is no believer in the innate virtue of humanity, particularly among the multitude. His reading and experience convince him that, in an emotional state, men who see themselves acting against tyranny too easily commit tyrannical acts. Authority and self-control are two faces of a single coin.

Winning the war required stability and order: this emerges as a key theme for Hamilton. To George Clinton, governor of New York, he complained bitterly in February 1778 of a weak and disorganized Continental Congress that fawned over French officers yet let its own men go unfed and that failed to see the "pernicious" effect of allowing the states to withhold funds for the Revolutionary army. To John Jay, in March 1779, he wrote in avid support of an effort to help secure the South by allowing black slaves to fight in the army, an idea he knew would enhance federal power over the states. The effort failed, but Hamilton's unique mix of Enlightenment sensibility and calculated strategy is, again, startling for one still in his early twenties:

> I foresee that this project will have to combat much opposition from prejudice and self-interest. The contempt we have been taught to entertain for the blacks, makes us fancy many things that are founded neither in reason nor experience. . . . But it should be considered, that if we do not make use of them in this way, the enemy probably will. . . . An essential part of the plan is to give them their freedom with their muskets . . . opening a door to their emancipation. (Hamilton 2001, 57)

Hamilton often turned his letters into dense intellectual arguments. Among the most famous, dated September 3, 1780, was to James Duane, a law school colleague and politician. It is here that Hamilton lays out a detailed critique of the Articles of Confederation and sets forth his own plan for correcting them—a plan that, in large part, would succeed even before he became America's first secretary of the treasury. The Articles, he wrote, suffer in three ways: (1) too much power given to the states, who must supply the soldiery; (2) a weak Congress, which constantly makes concessions; and (3) no means by which Congress can levy taxation or raise an army. He is sharpest about the first: "the idea of an uncontrollable sovereignty in each state, over its internal police, will defeat the other powers given to Congress, and make our union feeble." In a monarchy, "the danger is that the sovereign will have too much power . . . in our case . . . the danger is directly the reverse." Unable to cure this defect, "we shall have all the leisure and opportunity we can wish to cut each others throats" (Hamilton 2001, 71, 72, 73).

What to do? Congress must take back sovereignty in all things related to war, peace, trade, finance, foreign affairs, and the military. It must impose a war tax (and system of collection) to properly support the army, and it must set up a national bank as a reservoir of public and private credit. This would stabilize the national economy, allow the country to pay its debts, and provide it with capital after the Revolution. Also essential was to assign highly capable men to lead major departments of state. In this way, "we shall blend the advantages of a monarchy and republic in our constitution" (2001, 75).

Flowering of Federalism

With the war essentially over by 1781, Hamilton left the military, obtained his law degree, and set up practice in New York City. He defended loyalists whose property had been confiscated, maintaining that, as citizens, they should not be subject to vengeful acts or laws. His reputation as an army officer and forceful speaker led the New York legislature to select him as a state representative to the Continental Congress of 1782. Here, and again at the Annapolis Convention of 1786 on economic challenges facing the Union, he put himself forward as the most articulate proponent of the Federalist position, with its program for a strong central government. By this time, many of the Founders agreed that Congress had been a broken instrument during the war. Washington spoke of "a half-starv'd, limping government," Madison of "a Government . . . too feeble." Meanwhile, many farmers who had fought on the patriot side had not been paid yet and were now being taxed by the states to pay war debts. In Massachusetts, a merchant elite (who had loaned money to the state) began to foreclose on farms and homes whose owners could not pay the new tax. An enraged uprising began (Shay's Rebellion) that Congress proved incapable of handling. The merchants took matters into their own hands, funding a militia to defeat the insurgents. Washington was "mortified beyond expression." That all of Europe now saw a feckless government drew many to Hamilton's side (Chernow 2005; Rossiter 1953).

Indeed, the 1780s as a whole proved crucial to Hamilton's vision. In his letter to Duane he had spoken of "calling immediately a convention of all the states" to decide a new structure of government. It did not happen immediately. But in 1787, the all-important Constitutional Convention took place in Philadelphia, with aims that Hamilton had repeatedly stated. First, the Articles of Confederation, a dismal and dangerous failure, had to be tossed out. Second, a government with far greater powers, headed by the most able individuals, must be created. Third, this new government required a blueprint, a document laying out its powers and responsibilities, as well as its limits. All of this was achieved by the writing of the Constitution, a task lasting from May 25 to September 17.

Hamilton did not agree with the Constitution in all its parts when it finally emerged. A number of his own ideas were tossed aside. But he came to be its most assertive and effective defender. In order to be the law of the land, it had to be ratified by at least nine of the thirteen states. New York proved a major hurdle. When opponents in that state quickly began attacking the text for its "monarchical" cast, Hamilton rose immediately in its defense. Between October 1787 and May 1788, he and two collaborators, John Jay and James Madison, published no fewer than eighty-five essays—roughly one every three days—all signed by the pseudonym "Publius," to explain the principles expressed by the Constitution, why they are there, and why they are all needed.

These essays, later collected as *The Federalist Papers*, are often considered the most important single document of political theory ever written in favor of democracy (Wood 1992). Of the essays, it is now agreed that Jay wrote five of them, Madison twenty-eight or twenty-nine, and Hamilton fifty-one or fifty-two, with Hamilton conceiving the project and enlisting the other two (Chernow 2005; Wood 2007). *The Federalist* provided more than valuable arguments in support of the Constitution; it created an entire discourse of democratic philosophy, mainly on behalf of Federalism. Madison's famous words in essay no. 51 give some feeling for the whole: "If men were angels, no government would be necessary. If angels were to govern men, [no] controls . . . would be necessary. In framing a government . . . by men over men, the great difficulty is this: you must first enable the government to control the governed; and in the next place, oblige it to control itself" (Hamilton, Jay, and Madison 2001, 269).

With the extraordinary pace of the writing, we might expect *The Federalist* to seem hurried, even haphazard. Yet a careful plan guides the whole. The first twenty-two essays lay out the threats and instabilities facing the United States and thus the need for a strong union—titles include "Dangers from Foreign Force and Influence," "Dangers from Dissensions between the States," and "Union as a Safeguard against Domestic Faction and Insurrection." In echo, the next twenty-nine deliver answers to these concerns—the "General Power of Taxation" to build a military and protect the people; the "Powers Conferred by the Constitution" to regulate commerce and end interstate conflict; the "Particular Structure of the New Government" showing how it distributes and limits power by "proper checks and balances." The final section of thirty-four essays is a detailed look at each branch of government, beginning with the House of Representatives, followed by the Senate, the executive, and lastly the judiciary, whose independence from the other branches Hamilton strongly advocates. Particular attention is given to the executive, as the idea of a president drew the most bellicose criticism from the anti-Federalists.

Hamilton showed himself in these essays to rank among the few to fully comprehend that a strong military, especially a navy, was critical to the nation's future. Britain, to be sure, was his model but also his concern. Its fleets controlled the seas and defended the largest trading empire in history. They could operate as guardians, threats, police, and pirates. America would need ships to do the same, to expand and protect its own overseas commerce, as well as secure its coasts. Hamilton saw quite clearly that the place of sea power in the world meant America could not be safe by isolation. Its image as an "island empire," protected by oceans on both sides, was a mirage. Wars were now fought between European nations in places from the Caribbean to India—a key lesson of the Seven Years' conflict that Hamilton knew well.

No one who delves into these essays properly, therefore, will emerge with the idea of Hamilton as an aristocrat *manqué* or a monarchist unrepentant. He had compromised or abandoned most of the ideas (both his and those of others) that inclined in this direction—for example, that the president be chosen for life or that senators be selected by state legislatures. He argued not for a wealthy elite but for representation— "the cultivators of land," preponderant as they were in the nation, must be so in the government, not by moral principle (as with Jefferson) but by political truth. He repeatedly warns that the power of a king, accountable to none, *must* always be guarded against and that the Constitution does so by limiting the president to a four-year term. Such, however, was never enough for the anti-Federalists.

One of the more lucid of Hamilton's enemies, who also appeared in the *New York Journal*, took the name "Cato" (scholars believe this was George Clinton, governor of New York) and calls upon the great Greek orator, Demosthenes, in his attack:

> [T]here is one common bulwark with which men of prudence are naturally provided, the guard and security of all people, particularly of free states, against the assaults of tyrants—What is this? Distrust. Of this be mindful; to this adhere; preserve this carefully. . . . The plain inference from this doctrine [of Demosthenes] is, that rulers in all governments will erect an interest separate from the ruled, which will have a tendency to enslave them. There is therefore no other way of . . . warding off the evil as long as possible, than by establishing principles of distrust in your

constituents, and cultivating the sentiment among yourselves. (Storing 1981, 125)

So great is the threat of government authority that no president or Congress should ever gain the confidence of the people. For the anti-Federalist position, loyalty to one's country must be secondary to suspicion of its leaders; these are always to be bound by the cords of doubt. It is a position based on a fear grounded in human nature, its weakness before the temptations of power. Hamilton understood this fear but saw it in a different light.

In Federalist #1, he says the Constitution's greatest enemy may well be "a certain class of men in every State [who] resist all changes which may hazard a diminution of the power . . . they hold" (Hamilton, Jay, and Madison 2001, 2). That is, men who may have supported or even fought in the Revolution, but who now hold office (in *state* administrations), may be the real foe. Not power, in other words, but self-interest, a dividing force, forms the greater threat to the public good. Such is why a Constitution is needed—only "energetic rules and principles" could steer a republic safely between the reefs of tyranny and anarchy. Anti-Federalists, led by those such as Patrick Henry of Virginia, worried deeply about individual rights. Madison partly answered this by introducing the Bill of Rights to the first U.S. Congress in 1789. But there was also the question of fundamental concept: should the new country be closer to a league of largely independent states or a unified nation (the Union)?

The whole of *The Federalist* argues for the latter, without pause. And, as we know, this view would triumph. But so, in a sense, did Hamilton's own worries. For the theme that occupied Madison and Hamilton in *The Federalist* more than any other, and that shows the far-seeing and sobering realism of these essays, was indeed "the violence of faction"— the splintering of the public into competing, uncompromising, even absolutist interest groups. This constituted one of the objections to democracy that had been made since classical times. Madison in Federalist #10 identified it as the source of "instability and injustice under which popular governments have everywhere perished." How do such factions arise? They result from "an excess of liberty" (Hamilton's phrase) endemic to democracy itself, which permits people to be drawn toward "some common impulse of passion"—fear-based causes, charismatic individuals, religious opinion, the struggle between social classes. If one interest becomes a majority, it can act as a tyranny, disguised as the "general will." In Madison's own words: "the form of popular government . . . enables [the majority faction] to sacrifice to its ruling passion or interest both the public good and the rights of other citizens" (Hamilton, Jay, and Madison 2001, 45). How, then, to deal with the danger? In a large republic, says Madison, the matter will take care of itself. There will always be such a diversity of parties and interests that a majority will be weakened by the demands and representatives of the other parties. Factionalism becomes its own enemy. Republican government leads to frequent compromise. After so many words making clear the danger, however, this strikes the reader as less than reassuring news.

One other statement in this essay deserves our eye: "It is vain to say that enlightened statesmen will be able to adjust these clashing interests. . . . Enlightened statesmen will not always be at the helm." An ultimate test for any republic is to survive and prosper beyond bad leaders—poor choices by the public. Hamilton, at the end of *The Federalist* (#85), returns to this point:

> The establishment of a Constitution, in time of profound peace, by the voluntary consent of a whole people, is a *prodigy*, to the completion of which I look forward with trembling anxiety. I can reconcile it to no rules of prudence to let go the hold we now have, in so arduous an enterprise . . . I dread the more the consequences of new attempts [to begin all over again], because I know that *powerful individuals*, in this and in other States, are enemies to a general national government in every possible shape. (Hamilton, Jay, and Madison 2001, 458)

Hamilton's worries would long outlive him. America faced dire enemies from within, a shattered economy, and a world thundering with formidable monarchies and insatiable ambitions, eager for dominance and ready for war. In such a world, the United States, an "empire" in name alone, could only appear frail and "trembling."

Secretary of the Treasury: Builder of a Modern State

In its primary goal, *The Federalist* was a failure. New York State voted 46–19 against ratification. But the essays had their impact in Virginia, Madison's home, which was no less important. Why didn't corks pop when New Hampshire became the ninth state to officially ratify? Because, as all knew, without New York and Virginia, the most populous, rich, and powerful states, the new government would never succeed. Partly because of *The Federalist*, Virginia followed suit after New Hampshire. New York held back. Debate among its delegates continued, acrimonious as ever; there was even talk of "civil war." The anti-Federalists demanded that the Constitution accept a bill of rights and several other amendments. Hamilton, on the wrong side of history, had argued against such amendments. But a compromise, largely negotiated by Hamilton, was finally struck: a limited bill of rights would be added as amendments, satisfying many of the anti-Federalists. Hamilton was touted as hero of the hour, celebrated throughout New York City (Chernow 2005).

Scholars have often noted that the level of discord over the Constitution meant only one man could be the nation's first president (Wood 1998; Ellis 2002). This man, after all, had to be a figure of proven stature and known virtue, able to stand as both flesh and symbol for national accord. Hamilton himself went to plead the case. Washington agreed but demanded that Hamilton be his secretary of the treasury. Washington knew that no one would work harder and more effectively to tackle the country's economic problems, which were dire. He also knew from experience that Hamilton was a divisive figure, supremely confident, even impetuous. But Hamilton's brilliance was beyond all doubt; Washington had learned this firsthand, too. And the moment demanded confidence and boldness of ideas. The nation's gravest challenge was that it lay groaning under its war debt, enfeebling its reputation abroad. Here, all felt, lay the key to America's survival. Hamilton, however, knew different.

It would be futile to solve the present situation while leaving the future to perilous uncertainty. America could be good, a successful nation—or it could be great. The moment, therefore, was decisive. The

first secretary had the opportunity to set the country on a path of financial and political ascent, one informed by an understanding of where
the powerful nations of Europe were heading and which of them was
most likely to get there first (Britain). For America, it would involve
building institutions, creating a bureaucracy, forging trade relations,
launching a modern military. In all this, Hamilton proved himself
ahead of everyone.

His vision for economic and military power was expressed in three
main documents, written over a period of eighteen months: the reports
on public credit, on the need for a national bank, and on manufactures
(industry). Within months of his appointment in 1789, Hamilton was
called upon by the House of Representatives to produce a plan for "the
adequate support of the public credit." The country was not only broke;
its reputation had fallen to where it had no borrowing capability. *Report
on the Public Credit*, delivered in January 1790, brought considerable
debate, but, blessed by Washington and strengthened by compromise
with Secretary of State Thomas Jefferson, its proposals were enacted
with much beneficial result (Chernow 2005).

Hamilton moved not just to regain America's financial standing but
to transform it. In eighteenth-century terms, America had to secure its
"honor," which required "the punctual performance of contracts," that
is, payment of debts. These Hamilton calculated at $54 million for the
federal government, with $25 million more owed by the states, mainly
in the North (Hamilton 2001, 54–55). But how to eliminate this when
the country had so little capital? Hamilton's plan was as dazzling as it
was audacious. The federal government would take charge of its own
war debt, much of it in the form of highly devalued war bonds, but it
would also cover *all* the remaining debts of the states. It would do this
by a sophisticated system of funding: European debt would be repaid
by the selling of western lands, while the money owed to domestic creditors would be maintained as a perpetual investment in the country's
future, with yearly interest paid back on the full value of the original
bonds. In addition, a new (relatively mild) system of taxes and issuing
of government bonds would add to the sources of capital (Hamilton
2001, 553–74).

The plan's genius lay in its reduced financial risk and in its ability to form those "ligaments" tying wealthy interests—merchants, plantation owners, and speculators, who had bought the original bonds—directly to the government. Opposition was forecast, and it came, both from anti-Federalists who saw Hamilton doing exactly what they had feared (expanding government power) and from the South in general, which had paid over 80 percent of its war debt yet was now being asked to take some responsibility for northern states. Again, a compromise was needed and found: Jefferson and his southern colleagues agreed to Hamilton's plan in exchange for his support that the new national capitol be sited along the banks of the Potomac River.

Once put into action, Hamilton's plan proved nothing short of miraculous. With foreign debt soon reduced, European investment flowed into the country, and purchase of further bonds by the native elite rose as well. True to his indefatigable ambition, however, Hamilton moved quickly to gain congressional approval for the second part of his strategy, the establishment of a national bank. Such a bank was needed, he said, to fulfill the Constitution's requirement that the federal government collect taxes, regulate trade, coin money, and raise and support a military. When later challenged by Jefferson on the grounds that such a bank was in fact unconstitutional—no specific power being given to erect one—Hamilton called upon Article 1, Section 8, Paragraph 18, stating that Congress has the authority "to make all Laws which shall be necessary and proper" to fulfill its obligations. Here, then, was the "elastic clause," as it famously came to be known, that kept the door open to a true, if somewhat careful, extension of government power. Washington and Congress approved the bank, which remained in operation until closed by Andrew Jackson (after a long and brutal battle) three decades later (McCraw 2012; Eckes 1995).

Report on the Subject of Manufactures, presented to Congress in late 1791, constitutes Hamilton's most impressive, far-reaching, and influential document. It was not, as often claimed, a rejection of Adam Smith. *Manufactures* does say the government should use tariffs and subsidies to lower demand for foreign goods in favor of "domestic productions." America's newborn industries needed help and protection, Hamilton wrote, until they could fairly compete. This would take time. England was already harnessing "fire and water" to run its textile mills in a new, mechanized way; Hamilton was among the few at the time who saw the coming of the Industrial Revolution. Regulation of trade, using moderate "bounties," would supply revenue for the support of homegrown industry through the building of roads, canals, and other infrastructure, "discoveries and inventions," technology, and agriculture. This, in turn, would bring more immigrants to the country and help create real urban centers, perhaps one day to rival even Paris or London (Hamilton 2001, 649–64). Hamilton does take up and reject the invisible hand. Men too often fail to understand their own interest and resist change; the visible arm of government is needed. He thus appears to dispute *Wealth of Nations*. Indeed, the first fifteen pages of *Manufactures* is a kind of point-by-point debate with Smith, whose name is never mentioned.

But this only makes clear that Hamilton was, in fact, a child of Smithian economics. On nearly all his main points he borrows heavily from the Scotsman. From Smith, he takes the key idea that an economic system rests upon the back of labor, therefore on human capital, the greatest resource of any nation. He also agrees that industry is not parasitic on agriculture but increases it through the division of labor and innovation. Just as Smith did, Hamilton spends no little space arguing against the view that agriculture is the only productive form of labor. From the discussion in chapter 2 we certainly know who is called upon when Hamilton writes, "It has justly been observed, that there is scarcely any thing of greater moment in the economy of a nation, than the proper division of labour. The separation of occupations causes each to be carried to a much greater perfection, than it could possible acquire, if they were blended" (Hamilton 2001, 659). Hamilton on these topics provides what can only be seen as glossed summaries from *Wealth of Nations* (e.g., Book I, chapters 1 and 2). He varies not an inch from Smith's argument that stability in a society depends on a state's power to defend itself and on a system of law that allows people to pursue their own interests. And lest we forget, Adam Smith was not at all against government investment in infrastructure and education or the use of tariffs. (E.g.: "The expence of maintaining good roads and communications is, no doubt, beneficial to the whole society, and may . . .

without any injustice, be defrayed by the general contribution of the whole society" [*Wealth of Nations*, V.1.238]. "Those trades only require bounties in which the merchant is obliged to sell his goods for a price which does not replace to him his capital, together with the ordinary profit" [IV.5.2].)

But Hamilton is no epigone. To his mind, Smith wrote from a European perspective. Despite his treatment of colonies and support for the American cause, he did not fully understand the circumstances faced by a newly independent state with a sparse, scattered population and an infant government in need of "honor." Hamilton had his own powerful perceptions to offer:

> Men reluctantly quit one course of occupation and livelihood for another unless invited to it by very apparent and proximate advantages. . . . Manufacturers who, listening to the powerful invitations of a better price for their fabrics, or their labor, of greater cheapness of provisions and raw materials, of an exception from the chief part of the taxes, burthens, and restraints, which they endure in the old world, of greater personal independence and consequence, under the operation of a more equal government, and of what is far more precious than mere religious toleration—a perfect equality of religious privileges—would probably flock from Europe to the United States to pursue their own trades or professions. (2001, 662)

Hamilton here foresees America's future as a "promised land." More than two centuries further on in time, we recognize the vision as strikingly prescient for its time.

Overall, Alexander Hamilton brought large portions of *Wealth of Nations* to the New World, adding some crucial ingredients of his own. The Hamilton program of nurtured industries, public financing, and a national bank—the so-called American School of Economics—was no laissez-faire policy, to be sure. But its emphasis on human capital and technological progress, its favoritism toward paper currency and the selective, targeted use of government investment for the common good, its distrust of great wealth and inherited nobility, its association of economic power with urban centers, and its demand that citizens contribute toward the support of the government in proportion to the revenue they receive under its laws and protections—all of these are directly taken from Mr. Smith.

All is not sweetness and light, by any means. Criticisms are often leveled at Hamiltonian economics. As Hamilton's words hint, for example, the desire for immigrants is far from altruistic. It is *skilled* labor that Hamilton wants, labor that arrives already able to enhance America, not make demands upon it. There is irony here, perhaps: Hamilton, child immigrant himself, does not call for the tired and poor, yearning to breathe free, but instead the ambitious and educated, longing for advancement. To be fair, a preference for skilled newcomers reflected his own immediate worries for America. Still, it remains unclear if he would have favored Emma Lazarus's famous poem engraved on the Statue of Liberty, beckoning Europe's huddled masses.

Hamilton left his post as treasury secretary in 1795 and reentered private life to support his growing family. He would live another nine years before being mortally wounded in his duel with Aaron Burr. During this period, he continued to be consulted by members of the cabinet under the presidency of John Adams (not a great fan of Hamiltonian ideas). But he lost prestige when he threw his support in the close election of 1800 to Jefferson, leader of the opposition and his ideological nemesis, in order to defeat Burr, whom he considered a scoundrel. Further efforts to scuttle Burr's attempt to win the governorship of New York, plus derogatory comments Hamilton may have made to others, led to the duel. With poignant irony, the man who had done so much to make America stable and prosperous left his wife and seven living children heavily in debt, a situation remedied only by the kindness of friends.

Before his death, Hamilton performed one more service to his adopted homeland. With Jefferson's election and then the Louisiana Purchase, New England Federalists saw a dramatic loss of their power and also a move to weaken the North. Timothy Pickering, a former U.S. secretary of state under John Adams, gathered together a group of powerful Federalists in Massachusetts to discuss the idea of a northern secession. The new republic would include New England, eastern Canada, New

York, and New Jersey and would be centered in New York. Known as the Essex Junto (many of its members being from Essex County, Massachusetts), the group approached Hamilton to lead the secession and act as the new republic's first president. Aghast at the plan, Hamilton refused. The group next turned to Aaron Burr, who accepted. The Essex Junto then gathered its political forces behind Burr's run for the governorship of New York in 1804, while Hamilton, aware of what was at stake, campaigned night and day to defeat Burr. The election went to Republican Morgan Lewis by a paper-thin margin of seven thousand votes. Most scholars believe this defeat was most responsible for the duel (Chernow 2005).

Thomas Jefferson Dined Here

When we skim their lives and minds, Thomas Jefferson and Alexander Hamilton appear so remarkably opposed as to suggest political matter and anti-matter. Jefferson was born to a genteel family in Virginia, the oldest American colony, and received an excellent education; Hamilton entered life as an illegitimate child in the Caribbean and came to America an unschooled immigrant. Jefferson spent the Revolution engaged in political work and caring for his family; Hamilton was hot in the fray of the home front, a military officer and aide to Washington. Jefferson had no public speaking talent; Hamilton's voice could sway minds and alter decisions. Jefferson's more aristocratic nature made him shy away from public conflict; Hamilton's nitrous temper propelled him into challenges of honor. Thomas Jefferson lived long enough to see his ideas for America fail; Hamilton died before many of his triumphed.

If Thomas Jefferson and Alexander Hamilton can appear like negatives of one another, Jefferson on his own has presented historians with a perplexing reservoir of incongruities (Ellis 1998). A man who proclaimed a loathing for slavery as a "hideous blot," who wrote the ever-powerful words "that all men are created equal," lived his adult life as a slave owner and, at his death, left two hundred men, women, and children in servitude. As the grand libertarian who demanded limits on government and a strict interpretation of the Constitution, once becoming president he stepped well beyond such boundaries. He could argue, in his first inaugural address, for "Peace, commerce, and honest friendship with all nations, entangling alliances with none"—and thus provide the paean for American isolationism ever after—yet launch a vengeful war against the piratical Barbary states of North Africa, when Europe, subject to the same piracy, simply paid a tribute. Nurtured on Old World thought and art, Jefferson declared no American should visit Europe before thirty years of age to avoid its taint of corruption. Most perplexing of all, perhaps, is the epitaph he wrote for himself in his last year of life: "Author of the Declaration of Independence, of the Statute of Virginia for Religious Freedom, & Father of the University of Virginia," leaving out any mention of his two terms as president. Thomas Jefferson, it seems, wanted most of all to be remembered for his most noble ideas: two brief writings that condensed his thought on freedom and one institution where such thought might be studied.

Jefferson is rightly called the most intellectual of American presidents. His learning was legendary. Even the cultured, worldly, and multilingual John Quincy Adams stood in awe of him (Peterson 1975; Ellis 1998). In more recent times, there is this well-known story: while hosting a presidential dinner to honor American Nobel Laureates, John F. Kennedy commented, "I think this is the most extraordinary collection of talent and of human knowledge that has ever been gathered together at the White House—with the possible exception of when Thomas Jefferson dined alone." Theodore Roosevelt wrote many more books than Jefferson, on subjects like hunting, nature, and history. Woodrow Wilson was an author as well as a true academic, president of Princeton, and the only president ever to hold a Ph.D. Yet neither man was ever at home in the fields where Jefferson's mind happily roamed: Greek and Roman literature; French political and economic thought; British legal history; the fine arts; natural philosophy (science); engineering; agriculture. If he could converse on Plato, he could discuss with equal intensity the design of a chair. Jefferson wrote only three books, the flat-toned *Autobiography* (1821), the *Manual of Parliamentary Practice* (1811), and the magnificent *Notes on the State of Virginia* (1781), a type of narrative encyclopedia on his home state, its geography, natural resources, animals and plants, fossils, native peoples, climate, architecture, commerce, and more. He also produced the important pamphlet *A Summary View of the Rights of British America* (1774), a draft constitution for Virginia, a sizable number of bills put before the Virginia legislature, and, lest we forget, the Declaration of Independence (1776).

Jefferson's pen was most prodigious in writing letters. There are over nineteen thousand of these. They make up an enormously diverse and rich correspondence. He was in touch with French philosophers, continental literary figures, important aristocrats, and European scientists, including Joseph Priestly, Edward Jenner, and the Comte de Buffon, the greatest natural historian of the day. He also exchanged letters with many women, some in the United States, like Abigail Adams, others in Europe, including the formidable Madame de Staël. Many of his missives, like Hamilton's, are recordings of his thought on weighty subjects, spanning his innumerable interests. He shows himself to be most at home when reflecting, analyzing, and conversing—sharing what he knows and thinks in language that suggests a speech or lecture. A meaningful example to John Jay on August 23, 1785, just after the Revolution, shows this well:

> We have now lands enough to employ an infinite number of people in their cultivation. Cultivators of the earth are the most valuable citizens. They are the most vigorous, the most independent, the most virtuous, & they are tied to their country & wedded to its liberty & interests by the most lasting bonds. . . . [When] their numbers . . . become too great for the demand both internal & foreign . . . I should then perhaps wish to turn them to the sea in preference to manufactures, because comparing the characters of the two classes I find the former the most valuable citizens. I consider the class of artificers as the panders of vice & the instruments by which the liberties of a country are generally overturned. (Jefferson and Randolph 1829, vol. 2, 291)

Jefferson's voice is not that of a statesman but rather of a teacher, impelled by moral as well as ideational concerns. This aspect of Jefferson, his focus on ethical principle and his ability to do so in stirring, epigrammatic language, partly defines the force that his writings achieve,

even for Americans today, and explains why they are so often lifted out
of context.

He was born April 13, 1743, in Shadwell, Virginia, a prosperous settlement in the rolling foothills of the Blue Ridge Mountains. His father,
Peter Jefferson, had been an early settler in the area, taught himself many
crafts, including cartography and surveying, and amassed a plantation
with sixty or more slaves. He entered local politics, serving as a justice
and a representative to the Virginia House of Burgesses. His wife, Jane
Randolph, was from a prominent family in the Tidewater region, with
a presumed noble lineage reaching back to medieval times, a bit of family lore that likely played in the imagination of young Thomas, who, at
nine, was sent to the Latin school of the Reverend William Douglas
where he was introduced to Latin, Greek, French (in a Scottish accent),
and a sense of higher destiny (Kern 2010).

Such pastoral beginnings came to an abrupt end in 1757 when Peter
Jefferson fell ill and died, leaving his fourteen-year-old son as the patri-
arch of a family that included six sisters and one younger brother. Of his
father, Thomas writes in his *Autobiography*: "[His] education had been
quite neglected; but being of a strong mind, sound judgment and eager
after information, he read much and improved himself" (1904, vol. 1,
4). It is, we can only feel, a thin, strange caption.

For the next two years, Thomas studied with "Reverend Mr. Maury,
a correct classical scholar," before entering William and Mary in 1760.
It is at this point that the *Autobiography* shows the first signs of real life
(though the book was "for the information of my family," there is small
ink given to his father, mother, brothers, sisters, and early teachers, all
of them packed into a dozen, impassive lines). Once he is inside the
college gates, we learn interesting things:

> It was my great good fortune, and what probably fixed the desti-
> nies of my life that Dr. Wm. Small of Scotland was then professor
> of Mathematics, a man profound in most of the useful branches
> of science, with a happy talent of communication, correct and
> gentlemanly manners, & an enlarged & liberal mind. He . . . be-
> came soon attached to me & made me his daily companion when
> not engaged in the school; and from his conversation I got my

first views of the expansion of science & of the system of things in which we are placed. (Jefferson 1904, vol. 1, 5–6)

William Small and his brother, Robert, were members of the Scottish Enlightenment. After returning to Britain in 1764, William was elected to the Lunar Society, a prestigious group of scientists, philosophers, inventors, and early industrialists, and had a major impact on it, organizing its members and meetings into a true professional society. It is through Small that a connection can be made between Jefferson and Darwin, whose grandfather, Erasmus, was a Lunar Society fellow. From Jefferson's comments, it is likely that Small introduced him to such thinkers as David Hume and Francis Hutcheson. Certainly the latter had an impact on the young Jefferson, who eagerly became a loyal believer in Hutcheson's idea of an inborn "moral sense" (Ellis 1998; Malone 1974, vol. 1). Small invited Jefferson to dine regularly and discuss big topics with himself, Lieutenant Governor Francis Farquier, and the lawyer George Wythe. The scene held no small meaning: a seventeen-year-old boy regularly encouraged to converse and debate the issues of the day with sitting politicians and professional men.

At twenty-one, Jefferson came of age and inherited 2,750 acres. From this point on, he became a landowner, slave owner, and member of Virginia society, with a growing circle of acquaintances among the colonial gentry. He studied law, was admitted to the bar in 1767, and began a solid practice, attracting clients from many parts of the state. Most of his cases involved land claims, causing him to travel often and, with his capacious mind, to become knowledgeable about Virginia in all its aspects. After several years, he decided to build a country home, in the style of the Renaissance architect Palladio, on a hill surrounded by five thousand acres. Monticello ("little mountain") was his name for this elegant dwelling, where he would remain the rest of his life. In 1772 his wife, Martha Skelton, joined him there, and they began a family (Malone 1974, vol. 1).

He had been a rather shy suitor of Martha, the widow of a college classmate. Her father, John Wayles, a wealthy landowner, didn't much favor the red-haired, freckled young lawyer who played piano rather well but seemed lacking in the ambition needed to ever become a person of note. He did not formally object to the marriage, however. Indeed, within eighteen months he obliged the young couple by dying and leaving them 10,000 acres and 130 slaves, thrusting the couple into the upper levels of genteel society. But distinct complexities, of a particular kind, were also inherited. As a widower, Wayles had sought companionship in one of his slaves, Betty Hemings, who bore him six children— half brothers and sisters of Martha. In the Jefferson household, these people were retained as "servants," never being called "slaves." This was not mere dissembling. The term "slave" had legal as well as cultural associations (Bailyn 2013).

Thomas had entered politics by this time, named to the Virginia House of Burgesses in 1769. Demands of the position were now much greater than when his father had served. The march of new laws from Britain had lit many fires of resentment in the colonies, nowhere more so than in Virginia, where Patrick Henry had become a daunting voice of resistance. Jefferson found himself in close sympathy with Henry, sharing his rage at the Boston Massacre and his pride when the Townshend duties were repealed. Yet in the moment, the first of many tragedies occurred. February 1770 saw his birthplace, Shadwell house, burned to the ground, destroying a great many family possessions and, not least, his personal library, including the precious volumes pored over while at William and Mary. Jefferson was crushed; his mother and younger sisters had to live on nearby farms, while he did his best to hurry the construction of Monticello.

The Jeffersons set up house in the 1770s, as the country pitched toward war. For Thomas, it was a time of rising fame and responsibility, but it soon became a period of further loss and heartache as well, as death came to his young family. These trajectories—the Revolutionary War, colonial politics, and death in his home—greatly tested the mature man, not once but many times, in public and in private (Malone 1974, vol. 1; Peterson 1975). But it was also the period when Jefferson was most fertile and dynamic in his thought, when his most powerful ideas emerged. If his own life brought storms of brilliance and shadow, he never abandoned his family or nation.

MAN OF THE PEN

Jefferson's national career began when he came to the attention of colonial intellectuals beyond the rim of Virginia. This came from a position paper he wrote in 1774, when called to the Virginia Convention for choosing delegates to the First Continental Congress. Jefferson fell ill with dysentery on the trip and instead of attending sent a pamphlet: *A Summary View of the Rights of British America*. It announced an author of unexpected skill and learning.

Using points from England's own history, Jefferson addressed himself not to Parliament, source of the abusive new laws, but to King George III. The colonies, he said, owe their allegiance to the Crown, whose loyal subjects they remain. But loyalty is obligated only if a sovereign rules with the welfare of his people in mind. If not, the link of fidelity is shattered. Jefferson thus calls directly upon Hobbes and Locke, speaking to purpose. But then he does something bold—he pleads with and lectures King George as if an intimate counselor of the court: "Open your breast, sire, to liberal and expanded thought. Let not the name of George the Third be a blot in the page of history. . . . It behooves you, therefore, to think and to act for yourself and your people. The great principles of right and wrong are legible to every reader" (Jefferson 1904, vol. 2, 87). Virginia's legislators could only have been roused, and stood aghast, by such daring. They embraced *A Summary View* for its needed fervor but did not approve it. It was published and circulated ("leaked") anyway, without Jefferson's permission.

Within a year, Jefferson had become a name in the movement for independence, and his star rose rapidly in the constellation of politics. He was named a delegate to the Philadelphia Continental Congress (1776), where he was selected to write the Declaration of Independence. He then became a leading member in the Virginia House of Delegates (1776–79), governor of Virginia (1779–81) during the Revolution, and after this, minister to France (1784–89). In less than a decade, Jefferson had soared through the highly charged orbits of revolutionary politics, his value to the republican cause revealed in his dynamic ability to apply deep learning and rhetorical prowess to each new issue.

His wife, Martha, never physically strong, grew weaker with each new pregnancy. In the nine years after their marriage, she bore five daughters and one son; all but one died before reaching the age of three. Jefferson's mother also passed away in 1776. Because of these illnesses and deaths, he was absent from many sessions of the Virginia Assembly, for which he was often fined. After seventeen-month-old Lucy died in 1781 and Martha fell ill again, Jefferson resigned the governorship and came home to care for his ailing spouse. She finally succumbed on September 6, 1782, at the age of thirty-three. On her deathbed, recalling her own abuse at the hand of a stepmother and fearful for her two surviving daughters, she had Thomas promise never to marry again. He never did. All of this occurred eighteen years before he became president (Malone 1974, vol. 1).

The relentless march of tragedy threw the thirty-eight-year-old Jefferson into a chasm of depression. Guilt for having spent so much time away with political duties added to his private suffering and may have brought him even near suicide (Conkin 1993). Within months he rose from this dreadful state, the darkest of his long life, by relying on friends, the solace found in his books, and the new obligations his growing renown brought. His pen never went still. On the contrary, his correspondence expanded and was joined by *Notes on Virginia* and, at the outbreak of war in 1776, one brief but densely argued document that is perhaps familiar today:

> We hold these truths to be self-evident, that all men are created equal, that they are endowed by their Creator with certain unalienable Rights, that among these are Life, Liberty and the pursuit of Happiness.—That to secure these rights, Governments are instituted among Men, deriving their just powers from the consent of the governed—That whenever any Form of Government becomes destructive of these ends . . . when a long train of abuses and usurpations, pursuing invariably the same Object evinces a design to reduce them under absolute Despotism, it is their right, it is their duty, to throw off such Government, and to provide new Guards for their future security.

The Declaration of Independence is an explanation to all humanity of why separation for the colonies was necessary. It is a litany of offenses committed by Britain, wrapped in profound statements about the nature of government and human freedom. The lines quoted here provide one of the most concise, eloquent, and fervent elucidations of democratic theory ever written. We see Jefferson has grounded all in God's structure of the world. Yet if rights are divine gifts, governments exist to make them real and protected. Abuse of power that degrades the ability to enjoy these rights goes against nature and against divine law. But God does not intervene to set things right; he has left the working of the world to men: the deity of the Declaration is not among us. He is not mentioned anywhere in the U.S. Constitution or Bill of Rights either. The responsibility of freedom remains in the hands of those who suffer and triumph on its behalf.

Jefferson's rhetorical power soars in the Declaration. It is a resounding speech, which we are meant to hear as much as to read, and it makes us taste the rage of the moment in every line: "He has dissolved Representative Houses repeatedly, for opposing with manly firmness his invasions on the rights of the people. . . . He has erected a multitude of new offices, and sent hither swarms of Officers to harass our people, and eat out their substance. . . . He has plundered our seas, ravaged our coasts, burnt our towns, and destroyed the lives of our people." It is certainly no accident that this brief piece of writing would serve as a model for many other proclamations of sovereignty and rights over the next two centuries (Armitage 2007).

However, not every just complaint of Jefferson's survived to the final draft. Congress made some revealing deletions. Jefferson was part of a committee appointed by Congress to draft the Declaration. The committee also included John Adams, Benjamin Franklin, Roger Sherman, and Robert Livingston. Jefferson wrote the first draft, which was lightly edited by Adams and Franklin, then delivered to Congress, which altered it much more, deleting sections amounting to a third of the whole (Becker 1922, 166–92). One of them must work upon our conscience today:

He [the King] has waged cruel war against human nature itself, violating it's most sacred rights of life and liberty in the persons of a distant people . . . captivating & carrying them into slavery in another hemisphere, or to incur miserable death in their transportation thither. This piratical warfare . . . is the warfare of the CHRISTIAN king of Great Britain. Determined to keep open a market where MEN should be bought & sold, he has [suppressed] every legislative attempt to prohibit or to restrain this execrable commerce. And . . . he is now exciting those very people to rise in arms among us, and to purchase that liberty of which he has deprived them, by murdering the people on whom he also obtruded them. (Becker 1922, 180–81)

The passage was removed to appease South Carolina and Georgia specifically, and possibly Rhode Island, whose merchants were engaged in the slave trade.

So it is essential to understand what this deleted section indicates for the Declaration and its author. When Jefferson wrote "all men are created equal," he meant *all* men, of all races, not only white men who owned property. This universalism is at the core of the document; Jefferson is speaking not just of the American colonies but of all people and all governments at all times.

Like Jefferson himself, Madison, Washington, Jay, Patrick Henry, and John Hancock owned slaves but detested the trade in human flesh (only Henry spurned emancipation). Having inherited slaves from their families, most freed them later on. Jefferson never did, but in 1779 he put forward an entire plan for emancipation, including job training for all freed men, at public expense. In 1786, he advised that the Articles of Confederation forbid slavery in the Northwest Territory (land west of Pennsylvania and north of the Ohio River) to prevent its spread. His letters call slavery a "moral depravity" and "a fatal stain." Had he died in 1790, Jefferson might well be known today as a hero of emancipation (Davis 1975; Peterson 1975).

However, once attaining high office, he grew silent on the subject in public, where he had previously been bold (as a Virginian). *Notes on the State of Virginia* (Query XIV) expresses some of the reigning beliefs about black inferiority (e.g., their lack of reasoning ability, though he notes they are equal to whites in memory). Such beliefs had the imprimatur of science, not least from Buffon, whom Jefferson greatly esteemed and whose *Varietés dans l'espèces humaine* (1749) spoke of the "simplicity" of blacks. It would seem that in entering politics at the national level, Jefferson found reason to compromise one set of values for another. The period of the 1790s, in particular, saw him leading a new political party (something he did not care for), whose agenda was to counter Federalism and proclaim the need for small government, state authority, and the sacredness of private property. All of these principles were contradicted, in some measure, by the idea of using federal power to free slaves. It escaped no one, either, that prosperity in the South was greatly dependent on slave-based agriculture. Hamilton spoke of manumission yet never made it a core part of his program. He, too, accommodated the South for the sake of national stability, though he did so with resentment.

That slavery went unaddressed by these men was not lost on Europe. "We are told," said Samuel Johnson in an address responding to the Declaration of Independence, "that the subjection of Americans may tend to the diminution of our own liberties. . . . [But] if slavery be thus fatally contagious, how is it that we hear the loudest yelps for liberty among the drivers of Negroes?" (Johnson 1913, vol. 14, 143). That particular year, America had nearly 450,000 slaves, almost a fifth of its total population. Johnson's comment stings today, as it has since it was uttered, whenever the heroic image of America's Founders floats on high (Marx 1998).

Reforming Virginia, Advancing Democracy

As a member of the Virginia legislature and as governor, Jefferson's goal was to bring progress to his home state through reforms rooted in Enlightenment ideas. We recognize his plans as a distinct break from more medieval concepts of a fixed world system encoded at many levels of society. He advocated for an end to feudal property rights, for representation independent of property size, and for a more flexible and humanitarian penal system, public education, and no state religion.

Despite being part of the so-called Piedmont oligarchy, he joined Hamilton and most other Founders against entail (which restricted future ownership of land to an owner's own descendants) and primogeniture (property going to the oldest son) as tools for an aristocracy (Wood 2007). Adam Smith, in *Wealth of Nations*, wrote scathingly against entail in particular, which was common in England though less so in America.

Jefferson, like Hamilton, greatly valued education as a source of future progress. But where Hamilton never spoke extensively on the subject, Jefferson had a full program in mind, a secular one, based largely on his political ideas (Peterson 1975). The scheme was laid out in two documents, *A Bill for the More General Diffusion of Knowledge* (1779), sent to the Virginia legislature, and Query XIV in *Notes on Virginia*. In the first of these, the author justifies his plan:

> [E]xperience hath shewn, that even under the best forms [of government], those entrusted with power have, in time, and by slow operations, perverted it into tyranny; and it is believed that the most effectual means of preventing this would be, to illuminate, as far as practicable, the minds of the people at large, and more especially to give them knowledge of those facts, which history exhibiteth, [so] they may be enabled to know ambition under all its shapes. . . . [Moreover] those persons, whom nature hath endowed with genius and virtue, should be rendered by liberal education worthy to receive, and able to guard, the sacred deposit of the rights and liberties of their fellow citizens, and that they should be called to that charge without regard to wealth, birth or other accidental condition . . . and educated at the common expense. (Jefferson 1904, vol. 2, 414)

Education must be more than learning. It must make the people their own guardians against the power of tyranny. Jefferson draws from Locke, whose *Thoughts Concerning Education* (1693) begins with the simple statement "of all the men we meet with, nine parts of ten are what they are, good or evil, useful or not, by their education. It is that which makes the great difference in mankind" (Locke 1824, vol. 8, 6). But Jefferson is thinking politically: if education makes the man, it builds the society, brick by brick, and protects it against its more ambitious leaders. "Lessons of history" are key; from these, Americans can learn to recognize oppression, whether it glowers in the streets or whispers behind doors. But the capable system of liberal education can also shape the best and brightest into leaders who will be least likely to turn ambitious. Such is not, we might note, a plan for learning on its own merits. It is a strategy for guardianship.

Religion and Liberty

Jefferson thought the Bible too morally difficult and too self-contradictory for young minds to study. This went against centuries of educational practice, but it did not make Jefferson opposed to religion. Faith had an individual dimension, he felt, and helped keep society knit together by moral-ethical fibers. Belief must be protected, as a right, but never imposed or restricted. His *Bill for Establishing Religious Freedom* (first drafted in 1777, enacted into law 1786), in which these ideas are articulated, was always among the documents of which Jefferson was most proud. "Almighty God hath created the mind free," he begins, "and manifested his supreme will that free it shall remain." Thus,

> [T]he impious presumption of [those] who, being themselves but fallible and uninspired men, have assumed dominion over the faith of others, setting up their own opinions and modes of thinking as the only true and infallible, and as such endeavoring to impose them on others, hath established and maintained false religions over the greatest part of the world and through all time: That to compel a man to furnish contributions of money for the propagation of opinions which he disbelieves and abhors, is sinful and tyrannical ... that our civil rights have no dependence on our religious opinions, any more than our opinions in physics or geometry; and therefore the proscribing any citizen as unworthy the public confidence ... unless he profess or renounce this or that religious opinion, is depriving him injudiciously of those privileges and advantages to which, in common with his fellow-citizens, he has a natural right. (Jefferson 1904, vol. 2, 438–39)

This is one of the few places where Jefferson applies the word "sinful" in a serious way. If he is sermonizing, however, he is doing so with Enlightenment intent. Belief is a relative thing: "all men shall be free to profess, and by argument to maintain, their opinions in matters of religion" (1904, vol. 2, 441). Liberty is above faith. Jefferson's God does not like single interpretations. His statute, used by Madison to write the First Amendment, marks a distinct victory for secular government. It rejects the notion that America depends for its survival on shared religious practices or beliefs.

The story does not end here. In October 1801, a group of Baptist ministers from Danbury, Connecticut, wrote to congratulate the Sage of Monticello on his election to the presidency but also to complain about being the victims of religious discrimination. Congregationalism, the dominant sect, acted as a de facto state faith, so that "what religious privileges we enjoy, we enjoy as favors granted . . . not as inalienable rights" and at the price of certain "degrading acknowledgments," like taxes levied on their church that went to support the Congregationalists. Thus they asked their new president to "assume the prerogative of Jehovah and make laws" to right the situation (Dreisbach 1997, 460). Jefferson's letter in reply, dated New Year's Day 1802, was noncommittal but, in its phrasing, both careful and pivotal: "Believing with you that religion is a matter which lies solely between Man & his God . . . I contemplate with sovereign reverence that act of the whole American people [the Constitution] which declared that their legislature would 'make no law respecting an establishment of religion, or prohibiting the free exercise thereof,' thus building *a wall of separation* between Church and State" (Dreisbach 1997, 468–69, emphasis added). Jefferson promised no action. Any involvement on his part, as president, would have contradicted the First Amendment. Still more, he fully intended to display no obvious religious observances while in office, unlike his predecessors. His response to the Danbury Baptists, in fact, was revised on the advice of his attorney general, Levi Lincoln, to whom Jefferson had shown the letter and draft of a reply. Among other revisions, the word "eternal" was removed before the epochal "wall of separation" phrase. Jefferson, no doubt, felt there was too much of religion in the word. In any case, over time, through judicial decisions, most of all those by the Supreme Court, the wall would indeed be erected.

For his own part, Thomas Jefferson had no deep loyalty to any particular faith. In the 1760s, when still young, he had apparently subjected many Christian precepts, such as the holy trinity, to analysis and decided they were untrue. Using a razor, he physically cut and pasted together those parts of the New Testament he felt were true to Jesus' actual words. *The Life and Morals of Jesus of Nazareth*, as he titled his creation, makes no mention of angels, miracles, the resurrection, or even Jesus' divinity. It begins with the birth of its hero and ends with his death, deleting all that is supernatural. The book, as Jefferson wrote to John Adams, provides "the most sublime and benevolent code of morals which has ever been offered to man [in] forty-six pages of pure and unsophisticated doctrines" (Jefferson and Randolph 1829, vol. 4, 229).

More than any of the other Founders, Thomas Jefferson is responsible for the secularization of American politics and education. A strong believer in the value of history, he pointed out time and again that organized religion had not led humanity to live righteously but instead, far too often, intolerantly and violently. America would avoid this valley of grim event not by turning away from religion but by making it the very object of liberty.

Acts and Resolutions

The period of the 1790s, leading up to the election of 1800, was a raw and ruthless chapter in the new republic. This was the era of Federalism's ascent and the bitter battles it set loose, involving Jefferson, who, along with Madison (who now switched sides) and Monroe, became a leader of the Republican Party. The grip of battle, moreover, was tightened by conflict with France, which had been seizing American merchant vessels, damaging U.S. trade, and bringing on calls for vengeance. In his farewell address (1796), Washington warned of "The alternate domination of one faction over another, sharpened by the spirit of revenge, natural to party dissension" (Washington 1997, 969). But such prescient words did not find attentive ears.

Early in the decade, when Jefferson was still secretary of state, there were inklings of possible compromise. He had come to see that yeoman farmers could not support the nation. Manufactures and merchants were needed and deserved encouragement. He also recognized the good that Hamilton's plan on public credit had done for the nation. Jefferson, moreover, was no stranger to the idea of free trade, which he derived from his reading of Adam Smith and which he eagerly supported in his own 1793 *Report on Commerce*, where he wrote: "Instead of embarrassing commerce under piles of regulating laws, duties, and prohibitions, could it be relieved from all its shackles . . . the greatest mass possible would then be produced of those things which contribute to human life and human happiness" (Jefferson 1984, 443).

However, within a few brief years, the two men came to be enemies. Their political parties, newly built and belligerent, armed with the calumnies of an often defamatory press, roared and fired at one another like two ships of the line. Through the verbal splinters and smoke one could glimpse a conflict centered on ideas of government power, which Federalists felt should be strong but harnessed, Republicans hobbled and weak. On April 24, 1796, Jefferson wrote to his friend Philip Mazzei in Paris, expressing his own anxiety: "In place of that noble love of liberty, & republican government which carried us triumphantly thro' the war, an Anglican monarchical, & aristocratical party has sprung up, whose avowed object is to draw over us the substance . . . of the British government." Jefferson felt himself surrounded by "timid men who prefer the calm of despotism to the boisterous sea of liberty." But there was a sense of betrayal as well: "It would give you a fever were I to name to you the apostates who have gone over to these heresies, men who were Samsons in the field & Solomons in the council, but who have had their heads shorn by the harlot England" (Jefferson 1904, vol. 8, 238–41). There can be little doubt who was being invoked.

It was a potent and employable image: Hamilton and the Federalists edging America toward the evils of England's own governmental structure, so lately the enemy of freedom. In turn, Jefferson was vilified in the Federalist press for his support of the French Revolution, which had mutated into the Terror. Unscrupulous editors then exposed an affair that Hamilton had indulged years before and, on the other side, accused

Jefferson of fathering children by Sally Hemings, a slave and his wife's half sister. Jefferson called the election "the revolution of 1800," since it would decide whether the country caved to tyranny or embraced once more the true freedoms of the Revolution. There was great worry among party loyalists of both sides that the election would prove to be the last the United States would ever see, that the country would be ripped apart, disunited for ever after (Larson 2007). All of this anxiety, moreover, was given an even sharper edge by the war fever and paranoia generated by growing French attacks on American shipping.

The peak of hysteria came in 1798 when Congress passed, and President Adams signed, the infamous Alien and Sedition Acts. These raised from five to fourteen years the time required for immigrants to become U.S. citizens. They allowed the president to deport any resident alien deemed "dangerous to . . . peace and safety" or whose native country was at war with America. And they made it an actual crime to publish or say "false, scandalous, and malicious" things about the government. The Republicans foresaw these laws would be used by the Federalist-dominated Congress and administration to entrench themselves and intimidate Republican supporters, and they were right (only Republican editors were arrested, for example). Hamilton himself first balked at the acts, calling them violent and capable of engendering civil war, but ended up supporting them in their final, modified form (Chernow 2005, 715).

Jefferson, outraged, instantly seized upon them as unconstitutional and a Federalist ploy. But to invalidate them, he did something no less beyond the pale. Enlisting Madison's help, he secretly drafted resolutions for the Kentucky and Virginia legislatures declaring that the Constitution was not really the law of the land but instead a "compact" among the states—it merely "constituted a general government for special purposes" (Jefferson 1984, 449). Any powers not strictly given in that compact remained with the states, which were able to pass judgment on, and even *nullify*, federal law. Jefferson even went so far as to provide language for Kentucky to threaten it would secede from the Union, if it felt any congressional law worthy of resistance. Such language, coming from the sitting vice president, could easily have been seen as treason and brought the call for impeachment. That the same man who had authored the Declaration of Independence could be impelled toward actions that, at their limit, were capable of destroying the United States itself gives us some idea about the raw intensity of the historical moment.

Kentucky and Virginia approved these resolutions. Other states, however, did not follow. There was no "second revolution." But the resolutions came to serve as the basis for the states' rights theory of government. Known as the "Principles of '98," they were direct inspiration for debates regarding slavery leading up to secession. Only after the Civil War did the Supreme Court become the final authority for determining the constitutionality of legislation. Jefferson's gambit, "creative" as it was, turned out to be a greater "encroachment of power" than any of the presumed "aristocratical" acts or policies put forward by his nemesis, Hamilton.

What, then, of the Jeffersonian presidency? The vision of an American pastoral, shorn of power, did not last. In his first inaugural address, delivered on March 4, 1801, Jefferson already showed a more seasoned view, as a result of the previous two years' ugliness. He spoke of a need for the nation to come together, "to steer with safety the vessel in which we are all embarked amidst the conflicting elements of a troubled world" (Jefferson 1984, 492). He declared the necessity for "a wise and frugal Government, which shall restrain men from injuring one another, shall leave them otherwise free to regulate their own pursuits of industry and improvement, and shall not take from the mouth of labor the bread it has earned" (1984, 494). He favored:

> [T]he support of the State governments in all their rights, as the most competent administrations for our domestic concerns and the surest bulwarks against antirepublican tendencies; the preservation of the General Government in its whole constitutional vigor, as the sheet anchor of our peace at home and safety abroad; a jealous care of the right of election by the people . . . ; a well disciplined militia, our best reliance in peace and for the first moments of war, till regulars may relieve them; the supremacy of the civil over the military authority; economy in the public expense, that labor may be lightly burthened; the honest payment of our

debts and sacred preservation of the public faith; encouragement of agriculture, and of commerce as its handmaid; . . . freedom of religion; freedom of the press, and freedom of person under the protection of the habeas corpus, and trial by juries impartially selected. (1984, 494–95)

In short: states' rights, low taxes, small public debt, a mixed agricultural-industrial economy, and strict adherence to the Bill of Rights. Such were Jefferson's mature principles for governing. How well did he abide these, once taking the presidential seat?

The record is mixed. Certainly he did act in Jeffersonian ways, repealing certain taxes (e.g., on whiskey) and lowering military spending to reduce the national debt. But very soon he took to making Hamiltonian decisions. He left the Bank of America intact and continued Hamilton's program of moderate tariffs; they were working well. He pursued a war against the Barbary pirates of North Africa and a disastrous embargo against trade with both France and Great Britain, building more ships to patrol the East Coast. He made the Louisiana Purchase for $15 million, doubling the country's size, knowing there was no permit for such an act in the Constitution (he considered an amendment but dropped the idea for lack of time) and that this involved a major expansion of federal powers. He then used public funds to send an expedition, headed by Meriwether Lewis and William Clark, to explore this territory and authorized other such efforts by Zebulon Pike. In 1805, he sought to build on the Louisiana Purchase by offering to buy West Florida (coastal Louisiana, Mississippi, Alabama, Florida panhandle) from Spain.

A strict constructionist early on, Jefferson abandoned this view with time. At seventy-three, in a letter to his friend Samuel Kerchival, dated July 12, 1816, he wrote these striking words:

Some men look at constitutions with sanctimonious reverence, and deem them like the arc of the covenant, too sacred to be touched. They ascribe to the men of the preceding age a wisdom more than human, and suppose what they did to be beyond amendment. I knew that age well; I belonged to it, and labored with it. It deserved well of its country. . . . But I know also, that laws and institutions must go hand in hand with the progress of the human mind. As that becomes more developed . . . as new discoveries are made, new truths disclosed, and manners and opinions change with the change of circumstances, institutions must advance also, and keep pace with the times. We might as well require a man to wear still the coat which fitted him when a boy, as civilized society to remain ever under the regimen of their barbarous ancestors. . . . Let us [therefore] avail ourselves of our reason and experience, to correct the crude essays of our first and unexperienced, although wise, virtuous, and well-meaning councils. (Jefferson and Randolph 1829, vol. 4, 298)

A constitution is a document, says Jefferson, its words written by mortals. If treated like a holy tablet, it becomes funereal, as if engraved on standing marble. "Reason and experience" plead that we adjust our interpretations over time rather than seek the elusive ghosts of "original intent," which were rarely, if ever, clear to the authors themselves.

FORMS OF ORDER: JEFFERSON AND HAMILTON RECONSIDERED

At some point before he died, Thomas Jefferson had a bust of himself placed on one side of the entrance hall at Monticello and a bust of Hamilton on the other. This, he stated, was so they would be opposite "in death as in life." Jefferson's image gives him simple colonial garb, a noble gaze with eyes cast upward, a man of the people yet one who sees further. Hamilton, on the other hand, has a toga across one shoulder and a severe face, harsh with calculation, a close imitation of the famous head of Julius Caesar (now in the Vatican Museum), carved in classical times. That Jefferson had far more friends among aristocrats of the Old World and Hamilton thought Caesar a brutal tyrant was not relevant to marmoreal mythmaking.

Alexander Hamilton was killed in 1804. A year later, Andrew Jackson, a plantation and slaveholding politician from Tennessee and stalwart member of the Republican Party, welcomed Hamilton's killer to

Nashville with great fanfare. Such was the depth of bitterness between the two political parties that, in killing Hamilton, Aaron Burr restored his reputation as a Republican. The following decades were to prove no less cruel to Hamilton's image. With Jefferson's presidency, followed by Madison, Monroe, John Quincy Adams, and then Jackson, Federalism went into terminal decline. Hamilton became a routine symbol of aristocracy. It would not be until the last decades of the nineteenth century that he would be repatriated at a true founder (Knott 2002).

Rivers of ink have flowed into defining the differences and animosities between these two men (e.g., Cunningham 2000; Ferling 2013). Yet what they shared was, in some ways, no less primary. Both understood liberty as an absolute good; freedom from oppression was an absolute requirement for man to discover and develop his natural capabilities. America's own greatness lay in the chance to model this for all humanity. Both men therefore saw power as the problem and control of it the solution. Both felt that the most fundamental cause for worry was human nature—man's innate capability for virtue offset by that for weakness. This had to be dealt with in the very structure of government. Power for Jefferson meant the unending temptation toward tyranny; the more it rested directly with the people, the more dispersed and incapable of concentration and threat. Hamilton, too, saw that power was alluring, needful of perimeters. For him, danger came from too much direct authority given either to the less educated "multitude" or to the self-interested wealthy, whose desire for further gain and influence could work against the liberty of the public. For both men, then, liberty was the goal. But liberty was not enough. People needed education, health, occupations, rule of law, security. Both knew the warning of Aristotle's *Politics*: any people allowed to become poor, wretched, and derelict are no longer free; they lose faith and inevitably lean toward violence. This, too, was human nature—or, in the terms of Locke, the consequence of abandonment. To paraphrase Hamilton in *Manufactures*: liberty without prosperity is merely a word. Wealth was something that Jefferson spoke of in high tones, and poverty he spoke of very little. Hamilton was more a man of the larger world; he knew the deprivations and dependencies that poverty brought. He saw wealth in pragmatic terms. It was worthy only when it accepted a civic responsibility.

Robber barons or billionaire financiers could be no less destructive than demagogues.

There is another basic idea that these men shared. It came mainly from their reading of Greek and Roman thinkers. They both felt that a state is not merely a machine to protect life and property. It is a commonwealth that provides for its citizens so they can be the more decent ("virtuous" was their word) human beings, as well as prosperous ones. Politics and ethics must not be wholly divided. If, as Washington phrased it, virtue is a necessary spring of popular government, such government had to repay virtue by protecting its possibilities.

Hamilton and Jefferson could also be victims to their own principles. In the wake of Shay's Rebellion, which occurred just before the Philadelphia (Constitutional) Convention, Hamilton proposed that to counter any such "excess of democracy" the president and senators should be chosen for life and presidential power extended to appointing all state governors. Such ill-considered proposals shocked a fair number, who remained Hamilton's foes thereafter. As for Jefferson, his response, written in France to Colonel William Smith, was to endorse the rebellion—but not for its causes. "God forbid we should ever be 20 years without such a rebellion," he wrote. "What country can preserve its liberties if the rulers are not warned from time to time that their people preserve the spirit of resistance? . . . What signify a few lives lost . . . ? The tree of liberty must be refreshed from time to time with the blood of patriots & tyrants. It is its natural manure" (Jefferson and Randolph 1829, vol. 2, 268). It was naïve and callous.

The American "experiment," then, began under enormous tension from within. Victory over Britain did not bring peace. Revolutions in America and France proved beyond all doubt that new governments, even societies, could be formed on the basis of ideas. But this meant less security, not more. In Europe, it meant reaction and soon oppression, as elites responded in reactionary fashion to what happened in France, but it also meant philosophical longings for utopia. This did not happen in America—neither Jefferson nor Hamilton ever believed in the type of transformation that Marxist thought came to proclaim. Each man held a vision of America as a beacon in history, not a system that would grind paradise out of it.

Hamilton saw a future world power, adapting the best aspects of the British system (the most successful in Europe) to a democratic context. Its government and credit system would be centralized and run by a "natural aristocracy" of the best-educated and civic-minded individuals. Its judiciary and, to some extent, its executive would be insulated from the shifting passions of the popular will, and its Constitution would need to be interpreted, even a bit loosely, over time, as the nation matured and unforeseen circumstances arose. Still, America's unparalleled freedoms would magnetize the ambitious and enterprising, drawing the talented from unfree nations around the world to its teeming cities, vibrant agricultural sector, and most productive and efficient industries, all aided by the most advanced science and technology. Its government helps nurture all of this, providing legislative and financial support for new ideas, research, and inventions. Hamiltonian America is a big-government America, with powers directed to increase wealth, knowledge, and military capability. It uses tariffs moderately to help selected industries in their beginning stages only. Its economy generates high-quality goods for global export, and its trade relations extend to every corner of the globe (Eckes 1995). It is a superior power whom none would attack without grave consequence. Yet this America does not abandon its poor, disabled, or needy, for to do so would create a class of the wretched, a sign of national failure.

A Jeffersonian America would be a different place. If we hold to the ideas of the pre-presidential Jefferson, we can say that he favors a more small-town realm, filled with self-reliant planters, merchants, artisans, and manufacturers. Nearly all would own land; the country would be broad and wide and fertile. Instead of large-scale industries that utilized vast amounts of raw materials to make the goods needed by a highly advanced nation, Jeffersonian manufacturers would focus on lighter products needed in the agricultural, residential, and commercial sectors. Some big cities would exist, but millions of family farms, ranches, and plantations (no slaves) would be spread across the states, providing essentials for all and a surplus for export to many parts of the world. Political power would be focused at the state level; the federal government would use taxation mainly to support a reasonable military defense and to pay any national debts and for interstate infrastructure. Congress and the executive branches would be the servants of the popular will, and the Constitution would be treated as the strict and final word on legislative and legal matters, except perhaps in certain emergency situations. State militias would continue, and the citizenry could be armed, though not to excess. A peaceful nation, the United States would have a minimal but well-trained foreign service, its major overseas relations being the bustle of trade. Not a global power, America would hold itself a model of self-sufficiency.

America Revisited: A Brief History of Jeffersonian versus Hamiltonian Democracy

The past two centuries testify that the United States has largely remained a territory governed by the ideas of these two men. The struggle between Jeffersonian and Hamiltonian views on freedom, power, government, and economic destiny remains as fresh today as in the years following the Revolution and has lost none of its intensity. Anxiety that the nation was imperiled, torn in pieces, and unavailable to compromise was no less apparent in the election of 1800 than in that of 2008, when a black man ran for president and won.

Between those two dates, the conflict over which vision of American democracy would prevail never ceased. Victory, if we can call it that, changed hands more than once but was never settled. If we were to simplify this history in a few lines, we would have to start by observing that Hamilton's ideas, translated for later times, helped build most of the modern institutions and institutional systems of America, from industrial capitalism to the military. Hamiltonian capitalism for much of the late 1800s and nearly all of the 1900s was urged by Republicans and Democrats alike. It was encouraged by business interests who argued for federal protections, by progressives demanding laws and regulations to protect workers, by corporations and railroads who wanted grants of government land, by a defense establishment that grew into a global force, and by many millions of citizens, who have looked to government for help in hard times. Hamiltonian policies used federal and state funds to erect infrastructure—roads, canals, bridges, harbors, highways, airports, all vital to the U.S. economy and, as Hamilton foresaw, a means for binding the Union together. It was part of Hamilton's vision to also make government a main support of science and technology, a system often said to be inspired by Germany's example but in fact directly mentioned in *Report on the Subject of Manufactures*.

Jeffersonians tend to bemoan this history. Up to the Civil War, they stood in clear triumph while the country remained primarily rural in fact and mind. Federalism died a summary death under Jefferson's own presidency, and "Hamilton" became, for a good many, a foul word ("monarchist") associated with aristocracy and privilege. Andrew Jackson did a great deal to further this trend, though, as historians will readily attest, he grew the scale of government considerably and put his own people in favored positions. He also killed the National Bank, one of the most successful Hamiltonian institutions. During this era, Jeffersonian ideas were broadly embraced and especially seeped into the South, where they were used to defend states' rights and the "special" economy of slavery. Slavery was the source of Jackson's own wealth—his plantation near Nashville, the Hermitage, produced cotton as a cash crop— and remained closely tied to the issue of states' rights. Such was proven by the Missouri Compromise of 1820, prohibiting slavery in much of the Louisiana Territory, except for the proposed (and accepted) state of Missouri. The Kansas-Nebraska Act of 1854 followed suit by allowing popular vote in each territory to determine slavery's legality. Local sovereignty, a strong Jeffersonian element, continued as a guiding idea for large parts of the United States well after the Civil War. The relationship to slavery made it especially durable in the South, where it came to be woven together with religious conservatism, a most un-Jeffersonian factor.

But in national terms, this ideal of local autonomy, as a resistance and trump to federal authority, turned out to be doomed. It was, of course, rejected by the Constitutional Convention of 1787. It was rendered moribund by industrialization, which opened the American economy to foreign trade and the outside world. And it was denied yet again by the Civil War and Thirteenth, Fourteenth, and Fifteenth amendments. These new parts of the Constitution outlawed slavery, taking away a kind of ultimate power from the states to discriminate among the rights of citizens. Here Jefferson would likely have applauded yet also trembled at the sight of government using the means of war to impose its will on states, including his own Virginia. To a significant degree, the Civil War exposed the ultimate flaws and limitations of Jeffersonian concepts. To hold the Union together, Abraham Lincoln had to resort to a vast, if troubled, extension of central government power, including a new wartime bureaucracy, a draft, an unconstitutional income tax, and a temporary halt to some constitutional liberties. Lincoln, in fact, set a pattern by appealing to Jeffersonian sentiments about all things rising from "the people"—embraced by the Gettysburg Address ("government of the people, by the people, for the people")—while following Hamiltonian principles. Ultimately the result was an expansion of liberty for millions of blacks, something that both Jefferson and Hamilton would have welcomed but which those who carried on in the name of states' rights and Southern exceptionalism would fight intensely for a full century more (Marx 1998).

By 1880, the U.S. population stood at fifty-two million, larger than any European state except Russia. A mere three decades later, owing to high birthrates, improved public health, and massive immigration, it was nearly twice this figure. Sheer size and complexity, both of society and economy, along with the growing civil disorder and violence that industrialism had wrought among workers and the brutal response from companies, demanded an enlargement of federal involvement. The Gilded Age brought back Hamilton as its own heroic symbol, mostly for the wrong reasons. Essays and books about him multiplied, claiming his prescience about the need for an aristocratic class of wealthy capitalists and attributing to him, falsely, a dinner party remark about the common people being "a great beast" (Knott 2002, 73–74). Such misuse did more than a little to damn Hamilton's reputation for much of the twentieth century, even as his ideas continued to dominate.

The ideals of Progressivism made much use of Hamiltonian views, seeking to employ government power toward reducing inequalities and advancing equal rights (including those for women and blacks) over and beyond state laws. This included the Sixteenth Amendment, creating the federal income tax, and the Nineteenth Amendment, granting women the vote. There also came federal statutes against child labor and corporate monopolies. Jeffersonian conservatives who held to local sovereignty and the business elite who favored laissez-faire opposed every such change. Others who favored "strict constructionism," which Jefferson himself had discarded, also argued that such laws went beyond the limited powers allowed by the Constitution (Moreno 2013).

Such hostility to change Hamilton would have gladly mocked for its ignorance of what America had become. By the end of World War I, the United States had been transformed into a colossus on the world stage. It was now, beyond all denial, a massively industrialized, urbanized state, immensely wealthy, enormous in size, and replete with ethnic diversity and a host of social problems growth had delivered. Even without Progressivism, a global power on this scale could hardly operate under policies of pastoral libertarianism. There was the need to carry out the enlarged work of diplomacy, foreign policy, and military readiness, to monitor the national economy and federal budget, to deal with violence and degradation among the working class, to reduce the threats of political and corporate corruption, to explore and manage the expanded lands now under federal purview, to evaluate their natural resources, and more.

Major financial panics in 1893 and 1907 showed the vulnerability of America's complex economic system. But they also underlined the ability of a central power to moderate and end such a crisis. By 1913, Hamilton's idea of a national bank had been resurrected as the Federal Reserve. There was the necessity to protect the public welfare—to reduce unsafe working conditions, improve the state of sanitation and public health, eliminate unequal education, and battle interstate crime. It was a new America, in other words, whose major challenges had become hugely complex, dispersed, and diverse. If Hamilton would have been disturbed by the advent and influence of mass society, Jefferson would have found the hand of government grown huge and heavy.

The federal government grew far larger, however, in the 1930s when the U.S. government was faced with the Great Depression. This brought an unmatched crisis in liberal capitalism as well as real doubts about the future of democracy itself. Many millions calling for help and businesses of every kind failing badly made a hands-off, Jeffersonian policy simply impossible. Through many projects to advance public works, the U.S. government put a great many people to work and sought to protect the public in general from penury (and the "wretchedness" that Aristotle warned of) by providing a social safety net that included Social Security. But Franklin Roosevelt's Hamiltonian New Deal brought complexities of its own. Without a true coherent plan, it tried new things almost every year, some good, some damaging. A most un-Hamiltonian move was to let thousands of banks go under, causing a secondary crisis in credit, hurting business in general. Still, assistance flowed into all regions of the country, not least the South, where FDR built a large number of military bases, with federal defense plants and related industries nearby (thus making much of the South "democratic" and much of U.S. military culture "southern"). Southern power in Congress gave FDR what he wanted until segregation and race came into the mix. Any part of the New Deal that sought a change to the rule of Jim Crow met with a wall of resistance. Both the New Deal and Harry Truman's Fair Deal of the immediate post–World War II period fell back before this immovable object (Katznelson 2013). Jefferson's principle of state sovereignty, firmly entrenched in "the Southern way of life," stood fast, partly as a cover for racism.

Yet FDR achieved something that both Hamilton and Jefferson would have admired. By force of personality and leadership, Roosevelt drew the confidence and loyalty of the greatest number of Americans. Hope and a return of faith in liberal democracy were the result. No man or woman of the Revolutionary generation, particularly had they lived through the election of 1800, would ever question the value of such an achievement. Part of FDR's appeal, in fact, resided in following Lincoln's example. In the midst of pursuing Hamiltonian policies, Roosevelt adopted Thomas Jefferson as icon of the Democratic Party, commissioning the building of the Jefferson Memorial, placing Jefferson's face on the popular nickel, even using the life story of the Sage of Monticello for a mural in the Library of Congress. It was FDR's "magic" (or cunning) that he found a way to bring Hamilton and Jefferson together.

Few Americans have ever openly, proudly, labeled themselves Hamiltonians. The irony, at one level, is stunning: while Jefferson was born to gentility and privilege, Hamilton personified the highest prescriptions of the "self-made individual." No other founder began at such a low level, as an illegitimate child with no prospects and no country. No other statesman, of that era or any other, has so embodied the possibility of rising above "one's station at birth." That such an unfortunate could one day be instrumental to the very conception and launch of the United States is an immense fact, too often ignored. And contrary to what Jeffersonians feared, Hamiltonian capitalism did not enfeeble democracy and strengthen tyranny. The twentieth century was far more democratic in the United States than the nineteenth, and the twenty-first century carries this forward. Not only did women and racial minorities gain the full rights of citizenship, but many other freedoms were granted (e.g., the right of assembly for striking workers), and new ones were discovered, legislating nondiscrimination on the basis of age, race, gender, or sexual preference. Those who have sided strongly with Jefferson's small-government idea and his early libertarian impulses have typically opposed all of these efforts to make American democracy more inclusive. It is not easy to believe—when we recall Jefferson, the man of deep learning and reflection, author of the Declaration of Independence, and one who ascended to presidential heights—that he would have sided with those who rejected such efforts.

In other words, neither Hamiltonianism nor Jeffersonianism was ever a pure vision built of fixed and final policies. What they had in common was a faith in Enlightenment principles of liberty, democracy, and rationality. They understood the value and power of compromise as long as these core values were upheld. The Jeffersonian vision, representing his earlier thought, wanted to preserve the localism that existed before the Revolution. The realities of his own presidency, however, forced Jefferson to leave much of this among the intellectual toys of his youth. During his time in office, he abjured by many decisions his comment twenty years earlier about watering the "tree of liberty" with the blood of domestic rebellions. In his final State of the Union Address on November 8, 1808, he spoke not of creeping tyranny within the halls of government but of "the extraordinary character of the times in which we live," where "our attention should unremittingly be fixed on the safety of our country," which required a stronger army and assertive government (Jefferson 1984, 547; Crackel 1989).

Throughout the nineteenth century the example set by America, which remained more democratic than any other state despite its many imperfections, was watched in Europe. The French observer Alexis de Tocqueville toured the United States in the 1830s and concluded that it would be best for France, and Europe as a whole, if they adapted themselves to the "coming of democracy," just as the Americans had done. Always an acute interpreter of the scene before him, Tocqueville saw the American Revolution not as an eight-year war but as an evolving process of political, legal, social, and intellectual development far from complete in his own day. He saw the infusion of democratic impulses and the hesitant growth of democratic institutions—from the idea of liberty and beginnings of suffrage to a more assertive and critical press—as the signs of an inevitable change, one that would alter the nature of the world (De Tocqueville 2004). His words, near the end of *Democracy in America*, are striking in this regard:

> The world that is on the rise remains half buried beneath the debris of the world that is in collapse, and in the vast confusion of human affairs no one can say what will remain of old institutions and ancient mores. . . . Although the ongoing revolution in man's social state, laws, ideas, and sentiments is still far from over, it is already clear that its works cannot be compared with anything the world has ever seen before. Looking back century by century to remotest Antiquity, I see nothing that resembles what I see before me. (De Tocqueville 2004, 831)

The influence of the American example grew through the rest of the nineteenth century, in a mixed way to be sure, but with a gathering certainty. True, the United States itself did not intrude on the global imagination very much. It remained a distant domain until the end of the 1800s, when its industrial and economic power became impossible to ignore. From that point on, however, it increasingly became a model for those throughout the world who were drawn to Enlightenment principles of individual and collective freedom and who saw America, despite its many flaws and conflicts, as the best and most prosperous embodiment of those principles. With the rise of fascism and totalitarian communism after World War I, this perception faced some major challenges. Yet these did not last; the United States emerged from World

War II as something approaching a global savior of freedom. Presidents Truman, Eisenhower, and Kennedy all held up the American democratic example in terms that readily recall Jefferson's prediction that the country would stand as a "beacon of liberty." But this did not endure either, as we know. By the early decades of the twenty-first century, the beacon had dimmed as a result of both policies pursued abroad and a broader questioning of Enlightenment liberalism in much of the world. At home, too, the struggle between Jeffersonian and Hamiltonian ideas in the new century had become by 2010 more bitter and obdurate than perhaps at any time since the Civil War.

The Late Twentieth and Early Twenty-First Centuries: The Debate Continues

From the beginning, even in their most recalcitrant moments, Jefferson and Hamilton shared core ideas about what the United States should most embody. Individual freedom, equality under the law, religious tolerance, popular sovereignty, and separation of powers: such were foremost among these ideas. Where these two men parted company was in their more precise interpretations and the policies they promoted for putting such ideas into practice. Certainly there was some important overlap here, too. Neither man believed the Constitution to be a holy, immortal document; both of them, as true intellectuals, knew future history would demand changes to it. Regarding slavery, despite his unfortunate silence on the matter as president, Jefferson was never so deluded as to think that the United States could long continue with millions in bondage. That a terrible civil war would have to come to end this, with basic rights still functionally denied to blacks for a full century thereafter, would have bowed the heads of both men in shame. Beyond any doubt, they would also find disturbing, in more recent times, the expanded force of fundamentalist religion in political circles (a topic we will treat in chapter 6) and would be nothing less than appalled at the denial of large parts of modern science among elected officials.

But these kinds of agreement between Jefferson and Hamilton, important as they are, would never be enough to calm the intensity of their deep disagreements. And it is much more these quarrels, which also have their philosophical basis, that remain at the center of American political culture in the new century.

It does have to be said that both men's ideas have often been misrepresented and the basis of their disagreements and shared values misunderstood. We would be better-off if we could appreciate these and conducted our political arguments along such lines instead of veering off into absolutes neither would have found acceptable.

We are left, in the end, with the understanding that while there can be strong agreement between Jeffersonian and Hamiltonian ideas, there can be only a very partial synthesis. In truth, these ideas represent two overlapping yet also conflicting dimensions of the Enlightenment concept of freedom. The division was perhaps best articulated by one of the twentieth century's greatest liberal philosophers, Isaiah Berlin, in a famous essay, "Two Concepts of liberty" (Berlin 2002a). Adopting his definitions, we can say that Jefferson's view approximates Berlin's notion of "negative liberty," meaning the absence of external constraints and barriers on one's actions, thus a weak state that allows for maximum individual freedom. Hamilton, on the other hand, would side more with Berlin's "positive liberty," referring to the existence of some controls, within which one attempts to be self-directed, therefore a stronger state requiring some freedoms to be limited in order to allow greater freedom for all.

The persistence of Enlightenment ideals in both their more balanced Jeffersonian and Hamiltonian forms has saved America many times from full-scale regression and probably will again. Neither set of ideas can do without the other. It remains among America's most potent traditions, not without its important self-deceptions, to speak the ideals of Jefferson while living in the land of Hamilton.

Finally, we should consider one last time the bitterness leading up to and including the election of 1800. This was the primal clash of Jeffersonian and Hamiltonian philosophies, each viewing the other as a form of odium and a threat to the country's survival. Partisan warfare does not begin to describe the shudder of the historical moment. It tore apart the Revolutionary generation, those who had secured the country's existence and freedom from England. It ripped Madison away from

Hamilton, with whom he had authored *The Federalist*, and pushed him into Jefferson's camp. Jefferson had ceased to communicate with Washington, whose funeral he did not attend. Adams was not invited to Jefferson's inauguration. There were fights on the floor of the House of Representatives, and within a few brief years the sitting vice president, Aaron Burr, killed former secretary of the treasury Hamilton in a duel. Talk even reached the stage of proposing the country be split in half, one part to each political party.

Once the drawn-out election of 1800 was settled, both sides accepted the result. Bitterness continued, beyond any doubt; its acids burned the halls of Congress. But the transfer of power took place. Hamilton's Federalists lost to Jefferson's Republicans and would never rise again, though their ideas would come to rule the country for most of its history.

The political split of the early 2000s in the United States has not reached quite such a point, at least not yet, much less to the hatreds of the 1850s that led to the Civil War. But it is more than a bit ironic, and a testimony to the lasting power of their ideas, that the deep divisions in the United States today are along lines very similar to those that turned Hamilton and Jefferson into bitter enemies more than two centuries ago. It seems reasonable to hope that the outcome will similarly end by a retreat to intelligent compromise, such as the one that caused Hamilton to ultimately endorse Jefferson as president and refuse to take part in any secessionist movement.

Thomas Jefferson and Alexander Hamilton and the anxiety-laden struggles between them will not depart from the American political stage. Such is worth keeping in mind, since, as scholars like Merrill Peterson (1975) and Stephen Knott (2002) amply prove, many versions of "Jefferson" and "Hamilton" have been brought back from the grave over the past two centuries, dressed up and propped up to speak in epigrams that favor a host of both probable and improbable positions. Over time, we can see that it is the tension between the ideas each man introduced, the needed compromises and the vigorous balance these ideas have required to coexist, that has most granted the United States its long-term dynamism and its commitment, however troubled and sometimes stalled, to the hopes that both men shared.

PART II

SECULAR AND RELIGIOUS REACTIONS AGAINST ENLIGHTENMENT

CHAPTER 5

Counter-Enlightenment

From Antimodernism to Fascism

> War alone brings up to their highest tension all human energies and imposes the stamp of nobility upon the peoples who have the courage to make it.
>
> BENITO MUSSOLINI, "THE POLITICAL AND SOCIAL DOCTRINE OF FASCISM"

> The racial similarity of the German people in process of unification is, therefore, the indispensable precondition and foundation for the concept of political leadership of the German people. . . . Without the principle of the similarity of kind the National Socialist [Nazi] State could not exist. It would at once be handed back with all its institutions to its liberal and Marxist enemies . . . the new German law [must be] fully conscious of the force with which this concept of similarity of racial stock penetrates all systematic judicial considerations.
>
> CARL SCHMITT, *STAAT, BEWEGUNG, VOLK*

All of the major intellectuals we have looked at thus far were products of the Enlightenment or, as the French called it, *le siècle des lumières* (the century of lights), a celebratory phrase that suggested much lay in darkness before the advances of the later seventeenth century and the advent of truly rational, scientific investigations of the world. An inclusive dating of the Enlightenment would run from about the 1650s to the early nineteenth century, though more narrowly this "century" would be mostly the eighteenth. The phrase implies a future in which progressively brighter possibilities are revealed for human society, leading perhaps toward a form of near utopia. Obviously this did not happen. Indeed, the twentieth century brought something very close to the dark opposite, the near destruction of civilization itself.

We need to explain how and why this happened. What concepts and visions worked so forcefully, destructively, against Enlightenment ideas? Were there aspects of the Enlightenment itself, as many have said, that were actually antithetical to its liberal principles? What forms of antimodernism can we point to as most significant and powerful? Do any of them continue to find loyalists today?

To answer these and other relevant questions, we use the term "Counter-Enlightenment" and define it to include a set of reactionary responses that can be identified and traced. Some of these began in the eighteenth century itself, gaining further traction from the excesses of the French Revolution and Napoleonic Wars. They matured in the 1800s and eventually emerged in the twentieth century as full-fledged, violent hostility to individual freedom and other core tenets of a century of Enlightenment.

Indeed, it is just here, in the social and political realm, where the Enlightenment has faced its greatest, unflagging resistance in the West. A critical point: such resistance has not come predominantly from the irrational fears and thoughtless anger of the less educated masses. On the contrary, it has been the province of intellectuals who have formulated ideas able to be popularized and used by reactionary political elites. Immanuel Kant's hope that self-reliance in the realm of reason would strengthen Enlightenment everywhere remains as distant as ever.

The Birth of Modern Reactionary Politics

The Enlightenment in Europe faced opposition from the very beginning. That this would happen was clearly shown by the Catholic Church's rejection of the new science early on. The often-told story of Galileo Galilei (1564–1642) can serve as a reminder. His condemnation by the Church in 1633 for insisting that the Earth turned round the Sun was part of a very broad attempt to conserve the Church's authority. It was not merely a question of whether the Bible said the Earth is immovable at the center of the solar system. It did so indirectly in the Book of Joshua, when the Sun is made to stand still to prolong the day, but for those who wrote the Bible, that the Sun turned around the Earth was so widely believed that it did not have to be explicitly stated. More important, the Earth as the home to humanity had to be placed at the center of the universe because this directly revealed how mortal man lay at the core of God's plan. By publicly supporting the Copernican view of the solar system, Galileo was challenging far more than celestial arrangements. His became a test case for how far the authority of the Church could be challenged. That the Florentine astronomer deliberately provoked the Church in order to force the issue hardly helped his position (Wootton 2010). But Galileo's astronomical observations, using one of the earliest telescopes, altered our perception of the universe. Suddenly the Moon became a rocky world with features like Earth; Jupiter was shown to be orbited by four tiny dots of light, moons of its own; and the number of stars expanded immensely, suggesting the universe was far vaster than previously imagined. It was too much for some to absorb. The great seventeenth-century French mathematician and philosopher Blaise Pascal wrote in reaction to the new discoveries, "The eternal silence of infinite space frightens me" (Shapin 1996, 28).

Even at this early stage, science was not the only domain brought under suspicion and resistance. The Jewish community in the Netherlands excommunicated Baruch Spinoza (1632–77) on similar grounds that he questioned the divine authority of sacred texts. Spinoza's sin was not merely to take the rejection of dogmatism further than his predecessors, asking that human beings be viewed for what they were, not in an idealized religious way. He also initiated modern biblical scholarship by analyzing Scripture as a human-authored document. In his lifetime, he was reviled by religious Protestants and Jews as well as by the Catholic Church. Had he not been in the relatively tolerant Netherlands it is likely he would have paid for this very dearly, but he was actually able to continue to work as a lens grinder and write his books unmolested until he died. His influential books, according to Jonathan Israel, laid the foundation for the Enlightenment, and whether or not one agrees (some others point to René Descartes as the single most important original Enlightenment thinker), there is no doubt that Spinoza's influence was crucial (Israel 2001, 159–74; Lasker and Steinberg in Melamed and Rosenthal 2010, 68–71, 220–21).

Suppressing the voices of dissent, often brutally, has been a common response from autocratic authorities, not least religious ones, up to the present. Yet such voices have triumphed in more than a few cases, particularly in the modern era. How and why liberal Enlightenment thinking gradually won the day in western Europe is a complex story unto itself and has much to do with the entire rise of Western economies and power (McNeill 1963; Mokyr 2010). Our point here is that by the late eighteenth century, this realm of thought had been not only accepted but actively advanced by many of the intellectual centers in the West. We see this in the two great radical events that transformed world politics, the American and French revolutions. It was the latter, however, that shook the ground of Europe, igniting a response that would grow into a modern reactionary strain of thought, rejecting everything the Enlightenment philosophers stood for, leading eventually to catastrophic political outcomes in the twentieth century. And it is this determined hostility that survives to this day as a powerful base of resistance to Enlightenment liberalism.

In America, the Revolution that ended in 1783 solidified beliefs opposed to inherited privilege and favoring property rights but also accepted freedom of the press, protection of individual rights, and religious freedom. All these and the system of government instituted by the Americans were much inspired by the Enlightenment. Freedom of religion came from the perception, already expressed in Britain, that tolerance was the only way to avoid wars of religion such as those that had so troubled Europe in the sixteenth and seventeenth centuries. The new United States, however, went further even than John Locke by not excluding Catholics, whom the British still considered fundamentally disloyal to their nation. The new country did not recognize inherited privilege in the form of hereditary nobility, but if wealth rested on accumulated property, it was guaranteed. Because the American colonies already had a highly commercialized economy, defending property rights, as Locke and Adam Smith had said governments must do, was not at all difficult.

The American Revolution took place in what amounted to a unique society at the time. Not only did it already practice self-government, based on English law and tradition, but it lacked a true aristocracy.

Building a more democratic, liberal, and tolerant order was far easier here, in this distant frontier, than in Europe. As we saw in the previous chapter on the founding of the United States, the new country's leaders were very much inspired by the Enlightenment and disagreed more about how to implement it than on its essence.

Slavery, however, was accepted as a required condition for the founding of the United States; without this, none of the southern states would have joined the Union. The Founding Fathers hoped that the practice would decline and disappear with time. As this did not happen, the violent contradiction between Enlightenment liberalism and an ingrained culture of slavery finally led, eight decades later, to a devastatingly bloody civil war. Yet even that failed to solve the problem of racism that has troubled the United States ever since (Hartz 1955; Marx 1998). It is a contradiction as profound as any conceivable in a democracy. Later other violations of the more liberal and humane values of the Enlightenment would produce still more contradictions leading to lasting problems in the modern world.

Because the American Revolution did not produce a great social transformation but rather a political one, some historians, particularly Marxist ones, have denied it was a "real" revolution. The events in France that began in 1789 were an entirely different matter (Hobsbawm 1962).

Enlightenment intellectuals in Europe generally welcomed the American Revolution and, at first, the French Revolution, too. A warning, however, came from the socially conservative Anglo-Irishman Edmund Burke. Where he saw that the American wish for better treatment from Britain had merit, he perceived at an early stage that the French Revolution was going too far, in a wrong direction, and would lead to disaster. The Americans, he wrote, wanted to preserve freedoms they had enjoyed for many decades, through the "salutary neglect" of the home country. France, on the other hand, had suddenly thrown away every social and political institution and tradition on which the very nation and its stability had been based. Burke's *Reflections on the Revolution in France* (1790) appeared barely more than a year after events had begun. Louis XVI was still king (with his head on), the Reign of Terror and its murderous excesses had not occurred, and there was still hope that democracy would prevail. Yet Burke foresaw the troubles to come. Using abstract Enlightenment philosophy to create a wholly new social order, he said, while eliminating "the principle of reverence to antiquity" would necessarily degenerate into chaos and violence. Speaking in favor of respect for tradition and against all drastic revolutionary change, Burke wrote, "When ancient opinion and rules of life are taken away, the loss cannot possibly be estimated." And in reaction to the French Revolution's turn against religion, he wrote:

> We know, and it is our pride to know, that man is by his constitution a religious animal; that atheism is against, not only our reason but our instincts. . . . But if, in the moment of riot, and in a drunken delirium from the hot spirit drawn out of the alembrick of hell, which in France is now so furiously boiling, we should uncover our nakedness by throwing off that Christian religion which has hitherto been our boast and comfort, and one great source of civilization amongst us . . . we are apprehensive . . . that some uncouth, pernicious, and degrading superstition, might take the place of it. (1790, selection in Muller 1997, 105, 108)

What seems striking here is not merely Burke's desire for stability and use of tradition but the fear of what could happen if these were rejected in favor of man-made, supposedly rational but really dangerous and unworkable changes. Burke wanted to warn Britain not to follow the French example: "I would not exclude alteration neither, but even when I changed, it should be to preserve . . . I should follow the example of our ancestors . . . standing on the firm ground of the British constitution" (1790, in Muller 1997, 122).

Edmund Burke was proved prescient about the extremism of France's headlong attempt to abandon the past and all clear authority. Within two years, the revolution fell into the hands of the extremist Jacobins led by Robespierre. The king and his family were arrested, and the nobility and Catholic Church summarily dismantled. Resistance broke out in various parts of the country, and twenty thousand executions of "enemies of the Revolution" were accompanied by well over one hundred thousand deaths in the ensuing civil war. France, that is, provided the first modern attempt to use political theory as a means for imposing a totalitarian system and doing so in a sudden, revolutionary manner. For most of Europe, it was no less the physical slaughter than the shocking thought of such a plunge into the abyss, with its drive to destroy the very fabric of existing social order, that caused fear and rage.

It was not surprising, then, that the French Revolution had a massive impact on Europe's response to Enlightenment ideas. After Burke's worst fears had come true, the attacks against the Revolution and its principles took on a different tone. The most influential early reaction by intellectuals naturally came from France itself. Criticism did not merely call for a return to moderation but demanded a restoration of the old order, including the power of the Catholic Church and the repressive institutions of absolute monarchy. Liberalism as a whole was utterly rejected by the leading critics of the Revolution, not just its extreme version but in its very essence.

The most illustrious, imaginative, and eloquent of the reactionary intellectuals was Joseph de Maistre (1753–1821). Like Burke, whose elegant discourse he echoed, de Maistre stated that it was impossible to create a rational constitution as a political guide to change. "A constitution is a divine work . . . that cannot be written," he said. By this he meant that God, monarchy, and tradition all echoed one another, providing the only true basis for a social order. French liberal thinkers, the philosophes, who believed society could be remade on the basis of rationally conceived laws and rules, deserved scorn: "Promises, engagements, and oaths are mere words; it is as easy to break these weak links as to forge them. Without the dogma of a law-giving God, all moral obligations are chimerical" (1814, selection in Muller 1997, 136–37). The idea that society is made up of logical, self-directed individuals, able to decide how they would be ruled and by whom, was a pernicious fiction. Instead, people are imbedded in a web of order and authority stemming from cultural traditions backed by obedience to the authority of religion. The philosophes committed a terrible crime with their deification of reason, dissolving the real foundations of civilized society and releasing a godless chaos that inevitably led to a reign of terror. De Maistre's insistence on divinely legitimized monarchy and its right to use force to support a moral code were welcomed by those who saw the horrors of the French Revolution as the logical result of the Enlightenment rather than just an unfortunate divergence from its otherwise worthy liberal principles.

De Maistre did not stop here. He went so far as to consider the Terror a form of divine retribution. He also understood the Enlightenment well enough to realize he needed to attack science and reason because these were at the heart of political and social liberalism. Science did not have the only key to truth, and it lacked ethical content. Paraphrasing de Maistre, Stephen Holmes wrote that for him, "Science hardens man and desiccates his heart. Scientists make bad citizens and worthless statesmen" (1993, 23). Reason, meanwhile, was itself morally empty and could lead the individual to put his own judgment in place of accumulated wisdom and guidance from God. Science could not be accepted as a replacement for the Bible and its versions of the world, since it eliminated God's role and His lessons to humankind. Indeed, scientific discoveries ought to be kept from the general public, as they were inherently pernicious. (We will see in later chapters how closely this resembles some of the most antiliberal Christian and Muslim views in our own times.)

Much of what de Maistre believed became fundamental for conservative intellectuals in Europe and to some extent even in America thereafter. His works were widely read during the nineteenth century, and his ideas were selectively incorporated by a great many who rejected Enlightenment liberalism. Liberals, he claimed, are naïve in believing that humans can be rational and self-disciplined enough to govern themselves and to assume that without coercive morality they can behave properly. They are wrong to think that people have rights independent of their traditionally governed societies. And they invite evil by repudiating established and long-revered religious dogma (Holmes 1993, 25–36).

In France, however, the restoration of absolute monarchy after Napoleon's fall in 1815 did not take hold. In 1830, the last of Louis XVI's brothers, Charles X, a confirmed reactionary, was overthrown. At that time, the intellectual hero of French liberalism, Benjamin Constant (1767–1830), was lionized for steadfastly maintaining in his many publications that the original impulse of the Revolution had been correct and that the Terror had been neither necessary nor inevitable but instead a deviation from the principles of freedom and individual rights (Manent 1995, 84–92; Rosenblatt 2009, 351–58). Applauded as he was, however, Constant did not carry the day. Rather, what happened was a very restricted, timid opening toward democracy, followed by another revolution in 1848 that ended in 1852 with a new Napoleonic dictatorship. Constant's branch of liberalism would not emerge as an official set of ideas in France again until the Third Republic in the latter part of the nineteenth century, after the traumatic defeat of Napoleon III by Prussia in 1870 and the bloody radicalism of the Paris Commune. Even then, French liberalism remained contested, both by conservative forces on the one hand and by more radically leftist ones on the other, a situation that lived on until the second half of the twentieth century (Agulhon 1990).

The march toward greater individual freedom, of the sort that Kant had wished for and Constant had advocated, was anything but assured as a politically reactionary form of conservatism dominated Europe for decades after the fall of Napoleon I in 1815. But liberal resistance to this state of affairs also expanded. Aided by the Industrial Revolution and the writings of those like Constant, reactionary politics ultimately collapsed in the 1848 revolutionary uprisings that swept across the Continent. What emerged, however, fell far short of hopes for a new Europe. Only in Great Britain and ultimately the United States did Enlightenment liberalism largely (though not entirely) prevail.

The most influential liberal thinker in nineteenth-century Britain was John Stuart Mill (1806–73). An uncompromising defender of individual rights and freedom of thought, Mill expanded the Enlightenment conception of liberty while taking into account many of the complexities raised by industrialization and the vast social changes that had occurred since 1800. In his best-known essay, "On Liberty," he defended the need for arguing against any received idea in order to test its value: "Complete liberty of contradicting and disproving our opinion is the very condition which justifies us in assuming its truth for purposes of action; and on no other terms can a being with human faculties have any rational assurance of being right" (Mill 1956, 24). This repeated Kant's call to independent thinking and rejection of dogma.

Mill was a key influence. He advocated for expanded democracy, for the emancipation of women, and for greater social consciousness and intervention to help those in need. He defended the Irish peasants, whose poverty he ascribed to British misrule, and toward the end of his life he wrote against the injustices of colonial brutality. Mill was a most genuine example of the liberal reformer in all areas except one. He never entirely condemned colonial rule, stating instead that it should be more just, less corrupt, and aimed at raising the "less civilized" to a higher state. The Irish, in short, were accorded a level of respect wholly denied colonials, particularly in India. Liberalism, in short, was at this time still bound to the imperialism being imposed by the "superior" European races and cultures. It is significant that Mill's "On Liberty" appeared in the same year as Darwin's *Origin of Species*, which, mostly unintentionally, solidified the notion of racial hierarchies.

Here we must turn to the issue of slavery in the United States. The British outlawed this institution in 1833 and the French briefly during the French Revolution, only to have it brought back by Napoleon, but then again, and definitively, in 1849. Though increasingly opposed by a wide range of groups in the United States, it continued to operate legitimately. We should not be surprised to learn that a distinctly anti-Enlightenment strain of thought developed in the American South to defend slavery. This strain, however, did not merely argue the usual plea of "special economic circumstances" and racial design claiming that God and nature had intended blacks to be slaves. It also objected to the very idea of a free society whose view of nature was that all men are inherently free and equal in rights.

Encapsulating much of this sentiment was George Fitzhugh (1806–81), a Virginian who launched in the 1850s a spirited rearguard defense of slavery that adopted some of the themes of de Maistre and Burke. Fitzhugh contended that so-called free industrial laborers suffered a far more blighted existence than slaves, who, he claimed, were cared for by their masters:

> Our theory is that they [American slaves] are not free, because God and nature, and the general good and their own good,

intended them to be slaves. . . . They are, at the South, well governed and well protected. . . . The free laborer has no such securities. It is in the interest of employers to kill them off as fast as possible; and they never fail to do it. We do not mean to say that the negro slave enjoys liberty. But we do say that he is well and properly governed, so as best to promote his own good and that of society. (Fitzhugh 1857/1960, 77–78)

But he also declared that free society as a whole, in idea and practice, was a sham, an excuse for unlimited greed:

The moral philosophy of our age . . . is deduced from the existing relations of men to each other in free society. . . . If that system of society be wrong, and its relations false, the philosophy resulting from it must partake of its error and falsity. On the other hand, if [it] be true, slavery must be wrong, because that philosophy is at war with slavery. No successful defence of slavery can be made, till we succeed in refuting or invalidating the principles on which free society rests. . . . In fact, it is, in all its ramifications, a mere expansion and application of Political Economy—"Laissez-faire," or "Let alone." A system of unmitigated selfishness pervades and distinguishes all departments of ethical, political, and economic science. (Fitzhugh 1857/1960, 52)

All of Europe and the American North were in the grip of a philosophy that urged every individual to ignore others and grab all he could get—a society without social bonds. Only the South, in its rural essence, preserved the rule of nature and God. Here the supposed role of nature was important. There persisted in reactionary thought this notion that the natural order itself was against liberalism, that the ideas and hopes it embodied were not merely aberrant but inevitably destructive, ruinous (Burke had called them "monstrous"). Whether one began from consideration of God's plan, the biological hierarchy of races, or tradition as precedent, Enlightenment liberalism qualified as an enemy of the proper order, "an insolent irreligion" (again, Burke) that went against human nature. Somehow, people would always be better-off and better protected if governed by a patriarchal elite and did not overly question venerable norms and religion.

Nevertheless, the defenders of Lockean liberalism in America in the mid-nineteenth century, most notably the influential Ralph Waldo Emerson (1803–82), won over the majority of opinion in the North, and there ensued the election of Abraham Lincoln and the Civil War, which, according to the latest estimates, killed 750,000 men out of a population at that time of 30 million (Hacker 2011). Garry Wills has argued that it was this, and specifically, Lincoln's Gettysburg speech in 1863, one of the greatest statements of American liberalism ever made, that redirected the United States back to the Enlightenment principles of its Declaration of Independence (Wills 1992).

Despite the antiliberalism of slavery in America and colonialism by the British, both societies did gradually, unevenly, but with a certain momentum move toward greater liberty and democracy as the nineteenth century progressed. These changes were inherent in the liberalism these societies adopted. Particularly in the United States the ideals enshrined in the Declaration of Independence provided a constant standard against which political reality could be measured and found wanting. Such values clashed, in some ways, with industrialism and the creation of a large, increasingly organized working class that was supposed to remain subservient. But British and American elites slowly accommodated themselves to the opening of the political process to ever larger portions of their population. The ideals of the Enlightenment were too firmly entrenched in both opinion and institutions to be thrown overboard. This was not, however, a universal trend, and even in the western and central parts of Europe where such ideas spread, there remained a large body of opinion that was fiercely opposed.

Popular Reactions against Liberalism: The Role of Nationalism

Despite resistance that wanted to retain or return to an old order that privileged hereditary aristocracies and monarchies, and dogmatic Christian churches supporting traditional political systems, reactionary beliefs could not remain wedded to ideas that seemed increasingly archaic as societies modernized. Edmund Burke, who died in 1797, may have advised "infinite caution" in contemplating social change, but industrialization and urbanization impelled such change in every advanced nation of the nineteenth century. Antiliberalism had to adapt. The growth of an increasingly urban industrial working class that gradually became more self-assertive, creating unions and socialist parties, was one reason. Middle-class demands for political rights and more democracy that would liberate them from autocratic and aristocratic rule were another. New technologies not only improved communications, travel, and printing but created pressures for a higher level of mass education as nations were transformed from landscapes of farms and fields to those of cities and towns.

One of the clearest outcomes of these changes was the deliberate promotion by European states (and in the United States) of nationalism. Taught increasingly in schools, spread by newspapers and books, and used by political leaders who sought to mobilize their masses, nationalism claimed that all of the people governed by the state were really part of a large family related to each other by a common culture, common values, and, in most of Europe, a common ancestry. Nationalist histories were concocted to convince people of this (Gellner 1983; Anderson 1983).

The rulers of even the most antiliberal, antidemocratic states among the great powers, most prominently Prussia and Russia, saw that this was necessary. While maintaining the right of their monarchs to rule and of their landed aristocracies to keep their superior status and disproportionate power, they also promoted nationalism as something necessary to keep themselves in power and to be able to draw on the manpower and resources necessary to fight modern wars (Hobsbawm 1962; Tilly 1992).

Born of liberal idealism that sought to give voice to all of the people and to mobilize them in the cause of liberty, therefore, nationalism also became in much of Europe a tool of reaction, if of a modernized version. The fact that Russia, Prussia, and eventually Germany (once it was united by Prussia in 1871) used nationalism as a strategy to unify their people changed the nature of their conservatism. Nationalism had originally become such a powerful force as an ideology of the French

Revolution and as such was associated with liberal Enlightenment values, or at least a militant and militarized version of these ideas. But once it became evident that it could be spread and used by antiliberal elites to mobilize populations and instill a sense of loyalty to the state, it turned into an ideology that could function just as well to fight liberalism, socialism, and even greater democratization. As such, it broadened its appeal to include aristocrats and monarchs who had originally been suspicious of nationalism but included the masses, who were supposed to accept and legitimize rule by the rich and powerful because they were benign protectors of the nation.

By the late nineteenth and early twentieth centuries all the major states recognized that in order to remain strong they needed to modernize their economy, instill nationalism, and mobilize mass support. The idea had by then spread beyond the West to Asia, most notably to Japan where the preservation of a socially conservative elite and an autocratic regime was increasingly being based on a militarized ultranationalism (Bix 2000, 27–36). Later we will see how a highly mythologized, supposedly traditional but actually quite new, mystical version of this became the official doctrine of fascist Japan in the 1930s (*Kokutai No Hongi* 1937/1949).

There is a rich historiographical tradition of separating nationalisms into two types, "western" and "eastern" (Kohn 1944, 1955). "Eastern" Russia and Germany were said to have relied on myths of inherited kinship, or common blood, to promote nationalism, and this supported their autocratic, reactionary ways by discouraging class divisions. (Japan could easily have been included in this analysis, but as the study of nationalism began by those better versed in European history, "East" generally did not go beyond Europe in any detail.) As a superior, united "family" the nation was supposed to obey its fatherly monarch and defend itself against the outside world. Those who were not of the same blood, foreigners, Jews, and other supposedly disloyal minorities were to be excluded. "Western" France and England (as well as its offshoot, the United States) were supposedly different because their nationalism relied on a forged civic union. Therefore, outsiders could be integrated into the nation if they learned the proper culture, democratic organizations could be tolerated and even encouraged because they could become the basis of greater national unity, and union was guaranteed by democratic consensus (Greenfeld 1993).

Given that Russia was a repressive, autocratic state under its tsars, and later became a much more brutal communist tyranny, and that Germany produced that most anti-Enlightenment of all European ideologies, Nazism, this kind of historical determinism has always made sense.

Unfortunately it is a kind of ex post facto reasoning that is deeply misleading because by the late nineteenth century there were powerful intellectual currents throughout all of Europe that combined nationalism with ideas deeply hostile to the liberal side of the Enlightenment. In the more extreme cases this led to fascism, but even in Britain, France, and the United States racist types of nationalism became current, as did an increasingly aggressive kind of nationalism. This kind of attitude in Europe undoubtedly contributed to the hostility between nations that led to World War I and in the United States turned growing portions of public opinion against unrestricted immigration and in favor of overseas imperialist expansion.

In fact, these kinds of antiliberal, hypernationalist ideas remain widely accepted to this day in various forms and promote similarly intolerant, antidemocratic, and very antiliberal political movements and regimes. Had this happened only in Russia, Germany, and some lesser European states, these ideas would not have resonated so widely, even in more solidly democratic and supposedly liberal societies. Nor would they still live as the basis of Counter-Enlightenment reaction in large parts of today's world.

The Intellectual Roots of Fascism

Unlike communism, which drew its inspiration from a clearly identifiable source, Karl Marx and his followers, or liberalism, which had a broader but clearly identifiable lineage leading up to Adam Smith, Immanuel Kant, the Founding Fathers of America, Benjamin Constant, and John Stuart Mill, fascism never had a unified set of intellectual forefathers, though it also stemmed from the minds of intellectuals searching for an alternative to both liberalism and Marxist socialism.

What fascism's various manifestations all had in common was an admiration of violence and direct action, extreme nationalism that glorified traditional customs and exalted both the mythic origins of the nation and its racial purity, especially its rural portion, and the worship of a heroic national leader whose will and near divinity justified his power as representative of the national will. Extreme nationalism was an essential part of this ideology, but it was not sufficient to explain it because not all nationalists accepted the rest of this orientation. Important also was a sense of disgust with democratic capitalism because it supposedly was dominated by a commercially minded, crass bourgeoisie that cared more about money than national glory and honor. Revulsion to democratic governance that was deemed to be controlled by petty, mendacious, and definitely unheroic politicians therefore justified autocratic, even absolute dictatorship of the strong as something far better than weak democracy. A mysterious sense of community, unexplainable in purely rational terms but strongly felt at a deep, emotional level, was supposed to bind the various classes and interest groups in the nation together. Though some modern technology and science could be accepted in order to strengthen the nation's economic and military power, received dogma about the sacredness of the nation and mystical justifications of what was supposed to be ancient tradition were to be accepted. With this went a deep skepticism about the moral value of modern science and particularly of liberal openness to many new ideas.

A key part of this was a sense that modernization in the advanced parts of Europe had gone wrong and that Enlightenment liberalism was no longer a satisfactory model for future progress. Some who believed this turned to Marxism or other forms of radical anticapitalism, but for those who either disliked the idea of socialism or perceived that the growing socialist parties of Europe were themselves part of the corrupt capitalist system and not loyal to the nation because socialism was an international "alien" import, other solutions had to be found.

The roots of fascism, then, lay in a rejection of the excessive individualism and selfishness of capitalism, worry that this separated the parts of societies into antagonistic classes, and the belief that the consequence was the destruction of healthy, "organic" community values and national unity. This was compounded by fear of what were deemed polluting ideas and customs, particularly if they were carried by supposedly "foreign" and impure racial elements (Sternhell, Sznajder, and Ashéri 1994).

The rejection by so many late nineteenth- and early twentieth-century intellectuals of Enlightenment rationality and their skepticism about the worth of science might seem strange just at the moment when technological progress had become so evident and rapid. This, after all, was when discoveries in medicine, the spread of electric lighting, developments in communications and transportation, and widespread economic growth were vastly improving the lives of most people in the advanced countries. And this was also the end of a long period during which there had been no catastrophic wars in Europe since the fall of Napoleon except for the fairly brief Franco-German and Crimean wars. Europe's wars during most of the nineteenth century had been faraway colonial ones.

But somehow spontaneity, intuition, and emotion were deemed more authentic and creative by France's—and in the years before World War I perhaps Europe's—most popular living philosopher, Henri Bergson (1859–1941). His ideas were eagerly adopted by French ultranationalists who wished to reinvigorate French patriotism by appealing to this mystical sense of emotional solidarity meant to cleanse and refresh nationalist passions (Sorel and Jennings 1999, xxviii–xxix). This is not to say that Bergson was in any sense a fascist; in fact toward the end of his life in the 1930s, as a Jew himself, he explicitly rejected Europe's slide toward anti-Semitism and fascism. But his ideas were part of an intellectual environment that was turning away from Enlightenment rationalism in favor of a more intuitive religiosity and nonrational spontaneity that was greatly admired by those looking for a way out of the dullness of bourgeois materialism and the divisions and conflicts engendered by capitalist modernization (Hughes 1961, 113–25).

Much of this sense had already been captured by the seminal and widely appreciated writings of Friedrich Nietzsche (1844–1900). It would wrong to call Nietzsche a protofascist because he certainly would have rejected what turned into actual fascist movements. But his venomous dislike of the tolerant, liberal materialism that seemed to dominate the West certainly inspired others in exactly that direction.

He extolled the heroic "blond beast, the aristocratic violence of Homeric heroes ... crushing everything, and bespattering everything with blood" (1954, *Genealogy* 652–53). He decried what he called the slave mentality of kindly Christianity, the weakness of the modern world around him, and especially the narrow utilitarianism of democratic England, whose science and philosophy he dismissed as mediocre and whose parliamentary system of governance he despised. He thought he saw in peasants as well as in landed aristocrats the residue of his noble ideal, and he wrote approvingly of the militarization of Europe that he saw as a positive good (1954, *Beyond Good and Evil* 565–66; *Genealogy* 800–804).

These were themes that became very popular among what were more clearly fascist intellectuals, including, not least of all, Benito Mussolini (though Georges Sorel, who was deeply influenced by Nietzsche, was a more direct influence on him than Nietzsche), who drifted from socialism into militaristic nationalism and created the very term "fascism" (Sternhell, Sznajder, and Ashéri 1994, 199–200).

The New Anti-Semitism and the Growing European Rejection of Liberalism

Nietzsche, however, was seduced neither by anti-Semitism nor by anti-Slavic racism he saw being adopted by intellectuals and German nationalists and that would become an integral part of Nazism four decades later. He in fact apologized for having flirted with such ideas (1954, *Beyond Good and Evil* 562–64). That was part of his rejection of Richard Wagner, the musical genius whose notorious anti-Semitism and glorification of primitive, pre-Christian Germanic heroism would so strongly appeal to Adolf Hitler (Emden 2010, 308–12).

Some form of racist sentiment glorifying "our" national race and demeaning "others" who were deemed racially inferior was part of all forms of fascism, but anti-Semitism was particularly important in most of Europe, though far less so in Italy than in the rest of western, central, and eastern Europe.

Anti-Semitism was very old, as it originated in religious hostility toward Jews who did not accept Christianity (or, in the Muslim world,

Islam) because they rejected the divinity and very prophetic legitimacy of Jesus Christ (and of Muhammad). But Enlightenment ideas rejected this by promoting religious tolerance and skepticism of old religious dogmas, and by the first half of the nineteenth century it seemed that European anti-Semitism was rapidly declining as Jews were gradually emancipated from restrictive laws except in Russia and some other eastern European lands. In the United States, whatever prejudices existed, from the very founding of the republic there were no anti-Jewish laws.

But by the second half of the nineteenth century, that trend was reversed. It became a staple of right-wing nationalism in countries as different from each other as France, Germany, Romania, and Russia, and it influenced conservative opinion throughout much of the rest of the Western world.

The essence of the new argument against Jews was that they were responsible for the ills of modernizing capitalism. Using the old prejudices against Jews whose medieval urban merchant and moneylending roles had contributed to their image as greedy, money-grubbing Christ killers, the new version saw in the disproportionate presence of Jews in urban, market-related occupations the source of corruption and social displacement brought into the world by the spread of modern capitalism. Furthermore, as a culturally distinct community that had not accepted Christianity and that maintained ties with Jewish communities in other countries, Jews' loyalty to the newly mobilized nations that prized their own communal distinctiveness and solidarity was questioned. On top of this, because Jewish religious culture privileged book learning and literacy for its men, when Jews were emancipated they were more likely, on average, to do well in the increasingly literate, urban environments that became the centers of commerce and industry. Peasant migrants who came into these cities from illiterate families or elites with aristocratic pretensions who looked down on commerce and finance did less well, but they were considered by nationalists to be the more genuine and unspoiled parts of the newly conscious nations. So, as cities throughout Europe grew quickly because of industrialization and rapid population growth, many urbanites, including those in the aspiring middle classes, felt that they were disadvantaged by "alien" Jews who had some sort of mysterious and unfair advantage (Muller 2010).

This kind of prejudice was obviously not entirely new and certainly not limited to anti-Semitism. What are called "middlemen minorities," that is, culturally distinct groups who are seen as foreign but who do well in urban and commercial endeavors, have aroused and continue to provoke prejudice everywhere. Some of the more prominent examples have been the Chinese in Southeast Asia, migrants from India in East Africa, Igbo people in Nigeria, Lebanese in West Africa, and many others (Chirot and Reid 1997).

Before modernization societies had been dominated by landowning aristocrats and subservient peasants. The function of official religions had been to legitimize such social systems and thus to strengthen them. There had of course been cities and merchant and artisan classes, but they were less powerful except in a few key commercial cities. The rapid social change of the nineteenth century that began in western Europe and then spread elsewhere was economically dominated by striving capitalists and highly educated urban elites on the one hand and a growing poorer working class on the other. Both demanded a greater political say and seemed to be more attuned to Enlightenment liberalism or to socialism than to any traditional or religiously sanctioned rule.

To the many who found these changes disturbing, and for whom the new kinds of societies appeared rootless, unfair, and threatening, it was easy to blame Jews as well as the new liberal ideas extolling free markets and Enlightenment democracy. This was an opening for traditional conservatives who rejected liberalism but who needed the support of the masses to maintain political power.

We need to emphasize that anti-Semitism was not merely something that came from the anti-Enlightenment Right. As we pointed out in our earlier chapter on Karl Marx, he wrote one of the most viciously anti-Jewish essays of the mid-nineteenth century, "On the Jewish Question" (1844, in McLellan 1977). There he used all of the stereotypes of traditional anti-Semitism, accusing Jews of being little more than greedy capitalists.

Such theory, as already suggested, was much in favor in Marx's day and drew on biology for its legitimacy. It found huge support in the ideas of social evolution put forward by Herbert Spencer, one of the most influential thinkers of the late nineteenth century. Spencer was a great polymath and liberal utilitarian, who viewed society as a kind of living organism evolving toward greater complexity, with industrial societies the most complex and evolved of all. While his actual writings make it plain he thought society existed for the benefit of its members, not the other way, his ringing phrase "survival of the fittest" helped lead a great many to conflate his views with Darwin's and to interpret his theory as proposing a natural state of struggle among modern nations. Spencer, in short, was taken (wrongly) as offering "scientific" support for an organic nationalism—the state as a living body, one that could be healthy or infected.

This combined with the discoveries of one of western Europe's true scientific greats, Louis Pasteur, who established the germ theory of disease. Pasteur's work in the 1860s and 1870s proved that microorganisms were responsible for many diseases and acted like contaminants, spread by tainted air, unclean hands, and polluted foods like milk and beer. It did not take long for anti-Semitic spokesmen to begin using Pasteur metaphorically. Jews were not only purveyors of disruptive capitalism and offensive modern ideas but racial polluters spreading invisible but deadly degeneration by mixing with pure and healthier races (Chirot 1996, 52–53).

Racist "theory" had been presented earlier by the Frenchman Joseph Arthur de Gobineau (1816–82), whose book, *An Essay on the Inequality of the Human Races* (1853–55), is considered the foundational text of modern "scientific" racism. Gobineau was no scientist but a novelist who selectively collected ideas about human races and their ranking from other writers, only some of whom were well-known scientists. In his book, he labeled southern Europeans as members of a degenerate race and non-Europeans as inferiors, while northern Europeans were the descendants of an Aryan superior race with Germanic roots. Gobineau was not himself an anti-Semite, but he greatly influenced those in other parts of Europe, and in England, who wanted to place Jews into the ranks of the "inferior" races.

In France, however, it was not until Édouard Drumont's 1886 book, *La France juive*, became a best seller that anti-Semitism became a more popular creed. It excoriated Jews, blaming them for corrupting and swindling France. The very wealthy European Jewish banking family of the Rothschilds was his favorite villain. He wrote:

> The Rothschild family, which supposedly owns three billions in just their French branch, did not have this when they arrived in France. It has discovered nothing new, found no new mines, cleared no new lands, so it has taken these three billions from the French without giving anything in return.... If nothing is done to stop this, in 50 years, or at most a century, all of European society will have been delivered, bound hand and fist, to several hundred Jewish bankers. (1886, 2)

While capitalism drew attack from both Right and Left, it was only the reactionary Right that used anti-Semitism as the pillar of a program to keep France entirely "French." It was backed by members of the conservative elite, the Catholic Church, and traditional monarchists who had never accepted the democratic Third Republic, or even the French Revolution (Caron 1985, 459–62).

This exploded with the Dreyfus affair (1894–1906). A French Jewish army officer, Alfred Dreyfus, was condemned to prison on completely trumped-up charges of treason. French public opinion divided into two camps, the Catholic, traditionalist, anti-Republican Right on one side and the supporters of a democratic republic, anticlerical, liberal, and socialist Left. Both claimed to be nationalist and patriotic. But it was the Right that wanted to do this by favoring a more aristocratic army, traditional religion, and an antiliberal state. The various movements in France that would define its contentious politics for the next forty years were shaped by this drama whose final resolution, the complete exoneration of Dreyfus, solved none of the problems raised by the bitter divisions it had caused (Begley 2009).

In Germany, too, the new racism was spread from the top by leading intellectuals. As an example, German emperor Wilhelm II's Lutheran court chaplain, Adolf Stoecker, a popular speaker, launched an attack against Jews whose "temple was the stock exchange . . . and [who] were making Berlin a Jewish town." Particularly influential and revealing, however, was an 1880 tract, "A Word about Our Jews," by the prominent and highly respected German historian Heinrich von Treitschke (1834–96). A politically engaged academic who served as a Reichstag deputy for the National Liberal Party, Treitschke began his career as a liberal, then became progressively more nationalistic and concerned with "alien elements" after the unification of Germany in 1871. In his career, Treitschke provides a convincing example of how liberalism could deteriorate under the heat of nationalist fervor. In his tract, he admits to having "many Jewish friends [who] will concede, though with deep regret, that I am right when I assert that . . . a dangerous spirit of arrogance has arisen in Jewish circles." The nature of this "arrogance" was simple: "Semites bear a heavy share of guilt for the . . . insolent greed of fraudulent business practices, and that base materialism of our day." No less were they guilty of casting themselves as superior. The solution was for all Jews "to become Germans." And yet: "The task will never be wholly complete. A cleft has always existed between Occidental and Semitic essences . . . there will always be Jews who are nothing but German-speaking Orientals" (Treitschke 1879).

The essay reads today as unpolished bigotry, ugly and not particularly articulate. But to German readers at the time, especially other academics, university students, and the educated middle class, "A Word about Our Jews" was like a call to arms, written simply and directly, by a man of great knowledge who had descended from the clouds to bring a message of great import to his countrymen. At a deeper level—which many readers understood—Treitschke put blame on Germany's own lax laws and excessive tolerance, both inspired by liberalism. Liberal thinking, he said, had denounced a great deal of the German tradition, including Christianity, allowing Jews to think they could do likewise. Indeed, Treitschke noted, Jews were the most liberal people in Germany. As for its popularity, "A Word about Our Jews" outsold all other tracts and books, going through three editions in its first year of publication, followed by a fourth in 1881. Circulating through every major German university, it set loose a whole series of public debates about the "Jewish threat." In a line that would echo for decades, eventually to emerge in the speeches of Hitler, Treitschke proclaimed: "The Jews are our misfortune!" In 1881, as many as 225,000 Germans signed a petition addressed to their chancellor, Otto von Bismarck, demanding that immigration of Jews from the East be prohibited (Carsten 1967, 23–24).

East of Germany lay Poland, divided among the German, Austro-Hungarian, and Russian empires, and the rest of eastern Europe and the Russian Empire. Enlightenment ideas, as well as anti-Semitism, were translated differently here. Monarchs of the eighteenth century, such as Frederick the Great of Prussia, Maria Theresa and Joseph II of the Holy Roman Empire, and Catherine the Great of Russia, selectively adopted Enlightenment political and legal concepts to strengthen their own absolutist rule and, in the case of Russia, to Westernize a still largely medieval society so that it might stand with European powers. While there were some attempts to graft aspects of liberalism—partial freedom of speech and the press, limited rights to private property, and even religious tolerance—these changes, while real in Austria, elsewhere were weak, conditional, and often temporary, particularly in Russia. "Enlightened despotism," as the term goes, proved over time to be the contradiction in fact that it is in word. The more eastern portion of Europe, moreover, did not undergo a high level of industrialization and urbanization until very late. But from advanced Germany and France, the ideas of extreme nationalism, antimodernism, and other Counter-Enlightenment beliefs were introduced and became widespread by the middle of the nineteenth century. Russia adopted for itself the image of the great protector of the Slavic peoples, in opposition to a corrupt and dissolute western Europe. By the time of Nicholas II, the last absolute monarch in Europe, much of the Russian elite (including Nicholas) was completely hostile to "decadent" liberal ideas.

As for anti-Semitism, Russia also proved to be a special case because it maintained harshly discriminatory anti-Jewish laws at a time when they were disappearing farther west. It also became the source of an extraordinarily influential text, first published in 1903, that has remained a reference for anti-Semites around the world ever since. This text, *Protocols of the Elders of Zion*, was commissioned by the Russian police. An entirely fabricated document, it claims to be the proceedings of an 1897 meeting involving important Jews in Switzerland who hatched a plot to gain global domination by sabotaging the morals of non-Jews everywhere, taking control of the banks and economies, and seizing organs of the press. *Protocols* appeared in several Russian editions before finding its way into the rest of Europe and translation into many languages, including English. In 1920, even as British journalists were exposing the document as a fake, automaker Henry Ford financed its publication, as well as the distribution of five hundred thousand copies, in the United States. It was accepted as truth by Hitler and in more recent years has been further translated and reedited in many Muslim countries, where it is taken seriously by many (Filiu 2011, xii–xiii).

The Corrosive Effects of Imperialism and Elitist Theories

It was not just anti-Semitism that challenged liberal tolerance. Even at the heart of the most liberal nations, the United States and Great Britain, the effects of widely accepted imperialism, with its necessary corollary that the European races were somehow biologically superior, played an important role as well. Thus the widespread popularity of Darwinism and its social corollary, Social Darwinism, could be interpreted in any number of ways by those on the Left, among liberals, and by the Right. But when combined with ideas of racial purity and the inevitability of conflict between "races," it promoted a reactionary, anti-Enlightenment, antiliberal ideology that glorified not just anti-Semitism but widespread racism and aggressive militarism. The spread of European imperialism throughout Africa and Asia in the second half of the nineteenth century not only increased competition between the major European powers racing to expand their empires but also solidified racially based ideas that fit well into extreme nationalism. As a German imperialist wrote in 1879:

Every virile people has established colonial power. . . . All real nations in the fullness of their strength have desired to set their mark upon barbarian lands and those who fail to participate in this great rivalry will play a pitiable role in time to come. The colonizing impulse has become a vital question for every great nation. (Fieldhouse 1972, 120)

This was hardly an exclusively German sentiment. This combination of imperialism, a sense of superiority of "our" race, the alienation of large portions of Europe's populations from rising impersonal capitalist forces, and the rapidly accelerating arms race in late nineteenth-century Europe enhanced the influence of intellectuals like Treitschke and Drumont who offered an explanation of what had gone wrong and how to combat it to further the glory of the nation.

In the United States, which had created a continental empire by annexing western lands from Mexico and dispossessing native peoples, by the late nineteenth century a more aggressive, external imperialism was taking hold as well. President Theodore Roosevelt expressed his vision of American imperialism by talking of the need for "manly" and vigorous expansion (Morris 2001, and most specifically, 473).

In Italy sociology took the form of something approaching an "enlightened elitism" among influential analysts led by Roberto Michels (who was half German and half French but who made Italy his favored home), Vilfredo Pareto, and Gaetano Mosca.

Michels proposed in his most famous book, *Political Parties* (1915), that there was an "iron law of oligarchy" such that even the most democratically inclined movements like socialist parties would be taken over by numerically small but powerful elites. Elite rule was therefore inevitable.

Pareto, who was originally trained as an engineer, became a well-known economist and political philosopher drawn to measuring and explaining the distribution of wealth and power in society. In studying Italy, he discovered that 80 percent of the land was owned by just 20 percent of the people and that this "80/20 Rule" (or Pareto Principle, as it is still known) is generally true. A small elite always owns and controls the vast majority of capital and political influence in any country. All societies, then, are typified by gross inequities, with the mass of people at the bottom. This, he concluded, was "a social law" caused by primitive Darwinian competition among human beings of unequal talent. Theories like democracy seeking to treat people equally and provide them with level chances of success are false and deceitful as they go against the iron truth of human nature. A ruling class is inevitable; it will always arise, take the major share, and leave the bulk of the people much poorer and weaker. Late in his life Pareto embraced Mussolini and his early program to make Italy more heroic and less corrupt, though he died before ever seeing what fascist rule was really about (Hughes 1961, 270–74).

Gaetano Mosca, too, took pains to point out the defects, corruption, and indecisiveness of the prevailing forms of Western democracy. In the two decades following World War I, he solidified a theory similar to that of Pareto but argued this from the point of view of political history. First published in 1896, the book *Elementi di scienza politica*, later translated into English as *The Ruling Class* (1939), held that societies had always been ruled by a small minority, whether of a priestly, military, aristocratic, or other caste. The reason such elites formed was no accident. The masses of people were too irrational and too poorly prepared to rule themselves and too easily seduced by bad ideologies. He wrote that even in states "where the liberal principle prevails, we also find the two strata of the ruling class which we found in autocratic systems, the first very small, the second [of minor offices acquired through patronage] much more extensive. . . . The elective system, in fact does not preclude the formation of more or less closed cliques which compete for the highest offices" (Mosca 1939, 410). Thus, as with Pareto, democracy is largely a fraud and "the will of the people" a myth. Moreover, too often elected officials were corrupt and concerned with their own power, incapable of governing properly. The only solution was to accept the need for a powerful, well-trained upper class to guide the nation—an elite, however, that was not fossilized by hereditary inheritance but refreshed by men of superior talent and will from below (Hughes 1961, 249–74). Perhaps ironically, Mosca was here largely adopting the view of his ancient Roman countryman Cicero, who also saw democratic government as a dangerous "rule by the mob" unless headed by an aristocracy of superior individuals to guide the people toward their own best interest.

Indeed, even such politically moderate thinkers as Émile Durkheim and Max Weber expressed unease about the alienating and crass aspects of the new materialism and inadequacies of existing democracy. Durkheim, who was Jewish and is considered one of the founding fathers of modern sociology, also believed in the inherent biological differences between races, though the more conservative Weber, the other major founding originator of that discipline, did not. Both, however, were worried about the alienation of modern life (Hughes 1961, 278–335). Neither can be accused of promoting ideas that could be turned into fascist ideology, but they were part of a general disillusionment with the existing order.

It would take a good deal more than such thinking to produce the beginnings of fascism. But the many social and political analysts disgusted by the corruption of bourgeois democracy contributed to liberal, capitalist democracy's loss of legitimacy. For those who accepted some form of Social Darwinism and elitist theories, the inherent problem of democratic liberalism was twofold: it refused to accept the dictates of nature, which separated the strong from the weak, the superior from the inferior; and, as a result, it embraced the lower orders, preventing the best from rising to the top, thus enfeebling the state at a time when strength was most needed. This reflected in part the truth that intellectuals came mainly from affluent backgrounds. But it also flowed from some of the other elements of sensibility we have been discussing: nationalism, imperialism, ideas of race, end of the century pessimism, and the general perceptions of a civilization disintegrating under the inexorable forces of a capitalism that had severed every intimate and nourishing bond to the past. The longing for strong and vigorous leaders in the midst of this atmosphere was perhaps no less inevitable than the attraction of many to the mystical realm of national essence and destiny. As much as anything, the spectacular destruction of traditional beliefs and institutions by the advances of modernity left a good many thinkers in a kind of vacuum, grasping at primitive notions, yearning for the signs of power and order, and susceptible to the allure of violence as a promise of change. The remaining critical ingredient had to be theories about how to bring all this together. A precipitating event was needed to impose the necessity for a new kind of society.

Lenin's 1916 analysis of World War I may have exaggerated the role played by imperialist competition between the major powers, but he was certainly not entirely wrong (see chapter 2). That competition, particularly between rising Germany and previously dominant but weakening Great Britain, was behind the expensive, dangerous race to build bigger and more expensive navies (Kennedy 1980). Germany's rise and sense that it risked being hemmed in by a French-Russian alliance directed against its imperial growth fueled both German paranoia and its growing militarism (Kennan 1979). Everywhere, the spread of Social Darwinist ideas, the conflation of nation with biological race, and the certitude that only the most vigorous and expansionist of national races would survive contributed to the sense of crisis and an arms race that finally led to catastrophe. Without World War I there would have been no fascism, but well before the war, the intellectual groundwork for fascism had been planted in both high-level intellectual and popular discourse. The disastrous war then let the seeds sprout.

FASCISM EMERGES IN ITALY AND GERMANY

Zeev Sternhell's controversial contention that fascist ideology as it developed in France and Italy was "neither left nor right" is the key to understanding what fascism was about. Despite the fact that it came to be identified as being on the far Right when in power, the original intent and successful appeal to a wide range of Europeans, and then Asians, Latin Americans, and even some nationalist intellectuals and political activists in the Middle East, cannot be understood if we insist on sticking to the long-held but erroneous Marxist interpretation that fascism was merely the last gasp of an endangered monopoly capitalism and, therefore, the capitalist plutocracy's attempt to prevent socialist revolutions (Sternhell 1986, 4; Poulantzas 1974 for a widely cited Marxist explanation). Fascism emerged from a combination of French, Italian, and German ideologies that were intended to be revolutionary, to overthrow the existing bourgeois order, and to create a new world able to resolve the contradictions of modern industrial society without giving in to international Marxism and communism. While an extreme form of Social Darwinism emphasizing the need of nations and races to struggle victoriously in order to survive was a major component of these ideologies, and was very widespread, fascism also required a sense that revolutionary, violent upheaval was a necessary first step to national reconstruction.

Sternhell identifies the French theoretician of violent revolution, Georges Sorel (1847–1922), as a powerful influence on the creator of the first fascist state, Benito Mussolini. Sorel, who denounced anti-Semitism and called himself a follower of Karl Marx, had proclaimed in his *Reflections on Violence* (first published as a series of articles in Italian in 1905 and 1906) that both democracy and conventional socialist parties were simply ways of perpetuating a corrupt bourgeoisie. In order to free themselves, the working-class masses had to engage in a violent general strike that would bring the whole edifice down and create the basis for a more equitable, modern society. Later editions of *Reflections on Violence* included others of his articles and thoughts about Marxism, revolution, and the power of constructive myths in energizing revolution. In a 1919 edition of the book he added a praise of Lenin's Bolshevik Revolution. To say that this was somehow a doctrine that favored big capitalist interests misses the point.

This holds as well for another important intellectual precursor of Italian fascism, Filippo Tommaso Marinetti (1876–1944), whose futurist manifesto of 1909 was partly a call for a daring modern art and aesthetic and for a whole new way of life. Marinetti wrote:

> We intend to sing the song of danger. . . . We will glorify war— the world's only hygiene—militarism, patriotism, the destructive gesture of freedom bringers, beautiful ideas worth dying for, and scorn for woman. . . . We will destroy the museums, libraries, academies of every kind, will fight moralism, feminism, every opportunistic or utilitarian cowardice. (Sternhell, Sznajder, and Ashéri 1994, 28–29)

Mussolini backed away from the artistic side of futurism once in power but certainly made its notion of war, violence, patriotism, and masculine aggression the heart of the image he projected and tried to carry out in practice.

Also influential in the creation of Italian fascism was the poet and war hero Gabriel D'Annunzio (1863–1938). D'Annunzio came from the provincial elite and grew up an unrepentant nationalist. Known as Italy's "warrior poet," he was a figure of national pride who received praise for his writing from authors as disparate as Marcel Proust and James Joyce. A complex, histrionic personality, he became enraptured with Nietzsche's concept of the *übermensch* ("superhuman"). With the outbreak of war in 1914, therefore, D'Annunzio was eager for Italy to abandon neutrality. A year later, he began a campaign of dramatic speeches intended to inflame nationalist passions so that Italy might accept the call to its "trial by blood." In Rome, he told the crowds it would be just even to kill those in Parliament who opposed this trial of national virility. "If," he declaimed, "inciting citizens to violence is a crime, I will boast of this crime, assuming sole responsibility for it" (Kramer 2009, 36–37). As Italy was deciding to enter World War I in May 1915, D'Annunzio hailed this wonderful development by praising "an Italy that shall be greater by conquest, purchasing territory not in shame, but at the price of blood and glory. . . . After long years of national humiliation, God has been pleased to grant us proof of our privileged blood." Though D'Annunzio was too hysterical a figure to be a good politician, his heroism during the war and his demands right afterward to pursue territorial expansion won over many nationalists, and Mussolini was able to cleverly exploit this while maneuvering to take power himself (Carsten 1967, 47–49).

The reality of war, to be sure, was entirely different, and Italy, with its poorly organized, badly led, and underequipped army suffered greatly. Ernest Hemingway's semi-autobiographical novel about his time as a volunteer with the Italian army during the war, *A Farewell to Arms*, first published in 1929, is a better guide to the depressing reality of what the Italian war was like than the mythmaking that so enraptured D'Annunzio, Mussolini, and the Italian nationalists, but then, as Sorel himself had said in his *Reflections on Violence*, powerful myths hold greater sway than real history.

After the catastrophe of World War I shattered the illusion of permanent progress promised by the Enlightenment and then brought to the fore revolutionary movements that threatened the established order throughout Europe, the well-established intellectual denunciations of liberalism, democracy, bourgeois corruption, and Jewish conspiracies came into their own (though in Italy anti-Semitism would not play a role in the rise of fascism). Now habituated to extreme violence, many returned soldiers who were disgusted by the failings of the new liberal order that was supposed to be established joined movements advocating revolutionary, brutal cleansing.

Emerging fascist movements conjured up various plot theories to explain why there had been this terrible war and destruction, why it had not led to a better outcome, and why discredited, respectably moderate older ideologies no longer sufficed to make things right. Enlightenment liberalism had been nothing but a fraud weakening national resolve, and its hypocrisy had been exposed. On one side, Lenin's Russia offered an international revolutionary model that could appeal to the Left. But what of those who did not buy into a doctrine that claimed to abolish nationalism in favor of an abstract Marxist doctrine and yet who sought a drastic revolutionary solution to their societies' problems? Not only fearful upper and middle classes but more generally those of all classes who had thought they were fighting the war to save their nations and who remained intensely nationalistic were searching for a different, noncommunist solution.

This was precisely the niche filled by Mussolini, once a leading socialist journalist and politician who had become an ultranationalist proponent of violent revolution. Only this could energize Italy and propel it into the ranks of the great powers. He appealed to conservative forces that were uncomfortable with the idea of revolution but more afraid of the Marxist-Leninist version than of Mussolini's fascists who promised to make Italy great while breaking the power of the socialist unions who still adhered to Marxist ideas. So the elites struck a bargain with Mussolini, and fascism (a term first used in Italy, along with totalitarianism) became the strangely hybrid and contradictory form of government that it would be everywhere it came into power—protective of privilege but demanding drastic change, supportive of old elites as long as these backed the new order but also promoting new social forces, and, most confusingly, urging violence as a cleansing solution while claiming to be sustaining the order demanded by conservatives (Sassoon 2007).

The unifying idea that resolved these contradictions was brutal, cleansing ultranationalism and acceptance of conspiracy theories, which blamed outside forces for all the miseries of the modern age, including the disaster of World War I. Violence could be directed internally against those who were undermining the nation and externally against rivals who were blocking "our" nation's rightful place in the international order. Furthermore, national unity was to be assured not by the alliance of the old, soiled, and failed political parties of the past but by the leadership of an infallible, almost godlike man brought to power to save the nation and return it to greatness. This would replace the semiparalyzed, endlessly argumentative rule of democratically elected parliaments, and it could appeal to a wide variety of ideologies ranging from intellectual admirers of Nietzschean philosophy, to revolutionaries who detested the old order, to the embittered former soldiers who felt betrayed by their establishment leaders (Passmore 2009; Kramer 2009; Bessel 2009; Sluga 2009; Gregor 1969, 75–175).

The Nazi genocide of the Jews was so monstrous that it is all too tempting to forget the vicious if somewhat lesser brutality of other fascist regimes. Fascist Italy may have been less cruel at home and in its later European conquests than Nazi Germany, but in the late 1920s and early 1930s Mussolini conducted a genocidal colonial war in Libya that killed up to one-third of its population and perhaps half of those in the eastern Libyan province of Cyrenaica (Ahmida 2005, 35–54). Later Mussolini invaded Ethiopia where he used poison gas and then sent an army to fight for the fascist cause in the Spanish Civil War. Then, when it seemed that Hitler had established hegemonic control over much of Europe, Mussolini launched his own, unnecessary wars against Greece and British-controlled Egypt (Rodogno 2009).

If Mussolini was an intellectual and onetime journalist versed in European philosophy, the same was not true for Adolf Hitler. Hitler did read a good deal in his youth, particularly while in Vienna and Munich prior to World War I, but much of this was probably limited to popular histories and other light fare. The greatest intellectual influences on the youthful Hitler were Richard Wagner's operas. (Wagner lived from 1813 to 1883.) Hitler responded not primarily to Wagner's many artistic innovations in music and drama but instead to some of the more powerful regressive ideas and sentiments that the composer put into his work. Resurrected versions of ancient German mythology, mixed with a mystical form of heroic nationalism were the ingredients that most appealed to Hitler. It is here, in fact, that the future Nazi leader eventually came to see himself as Wagnerian hero, destined to be the Parsifal of the German race (Kershaw 1999, 42–43). Such grandiose dreams were furthered by Hitler's time in Vienna, where he lived from 1908 to 1913, immersed in protofascist ideas. Such sentiments, for example, flowed freely from the lips of Georg Ritter von Schönerer (1842–1921), a prominent Austrian political leader who impressed the young Hitler. Schönerer called himself "Führer" (leader) and had followers celebrate him with "Heil" ("All hail"), which Hitler would later adopt. Equally important was Vienna's populist mayor, Karl Lueger (1844–1910), who combined hatred of Jews with a mass appeal to a middle class that felt threatened by big capitalists, immigrant laborers, and Jewish financiers. Lueger had famously said that the "Jewish problem" could be easily solved if all Jews were sent out on a large ship and sunk at sea (Kershaw 1999, 33–35). Yet another probable influence was the Viennese magazine *Ostara*, which drew on mythology from German, Hindu, and even Buddhist sources to glorify an Aryan master race. The magazine's founder was himself a follower of Guido von List, the man who first proposed the Hindu swastika as an "Aryan" symbol (Kershaw 1999, 49–50). That this was not the high philosophy of Nietzsche but a mishmash of vulgarized racism and nationalist fantasy did not make it any less powerful for the young Hitler.

There was, too, Vienna's role as a center of modern journalism, art, literature, and science. Here Jews were particularly prominent, as well as in the economy, and this fact aroused much resentment (Beller 1989). For a provincial youth like Hitler, whose hope was to be an artist, this seeming Jewish dominance would prove decisive in shaping his thinking. Yet all of these threads to Hitler's worldview would not coalesce until he moved to Munich, eagerly joined the German army to fight World War I, and then agonized about Germany's defeat. This experience and Germany's subsequent humiliation at the hands of the Allies began Hitler's desperate search for an explanation of what had gone wrong.

Hitler's sense that the heart of the problem was Jewish influence and power led to German fascism's obsession with genocidal anti-Semitism. But there was much more to his popularity, which was genuine, because he persuaded much of Germany during the desperate, insecure, and politically unstable years of the early 1930s Depression that he could fix the economy, bring back order, regain German greatness, and prevent Marxism from gaining ground. In the parliamentary elections of 1932 the Nazi Party became the largest, though it never gained an absolute majority. Once in power in 1933, he fulfilled his promises. He launched a rearmament program that ended unemployment and the Depression, he rearmed Germany and made it a great power once more, and he ended political instability by eliminating all other political parties. To a great many Germans, he proved the weakness of the great power democracies when he first militarized the Rhineland, in direct opposition to the Versailles Treaty, then annexed Austria and Czechoslovakia without any significant opposition. That is not to say that German popular support was anything close to unanimous or that all social, economic, and political problems went away. On the contrary, there remained opposition to what the Nazis were doing, but the combination of their widespread popularity on the one hand and brutal repression of dissent on the other allowed Hitler's regime to present an outward face of unanimity and adoration for his leadership (Peukert 1987).

Despite Hitler's obvious charisma and success, however, it would be an error to attribute everything to one man. Hitler's rise to power was never assured or fated. It depended on miscalculations by other politicians and by military authorities. Scholars now generally agree that, absent these blunders, the army, not Hitler, would have taken power in 1933 and created a military dictatorship, then moved to rearm and retake territories lost to Poland after World War I. That would have made history different; war might well have ensued but without a Holocaust and perhaps without the intervention of the French and British to save Poland. At the same time, however, the prevailing antiliberal environment would not have dissipated. Henry Turner, whose book about the way Hitler came to power is a key source for understanding how far it was from inevitable, nevertheless acknowledges that if so many of Germany's intellectuals and elites had not been so determinedly antiliberal and hostile to the Enlightenment ideals of personal freedom and democracy, Hitler himself never could have established his dictatorship so quickly, so thoroughly, and with so much popular approval. Without such support, even once he gained power, it would have been very difficult for his Nazi Party to turn Germany so easily into a totalitarian, genocidal monster (Turner 1996, 163–83).

Admiration of violence, desire for strong and decisive leadership, ultranationalism, "manly" aggressiveness, and rejection of "weak" tolerance for divergent views and for cautious, carefully considered rationality were what cemented various nationalist ideologies and even contradictory economic and social goals in both Italy and Germany around the person of the all-knowing, all-powerful leader, the "duce," Mussolini, and the "führer," Hitler. The ideas put forward by intellectuals hostile to the Enlightenment, disseminated through more simplistic, more popular publications well before World War I, prepared the way for the subsequent rise of fascism and continued to legitimize its spread during the 1930s.

VARIETIES OF FASCISM FROM EUROPE TO EAST ASIA, LATIN AMERICA, AND THE MIDDLE EAST

The protean nature of fascist ideology and its many varieties might make it seem that there was no common ideological base. This was not the case. If we look not just at Italy and Germany but also around the world at other movements and regimes that could be called fascist, we see more clearly how they could differ in many details, depending on local political cultures, but still have important common elements that together defined the essence of what it was about. Furthermore, in the 1920s and 1930s, both Italy and, after Hitler came to power, Germany were models all over the world for those wanting to construct similar societies. The ideas behind fascism have hardly disappeared since then, though the defeat of the fascist powers in World War II made it unfashionable to cite Mussolini or Hitler as models.

A Community United by Blood under the Guidance of an Infallible Father-Leader

What were the fundamental ideas on which all fascist regimes were based? Basic was a rejection of any ideology that accepted class warfare as a natural outcome of capitalist industrialization. Thus, even as revolutionary fascist movements often denounced high finance, this was tied more often than not to accusing it of being somehow foreign or, in many cases, "Jewish." The very term "Nazi" is a short form of Nationalsozialismus (National Socialism), so named after the official name of Hitler's Party, Nationalsozialistische Deutsche Arbeiterpartei (National Socialist German Workers' Party). Socialism as practiced by both the democratically inclined Social Democrats and the Communists in the 1920s and 1930s was rabidly rejected because it fed on internal class conflict, which weakened all-important national solidarity. Thus independent unions were also hated. Instead, what was sought was some kind of national, usually race-based communal union, or what the German Right idealized as a Völksgemeinschaft, a term not easily translated. The "Völk" were the members of the nation, joined by blood relationship and a supposedly common but actually mythologized ancestry. Gemeinschaft was the warm, familial, small community in which positions were assigned by gender, age, tradition, and close personal ties rather than by the impersonal, bureaucratic, and coldly formal relations that were deemed to characterize modern firms and societies (Gesellschaft, also the German term for the modern business corporation).

The emphasis on the familial, close community as a remedy for the alienation and impersonality of modern life was a universal aspect of fascism. It was emphasized in the most prominent Japanese expression of the official national ideology published in 1937 once Japan had become genuinely fascist, *Kokutai No Hongi* (the fundamentals— sometimes translated as the cardinal principles—of the national polity or, literally, the national body). Aside from stressing the unbroken line of the supposedly divine imperial family and the duty of the Japanese to be guided by the fatherly, all-knowing emperor, the document "emphasized the centrality of the family, state, home, and ancestors." *Kokutai* was similar to what the Germans called *Völk*, a people tied together by common blood into the national family. The text idealized Japan's culture as far purer and nobler than crass, alienating Western individualism and stressed the myth of Japan as a "tightly unified, monolithic state and society" (Bix 2000, 313–15).

The Japanese philosopher Kuki Shūzō, inspired by his years of study with French and German philosophical proponents of antirational and antimodern nationalism such as Heidegger, wrote approvingly of this orientation, of the superiority of Japan's "culture folk" (*buka minzoku*), and of Japan's right to impose its superior "pure" culture on China by force (Pincus 1996, 229–32).

Reading through *Kokutai No Hongi* we can find all the elements present in the pre-1914 intellectual writings and ideas that would inspire fascists, including an emphasis on the unbroken rule of the imperial family descended from the gods, something more uniquely Japanese and meant to replace the virtually divine and infallible fürher or duce, and an insistence on the inherent unity and superiority of the Japanese race. Ancient mythologies mixed in with a late nineteenth-century interpretation of the traditional, pre-Buddhist practice of Shinto, while uniquely Japanese in detail, were not so different from Mussolini's exaltation of Rome and Hitler's obsession with Germanic and "Aryan" myths in their intent. There was, of course, an acceptance of the need to maintain a technologically powerful, modern society, but this was balanced by utter contempt for the supposedly failed liberal individualism of the Western Enlightenment (*Kokutai No Hongi* 1937/1949). Total subservience to the state and emperor worship would then legitimize the brutality of Japanese imperialism that culminated in the complete militarization of society and the launching of a series of wars that ended only in 1945 (Kersten 2009; and more broadly Maruyama and Morris 1969; Bix 2000, 317–85). The historian Walter Skya, documenting the adaptation of traditional Shinto into a new religion glorifying the emperor and justifying a kind of holy war to expand the Japanese Empire, used the term "disenlightenment," something that would have applied to all the fascist movements and parties proliferating between the two world wars (Skya 2009, 263).

In Romania both the virulently anti-Semitic League of the National Christian Defense and its more successful later rival, the Iron Guard in the 1920 and 1930s, preached a form of Orthodox Christian xenophobia, a worship of blood (that is, familial) ties within the pure Romanian folk, an idealization of peasant communal solidarity that was almost entirely myth perpetuated by nationalist poets, writers, and philosophers, and an insistence on the superiority of Romanian culture over that of its neighbors. The various Romanian fascist movements exalted their leaders, most prominently the would-be Romanian führer, Corneliu Zelea Codreanu, leader of the Iron Guard, who was murdered by Romania's authoritarian King Carol II in 1938. A local twist was the proclaimed Christianity of Romanian fascism and its alliance with the Romanian Orthodox Church. Romania could not, of course, claim the same great power status as Germany, Italy, or Japan, but it did its best. Under the rule of its openly fascist military dictator, Marshall Ion Antonescu, who ruled from 1940 to 1944 and styled himself "conducător" (Romanian for leader, in other words, führer), Romania allied itself to Nazi Germany, invaded the Soviet Union with the Germans, and attempted to annex Soviet territory as far as Odessa along the Black Sea Coast. It also launched efforts to racially purify the country, sanctioning mass killing of Jews in its own eastern province of Moldova, in Bessarabia (today mostly the Republic of Moldova), and in the Ukrainian territories it briefly annexed that it called Transnistria. The popularity of fascism in Romania had much to do with that country's strong anti-Semitic tradition that dated to the mid-nineteenth century and to the fact that its intellectuals widely shared delusions about the uniqueness of their supposed mix of "Latin" and "Dacian" (the pre-Roman Thracians) racial origins and purity. Equally important was a strong sense of resentment, jealousy, and inferiority caused by the relative weakness of their nation that had not been sufficiently recognized as great by the major European powers (Ioanid 2000; Solonari 2010; Weber 1966).

In the 1930s, major Romanian intellectuals, some of whom would later become internationally known, such as Mircea Eliade and Emil Cioran, along with the majority of the non-Jewish intelligentsia went along with this cult of the nation, the anti-Semitism, and the contempt for neighboring peoples whose languages were either Slavic or Hungarian rather than the Latin-based Romanian. Romania also produced an internationally known economic theorist of fascist corporatism, Mihail Manoilescu, whose work influenced later Brazilian and Argentinian economists. An admirer of Mussolini's "corporatist" state, Manoilescu promoted economic autarky, dictatorship, and national solidarity as ways of overcoming backwardness (Love 1996).

An interesting aspect of Romanian fascism was that two and a half decades after it collapsed and was replaced by Soviet-imposed communism, Romania's communist leader, Nicolae Ceauşescu, began to rehabilitate the memory of those very ultranationalist fascist ideologues of the 1930s and to move Romania into the kind of racially based, autarkic state that they had wanted to create. Whether this was fascism or communism is, of course, partly a matter of definition, but the resemblance between the two forms is more than coincidental. Both wanted to overcome the class conflict and alienation of industrial society with more communally solidary social forms, and as time went on, Romanian communism itself came to rely ever more on the same ultranationalism as fascism, as well as on the glorification of its leaders and the promotion of a mythologized history claiming that Romania had somehow been in the forefront of Western civilization and should be recognized for this (Verdery 1991).

In the most extreme communist cases, Albania under Enver Hoxha, the Soviet Union under Stalin, China under Mao, Romania under Ceauşescu, and North Korea under the Kim family, the leader himself replaced Marx as the fount of all wisdom and knowledge and the difference between fascism and communism narrowed greatly (Tismaneanu 2012; Chirot 1980; Cumings 1982).

Fascist Corporatism: The Theory That Never Worked

Raising the notion of corporatism brings up another of the major commonalities in fascist ideologies around the world as well as one of fascism's basic contradictions. The very term "corporatism" is somewhat confusing as it has a meaning very different from that used to describe modern large firms. But in fascist ideology, particularly where it was first developed, Mussolini's Italy in the 1930s, the meaning was clear. The goal was to overcome the class conflict between the working classes and farm laborers on the one hand and the owners of enterprises and land on the other by creating functionally based institutions that would unite employers and employees in harmonious "corporations." These would be combined into large groups by types of industries and professions, and conflicts within them would be mediated by the fascist state. Over time, the economy would be evermore regulated by the state, creating a kind of non-Marxist or "neo" socialism focused on achieving national self-sufficiency, that is, economic autarky, as well as social harmony. In practice, of course, all this meant was that independent labor unions were crushed, pleasing Mussolini's conservative allies (Gregor 1969, 293–303).

The Nazi Party's original "socialism" was connected to such ideas and promoted by the left wing of the party, whose ideologues spelled it out before Hitler's accession to power. The chief Nazi ideologue tasked with this was Gottfried Feder. But such ideas did not appeal to German industrialists, and Hitler's goals were much more oriented to imperial expansion, economic self-sufficiency by any means as a way of preparing for war, and racial purification. Vague notions of socialism could be thrown overboard if necessary. Feder's ideas were put aside once Hitler was in power (Neumann 1944/1963, 228–34). After many of the leaders of the left wing of the Nazi Party were murdered or otherwise pushed aside by Hitler in 1934 in order to placate more conservative forces, particularly the German army, and to consolidate his own power, the "socialism" part of Nazism vanished, though not the continuing drive to centralize the economy and put it on a war footing (Kershaw 1999, 506–17).

In Italy, corporatist institutions never really functioned, and it was only after he had been overthrown in 1943, imprisoned, rescued by the Germans, and then turned into a German puppet in northern Italy that Mussolini tried to reestablish his corporatist goals. By then it was just a fantasy, and the corporatist ideas he spun out had no real meaning (Morgan 2009, 154–65; Gregor 1969, 306–9).

Nevertheless, the idea of corporatism was very appealing to anti-liberal intellectuals in Europe, Latin America, and even part of Asia because it seemed able to solve the problem of modern class conflict while also cementing national unity and promoting what they all desired: centralized state control and economic growth freed of the international capitalist system dominated by the United Kingdom, France, and increasingly the United States. Mussolini's claim, taken originally from ideas put forth before World War I by Enrico Coradini, was that Italian fascism would raise the "proletarian" nation of Italy to its rightful place against the "plutocratic" rich nations that had dominated the world (Berend 1998, 70–71). The point was for corporatism to transform Marx's ideas of class conflict from something that took place within states to a conflict between nations, with deserving subordinate nations on one side and undeserving, degenerate ones on the other. For this, obviously, it was necessary to unify the nation and prepare it for war.

As an afterthought, it is interesting to note that in the later part of the twentieth century this idea of turning Marxist class conflict into a struggle between poorer, or "peripheral," nations and richer, or "core," ones became a staple of much left-wing theorizing (Love 1996; Packenham 1992). Here, as in the adoption of ultranationalism and the worship of an omniscient father-leader, the far Left in many cases transformed itself into something very close to its formerly hated enemy, fascism.

The Spread of Fascism in Europe

Fascist movements arose in all European countries, but at least until Germany conquered most of the continent, the more extreme variants did not come to power except in Germany itself (in 1933), Italy (1922), and Spain (1939). There were, however, dictatorships in almost all of southern, central, and eastern Europe that included some aspects of fascist ideology: contempt for democracy, repression of labor movements, autocratic leadership, persecution of socialists and communists, hypernationalism legitimized by myths about a grander past, purifying racism, and resentment of supposed enemies of the nation (Rogger and Weber 1966). By early 1938, aside from western Europe (France, the United Kingdom, Belgium, Luxemburg, the Netherlands, Switzerland, and the Scandinavian countries), there remained only one European democracy. That was Czechoslovakia, which would soon be dismembered in 1938 by Hitler's Germany. All the others, except for the Soviet Union, which was ruled by the exceedingly brutal communist dictator Joseph Stalin, were guided by ideologies that were at least partly if not entirely fascist. Even in most of democratic western Europe there were fascist kinds of parties of varying strength, particularly in France and Belgium but in the others as well (Riley 2010; De Wever 2009; Rogger and Weber 1966; Nolte 1965).

Not all historians of fascism agree. For example, Walter Laqueur begins his comparative book about fascism asserting that "Twentieth-century dictatorships may be detestable, but they are not necessarily fascist. Japan in the 1930s was not a fascist country, nor was Ataturk's Turkey, nor Poland under Pilsudski, nor Spain under Franco" (Laqueur 1996, 13). This misses the point. Of course they were all different, but all shared some aspects of fascist violence, suppression of working-class socialist and communist movements, antiliberalism, ultranationalism, purifying racism, and worship of the leader, and even in most cases some vague if unfulfilled pretentions toward a kind of autarkic corporatism.

A better approach than to insist that only Germany and Italy (or perhaps only Italy because it invented the terminology of fascism) were fascist is Robert Paxton's succinct definition of fascist movements as ones "marked by obsessive preoccupation with community decline, humiliation, or victimhood and by compensatory cults of unity, energy, and purity, in which a mass-based party of committed nationalist militants, working in uneasy but effective collaboration with traditional elites, abandons democratic liberties and pursues redemptive violence, and without ethical or legal restraints, goals of internal cleansing and external expansion" (Paxton 2009, 549). Furthermore, even though fascist ideology had to be imagined and described in its various ways, the movements themselves were "contemptuous of human reason and intellectual enquiry." Their ideologies, therefore, unlike those that underlay liberalism and socialism, appealed to visceral emotion rather than to coherent doctrine (Paxton 2009, 554).

In Spain, for example, the fascist Falange Party called for purifying violence and antidemocratic dictatorship to rescue Spain from its chaotic governments and economic ills. It also, like the Romanian Iron Guardists, was tied to reactionary religious sentiment, in this case, the Spanish Catholic Church. The controversy about Spanish fascism arises from the fact that ultimately the Falange did not gain power. Instead it was the army, led by Francisco Franco, that started the civil war in 1936 that overthrew the Spanish Republic in 1939. During this very bloody war, Franco (who would eventually rule as dictator until his death in 1975) would probably have lost without major help from Mussolini and Hitler, while the republic fell increasingly into the hands of communists because Stalin's Soviet Union was the only major power willing to help it. The Falange was allied to Franco, but after his victory he gradually sidelined it and by the end of his rule in the 1960s and 1970s Spain had moved decisively toward a more open, less violent, and less aggressive form of dictatorship. Corporatism, which had been part of the Falangist program, was never seriously tried (Payne 1966, 203–5; and more generally, Payne 1999).

Nevertheless, in 1939 and 1940, as Franco tried to enlist Nazi Germany into his nationalist goals, and while conducting a brutal bloodbath against the defeated supporters of the republic, his regime had all the hallmarks of fascism. As part of this, he demanded that Hitler grant Spain large parts of the French West African colonial empire, plans were made to go to war with the United Kingdom to seize Gibraltar, and there was even a serious project to invade Portugal. This all foundered on Germany's evaluation of Spain's weakness, the backwardness of its economy, and the fact that Germany had too many other commitments to help Spain. Partly as a result of this failure, the Falangists closest to Franco lost influence. Many of the most enthusiastic young men who made up its shock troops were encouraged to go off in a special Spanish division to fight the Soviet Union after Hitler invaded it in June 1941, and that was where most of them died. Then, when it became obvious by early 1943 that Hitler and Mussolini were going to lose their war, Franco cleverly backtracked, and the prospects for creating a real fascist regime faded (Payne 2008; Vincent 2009). In the end, Franco turned out to be the only friend of Hitler and Mussolini to survive in power, but of course, had World War II turned out differently, if the fascist powers had won, it seems certain that Spain would have become a more fully fascist state instead of the somewhat reformed, stodgily religious, and conservative monarchist regime that Franco tried but failed to leave as his legacy.

Of course fascism was hardly limited to Europe and Japan as it was admired and partly imitated in many other parts of the world where Mussolini's example was particularly seductive because it aimed to turn a relatively poor country into a great, modern power while honoring national tradition and protecting elites from the dangers of socialist revolution. It would take too long to go into any detail about many other cases, but a few more can be mentioned.

Argentina: Latin America's Version of Fascism

Argentina under the rule of Juan Perón from 1943 to 1955, but particularly during the early part of his rule, came close to being genuinely fascist. Perón himself was an open admirer of Mussolini and Nazi Germany and tried to create a kind of corporatist state. He was, however, much more concerned with actually bettering the working class than European fascists, and the Argentinian union movement that he favored has remained to this day mostly loyal to his memory. Because of this Perón's version was in some ways far more populist and hostile to business and landowning elites than were fascist Italy and Nazi Germany. It was in that sense closer to the original impulses of Mussolini's fascism and even Hitler's Nazism than what those more clearly fascist regimes became once in power (Rock 1993, 145–56).

With the collapse of fascist Italy and Nazi Germany Perón moved partly away from the drift toward totalitarian fascism that had characterized his first years in power, but he never completely abandoned its ideology. Nationalist resentment against foreign domination was a major part of this. In Argentina's case at that time this was originally frustration over British control of much Argentinian investment and Britain's role as the main importer of Argentinian wheat and beef. Nationalism and a sense of superiority over the rest of Latin America were widely accepted not just by Perón but also by his enemies who were equally nationalistic. At first the Catholic Church supported him but then became uneasy as Perón and his charismatic wife Eva (popularly called Evita) promoted a mystical, emotionally powerful worship of the dictator. Eventually the Church became his enemy because he was trying to substitute worship of himself over loyalty to Catholic doctrine, and it helped turn the population against him, which allowed an army-led coup to overthrow him in 1955 (Rock 1993, 149–83).

There is no need to go into the details of Argentina's political history but only to emphasize how much fascist ideas appealed to many of its people. The cult of violence, the worship of the great leader, the search for an alternative to both liberal capitalism and to socialism, the cultivation of resentful nationalism—these were appealing in other parts of Latin America as well, though Argentina developed such ideas more thoroughly than others.

Argentina also had the largest Jewish community in Latin America, and its right-wing inclinations included a strong element of anti-Semitism along with rejection of the Enlightenment. A prominent nationalist theoretician of the 1940s, Salvador Ferla, wrote that nationalism rejected "modern errors that started with Descartes and reached a climax with Kant." He also denounced democracy as "the tool of the Jews" and decried giving women the right to vote (quoted in Rock 1993, 168). That this was much more than mere fantasy by a marginal intellectual but part of mainstream Counter-Enlightenment thinking in Argentina is shown by what eventually happened after Perón's return to power in 1973. He came back as an old and dying man in that year and was then succeeded by his utterly incompetent wife Isabel (Eva had died of cancer in 1952). She was overthrown in a military coup in 1976. Then the military regime that followed adopted many of the same nasty ideas and practices of the fascist regimes of the past.

The military was not a friend of the Perónist unions, but it was brutally, violently dictatorial, hostile to any form of Enlightenment liberalism, and aggressively nationalistic. Its leading intellectual monthly journal, *Cabildo*, favored a rebellious branch of the Catholic Church led by the French Cardinal Lefebvre that denied the reality of the Holocaust and rejected the liberalizing reforms of Vatican II, which had become official Church doctrine in 1965. *Cabildo* "listed the teachings of Jews, Marxists, Freudians, Jehovah's Witnesses, Seventh-Day Adventists, and Mormons" as the enemy, in other words, anything that might threaten the religious hegemony of the most reactionary elements of the Catholic Church (Rock 1993, 227). The military regime launched an internal war against any possible opposition, tortured and murdered tens of thousands, and then went to war in 1982 with the United Kingdom to satisfy a claim to the Falkland Islands (*Nunca Más* 1986; Rock 1993, 224–31).

The prominent Jewish journalist Jacobo Timerman was imprisoned and tortured, and his life was saved only because he was internationally famous and pressure was put on the military regime to release him. He wrote in his memoirs about what he had undergone. His jailers had told him that:

> Argentina has three main enemies: Karl Marx because he tried to destroy the Christian concept of society; Sigmund Freud because he tried to destroy the Christian concept of the family; and Albert Einstein because he tried to destroy the Christian concept of time and space. (1982, 130)

Enough said! It was all the fault of these three major Jewish intellectuals.

The incompetently led expedition against the Falklands (known by the Argentines as Los Malvinas) ended in disaster, and the military junta that had ruled was overthrown. Argentina, however, still claims the islands and still elects Perónists as its presidents.

Fascism as an Inspiration for Anticolonial Intellectuals

The Arab Middle East also saw admirers of fascism, and intellectuals whose ideas about how to blend fascist ideas with modernizing Arab nationalist programs greatly influenced the course of politics in that region; however, we have to be careful about labeling every form of antiliberalism as fascism. Used that way, the term can lose its meaning.

What is important is not to insist on finding the proper label but to recognize how well the same ideals that underlay fascism appealed very widely in a variety of cases. Resentful, angry nationalism combined with a desire to violently cleanse an existing corrupt political system seen as a barrier to national redemption was understandable in the colonial part of the world dominated until well into the mid-twentieth century by Europeans. As such sentiments almost invariably came from relatively well-educated minorities but appealed to the less fortunate masses as well as to young intellectuals embittered by the subservience of their people, it was an easy step to claim that revolutionary elites were better interpreters of the nation's needs than the untutored masses and therefore that true democracy should mean rule by the elite who were more genuinely "democratic" than what the corrupt and evil West called "democracy." This certainly characterized fascism but also communism and other forms of autocratic nationalism.

Arab nationalism gradually turned away from resistance by traditional elites against European colonialism in the 1920s and 1930 to a movement led by young Western-educated men looking for ways of combating Western domination while also modernizing their societies. Mussolini's Italy, despite its brutality in Libya, was an obvious model (Ajami 1998, 224–25). The rise of Nazi Germany from its defeat in 1918 to great power in the 1930s also appealed to growing Arab nationalists, and Hitler seemed to some an ideal nationalist able to mobilize his people to greatness (Dawisha 2009, 98).

Michel Aflaq (1910–89), a Christian from Damascus who was educated in France, set out a doctrine of pan-Arab nationalism in the late 1930s that became, in 1947, the Ba'ath Party. By the time the Ba'ath took control of Syria and Iraq in 1963, Aflaq had been politically sidelined, but he remained the intellectual inspiration of Iraqi Ba'athism and died as an honored guest in Saddam Hussein's Iraq. His ideology and that of the Ba'athists is often labeled fascist, particularly by those eager to associate Arab nationalism's hatred of Israel—and for many, of Jews in general—with Nazism (for example, Patterson 2011, 225–38). The problem with this is that it tends to make all anti-Israeli Arab or for that matter Muslim sentiments "fascist."

We will deal with this particular issue in a later chapter on Islamic religious fundamentalism, but it has to be pointed out that while the association of Arab nationalism with fascism and Nazi racism is not entirely baseless, it neglects some of the reasons why Israel has been so objectionable to Arab nationalists.

Aflaq's final home, Saddam Hussein's Iraq, was unquestionably vicious and violently aggressive. It combined the kind of state-directed but still partly private and corrupt economy that characterized the European fascist states, and it merged anti-Israeli Arab nationalism with what could only be called racist anti-Semitism. Its official ideology, as in a similarly run Ba'athist Syria, drew from communism and militant Third Worldism as well as from older fascist ideas (Makiya 1989). (See chapter 2 for a fuller description of the origins and meaning of the term "Third World.") As far as Aflaq's obvious admiration of fascism before

World War II, his later revised written works took out early references to fascism, though the ideas remained the same (Makiya 1989, 223). But was this same as European fascism?

Walter Laqueur, analyzing Arab anti-Semitism, has written that "Muslim antisemitism was the result of, not the reason for[,] the hostile Arab attitude toward Israel. . . . [I]n Europe the stereotype of the Jew was that of the parasite, in the Arab world . . . especially after 1948 that of aggressor, assassin, and warmonger." Jews, who had previously been considered weak, cowardly, and subservient, had turned into something completely unacceptable, frightful robbers of Arab land (Laqueur 2006, 196–97). Without Israel's presence, it is unlikely that anti-Semitism would have played so large a role in Ba'athist or other Arab nationalist ideologies. Even the mufti of Jerusalem, Amin al-Husayni (1897–1974), who during World War II wound up in Germany where he was able to talk to Hitler and other Nazi leaders about cooperating to destroy the possibility of a Jewish homeland, turned in this direction as a result of his hostility to British rule in and Jewish immigration into Palestine (Mattar 1988, 100–104, 140–53; see also Segev 2000, 462–64).

The same could be said of Rashid Ali, an Iraqi general who briefly took power in Iraq in 1940 and 1941. He tried to establish an alliance with Hitler to better drive out British influence and openly admired Nazi militarism, as did many other Iraqi military men who saw fascism as a model for cleansing their society of corruption, freeing it of European domination, uniting it, and modernizing it. As it happened, however, the British army invaded Iraq and overthrew him, reinstating the pro-British monarchy that lasted until it was bloodily overthrown in 1958 (Wien 2006; Makiya 1989).

A similar sequence of events took place in neighboring Iran. It was ruled by Reza Shah, an army officer who made himself king (shah) in 1925 and established the dynasty that would last until 1979 when his son was overthrow by the Iranian Revolution. Reza Shah was intent on modernizing his country and in the 1930s looked increasingly to Germany as a model. Nazi Germany appeared to be modern and orderly, and it showed that dictatorship was more efficient than liberal democracy. Furthermore, it was a counterweight to Britain at a time when the British regularly interfered in Iranian affairs and controlled its oil production. Hitler recognized Iranians as racially superior Aryans (Iran and Aryan are derived from the same Sanskrit word meaning "noble"), which flattered the shah as well. But with the start of World War II, the strong German economic and political influence in Iran threatened the British and, after Hitler's invasion of the Soviet Union, Russia as well. Soviet and British armies invaded and overthrew the shah in September 1941, putting his son on the throne and effectively taking over the country for the duration of the war. Fascist ideology here, as elsewhere, had seemed to be a promising path to rapid economic development and escape from European colonial power (Keddie and Richard 2006, 101–6).

In short, while we cannot say that all anticolonial parties and regimes in the Middle East that took some elements of fascism can be called specifically fascist, there is no denying that when we look at the intellectuals who originally provided ideas for these movements it is very clear that they were influenced by the major European fascist powers.

This was obviously not just a Middle Eastern phenomenon. The rest of the world also took notice. Needless to say, both extreme socialism in the form of communism as well as European fascism appealed to intellectuals in the non-European world. The Soviet Union was one model of a poor, marginalized European power that had turned itself around and become a seeming model of how to fight back against the hypocrisy and domination of the West. But so were Italy and, even more, Germany, as it was the British and the French, Germany's enemies, who were the main colonial powers throughout Africa and Asia.

By the 1930s there were movements throughout much of the world that mixed admiration of communist and fascist strategies for modernizing society, but when combined with nationalist pride, the rightist version seemed better for many. Aside from the examples already given, in both Turkey and nationalist China there was open admiration of Nazi Germany in the mid- to late 1930s (Kirby 1984, chapters 5 and 6; Adanır 2001). After World War II, however, it was no longer fashionable to admit being inspired by Mussolini and Hitler, and the revolutionary, youthful impulse behind fascism became leftist as it began to inspire much of the Third World.

The important fact is that the intellectual inspiration for both the far Right and the far Left leaned heavily on Western thinkers who had initiated these movements and whose ideas proved to be easily adaptable to anticolonial, modernizing nationalisms. But by the 1950s and 1960s, this was always associated with the Left (Kautsky 1967).

Third World nationalism and the brutal modernizing dictatorships and military rulers that came to dominate much of the Middle East, including Algeria, Libya (under Muammar Qaddafi), Nasser's Egypt, and Ba'athist Syria and Iraq certainly took on many fascist as well as communist trappings without ever becoming entirely one or the other. They all saw themselves as leftists bent on overthrowing corrupt old elites as well as standing up to Western imperialism, of which Israel came to be defined as a hated offshoot. Then these Third Worldists actually did go far in trying to destroy the old elites who had collaborated with European colonialism. But ultimately they created their own corrupt economic elites, their autarkic economic policies did not work, and their internal violent repression turned many of their people against them. They all failed (Malley 1996, 168–203; Dawisha 2003, 214–313). But then, this was the fate of all the twentieth-century revolutionary regimes that relied to a considerable extent on Counter-Enlightenment ideas and practices, on both the Right and the Left.

Philosophical Support for Fascism and Its Continuing Allure

Though this may not at first sight be obvious, the discussion of a sample of fascist and semi-fascist movements outside Europe can provide an insight into one of the more controversial and in many ways puzzling aspects of fascism in Germany itself, namely, its attraction for some very prominent, brilliant intellectuals.

It is not too difficult to understand why among so many European intellectuals of many ideological persuasions before World War I there was considerable dismay about social change. Increasing material well-being was accompanied by growing class conflict; urbanization and industrialization seemed to be weakening traditional family and community ties; better education made far more people aware of continuing, and perhaps even growing, immense inequality; traditional religions no longer seemed able to answer questions about their validity, particularly as scientific advances raised ever-increasing doubts about the value of religious dogma; and finally, the promises of the Enlightenment, which had certainly brought huge technological advances, were failing to create anything close to the ideals of general personal liberty and freedom. In short, modernization was not fulfilling its promises.

Albert Hirschman has identified three great waves of political reaction against modern classical Enlightenment liberalism. The first was against the excesses of the French Revolution, the second was this late nineteenth-century attack against the social change and democratization brought about by modernizing industrialization, and the third began in the 1980s in reaction to the seeming overbureaucratization of welfare states in the West and is still going on against increasing globalization (Hirschman 1991, 3–8). The late nineteenth-century version (as today's) was as much from the Left that wanted to move toward some form of egalitarian socialism as it was from the Right that hoped to reject the most unsettling effects of modernity. That is why the roots of fascism were originally, as Zeev Sternhell put it and we have already noted, "neither right nor left."

World War I only increased disillusionment with the liberal Enlightenment. Progress and liberty had failed to prevent this immense, pointless tragedy. In Europe, the reactionary side of discontent soon found that it had potential allies among conservative forces because it rejected both socialism and communism as alien, antinational forces feeding on class conflict rather than focusing on rebuilding unity and preserving national traditions. For those intellectuals who were both nationalists and hostile to the idea of radical socialism and failed liberalism but who nevertheless saw that returning to a simpler religious, conservative trust in traditional rulers and elites could no longer work, something that eventually came to be fascism was a welcome solution. It combined reaction with an appeal to the masses without endorsing corrupt democracy. It was antisocialist while ideally promoting the general welfare and the unity of all economic classes. It called on the enthusiasm of youth to redeem the nation from temporizing and inept politicians.

These were the same kinds of sentiments that later led to Third Worldist movements, which appealed so broadly to revolutionary intellectuals outside Europe. They were seeking solutions to a similar problem: how to deal with the contradictions of modernity when Enlightenment liberalism no longer seemed to provide a good answer, so either the communist far Left or the fascist far Right, or some combination of the two, seemed promising.

What does this have to do with two of the most prominent German intellectuals of the twentieth century, Carl Schmitt (1888–1985) and Martin Heidegger (1889–1976)? Whether or not we agree with their ideologies, turning to fascism was an entirely reasonable and appealing choice for them because those kinds of ideas seemed to provide solutions to their deeply felt frustrations and anger about Germany's failures during and right after World War I, and for them communism was too alien, too international, and too removed from nationalist passion and their own cultural traditions to provide an answer.

Schmitt, a legal scholar, brilliantly and persuasively excoriated the liberal basis of the post–World War I Weimar constitution. Liberal democracy imposed on Germany by the Allies was ineffective and alien. It needed to be replaced by a strong state that would guide Germany back to greatness. The German historian Karl-Dietrich Bracher has written about Schmitt's approach: "By comparing a theoretically idealized parliamentary democracy with the empirical circumstances of power in the Weimar Republic, he constructed an unresolvable contradiction within pluralistic democracy as such, and thus eventually came around to justifying the total state." This was "a method that was disastrously influential" (1995, 247). Schmitt was hostile to individualism and worried about the decadence, moral weakness, and materialism of modern life. He wrote, "[T]he value of life stems not from reasoning; it emerges in a state of war where men inspired by myth do battle" (quoted by Holmes 1993, 42). Once the Nazis came to power, he joined the party, and in a book on Hobbes published in 1938 he wrote, "[T]he Jews . . . observe how the people of the earth kill each other. For them this mutual butchery is lawful and 'kosher.' Accordingly, they eat the flesh of the slaughtered peoples and live off it" (quoted in Holmes 1993, 51; see also the quote at the beginning of this chapter).

Strangely, or perhaps not so strangely, Schmitt became the darling of quite a few leftist antiliberals after World War II. For example, the onetime New Leftist and now just antiliberal quarterly journal *Telos* published seventy-four articles between 1968 and 2013 with "Carl Schmitt" in the title, as well as several special issues devoted to him. While recognizing his Nazi period from 1933 on, many of these articles more or less excuse it and admire instead his critique of liberal democracy. (A good recent example is issue 142, Spring 2008, and particularly Emden 2008).

Martin Heidegger's career as a philosopher, considered one of the most influential in the twentieth century, is even more to the point. Seeking to promote a more united, stronger Germany, Heidegger was also deeply hostile to the entire Enlightenment. For him modern technology was proof that humanity had "lost its way" (Holmes 1993, 123). He was very much a part of a Counter-Enlightenment tradition that we have traced from the reaction against the French Revolution into the twentieth century. This fit well into the romantic German mysticism that was part of the appeal of Nazism (Gray 1996, 133; Berlin 2002, 206–7). Like many politically inexperienced intellectuals, Heidegger was not particularly successful in his attempts to curry favor with the Nazis to secure a better position for himself, though he remained a respected and influential pro-Nazi academic philosopher. After World War II, Heidegger's views hardly changed, and he argued that "it made no difference to European civilization whether Europe was smothered by America or Russia in the process of technologization and mass leveling" (Bracher 1995, 210).

Because Heidegger influenced much post–World War II philosophy around the world, his Nazism and anti-Enlightenment writings have remained controversial. He was, for example, a strong influence on French thought, notably that of Jacques Derrida, one of the heroes of what is considered leftist postmodernist deconstruction, which is at its heart a plea against the consequences of liberal modernization and materialism. Derrida, like another of the heroes of postmodernism, David Harvey, struggled mightily to disentangle Heidegger's Nazism from his more "useful" critique of modernity (Harvey 1990, 207–10; Faye 2009, 171). This is not to suggest that Derrida, Harvey, or for that matter postmodernism itself is fascist (though some of its founders were) but rather to point out the continuing appeal of Counter-Enlightenment skepticism about the values of liberalism and modernity. And in a cultural atmosphere that has systematically delegitimized those values, when Counter-Enlightenment ideas become the basis of political action, frightening outcomes are likely to occur.

The argument here is not that noted intellectuals like Schmitt and Heidegger shaped Nazism. The intellectual basis for all forms of fascism was laid well before they began to write. Rather, their work helped give Nazism a greater patina of intellectual legitimacy. More important, despite their brilliance and learning these two men were seduced by Hitler and Nazism, and so became their spokesmen. We do not need to completely agree with an argument like that of Emmanuel Faye (2009) that tries to suggest that Heidegger's philosophy and Schmitt's jurisprudence made no real sense to agree with Faye's conclusion:

> We must be mindful that behind its masks of legal "erudition" and political "vision" the works of a Carl Schmitt signal the demise of justice. . . . and that beneath the cover of philosophical "greatness" those of Martin Heidegger aim at the destruction of philosophy and the eradication of human meaning. . . . [They] strive toward the goal of the eradication of all the intellectual and human progress to which philosophy has contributed. (2009, 322)

The danger is not that such Counter-Enlightenment ideas lack sense but rather the opposite. Ideas such as these, when they begin to form the basis of a rejection of the Enlightenment, no matter how difficult they may be to interpret without subsequent vulgarizations and simplifications, can have a profound effect. In their original form, they can seduce even the most learned and powerful intellects. In a simplified version, they can appeal to many more. We ought not underestimate how attractive they can be to those disenchanted with the ineptitudes, corruption, and bad decisions made by all too fallible leaders of liberal democracies. But this makes it even more essential to remember that Counter-Enlightenment ideologies need to be analyzed seriously and met with equally learned and persuasive arguments. Otherwise they can poison a whole era, as they did in so much of Europe in the first half of the twentieth century and as they continue to do in parts of the world to this day.

CHAPTER 6

Christian Fundamentalism

The Politics of God in America

And he said unto them, Go ye into all the world, and preach the gospel to every creature. He that believeth and is baptized shall be saved; but he that believeth not shall be damned. And these signs shall follow them that believe: In my name shall they cast out devils; they shall speak with new tongues. They shall take up serpents; and if they drink any deadly thing, it shall not hurt them; they shall lay hands on the sick, and they shall recover.

MARK 16:15–18

They have often heard that conversion is a work of mighty power, manifesting to the soul what neither man nor angel can give such a conviction of; but it seems to them that these things are so plain and easy, and rational, that any body can see them.

JONATHAN EDWARDS, "A FAITHFUL NARRATIVE OF THE
SURPRISING WORK OF GOD"

Once, not very long ago, modernity meant the eventual departure of God from the scene. Through the decades of the nineteenth and then the twentieth centuries, modern Western societies had become progressively more secular, worldly and science based in an evolution as certain as that of *homo sapiens* from a more primitive ancestor. We now know that this did not exactly happen. In fact, to a significant degree, the very opposite has come to pass. Not just religion per se but assertive, fundamentalist religion has risen and spread to many parts of the world—the Middle East, Africa, South Asia, Israel, and, not least, America. This might dismay some and delight others. It cannot be denied as a truth of the twenty-first century.

In the making of the modern world, God as an idea has done its part, though not with universal welcome. Struggles over the role and place of faith in society are no less urgent today than at any time during the last 250 years. In America, more than in any other advanced nation, conservative religious belief, particularly evangelical Protestantism and its offshoot, fundamentalism, has proven to be a key source of meaning, institution building, and political engagement ever since the middle of the eighteenth century, with no prospect of an end in sight. It has been Protestantism—especially its branches that take the Bible as divine truth and that stress the need for spiritual "rebirth" and the salvation of every individual—that has been the most dynamic, rapidly growing, and politically sophisticated part of Christianity. Indeed, the theologically conservative side of Protestantism, taken as a whole, has transformed itself into a global faith with hundreds of millions of new followers in developing nations.

It is essential to make clear that Christian evangelicalism and fundamentalism are not two names for the same phenomenon. Both place great emphasis on personal conversion (the "born again" experience), the sacrifice of Christ on the cross, and the need to live the principles of the Gospel and spread its benefits to others. Fundamentalists, however, tend to be uncompromising about the literal truth of the Bible and the lack of validity and value in other religions. They deny sizable portions of modern science and put in its place one or another eschatology founded on a divine unfolding whose key event is the second coming of Christ. Some religious historians hold fundamentalism to be a militant, antimodernist Protestantism that separates itself from the rest of Christianity (Marsden 1991). But as other scholars like Martin Marty point out, it is a faith born in the early 1900s and can be better thought of as a strand of modernism that seeks to remake aspects of society in the image of a sacred former world (Marty and Appleby 1992).

Christian fundamentalism is a branch of the much greater tree of evangelical faith. Evangelicals, in general, have comprised an extremely diverse and adaptable realm of belief in America since before the

Revolution. During the course of the twentieth century as strict religious faith, particularly in the South, increasingly became the object of criticism from urban intellectual culture, generating anger and resistance, elements of fundamentalism seeped into large portions of the evangelical community, such that it became ever more difficult to draw any sharp boundaries. This grew to become especially true in the arena of politics. Here, conservative evangelicals and fundamentalists have been close companions. As we will see, however, the greater evangelical community has gone in many directions, including those, opposed to the fundamentalist view, that have kept alive a more progressive tradition.

The term "evangelical" comes from the Greek *euangelion*, meaning "good news." The "news" referred to is the Gospel of the New Testament and the possibility of salvation brought by Jesus Christ for all sinners, attained through the process of being born again in his mercy and forgiveness. Widespread use of "evangelical" in writing was first done by the fiery Martin Luther, who used the word to sever Protestantism from the Roman Catholic Church and its lavish evils. It came to include obedience to the Bible as final authority and the centrality of individual piety. Above all, it meant spiritual renewal by rebirth in Christ. Such were the bones of faith; over these, the flesh took protean form (Marsden 1991).

Evangelicalism as we know it had its theological origins in Germany during the late 1600s, soon after the end of the Thirty Years' War. It arose from a movement known as Pietism, whose originator was a quiet Lutheran scholar of the humanities named Philipp Jakob Spener (1635–1705). Spener was no ordinary product of Luther and the Reformation. He perceived that an essential fire had gone out, that the Church (Lutheran, especially) had settled into its own stagnant, often corrupt rituals of earthly power and that there was intense need for renewal and cleansing, thus for what amounted to revolutionary change (Stoeffler 1965; Noll 1992, 2010).

As delineated by Spener, Pietism stressed four main needs: for a literal reading of the Bible; for missionary work; for a pious lifestyle; and, above all, for a central role to be given to a passionate, emotionally charged experience of rebirth, one that was entirely personal and independent of ministerial witness or direction. Its most radical aspect was its demand for a "universal priesthood," for acceptance of lay preaching. This meant doing away with the ultimate authority not only of ministers as spiritual leaders but of denominations. Spener also argued for small Bible groups to study and discuss the Scriptures on their own and for missionary efforts that would expand beyond Protestant communities. These were ideas that rejected large parts of the institutional Lutheran Church. Such lack of respect for existing religious authority earned Pietism's followers persecution in a number of the German states. Indeed, the movement never became very large, numerically speaking. But its influence spread, first to other parts of Germany, then to Switzerland, Denmark, and Bohemia. By the early eighteenth century, representatives of the movement had migrated to Britain and then, with epic results, to the American colonies.

BACKGROUND AND CONTEXT

Christian fundamentalism today has a truly global context. Its missionaries have been enormously successful—or rather, the attractions of fundamentalist ideas have gained a vast following in nations with radically different religious traditions than those of the United States. If, in the opening years of the twentieth century, the great majority of Protestants lived in the United States, Canada, and Europe, by 2010 no fewer than 67 percent inhabited very different parts of the world: 37 percent in sub-Saharan Africa, 17 percent in Asia-Pacific, and 13 percent in Latin America (Pew Forum on Religion and Public Life 2011). A video on the life and death of Christ known as "The Jesus Film," created in 1979, later remastered for DVD and made available through the Internet, has become perhaps the most widely distributed movie in history, translated into over 1,100 languages. (See http://www.jesusfilm .org/.) Most of these are unwritten, oral indigenous ones, and the DVD is part of the effort to translate the Bible into every existing language.

Protestant Christianity has been the most rapidly growing faith worldwide since the 1980s, bar none. Such growth, moreover, has been overwhelmingly concentrated in the Pentecostal and Charismatic sects (now over 550 million strong), those especially rich in what used to be called "religious enthusiasm," that is, emotional outbursts and supernaturalism. They share many aspects with fundamentalism. They emphasize possession by the Holy Spirit and, to varying degrees, the appearance of wonders and signs in the form of divine healing, speaking in tongues (glossolalia), prophecy, and miracles—the active and immediate hand of God—as well as literal interpretations of the Bible. Western critics have wondered why these most "backward" and "regressive" sects could have so deep an appeal. One interpretation holds that supernaturalism fits well with sub-Saharan Africa's animistic traditions, said to be antimodern in their essence. But authors like Philip Jenkins (2002) have a different message: in African nations, the Bible is not a text of ancient stories and long-ago history but a reflection of lived reality today. Old Testament narratives depict a world of tribalism and blood sacrifice, ethnic loyalty and vengeance, chronic war and brutal justice, all things known firsthand by many millions of Africans.

Might evangelical Christianity have certain modernizing aspects, too? It helps to be clear about some points of history. Much of the violence and suffering in Africa, as well as in Latin America, are the result of inequality, poverty, corruption, and struggles for power that date back to colonial and even precolonial times. In these places, evangelicals have offered a hopeful mixture of goals. Pentecostalism, the most widespread of the new churches, has been demanding of social and political reform. Its ministers have encouraged self-improvement, economic advance, opposition to corruption, and helping the poor. There is health evangelism to minister the ill, holistic evangelism to aid the entire person, and evangelical nongovernmental organizations (NGOs) focused on children and education. But there has also been violence against homosexuals, denunciation of condom use, rejection of family planning, and intolerance toward Muslims where the contest for conversion between Islam and Christianity is fierce. Many pastors in the Global South feel, as fundamentalists do, that the Bible should be made the law of the land, that the first five chapters of the Old Testament known as "books of the law," since they contain the rules given by God through Moses to Israel, should guide the legal system. For example, adultery should be punishable by imprisonment or even death. A 2006 survey from 166 different countries by the Pew Research Center showed that such pastors felt secularism, consumerism, and popular culture are the greatest threats faced by the human species as a whole (Pew Forum on Religion and Public Life 2011).

As for the United States, scholars like Mark Noll (1992), George Marsden (2006), and Karen Armstrong (2000) have emphasized that conservative evangelicals and fundamentalists are fully modern and unlikely to disappear. They have been expert at employing media for their purposes and have further adopted many forms of organized political action, from fund-raising to block voting. They have done this, moreover, while mainline Protestant churches have declined year by year in membership and while the percentage of young Americans (ages eighteen to twenty-nine) choosing to be nonreligious soared from about 12 percent in 1972 to 26 percent in 2010. One might assume that this fall from faith would have weakened the ranks of conservative Protestants. But it hasn't. Fundamentalist-leaning evangelicals, including megachurches, have seen their own numbers rise and their overall percentage surge to over 55 percent of all American Protestant churches by 2010 (Pew Forum on Religion and Public Life 2011). There are now many thousands of pastors with their own, unique congregations offering "personalized" versions of evangelist/fundamentalist doctrine and practice. Such proliferation of communities has been greatly aided by sophisticated use of communication technologies, from televangelism to the Internet. Indeed, the number of websites, blogs, listservs, glossy periodicals, apps, gift stores, and so on make it evident that fundamentalist-leaning evangelicals have succeeded in making themselves the techno-experts of God's Word.

However, a pause is needed. For even as they have made such competent use of technology, a significant portion of conservative evangelicals in the United States, and nearly all fundamentalists, reject much of the society that gave such technology birth. The largest part of this overall group, which numbers in the tens of millions, comprises a highly influential, reactionary political bloc that refuses to accept many of the liberties of modern Western society, even while benefiting from others. In fact, "refuses" does not quite capture it. Fundamentalists even deny the validity of these liberties and often blame them for the moral degeneration of the West. That these believers have become a distinct influence on American political and social life in the late twentieth and early twenty-first centuries presents a decided conundrum, as well as several essential questions.

In the Beginning: The Power of Pietism in America

When Pietism was imported to frontier America, Methodists, Baptists, Presbyterians, Congregationalists, and still others avidly took up the evangelical word. It caught fire during the spiritual paroxysm of the 1730s and 1740s known as the Great Awakening. The term "awakening" in this case refers to a vitalization of religious fervor that swept through the colonies in a series of pulses lasting a total of about four decades, from the 1730s to the 1770s. Its zeal was first centered in New England, from which it spread to the mid-Atlantic and southern colonies and eventually came to play its own part in the Revolutionary passion against monarchical and Anglican Britain. It started locally, sporadically, as a series of highly emotional born-again events, such as those in the Northampton, Massachusetts, parish of Jonathan Edwards (1703–58).

Edwards was no common minister; he was the greatest American religious intellectual of the century. Yet he found himself responding to the events before him with a mixture of joy, awe, and anxiety, as the outpouring of emotion reached a summit. People fell into states of terrible depression, even terror, at the realization of their sins, then soared to heights of trembling ecstasy as they felt the rebirth granted by embracing Jesus' sacrifice. There were divine visions and signs, with some parishioners shrieking or going into trances, even during services. All was said to be the work of the Holy Spirit, taking each soul into its beneficent grip. Edwards witnessed dozens of such conversions, including those of children, and described them in detail in *A Faithful Narrative of the Surprising Work of God* (1737), a volume he felt compelled to write after the paroxysm had passed on. In his parish, the fervor finally dimmed after several weeks, quite suddenly, when a suicide took place, chilling the communal air.

But the movement surged ahead, bursting into flames in 1740–41 after the arrival from England of George Whitefield (1714–71). Still in his early twenties, Whitefield was already an orator of the first rank, and he proved this in America, where he preached to many thousands in open-air fields and town halls, as well as in churches. He was the first preacher to become a national sensation. The message was always simple and direct: every person, every individual, was a sinner in God's eyes, thus they could be damned by their earthly acts or saved through Christ and thereby blessed with God's grace and love. It was a message delivered with sufficient eloquence that even skeptics like David Hume and Benjamin Franklin were wholly charmed by it. In his *Autobiography*, Franklin relates how he was so swayed by one of Whitefield's sermons that, against his own resolution, he emptied his pockets when the collection plate came round (Noll 2005, 2010). Whitefield's impact was often enhanced by skillful promotions and advertisements in local newspapers, a distinct innovation in religious culture that was to be used again and again, into the twentieth century. Crowds who beat their way to hear him were made up of people from all backgrounds, ages, races, and denominations; they were rich and poor, baptized and not, native born and immigrant (Maxson 2006). Nowhere else in eighteenth-century America did "the people" make such an appearance.

Evangelicalism thus began in colonial America in a wholly different way from the intimate, slowly expanding, then persecuted beginnings it had in Europe. In New England and then in the mid-Atlantic colonies it was born as a grassroots crusade led by an entrepreneurial communicator. Why did it succeed? Historians have pointed to two ideas: first, that America was God's chosen land, the New Israel, and thus Americans were playing out a greater part in the divine plan; second, that in this New Israel, every man, woman, and child, of whatever background or race, was equal before Christ and so could be saved (Miller 1953; Cherry 1998).

How did all this interact with the American Enlightenment, the republican values underlying the Revolution? We can perhaps guess that they shared ideas quite willingly. Concern for the individual soul and rejection of denominational supremacy meant a potent compatibility between Enlightenment liberalism and evangelical belief. It is not too much to say that in the early stages of the new republic when civil institutions were few, the blending of Enlightenment ideals with evangelical practices formed a major part of the society that emerged (Marty 1989; Noll 2005; Howe 2007).

Religious republicanism had a companion idea to compel its cause, as we have said. Since the first landings at Jamestown and Plymouth, the narrative of America as God's chosen land had been a staple among the faithful (Hall 1990). In the seventeenth and early eighteenth centuries, Increase Mather and his son Cotton, the most eminent Puritans of their time, included this sentiment often in their writings. Jonathan Edwards, in his well-known sermon "The Latter-Day Glory Is Probably to Begin in America" (1745), saw it revealed in the Great Awakening: "This work of God's Spirit, so extraordinary and wonderful, is the dawning, or, at least, a prelude of that glorious work . . . so often foretold in Scripture, which, in the progress and issue of it, shall renew the world of mankind. . . . And there are many things that make it probable that this work will begin in America" (Edwards 1839, vol. 1, 381). America was thus a land selected by God to begin the deepest spiritual renewal. As the Revolution approached and then exploded into war and final victory, claims regarding America's divine calling found a high pitch. So routine did this idea become that Washington felt required to include it in his 1789 inaugural address: "No people can be bound to acknowledge and adore the Invisible Hand which conducts the affairs of men more than those of the United States. Every step by which they have advanced to the character of an independent nation seems to have been distinguished by some token of providential agency" (Washington 1997, 731).

Evangelicals became the root and branch of this American religious nationalism. They took note that God was present in the Declaration of Independence but failed to appear in the Constitution. And though Jefferson saw Christ as a great teacher, not a deity, and abhorred supernaturalism and even sliced up the New Testament with a razor to create his own version, evangelicals still largely voted for him in the brutal election of 1800. Why? They were drawn to Jefferson exactly because his political words carried the spiritual meanings they held dear. He was against authoritarian constraints, against European-type limits on religious freedom, against rule by single denominations, and for the belief that all earthly rights and powers came from God, and he was most assuredly in favor of individual responsibility (Noll 2010). Just as they had turned to liberty to reject ecclesiastical tyranny in its old world forms, so were evangelicals repelled by the image of John Adams (Jefferson's opponent), whom the Federalists were successful in associating with established churches and with a powerful centralized government.

After Jefferson left office, evangelicals were further brought to the Republican Party by the argument of separating church and state. The First Amendment, that is, applied only to the federal government, not the states, and in a number of these in New England—Vermont, Connecticut, New Hampshire, and Massachusetts—the Congregationalist denomination remained a de facto official religion, supported by local taxes. To wrest these states from their Federalist majorities, Republicans made the disestablishment of religion from state control a heated issue, employing Jeffersonian language about religious freedom and self-determination. The strategy proved a brilliant success. By 1818, Vermont, Connecticut, and New Hampshire had all disestablished themselves; Massachusetts would follow a decade and a half later.

We would be wrong, however, to assume from this that a weakening of the bond between religion and politics took place for evangelicals. Exactly the opposite happened. To a significant degree and in various ways, evangelicals were republican in outlook from the beginning (though the reverse could certainly not be said). In this they departed greatly not only from the Puritans, their religious predecessors, but from Europe and its traditions of faith. Evangelicals were innovators of belief, no less original than the Founders themselves.

Evangelicalism in the Nineteenth Century

By the first decade of the 1800s, all the elements of American evangelism were in place. The religious ideals of Philipp Jakob Spener, the seventeenth-century founder of Pietism, had found a home, the best they would ever know. But it was a home that would come to be divided against itself, where faith and politics, the word of Scripture and the worldly Enlightenment, would separate into two great realms. The harmony, at first, was real enough. But it began to thin and evaporate in the decades ahead, as a second wave of revival spread and the issue of slavery became invested with religious meaning.

Signs of the new revival, known as the Second Great Awakening, are apparent from the 1790s, particularly in the South. By this time church attendance had fallen off, and people's concerns were primarily material and economic. Revival began when certain denominations tried to revitalize their memberships. But full national flowering of the new episode came in the decades after 1810, especially during the presidency of Andrew Jackson, with its intense political conflicts, violence, and early industrialism creating widespread uncertainty and unease.

Like its predecessor of the 1740s, the Second Great Awakening was a grassroots spiritual movement, devoted to conversion and carried forward by itinerant preachers, many of whom developed charismatic speaking abilities. Methodists and Baptists were the dominant groups, gaining millions of new members by 1840, with Baptists becoming more concentrated in the South over time. Yet the phenomenon was highly interdenominational, often localized, with some of its most energetic and influential leaders breaking away from their sectarian beginnings in pursuit of new ways to save souls. This helped make the movement one of lay preachers and unofficial organizations, with domestic missionaries venturing by the thousands into rural areas north and south, pioneer settlements along the western frontier, as well as cities and towns of the eastern seaboard. Rooted in such volunteerism and self-appointment, the revival has been interpreted as a "democratization of American Christianity" (Hatch 1991). In another sense, however, we can understand it as America's most widespread nativization of Protestantism. Though not a state religion, evangelical Protestantism nonetheless became a national faith. Its blending with politics was never far from sight, and often in the open. This comes through in much of the language of the time. Lyman Beecher, one of the spiritual leaders of the time, for example, spoke of the new preachers and volunteer organizations as "moral militia" (Howe 2007, 167).

Inspired by Beecher and other influential groundbreakers, above all Charles Finney, the new movement took seriously the task of making society an embodiment of the pious life. This included the spiritual care

of every individual, male or female, black or white, rich or poor, educated or illiterate. The saving of souls also meant the preserving of liberties, though this had a different meaning in the South than it did in the
North. By the 1830s, evangelicals were highly active at every level of the
political process. Their power to shape public opinion had much to do
with their use and development of new forms in communication. Technological advances in printing allowed for much faster and cheaper
production of books, newspapers, and tracts and soon led to a flurry
of creations such as magazines, weeklies, pamphlets, and more. The
1792 Postal Act created the modern mail system, offering special rates
to newspapers and growing the number of post offices from under two
hundred to roughly eight thousand by 1830, all at government expense.

Evangelicals turned all this to advantage. Teachers, ministers, and
parents established Sunday schools in every community and formed
organizations to send Bibles to every city, farm, and frontier town. National evangelical publishing organizations, coalescing from local societies, moved to create their own newspapers and to distribute brochures,
pamphlets, magazines, and the holy book systematically, cheaply, even
freely. In a number of ways, this represented the true beginnings of the
mass media in America (Nord 2004). But it also intended to expand
literacy and self-reliant learning in the name of Jesus. So successful
was the effort, so ardent and widespread the missionary work, that by
1850, 40 to 50 percent of Americans, including many politicians, were
attached to evangelical churches, with numbers much higher in the
southern states (Marsden 1991; Hatch 1991; Noll 2005).

For the twenty-first-century reader, this era brings an arresting fact.
For most of the 1800s, but particularly leading up to the Civil War,
evangelicals were the most socially progressive reformers in the nation,
and the most effective. It was evangelicals, not the socialists or utopi-
ans, not the liberal Whigs alone or even the labor parties, but the religiously awakened who most compelled the United States to broaden
the freedoms and protections of ordinary people. A list of causes championed by evangelical groups between 1800 and 1875 would lift today's
liberal from his or her seat: abolitionism, women's rights, poverty al-
leviation, programs on domestic abuse, temperance (as a way to fight
violence and broken families), better working conditions, reducing

capital punishment, better treatment for the insane and for alcoholics, improved sanitation, and universal education. Evangelicals fought for the downtrodden of society, for the poor and dispossessed, for the sick and enslaved, whose presence had grown enormously in an America of surging industry and swelling cities. They fought to give the rich a conscience. And they battled to try to force government toward taking responsibility for all its citizens. One measure of their success can be found in the penetration of political oratory by religious references, including quotations from the Bible, and often by a righteous fervor and crusading tone (Howe 2007).

The goal of revival was always a Christian society. Politics was a means to build it. This was to be a society made up of disciplined and moral individuals, freely united in Christ and therefore in uplifting social action. Historically, it would be a wholly different kind of religious society than anything Europe had ever seen, with faith separated from the state, individuals free to form any kind of pious organization they desired, from new colleges and large antislavery societies to the Methodists' small collectives resembling the Bible study groups that Spener had proposed. To redeem American society, however, meant to reform and revitalize it, politically and legally, given the brutalities and inequalities of industrial society. The calling was to create, as Alexis de Tocqueville said, a "benevolent empire" (McLoughlin 1980).

But there was always another side to this benevolence. The rise in religious fervor did not come without useful enemies. Evangelicals perceived a major threat in the masses of immigrant Catholics from Ireland who arrived in the 1840s and 1850s as a result of the great potato famine and continuing oppression and poverty at home, declaring them "un-American" and a national danger. They adopted the conventional Protestant suspicion that Catholics were loyal only to the "King of Rome" (the pope) and translated this distrust into a threat against American values of democratic equality and individual freedom. In the face of mass immigration, evangelicals played a central part in redefining "Americanness." As late as 1830, over 98 percent of the U.S. nonslave population was native born, overwhelmingly white, and Protestant, a situation that then began to rapidly change (Howe 2007). Evangelicals were in the forefront of an ugly turn toward nativism. They turned against not only Catholics but also other non-Protestant newcomers, as well as the Mormons, whose faith was itself an outgrowth of the Second Awakening. Another damaging aspect came directly from the mixing of religious zeal and politics. Too often, it made compromise impossible. Political issues became moral crusades; opponents turned into malevolents, apostates against God and the Constitution (Goldfield 2012). Debates became symbolic battles between the righteous and the sinful. Candidates for office were christened or condemned on the basis of their religious credentials. Above all, the issue of slavery, viewed by the South as sanctified by the Old Testament and by the North as "an abomination in the eyes of the Lord" according to the New Testament, became a kind of ultimate benchmark. By the 1840s, evangelicals had divided themselves into regional factions: slavery divided the Methodists, Baptists, and Presbyterians in the North and Midwest from those in the South, where church leaders were often slave owners. In 1845, Baptists met in Augusta, Georgia, to found the Southern Baptist Convention, an organization that would later grow to include millions of southern evangelicals. The religious-political atmosphere thus swirled with holy ultimatums. To believers and nonbelievers alike, the Union seemed a ship broken upon a rock. Some sense of this can even be found in Abraham Lincoln's famous "House Divided" speech of 1858 accepting the Republican nomination for the United States Senate, where he calls directly upon the words of Jesus in Mark 23:5:

> "A house divided against itself cannot stand." I believe this government cannot endure, permanently half slave and half free. I do not expect the Union to be dissolved—I do not expect the house to fall—but I do expect it will cease to be divided. . . . Either the opponents of slavery will arrest the further spread of it and place it where the public mind shall rest in the belief that it is in the course of ultimate extinction, or its advocates will push it forward till it shall become alike lawful in all the states, old as well as new, North as well as South. (Lincoln 1858)

Lincoln implies that America is indeed God's house, but it is a home whose troubles extend well beyond politics to the highest spiritual level.

What impact did the Civil War have on evangelicalism? The conflict did indeed involve a religious battle as well as a military and political-cultural one. This means a struggle over ideas about the Bible, God, and His design for America (Rable 2010). In the South, evangelicalism was a core support of slavery. Biblical teachings, Southern evangelicals believed, held slaves to be part of the divine plan, not least for America. They also held up the principles of self-determination, a Jeffersonian concept, and a manly culture of honor, chivalry, patriarchy, and violence. Northern evangelicals, meanwhile, argued that Christ demanded every person must be free and that slavery laid an intractable sin upon America, one that must be cleansed. Only the defeat of the Confederacy could ensure that the Kingdom of God might be realized among men and that America would not fail in fulfilling its divine role as the light of democratic ideals and Christian values. Northern victory confirmed this; Southern evangelicals felt the Confederacy to be a rebirth, defeat to be a form of divine punishment, a cleansing in blood. Thus the war acted both to strengthen evangelicalism and to divide it further. If Southern evangelicals retreated into local communities and a resistance to change, their Northern relatives embraced their victory as a sign of both spiritual and industrial advance, a revelation that America had been given the blessing of progress and was on its way to a new era of national greatness. The South, that is, lost more than the Civil War. It gave up for many decades any central role in the drama of America's modernization, retreating into a past of sanctified yet broken ideals, a realm of poverty, segregation, and alienation, all given a provincial legitimacy by religion (Howe 1991; Goldfield 2012).

Such was not true for black evangelicalism. While the South underwent Reconstruction and built for itself a still more racist outlook, blacks "seized control of their own religious lives" (Noll 2010, 336), establishing a great number of independent, self-sustaining congregations that became centers of communal identity and support. Blacks had been very much part of both Great Awakenings and, in the early nineteenth century, were given places in white Baptist and Methodist congregations. White authoritarianism and exclusionism, however, returned with a vengeance after the 1831 slave revolt led by Nat Turner in Virginia. Still, black churches continued to grow in urban areas, often led by lay black preachers, while underground or "invisible" churches found life in plantation areas. Belief centered on personal conversion, on the equality of Christians in the sight of God, but also on the promise that God would one day bless the enslaved with freedom. Jesus began as savior but evolved into a fellow sufferer during the antebellum period. With most slaves illiterate, biblical inerrancy (the idea that the Bible was entirely free from error) was not a core principle for many churches. And because whites had used such inerrancy to justify slavery in the South, and in the North to treat blacks as "God's children," that is, as lesser citizens, it remained a marginal idea. But well into the twentieth century, evangelicalism proved to be a source of dynamism and positive separation for many American blacks and their communities, as well as a key force in the struggle for freedom and survival (Sernett 1975). That it was not the same faith as that in white society is one reason for this. For many decades after the Civil War, most blacks continued to live in rural areas, especially in the South. It kept them apart from the massive changes occurring elsewhere in the nation.

Indeed, by the end of Reconstruction in 1877, America was no longer a nation of farms and fields, speckled with cities and factories. It had become a major industrial nation and a society of great urban masses and challenges. Numbers give some color to the historical reality: in 1830, the nation's people numbered about 12.8 million, and 92 percent of them lived in rural areas; five decades later, the population was over 50 million and by 1900, 80 million, over a third of whom now lived in cities (U.S. Census Bureau 2014).

The new era remade large parts of American society. Social mobility, secular education, links with Europe that introduced more cosmopolitan fashions and attitudes, commercial and financial expansion, the role of expertise, and the place of science and technology were all part of this modernization in the decades after 1865. There was little hope for the greater evangelical community to remain unchanged in the face of all this. The new scientific age and a growing secularism in many aspects of daily life caused the evangelical movement to splinter still further. Politically and culturally, but most of all religiously, it came to be divided into three broad factions: liberal, conservative, and undecided (Noll 2005).

Liberal evangelicals sought to revitalize the tradition of reform in the name of Christ. Coining the name "social gospel" for their efforts, they organized and worked to alleviate the failures evident in the new urban centers, from poverty and disease to child labor and alcoholism.

They shared a powerful belief in progress as an indicator of material but also spiritual advancement. Key to their motives was the doctrine of postmillennialism, which maintained that the Kingdom of God had been formed on Earth but could not be completed, and thus the Second Coming of Christ and the opening of heaven to the righteous could not happen until society was cleansed of its evils. Yet liberal evangelicals accepted modern science. Moreover, they accepted the "Higher Criticism," an interpretive approach to the Bible based on linguistic analysis, pioneered by German scholars, revealing that Scripture was in fact the work of many hands and periods, an effort of inspired literature not divine dictation. Liberals were therefore modernists and broke entirely with honoring the Bible as the inerrant word of God. They brought Jesus down from the heavens and made him an ethical leader among the millions, even an ideal American. Henry Ward Beecher's widely read and taught *Life of Jesus, the Christ* (1871) expressed this in no uncertain terms: "Jesus was a citizen. He knew the fatigues of labor, the trials which beset poverty, the temptations arising from the practical conduct of business. He lived among men in all the innocent experiences of social life, a cheerful, companionable, and most winning nature" (343). In an age of vast wealth and inequity, Jesus was transformed into a man of the people, one who had lived the life of the lower classes. It is not surprising that the social gospel became an integral part of the Progressive Movement in the early twentieth century.

Conservative evangelicals denied and hated all of this. They found science, in the form of evolution and geologic history, impossible and anathema. But their greater enemy, they felt, was liberal Protestantism, which defamed the true faith and threatened to spread like a disease. Holding firm to biblical inerrancy, which they now made a sine qua non of faith, conservative evangelicals found the Higher Criticism particularly offensive, a form of hostile and destructive atheism. Their numbers were particularly strong among southern Baptists and Methodists, but they were present in the North as well. Among them were many well-educated, middle-class believers, including academics and other religious intellectuals. They also included members of the newly formed Holiness Movement that added to evangelical principles the idea of a second conversion experience (rebirth) that would purify the believer of all future sin. Out of this movement there emerged in the early twentieth century the new sect of Pentecostalism, deeply immersed in faith healing, speaking in tongues, the working of miracles, and other supernatural signs of God's immediate presence. Conservative evangelicals were not at all blind to the problems of the new cities; but their guiding ideas of religious meaning cast these social evils as signs of degradation and degeneracy. They, too, had a view of God's earthly kingdom and the Second Coming, but it was based on prophecies about the decline of civilization and its fiery end at Christ's own hand. We will discuss this view, called premillennialism, in more detail later, as it has been central to conservative evangelicalism up to the present. Suffice it to say here that, far from a man of the people, Jesus in this telling is a deity of infinite power, hard judgment, and world-ending force. From the midst of evangelicals who held such beliefs came the most militant group of all, the Fundamentalists (Marsden 1991, 2006).

The Gilded Age, then, was a turning point. Between the 1860s and 1890s, the place of religion in America shifted beyond all expectation. To measure the extent of this shift in only a few lines, we might turn to Andrew Carnegie's well-known essay "Wealth" (1889). Carnegie wrote of "the true Gospel concerning Wealth," coining a phrase ("gospel of wealth") he hoped might sway others of the *opulenta classis*. His claim was simple: gaining a vast fortune had a holy mission in the form of philanthropy. Giving away great wealth for social betterment would earn the rich man a ticket to heaven. It was an idea that, rather than calling upon the words of Jesus, utterly inverted one of his most famous phrases: "it is easier for a camel to go through the eye of a needle than for a rich man to enter the kingdom of God" (Matt. 19:24). For the robber baron, paradise lay open and ready; all that was required was the giving of generous alms. Then, too, there was Charles William Eliot, chosen president of Harvard in 1869, a scientist who ended two hundred years of clerical leadership over the nation's oldest college. Eliot was no mere token of a new era, however. He set quickly to work reforming

Harvard's petrified curriculum, elevating the sciences, creating new departments, turning the college into a modern university on the German model. Religion, formerly a core subject, became an elective. Later in life, Eliot created the Harvard Classics, a fifty-one-volume anthology of "great works" from classical to modern times. Published in 1909, the series sold 350,000 copies in its first two decades. We would expect, of course, the Bible to be included. And it was, in pieces. Indeed, these were intermingled with Confucian, Buddhist, Hindu, and Islamic religious selections. To the modern American mind, Scripture had become one entry among "religious works of the world."

THE BIRTH OF FUNDAMENTALISM: THE MILITANT ALTERNATIVE

Some form of angry, militant reaction to the new era of secularism and science therefore seemed inevitable. To those whose lives and beliefs were steeped in a more traditional evangelicalism, this era demanded that too much be abandoned, too quickly and completely.

In the whirlwind of change before them, conservative evangelicals clung above all to the inerrancy of the holy book, a principle going back centuries that now became the iron gate of the faith. Letting go of the perfection of God's Word meant forsaking a sphere of sacred meanings and authority that could guide one's journey through the turbulent, unmoored age. If liberal evangelicals like Henry Ward Beecher could declare that Darwin and Newton had discovered the laws of God's own workings, to conservatives this was giving up holy ground. Genesis could not be taken as story or metaphor. Science could not be an alternative to biblical truth. God's Creation could not be despiritualized, debased into the merely material. Astronomy, geology, and biology could well roar ahead and claim their many discoveries, but none of this would prove permanent if it ran counter to the evidence of God's own plan, inscribed in the divine phrases of Scripture.

Herein lay the logic of the response at its most intellectual level. As late as the 1880s, there remained many evangelicals in academia, most of them trained before the Civil War, when science was still "natural philosophy," species were fixed by Creation, and Charles Darwin a name unknown outside the precincts of geology. But in the new industrial era of progress and discovery, evangelicals in academe felt religion had to "fight for its life" against the new class of scientific men, as expressed by Charles Hodge, president of Princeton Theological Seminary. And the way to do this was to employ the very powers of science to prove the infallibility of the Bible. As Hodge defined it, "the facts of nature are all related and determined by physical laws, so the facts of the Bible are all related and determined by the nature of God. . . . And as He wills that men should study his works . . . so it is his will that we should study his Word, and learn that, like the stars, its truths are not isolated points, but systems, cycles, and epicycles, in unending harmony and grandeur" (Hodge 2005, 21). Not all of science could be accepted. Darwin's law of natural selection Hodge called "a road to atheism." Darwinism took God out of nature. Scientific study of the Bible, known as "scientific theology," would put Him back.

At the same time that scientific theology was born, a large part of conservative evangelicalism became infused with premillennial Dispensationalism. Inspired by the Irish theologian John Darby (1800–1888) and popularized by William E. Blackstone's *Jesus Is Coming* (1878), Dispensationalism opposed geology and biology directly by proposing an alternate, era-based history of Earth and life rooted in biblical prophecy. It held there were seven great eras, each a period of dispensation when man was to be tested regarding his obedience to a specific revelation of God's will. Failing this test each time, man therefore becomes subject to divine judgment and retribution. The first era began with Eden and ended with the Fall; the second brought the Flood; the third, the Tower of Babel. Humanity now lives in the sixth or "Church" era, following the Crucifixion, which brought forth the Christian faith and grace to the world (Jesus' death for man's sins). This, the doctrine states, will also end badly. When God decides it is time, there will come seven days of calamity, the "Tribulation." Israel will then recognize Christ as the Messiah, and Jesus will return to install the "Millennial Kingdom," a thousand-year rule, which will be conducted from Jerusalem. Whoever among the dead and living has accepted Christ as savior will be swept up in a final resurrection known as the "Rapture." As for when all this will happen, God will provide signs that can be read—the founding of

Israel, for example. Despite many attempts at prediction, no one can truly say when the "end of days" will begin. Israel plays a central part; the Jews are God's first chosen people. Thus any form of anti-Semitism must be opposed. Relevant to science, various natural phenomena will be part of the event, too: "Immediately after the tribulation of those days shall the sun be darkened, and the moon shall not give her light, and the stars shall fall from heaven, and the powers of the heavens shall be shaken: And then shall [all] . . . see the Son of man coming in the clouds of heaven with power and great glory" (Matt. 24:29–39). Before the plan of God, science must be silent and accept irrelevance.

Premillennialism as a system of belief grew steadily in the late nineteenth century. But it truly gained a primary place in conservative evangelicalism only after 1900 as a result of the work of Cyrus I. Scofield (1843–1921), specifically his *Scofield Reference Bible* (1909, revised 1917). This text had an enormous influence in the history of American Protestantism. With its extensive, explanatory annotations on every chapter, its accessible style, and its learning, it quickly became the new basis for interpreting and studying God's dispensational plan. Another reason for its popularity and longevity is its complex, diverse narrative. While it popularized Dispensationalism for the evangelical masses, it did this while accepting some parts of science, rejecting others, and modifying or proposing still others such as the idea of a very young Earth. According to Scofield, the world was about six thousand years old. This was based on a date originally fixed by the Anglican Bishop of Ireland, James Ussher, whose calculation, published originally in 1650, had the Earth's creation occurring on Sunday morning, October 23, 4004 B.C. This calculation, it must be said, was consistent with similar estimates made by various other Christian and Jewish scholars (Newport 2000).

Scofield, in essence, modernized the Bible. He did this by seeking its compatibility with science and by turning it into a textbook. During his own life, Scofield fit the tale of the wayward soul who finds and serves God. He fought for the South in the Civil War, then set himself up as a lawyer of uncertain scruples. A heavy drinker, he abandoned his first family after resigning as U.S. District Attorney for Kansas under accusations of financial malfeasance. He came late to faith, being ordained in 1883 when he was forty, yet he showed himself an ardent agent of the Gospel and, eventually, a popular teacher. With a lawyer's feel for rhetoric, he wrote crisply articulated books and tracts that built a following, then turned his hand to a correspondence course from which the *Reference Bible* eventually emerged. The book was published by Oxford University Press, granting it an added measure of respectability. There is indeed much learning and subtlety in it. Scofield's notes range from definitions of Greek terms to literary analysis. But when he lights on scientific matters, another side is revealed. Note, for example, the author's annotation on Genesis 1:26 ("And God said, 'Let us make man in our image'"):

> Man was *created*, not *evolved*. This is (a) expressly declared, and the declaration is confirmed by Christ (Mathew 19:4; Mark 10:6); (b) "an enormous gulf, a divergence practically infinite" (Huxley) between the lowest man and the highest beast, confirms it; (c) the highest beast has no trace of God-consciousness—the religious nature; (d) science and discovery have done nothing to bridge that "gulf." (Scofield 1917, 5)

It is a key passage, for it shows how Scofield, and conservative evangelicalism as a whole, drew a line in the sand over evolution. As a religious intellectual, Scofield agreed with the tenets of scientific theology, and he here seeks an accommodation to science via the demand for evidence.

But there is none to be had. Wherever it appears in the *Reference Bible*, such "evidence" comes down to biblical citation, mere declaration, and odd mixtures of misunderstanding and inaccurate statement. In the passage from Genesis we find all of these: testimony from Matthew 19:4 ("He who made them at the beginning made them male and female"); a quote from Thomas Huxley out of context: a presumption on animal psychology; and an incorrect observation (Scofield was no biologist). Most strikingly, Jesus Christ and Thomas Huxley share bread over the denial of human evolution. In Scofield's influential hands, science and discovery fail in explanatory power before the truth of Scripture.

Scofield marks a historic step on the path from evangelicalism to fundamentalism. The huge success of the *Reference Bible* helped spread the popularity of premillennialism among conservative evangelicals everywhere and thus built a beachhead against liberal religion and modern secularism. The next step was taken by academic dispensationalists who set the stage for a still more radical line of angry defense.

Here again, the Princeton Seminary was at the heart of things. This highly respected institution had become, by the late nineteenth century, the intellectual center for much of conservative Protestantism as a whole. In truth, its faculty hewed to a tradition that mixed together aspects of Calvinism and Presbyterianism that came to be known as the "Princeton Theology." As described by religious historian Mark Noll, this put priority on defending the glory of God (not human happiness or welfare); affirming the role of the Holy Spirit in conversion; and maintaining faith in the Scriptures as the basis of theology and the holy word of God (Noll 2010, 237). According to Noll, Charles Hodge (whom we encountered earlier) was a leading light of the seminary for over five decades and "once remarked proudly that there had never been a new idea at Princeton, by which he meant that Princeton intended to pass on . . . faith as it had been defined in the 16th and 17th centuries" (Noll 2010, 237).

Between 1910 and 1915, Princeton Seminary professors and their colleagues in other institutions wrote a twelve-volume collection of ninety essays called *The Fundamentals: A Testimony to the Truth*. The hope of these writings was to vindicate tradition and define orthodox doctrine by a return to "first principles." This meant the supernatural aspects of Christ's life and resurrection, his virgin birth and Second Coming, the miracles of the New Testament, and the necessity of God's grace. Volumes in the series were published through a grant by Lyman Stewart, cofounder of Union Oil, and his brother Milton by the Bible Institute of Los Angeles, founded by Lyman. The grant allowed for three hundred thousand copies to be sent free of charge to ministers, missionaries, theological professors and students, Sunday school superintendents, YMCA/YWCA secretaries, and Protestant organizations throughout the nation. Anyone involved in spreading God's Word was likely to encounter *The Fundamentals* before long. The term "Fundamentalist," meanwhile, was first used in the early 1920s and referred not to these original academic authors but to more ordinary people, mainly southerners, who subscribed to the tenets of *The Fundamentals* and were particularly combative toward liberal Christianity (Marsden 1991, 2006).

In total, the essays represent a jeremiad, a genre of complaint about the wickedness of Christians who have lapsed and wandered. *The Fundamentals* gives the genre a calm, lecture-room voice, in contrast, say, to the emotional intensity of Puritan versions. Coming from Princeton, greenhouse of scientific theology, it also has calls for "Proof," "Evidence," "Demonstration and Illustration." Throughout, we hear the appeal to reason and evidence. Yet when it comes to the creation of man, the link to Scofield seems evident:

> Man was created, not evolved. That is, he did not come from protoplasmic mud-mass, or sea ooze bathybian, or by descent from fish or frog, or horse, or ape; but at once, direct, full made, did man come forth from God. When you read what some writers, professedly religious, say about man and his bestial origin your shoulders unconsciously droop; your head hangs down; your heart feels sick. Your self-respect has received a blow. When you read Genesis, your shoulders straighten, your chest emerges. You feel proud to be that thing that is called man. Up goes your heart, and up goes your head. The Bible stands openly against the evolutionary development of man, and his gradual ascent through indefinite aeons from the animal. (Dixon 1910, vol. 8, 82).

Man's faith that a Creator brought him forth thus provides the fount of his confidence as a special being. Without it, he is mere animal, no more important in the unfolding of the world than a fish or frog. To accept an amoral, antispiritual process like natural selection is to debase man, to strip him of all that is unique and sacred. As *The Fundamentals* avers repeatedly, man is not merely central to God's plan but the very *reason* for it. Christ's sacrifice, his pure birth and resurrection, each era of dispensation, the Second Coming—all have meaning only in view of man's need for salvation. Biblical cosmogony exists entirely to further this purpose. It collapses utterly into ash and dust when Darwin is allowed to enter. *The Fundamentals* therefore tells us why the Scopes trial, when it arrived ten years later (1925), would be a crushing defeat for believers.

THE TWENTIETH CENTURY: FUNDAMENTALISM MATURES, SUBSIDES, THEN RETURNS

Fundamentalism may have had its intellectual roots in New England and its modern formulation at Princeton, but it found far richer soil in the South. White southern evangelicals had remained loyal to inerrant Scripture and had progressively absorbed the scheme of premillennial Dispensationalism. To a significant degree, their faith was already largely "fundamentalist" in the sense of that term today. The only things still missing were a more militant rhetoric against modern society and a political agenda to match. While fundamentalism eventually spread to include conservative evangelicals in other parts of the country, its core area remained the South, where there existed to varying degrees an element of long-term resentment toward the North and its great cities. Rising militancy found reason in new waves of immigration, which brought an end to the domination of traditional Protestant America. It also grew from the lead-up to World War I. Religious patriotism took on the character of a deep hatred of Germany, source of the Higher Criticism, antibiblical science, and socialism. Against these modern blasphemies stood the Bible as well as the Declaration of Independence, written by a southerner, Jefferson, stating that America was the favored realm of "Nature's God." Jefferson's other words—about religious "superstitions" and his own version of the New Testament with Jesus shorn of miracles—were less pertinent to the perception that these threats were undermining America.

After the war, a large segment of this expanding group of fundamentalist believers entered the theater of political activism and seized upon one issue in particular: education. The teaching of evolution in public schools provoked their anger and fear most of all (Laats 2011; Lambert 2008). Why, we might ask? Compulsory schooling was new in the South; it had been resisted for decades. First instituted in Massachusetts in 1852 as a result of the work of Horace Mann, it did not succeed in most southern states until the 1910s. Requiring children to attend school was felt to be a massive intrusion of government power into the home and community, a loss of vital territory that belonged to families and the church. Especially in rural areas, such schooling took children away from their parents, preventing them from helping run the household and family farm. It presumed that officials in a far-off city knew what was best for the minds of the young everywhere and had the right to impose their will. That this "best" turned out to be tainted with modern science and rejection of biblical teachings raised the level of felt invasion still higher.

By 1920, the fundamentalist movement swelled its ranks well into the millions. A few years later, it found common cause with violent, reactionary groups, such as the Ku Klux Klan, and now opposed not only modern science, government intrusion, and liberal Christianity but immigration, unions, and bolshevism. Many evangelicals drawn to fundamentalist militancy were angered by the Nineteenth Amendment, giving women the right to vote, because they believed it would disrupt the traditional family, and were fearful of blacks migrating into southern cities for factory work during the war. They were further scandalized by the Jazz Age, with its overt sexuality and secular youth culture. And to all this conspicuous decay, occurring in God's chosen land, there was added a potent theological element: the dire events of the Great War, the Russian Revolution of 1917, and the influenza pandemic of 1918. All coming in a few short years with monstrous levels of destruction and death, these were the unmistakable signs of God's wrath or the coming of the Tribulation or the Anti-Christ or some other form of divine punishment.

Finally, fundamentalism benefited greatly from a charismatic leader, though an unfortunate one. This was William Jennings Bryan, secretary of state under Woodrow Wilson, three-time candidate for president, devout Christian, and orator of the first rank. In fact, though highly religious himself, Bryan was no fundamentalist. His career had been that of a populist democrat, one who had favored many progressive causes and who had little problem with modern science. Bryan objected less to Darwin than to Darwinism, the application of evolution to society. Such ideas, he believed, had ruined moral standards in Germany, where a "might makes right" ethos had impelled the march to war. Bryan was willing to join the fundamentalist cause as a way to prevent this from happening in the United States and to reverse a decline in mores linked to a loss of traditional faith. He saw fundamentalism as a growing movement that might sweep not only the South but much of the nation into a revival of piety and renewed moral fiber. Fundamentalists, for their part, were not loath to claim a man of Bryan's stature as a spokesman. Already the movement had been able to get anti-evolution bills taken up and approved by the legislatures of eleven states. But with Bryan, they were sure to gain entrance to still higher levels of political contact and effect (Numbers 2006).

Everything came to a head in the summer of 1925. The Scopes trial, held in Dayton, Tennessee, with a vast media attendance, turned out to be a Waterloo moment. Indeed, through the new medium of radio, it was transformed into a national and international drama. But it was a drama that ended in tragedy for fundamentalism and Bryan. John Scopes, who had broken Tennessee law by teaching evolution in his high school biology class, was found guilty and fined, but this was later overturned and never comprised more than a sideshow. The real contest, between biblical inerrancy and organic evolution, finished with Bryan largely humiliated by the scientifically literate Clarence Darrow, who essentially reduced the Great Commoner to a befuddled elder of antimodernism. Or so it was widely reported. Within a week of the trial, Bryan had died yet was still lampooned in the press from sea to shining sea. The most damning and influential portrait was surely that of H. L. Mencken, who brutally satirized the fundamentalists as "Neanderthals" and "*homo boobiens*" and unfairly but effectively cast Bryan as "ignorant, bigoted, [and] deluded by a childish theology" (Mencken 2006, 109).

The ultimate result was a major defeat for fundamentalism as a whole. Having lost a great leader, having suffered a flood of ridicule in the national press, the movement soon retreated from public life for a half century. Further attempts to get laws passed against the teaching of evolution failed, though a few, including that in Tennessee, remained on the books. Overall, conservative evangelicalism remained a vital presence in American religion but as a massive but marginal subculture.

It built many schools and colleges, media outlets, and missionary programs but stayed largely out of the national limelight. What this meant, however, was that when fundamentalists decided it was time to reenter politics in the late 1970s, they had a well-established infrastructure to draw upon that would prove central.

Fundamentalist Resurrection: 1940s–1970s

Indeed, though they departed from mainstream politics, their numbers grew impressively. Between 1945 and 1980, membership in the Southern Baptist Convention, the premier evangelical organization in the country, soared from under five million to over fourteen million. With such numbers, it was unlikely white evangelicals would remain long out of politics. But it was certain events of history most of all that impelled fundamentalists toward revitalized political action. These events occurred over a thirty-year period and built to a kind of crescendo in the 1970s, one that combined deep anxieties related to social, cultural, and religious change.

Among these selected events was the founding of Israel in 1948, a matter of huge importance. As it heralded the Tribulation and all that followed (Armageddon, the Second Coming, Judgment Day), it inspired an outpouring of overheated predictions and discussions regarding other signs related to the end of days. The Cold War, which had sundered the world into two great opposing forces, one being the people of faith and democracy, the other, its enemy, godless communism, seemed to have arrived on time (Leffler 2007). To many, the Soviet Union was clearly the land of Gog, as described in Ezekiel (books 38–39), a great enemy from "remote parts of the north" that, in league with other nations (the Arab Middle East), would invade Israel and set loose God's wrath to rain down "hailstones, fire and brimstone." Almost on cue, the phrase "nuclear Armageddon" became popularized by the mainstream American media in the 1950s and 1960s. Books on biblical prophecy predicting humanity was at its climactic hour grew in number and readership from the late 1940s on. The genre culminated in *The Late Great Planet Earth* (1970) by evangelist Hal Lindsey (with Carol C. Carson), appearing in the wake of the Six-Day War. Updated several times, the book has been one of the best-selling English-language volumes of the twentieth century (Marsden 2006).

These events set the background for what fundamentalists perceived as a new stage of decline in America. Believers did not long remain passive in the face of such decay. Though God's plan was fixed and certain, America still needed to be morally solid and strong in divine favor for the coming struggle (Lambert 2008). Fundamentalist evangelicals saw threats of all kinds to this, many of them representing intensified renewals of traditional enemies and dangers. One of these emerged in the growing success of Catholics who were now affluent enough to found their own schools, colleges, and publishers and whose authority became all the more apparent with John F. Kennedy's election as the first Catholic president. Within fundamentalism itself, moreover, there arose a division, as the so-called neo-evangelists, with Billy Graham at their head, pursued a moderate course of engagement with mainstream American culture (Noll 2010).

In 1954, the U.S. Supreme Court declared segregation unconstitutional in *Brown v. Board of Education of Topeka*. To southern evangelicals, this meant the federal government intended to take away all local control of public schools. Such seemed confirmed in 1957 with the Little Rock Nine incident. When nine black students tried to enroll in Little Rock Central High School, thousands of Arkansas whites raged into the streets to stop them and Governor Orval Faubus ordered the National Guard to surround the school and bar entry. President Eisenhower sent in the 101st Airborne to restore order and escort the students into the school. Soldiers remained for the entire school year to protect the black students. For much of the South, this qualified as an illegitimate government assault on an autonomous community. So emotional was the local reaction that Eisenhower, the Supreme Allied Commander in World War II, was accused of "Nazi tactics." Despite such absurdities and the ugliness of the incident, it helped politicize the fundamentalist cause. A century after the Civil War, conservative evangelicalism remained a support for segregation and antigovernment sentiment.

Still more was to come, however. The civil rights movement had only just begun. Black religious leaders of the movement now declared themselves, in the words of Martin Luther King Jr., to have taken over the task of trying to "redeem the soul of America." In essence, the movement exposed to all Americans the deep moral failures of those who opposed desegregation yet considered themselves the true representatives of God. Cultural turmoil during the 1960s added many new threats and insults. Conservative white evangelicals found themselves deeply offended, even outraged, by the sexual revolution and women's liberation, as well as by the widespread embrace among young people of New Age spiritualism and Eastern religion. Fundamentalists were again ridiculed by a liberal media now highly critical not only of evangelical belief but, the evangelicals felt, of patriotism as well.

The final straw, however, came with the next round of Supreme Court decisions. These outlawed prayer in the classroom (*Engel v. Vitale*, 1962), enforced the separation of church and state (e.g., *Lemon v. Kurtzman*, 1970), and upheld forms of pornography as "free speech" (*Miller v. California*, 1973). It was apparent to fundamentalists that America was undergoing spiritual failure. The camel's back finally broke in 1974. Once again, the issue was education. Two fundamentalist colleges, one the prestigious Bob Jones University, were stripped of tax-exempt status for failure to desegregate. The schools sued and won, but the decisions were overturned by federal appeals courts and the Supreme Court itself (*Bob Jones University v. Simon*, 1974). It now seemed clear to fundamentalists that the government aimed to take away all rights in this critical domain. For decades after the Scopes trial, during economic depression and war, schools in the South were left relatively alone; Jim Crow prevailed, and evolution was not widely taught. With *Brown v. Board of Education* and its aftermath, Washington showed its determination to seize education, by force if necessary, and remove protections that would allow evangelicals to operate their own schools in their own image. The attack on Bob Jones University seemed nothing less than a declaration of war against Christian schools everywhere. All that was needed now for a massive political response were leaders able to harness and organize the enormous well of fear, injury, and resentment that had come to exist among religious conservatives.

Such leaders were not long in coming. Among those who stepped forward at this critical moment, the most effective was the televangelist Jerry Falwell (1933–2007). Media savvy, outspoken, provocative, and fully energized by events, Falwell adopted the example of the great evangelical preachers of the past, who knew the sway of simple messages endlessly repeated and sonorously delivered. Earlier leaders had to be itinerant to gain their full impact. Falwell had the force of technology at his disposal, and he employed it expertly: radio, television, films, videos, many forms of print, and live sermons all created a massive national presence. In 1979, after intense discussions with several colleagues, he founded the Moral Majority, a southern-oriented, grassroots organization with a distinct agenda described as pro-family, pro-life, pro–national defense, and pro-Israel. It proved a great success. In 1980, the Moral Majority delivered millions of conservative votes for Ronald Reagan's presidential campaign, aiding one of the largest landslide victories in American history. A new political-religious revival had begun.

Newly Risen: 1980s–2000s

Because of its passionate focus on both individual piety and the state of American society as God's chosen kingdom on Earth, evangelicalism has always sought, and found, a political dimension. Such dimension has shifted over time, for example, from the defense of republican ideals to the politics of public education. At certain times, however, more than at others, the fusion of religious and political goals has worked against the democratic process as envisioned by those such as Jefferson, Franklin, Hamilton, and Madison. These men distrusted religious "enthusiasm" as a stimulus to political decisions. They worried about the inflammations and loss of compromise that would result if sectarian aims were to set themselves forward as ambitions for the nation. Fundamentalist revival in the late twentieth century shows they were right to worry.

It has often been said that Reagan Republicans used the Christian Right for their own purposes. Reagan himself was mildly sympathetic to evangelical causes, but he was no fundamentalist. He was a pragmatic conservative concerned about the economy and national defense, a skillful orator who plied biblical language of God and Country to win support (Domke and Coe 2010). His 1980 nomination acceptance speech carried such phrases as the "spirit that flows like a deep and mighty river through the history of our nation" and a "vast continent that God has granted as our portion of this creation." Reagan framed an uplifting message of the greatness that could be reclaimed for America after the dismal economic and wartime failures of the 1970s. It was a powerful message, wrapped in a rhetoric of hope and moral responsibility.

What Reagan and his team did not fully appreciate was that the Republican Party would itself come to be used in turn by the fundamentalists. Together with other religious leaders with political connections, like Pat Robertson, Tim LaHaye, and James Dobson, Falwell saw the Democratic Party and liberals in general as responsible for America's decadent state and guilty of egregious wrongs against God and biblical truth. For religious conservatives, Republicans offered a path to save the nation through political change. This meant undoing laws that worked against the dictates of faith and that gave the government too much power over society, over the individual, and over religion, and thus over God's kingdom. In the 1990s, conservative Protestants were a rapidly growing faction of Congress, and right-wing discourse had adopted fundamentalist tones of accusation, anger, and even the rejection of science. By the 2000s, the Republican Party platform had adopted every major issue of the Religious Right. It was now de rigueur for party candidates to declare their support for school prayer, the traditional family, the defense of marriage (anti-gay), God in government, Creationism, skepticism toward climate change, and, above all, anti-abortionism.

These issues reflect a revival of concerns held by conservative evangelicals since the late nineteenth century: education, the family as a moral center, and the necessity of faith as a guide in governing. Homosexuality? This was a forbidden subject in 1880 or 1915, yet its offense in the 2000s was its presumed denial of the marriage sacrament and the traditional family. An antiscience position, as we have seen, has always been part of fundamentalist belief. Creationism, and its more refined companion, Intelligent Design (ID), are constructs from the legacy of "scientific theology." As for the rejection of climate change, there is claimed to be a theological argument here, too. An example is the well-known "Evangelical Declaration on Global Warming" by the Cornwall Alliance, stating: "Earth and its ecosystems—created by God's intelligent design and infinite power and sustained by His faithful providence—are robust, resilient, self-regulating, and self-correcting. . . . We deny [they] are the fragile and unstable products of chance, and vulnerable to dangerous alteration because of minuscule changes in atmospheric chemistry." Biblical passages have also been cited, for example, Genesis 8:21, where God proclaims after the flood: "I will not again curse the ground . . . neither will I again smite any more every thing living, as I have done."

Abortion defines a different story, and an important one. Though widely believed to have been a core issue for conservative evangelicals for many decades, such is not the case. Before 1979, abortion was not widely discussed. Nor was *Roe v. Wade* (1973) viewed as a key decision in its day. Fundamentalist and Pentecostal leaders such as Carl Henry, Pat Robertson, D. James Kennedy, and even Falwell had little problem with abortion in instances of fetal deformity, rape, or incest or when the mother's life was threatened. A 1976 resolution against abortion passed by the Southern Baptist Convention, reaffirmed in 1978, spoke only against the practice "for selfish non-therapeutic reasons." Indeed, the Right to Life movement was founded in 1973 by American Catholics, for whom the issue *was* central. The fetus simply had not yet been adopted by the conservative Protestant community as a victim of overriding consequence. Indeed, its most staunch defender in Congress was none other than the liberal senator from Massachusetts, Edward Kennedy. A close colleague of Jerry Falwell's, Ed Dobson, tells us that "[the] New Right did not start because of a concern about abortion. I sat in the non-smoke-filled back room with the Moral Majority, and I frankly do not remember abortion ever being mentioned as a reason why we ought to do something" (Balmer 2007, 16).

What changed this? Pastor Falwell and other public evangelical figures were deeply affected by the arguments of Francis Schaeffer, an eloquent, unconventional minister of Christian apologetics. Schaeffer characterized American society not merely as morally degraded but mechanized and murderous under the influence of "secular humanism." Abortion was the decisive sign of a loss in the value of human life. Schaeffer, who had had a long ministerial career starting in the 1940s, began in the 1960s to publish and speak out, styling himself as a kind of Christian guru with long hair and goatee. He took a cue from the civil rights and student movements to promote political activism as a means to necessary change and, like evangelicals before him, made effective use of various media. His 1979 book and film, *Whatever Happened to the Human Race*, made in partnership with C. Everett Koop (later, President Reagan's surgeon-general), focused on abortion, using amateurish and lurid yet effective imagery. The film toured twenty major cities in 1979, gained nationwide attention, and came to have a major impact on parts of the evangelical community. Abortion was nothing less than state-sanctioned infanticide, the killing of *millions* of innocents by a supposedly freedom-loving government that had only recently gone to war to stop the horrors of fascism. These were formidable ideas, and they fit excellently with Falwell's own understanding of America's plight. They also struck a chord with conservative Baptists throughout the South, who had become increasingly angry at the move toward moderate positions by portions of the Southern Baptist Convention over the preceding two decades and who staged a "coup" at the 1979 meeting in Houston, installing a more fundamentalist administration that quickly fired or otherwise eliminated any remaining "liberal" elements. Within less than two years, abortion (for any reason, under any circumstance) had become a topic of resistance and activism.

It was clear that abortion *should* be a key fundamentalist issue. Adopting the discourse of "the unborn child" and "abortion is murder" was, Falwell felt, accurate and needed. It would help people realize the depths into which the country had fallen. These instincts proved spot-on. Once added to his agenda for the Moral Majority, "pro-life" rang true for conservative evangelicals everywhere as a frightening and vital issue.

Like a colossal magnet, abortion seemed to encapsulate a great many of the evils that fundamentalism had identified over the course of the twentieth century: intrusion of government power, vulnerability of children, the sexual revolution ("sex without responsibility"), feminism and homosexuality (immoral sterility), and of course attack on the traditional family. All of these domains found consecration in the "unborn child," the most innocent of God's creatures, the most vulnerable to modern barbarism, the most brutally handled by a godless society.

Abortion quickly became the decisive issue for evangelicals. Starting in the 1980s, it gathered the political activism of the Christian Right to try to repeal *Roe v. Wade*, both at the state and national levels, and to push for a constitutional amendment banning abortion forever. It came to act, less officially, as a test for any conservative candidate to public office. It mobilized radical, violent groups, like the Army of God, founded in the early 1980s, and Operation Rescue, founded in 1986, which vandalized many abortion clinics and harassed female patients. At the extreme, it has been taken to justify beatings, shootings, arson, and murder. Data provided by the National Abortion Federation record over 3,240 acts of physical violence against abortion workers and clinics between 1977 and 2012, over 95 percent of which occurred after 1980, including eight murders and seventeen attempted murders (National Abortion Federation 2010). Such acts of domestic terrorism are routinely denounced by fundamentalist leaders, but in fact they are wholly consistent with the logic of proclaiming that millions of "unborn children" have been "murdered." This logic, in fact, is perfectly exposed in the slogan originally used by Operation Rescue: "If you believe abortion is murder, act like it's murder" (Hadley 1996, 163).

However, theologically speaking, there is a problem. Nowhere in the Bible are there any clear statements equating the fetus to a child. The most direct indication of how a fetus might be valued is Exodus 21:22: "If men strive, and hurt a woman with child, so that her fruit depart from her . . . he shall be surely punished according as the woman's husband will lay upon him; and he shall pay as the judges determine." On the other hand, it is apparent that God himself will order the killing of pregnant women, if they be among the enemies of Israel (e.g., Num.

31:17). These biblical passages are seldom noted by fundamentalists. To a large degree, they are irrelevant.

Christian conservatives are not against violence or even killing. In contrast to evangelicals of the Second Great Awakening, they are not interested in gun violence, domestic abuse, capital punishment, or the brutalities of poverty as key issues. Most strongly favor gun rights and state violence in the form of execution and foreign wars. The latter, after all, are rife in the Old Testament. Moses himself declares, "The Lord *is* a man of war" (Exod. 15:3). And the Old Testament has many references to God's order to commit genocide, for example, against the Amalekites and Canaanites.

Thus, with regard to abortion, the taking of life is not the real issue; the "pro-life" label means something else. We get some idea of what this is from the Southern Baptist Convention in a statement they released on the fortieth anniversary of the *Roe v. Wade* decision:

This is a tragic milestone that should cause us to repent and weep. These [millions of] unborn children are the most vulnerable human beings among us, yet they are afforded no protection by society. . . . We must never allow ourselves to accept abortion-on-demand as the new normal. Abortion kills innocent unborn people, wreaks havoc on the women who have them, desensitizes our culture to the value of human life, and subjects our nation to the judgment of God. (Duke 2013)

In the Valley of the Shadow: Fundamentalism and Evangelicalism in Today's America

What, then, is the role for fundamentalist ideas in an America that continues to secularize, to educate its young in nonreligious settings, to reward science in innumerable ways, an America that also develops new alternatives to traditional belief with every passing decade?

For this, we might turn once more to history. Without doubt, the most profound developments in America for evangelical Christianity since the late nineteenth century are: (1) the shedding of its more progressive elements, particularly the social gospel; (2) the birth of fundamentalism and the spread of its ideas into the larger evangelical community; and (3) the recent dynamism that has led to many new forms of evangelical worship, from small neighborhood gatherings to megachurches. Here is the place to try to bring all three of these trends together in a certain fashion, beginning with the social gospel.

Followers of this movement in the early 1900s revived the sympathy between Enlightenment republicanism and Christian fellowship. This, of course, had supported the American Revolution and helped liberalize American society in the following decades of the nineteenth century. Now it returned to do battle on behalf of labor and related needs. One of the new movement's primary leaders, Walter Rauschenbusch, author of *A Theology for the Social Gospel* (1917), wrote about the need to better what he called "the sinfulness of the social order" through the application of Jesus' lessons regarding compassion, succor, and justice. Rauschenbusch perceived that the combined desires and actions of a modern people, struggling for success in great cities, will create immoral conditions for many who inevitably fall into poverty, illness, unsafe working conditions, or various forms of oppression. Alleviating these "collective sins" would help advance the Kingdom of God. "The social gospel," he explained, "seeks to bring men under repentance for their collective sins and to create a more sensitive and more modern conscience. It calls on us for the faith of the old prophets who believed in the salvation of nations" (1917, 53). Such did not mean a liberal attitude toward all things, however. Loyalists of the social gospel found little fault with eugenics and were strongly in favor of prohibition. Yet their message of alleviating suffering became a standard for mainstream Protestantism.

The social gospel ended as a force after World War I. But liberal white evangelicals never went extinct. Suppressed by the rise of fundamentalism, such people emerged in the 1960s to join the civil rights movement and to work for other causes related to social justice. They were overshadowed and their voices made thin by the rise of the Christian Right. However, before 2000, they had grown to where leaders like Jim Wallis were openly critical of the fundamentalist agenda. In stirring fashion,

Wallis updated the social gospel to include contemporary notions of activism: a true evangelical movement, he stated, was not frozen by issues like abortion and school prayer but instead "relates biblical faith to social transformation; personal conversion to the cry of the poor; theological reflection to care of the environment; core religious values to new economic priorities; the call of community to racial and gender justice; morality to foreign policy; spirituality to politics; and, at its best, transcends the categories of liberal and conservative" (1995, 39). Wallis wanted a "progressive evangelicalism," one that would engage actively in a variety of causes to advance social justice.

In the 2000s, this embrace of activism began to expand. A host of new groups, repelled by the immobile and anger-soaked views of fundamentalists and concerned about the state of humanity and the environment, emerged onto the evangelical scene, with names such as the Green Evangelical Movement, Evangelicals for Social Action, the Christian Alliance for Progress, and the Misión Integral, to name but a few. Millions of younger Christians migrated from conservative churches to form or join a new denomination of similar character. Inspired by the global humanitarian work of Christian organizations like World Vision (focusing on aid for children), they adopted more flexible beliefs, leaving politics to the individual conscience, finding more (though varied) openness toward gays, feminists, science, and so forth. Some nonfundamentalists became willing to consider a more pliable view of biblical inerrancy, accepting that poetic, metaphoric language is employed to express God's truth. It is still Truth, however.

Abortion, on the other hand, has remained a difficult issue for progressive Christians. Most continued to oppose it, now along with other forms of "taking life," such as capital punishment. But these newer evangelicals refused to join the Christian Right's rigid pro-life agenda and its Republican supporters. The real problem, they said, reviving a claim from the social gospel, was the number of unwanted pregnancies, particularly among the poor.

Fundamentalists, who in the 2010s remain strong and politically highly active, reject this kind of social engagement. In general, they do not look fondly upon the dynamism of the American evangelical community, its innumerable, local, and ever-mutating forms of worship and gathering, its thousands of single, charismatic pastors (ordained or not), each with his or her individual take on issues and biblical interpretations, often circulating among various parishes. Fundamentalist ministers (all male) try to resist all such adaptions. Though often differing among themselves, they continue to adhere to the main principles set down in *The Fundamentals*, including Dispensationalism. In their politics, too, they retain an absolutist stance on abortion, on homosexuality, on intolerance toward other faiths, and in denouncing much of modern science.

And so we need to ask: given their political activism and demands, what would American society look like if fundamentalists were placed in power? What sort of America would this be? Let us count the ways.

We'll begin with government. All policy decisions, domestic or foreign, would seek guidance and legitimacy in Scripture. The Bible would become as important a document in governing the country as the Constitution. Candidates for office, at any level, would be tested for loyalty to Christian principles before being allowed to run. Presidents would be required by law to offer public prayers, to celebrate Christian holidays, and to attend services held in the White House and Capitol prior to any important proceeding. Ministers would offer Christian prayers at all civic functions, a role granted no other faith. Women would be allowed to hold public office but not the presidency and not leadership positions in Congress. Foreign policy would be redirected toward identifying those nations on the correct side of God and the Pentateuch; the rest would be divided between potential enemies and those in the hands of Satan. The United States would withdraw immediately from the United Nations, knowing that it is the forerunner of a global takeover to establish the single world government of the Anti-Christ.

As for social norms, all rights and access to abortion would be rescinded and the practice criminalized, as would any and all forms of euthanasia ("right to die"). Contraception would be curtailed, then restricted, and possibly outlawed. Homosexuality would find itself redefined as a pathology (once again), and same-sex marriage, like abortion, would be prohibited by constitutional amendment. Freedom of expression would be curtailed, since material deemed pornographic or obscene or offensive to religious views would be prohibited in film, print, literature, music, art, theater, social media, and the publicly spoken word. Capital punishment would be used more often and possibly extended to additional crimes, based on biblical readings. Schools would begin and end with Christian prayer, and the curriculum would include study and memorization of the Scriptures, no matter the ethnic or religious background of students. All material deemed supportive of "secular humanism" and inappropriate "to young Christian minds" would face rigorous censorship. Geology, biology, and astronomy would be reconceived to accord with Creationist "truth." Corporal punishment would be reintroduced. Schools that did not abide by these standards would lose all government funding. States and local communities would be allowed to set their own school standards, as long as they abided by Christian precepts.

As for universities, we would find the teaching of the subjects just mentioned redefined in terms of Intelligent Design or natural theology. Similar adjustments would be made to all sciences that deal with space and time (archaeology, cosmology, particle physics, etc.). Textbooks would discuss miracles, omens, divine signs, and supernatural events and would emphasize God's ability to overturn or alter natural laws at any time. Studies on environmentalism, biodiversity, and climate change would be allowed but receive little or no government support. All areas of research employing fetal and embryonic material, such as embryonic stem cells, fetal tissue transplantation research, and possibly in vitro fertilization work would be prohibited. Most areas of genetic engineering dealing with humans would also be banned. Other types of investigation using humans (e.g., psychology) would be phased out.

We can stop here. Such is but a paltry list of the mutations fundamentalism would eventually demand, but it offers some flavor as to the bitter outcome. America would not be a theocracy per se or a state ruled by "Christian fascism." It would, however, be a land of broken freedoms. Religious bigotry, intolerance, and gender inequity would become the norm. A state religion might not be declared (because of the First Amendment) but would rule in effect. A belligerent stance toward much of the non-Christian world, especially Islam, would prevail. Scientifically, the United States would regress to become decidedly backward. The humanities would fare no better, perhaps worse.

America's universities, formerly among the best, would turn into paper institutions, starved of support, intellectually dead. The Founders—Madison, Adams, Jefferson, Hamilton, Washington, and Franklin—would be recast as noble Christians. Yet were they to return, they would find the country an alien and repellent place. America would turn its back on the cultural achievements of the world.

Such common anti-intellectualism should not be viewed as a mere option. Why? Because it is endemic to any set of fundamentalist-type ideas. These ideas, in other words, however they may differ from one faith to another, or even within a single religion, share a basic sensibility. Above all, they seek a final narrative about the origin and destiny of the world, how humans should structure their minds, live their lives, and accept retribution if they fail. There is a yearning after purity, for primary absolutes revealed by direct contact with the divine. Its other side is an abhorrence of the present, fear and wrath at a world that has been corrupted, ruined. Purgation is essential. Opponents are malevolent. Deniers of the truth are obstacles to its assumption. Purist forms of faith, like their secular counterparts—fascism, totalitarianism, Maoism—are by nature deaf, fanatical, and violent. When they achieve political power, extremism quickly follows.

Fundamentalism in Christianity therefore shares some key aspects with its Islamic counterpart, particularly its closed mindedness, illiberalism, and rage. But it is also different in crucial ways. First, it has far more adherents, with millions in the United States alone, and is therefore integrated into society, not isolated from it. Second, it has abstained from terrorist violence on a large scale—there is no Protestant al-Qaeda. This is almost certainly due to the larger culture of democratic values in the United States, with its ingrained respect for the individual and political process. Fundamentalists in the American South from the beginning sought to turn the legislative and judicial system to their advantage, not to destroy it or murder its sitting leaders. They continue to see elections and the courts, civil disobedience and the media, as the primary tools to impose their will, not suicide bombers and assassinations. Thus, while the rationality of fundamentalism, with its indictment of secular society, does suggest a need to overturn the given order, this is powerfully countered by the ethics of democratic citizenship. For most of the Islamic world, such a form of citizenship has never existed.

Such reflections bring forward why fundamentalism will most likely continue to fail in its major goals for America. This one group, though comprising millions, calls for state power and public resources to regulate individual liberty in the form of private morality. It also wishes to take control, for hundreds of millions, over which choices of personal behavior should be redefined as criminal or deviant. In this way, that is, fundamentalists wish to become the moral lieutenants of a society whose democratic origins and history recognize no such position.

The other limiting factor has to do with modern science. Attempts to deny its validity in favor of biblical inerrancy are doomed. They were doomed at the time of the Scopes trial, and they are all the more predestined to fail a century later. To put it nicely, biblical arguments about the nature of the world exist on a wholly separate plane of meaning than does science, on a planet with a different atmosphere and gravitational constant. Our glance into the Scofield *Reference Bible* showed this well enough. Another way of saying this is to emphasize how unlikely we are to derive any new techniques for treating malaria, understand how various infectious agents mutate and adapt to antibiotics, or predict the effects of the melting of the Greenland glaciers from biblical passages, not to say Creationist or Intelligent Design "studies." Similarly, victories briefly won by fundamentalists with local school boards regarding evolution or climate change are neither factual nor spiritual victories; they do nothing to weaken science or spread the gospel of Jesus Christ. The last two hundred years have been unequivocal: truth about physical reality is the province of professional science, which is neither infallible nor final but unprecedented in its power to produce knowledge that is reliable, testable, often of enormous benefit, and always advancing. The place of science is globally secure; its financial and institutional support now comes from governments everywhere, which look to it as a source of progress and development.

The philosopher Charles Taylor (2007) has stated that a fundamentalist society is not necessarily a religious one, that is, one that satisfies spiritual needs and longings. A secular society, moreover, is not ineluctably an atheistic one. "Secular," he suggests, should be taken to mean fluid and diverse in forms of belief. That an overwhelming number of Americans continue to say they believe in God, even as church membership and attendance have fallen to historic lows, is no contradiction in this view. Institutional churches in the United States are no longer the center of faith. Secular society gives people the liberty to explore and alter their ways of pursuing belief, even to invent new ones. Nothing could be more American than such exploration, Taylor implies. Nothing, perhaps, except the authoritarian response to it that fundamentalism came to be.

It is quite possible that progressive evangelicalism, under its many forms and guises, will gain a new dominance in time. The abortion issue, however, could remain a sticking point. There is now little common ground between those who view this as a women's rights issue and those who see it as a matter of infanticide; however, that evangelicals had to discover it in the 1980s, urged to do so by angry and frightened leaders, implies the possibility for future changes. The Bible, too, can say a great many things. Evangelicals who revive the commitment to equality, dedication to the underprivileged, and care for "God's chosen land" in environmental terms will be more likely to contribute positively in the long term in a world that requires flexibility and negotiated solutions. No less, they would be closer to the "righteous land" or "benevolent empire" that those of the Revolutionary generation envisioned. For this was an America not as a failed spiritual state or as a society blinkered and rigid and distrustful of mind. It was a nation that continued to explore freedom, knowledge, and forms of social betterment as a matter of God-given responsibility.

CHAPTER 7

Purifying Islam

The Muslim Reaction against the Western Enlightenment

> This generation (the "Salaf" or original followers of Muhammad) drew solely from this source (the Qur'an) and attained something unique in history. However, it subsequently came to pass that other influences intermingled with this source. Successive generations thus drew from sources such as Greek philosophy and logic, Persian myths and their ideas, the Jewish scriptures and Christian theology, along with the residue of other civilizations and cultures. All of this came to be mixed with Qur'anic commentaries, Islamic theology, and principles of jurisprudence. As a result, subsequent generations were educated by a corrupted source, and so a generation like the first has never again appeared.
>
> SAYYID QUTB, *MILESTONES*

Religious extremisms, whatever their particular faiths, share several core traits. What might they be? These are the major ones: insistence on their exclusive possession of divinely decreed truth, contempt for outsiders who deny this, and refusal of the right of individuals within the group to question those truths or to deviate from orthodox practice. There are also key differences. Some extremists may be proselytizers, others not. Some are more violent in enforcing or imposing their beliefs, others much less so or not at all. Some base their orthodoxy on long traditions of textual analysis and highly intellectual commentary. Others rely more on raw emotion or combine both forms of self-definition to energize their followers. Even within the very large body of devout Christians and Muslims, there are very different versions of the "true" faith, often with little in common except for a general acceptance of the sacredness of Jesus Christ and His mission on Earth for Christians and the absolute truth of the divinely determined role of Muhammad as the ultimate prophet for Muslims.

Clearly not all or even anything close to majorities of practitioners of either religion are extremists of the sort that we are examining, and within each tradition there have been many whose beliefs can be reconciled with liberal Enlightenment ideals. Nevertheless, there is no doubt that however much resistance there has been in the West, particularly in the United States, among some Christians to Enlightenment science and social liberalism, that has remained a minority position within Western societies, and such versions of Christianity have been unable to overthrow the Enlightenment tradition that has developed since the eighteenth century. In fact, the greatest threat to that tradition in the twentieth century came from two European antireligious movements, Nazism and communism.

The Enlightenment has had a much harder time of it in the Muslim world, even if much of the opposition has not been as extreme as that of the violent Salafists who are so much in the news since the late twentieth century. (The term "Salafist" is more appropriate for Islam than "fundamentalist" because of the explicit references in their program to the original generation of Muhammad's followers, but the idea of returning to the "fundamentals" of the religion is very similar.) This can be explained in part by the fact that the Enlightenment was a Western, European invention and thus remains somewhat tainted everywhere else as a foreign imposition that often arrived as a companion of colonialism. That is not, however, a sufficient explanation because at least parts of the Enlightenment, and in some cases quite a bit of it, have gained successful entry into some Asian societies, but also because a century ago, at the height of colonial European power, it seemed quite likely that this could happen among Muslims as well. There were distinguished Muslim thinkers who tried to work out a compromise that accepted modern, even partly liberal ideas and tried to blend them with religious faith. There were also secularist intellectuals who were even more eager to Westernize their societies by adopting much of the liberal Enlightenment agenda. But today such thinking appears more unlikely than ever to succeed in Muslim societies.

Part of the reason the contemporary rise of specifically anti-Enlightenment religiosity in much of the Muslim world is astonishing is that in the more distant past, at a time when there was practically no hint of Enlightenment thinking in early medieval Europe, Islam produced thinkers and whole intellectual trends that had the potential to develop something similar to Enlightenment openness to new ideas, scientific inquiry, and the questioning of established religious tradition. Thus trying to find a reason for what has happened within Islam by going back to its foundational texts, the Qur'an and the Hadith (stories about sayings and actions of Muhammad that were not incorporated into the Qur'an, that were written later, but that serve as divinely inspired elaboration of religiously sanctioned law and practice), leads us nowhere. Had the original texts entirely closed off open inquiry, the intellectual history of Islam would never have been so rich. It is, we should add, just as useless to try to find, as some have, the opposite seeds of the Enlightenment in the most ancient foundational Christian texts. They tell us almost nothing useful about the astounding transformations of the past few centuries that were manifested in the thinking and influence of the intellectuals we have been studying.

A Chinese scholar visiting Muslim Baghdad or Cordoba and then Christian Rome or Paris in the late tenth century, to take an imaginary possibility, would certainly have been impressed with how cultivated and knowledgeable the Muslim intellectuals were compared to their benighted Christian counterparts. Nine hundred years later, a Chinese scholar visiting London and Paris, and then Baghdad and Tehran, would have been astonished by exactly the opposite difference. Trying to explain why this is so goes far beyond what we are trying to do here, but it is necessary to mention it, particularly to counter those who somehow think that Islam is impossibly fixed in obscurantist ancient texts while Christianity is not.

There are several explanations for why this "golden age" of Islamic scholarship and science failed to continue and, in fact, declined to a small rivulet by the fourteenth century (Huff 1993; Lewis 1982/2001). One account blames the enormous destruction brought by the Mongol invasions, in particular the siege of Baghdad in 1258, which led to a terrible sacking of the city, with many of its scholars massacred and its magnificent libraries and famed House of Wisdom utterly destroyed. Modern historians, however, emphasize that other thriving portions of

Islamic culture, such as Spain, were not affected. Another explanation focuses on the enormous influence of the Persian Arab philosopher Abu-Hamid al-Ghazali (1058–1111). His exceptionally learned writing concluded that ultimately most of the Greek-inspired high Arab philosophy was unworthy except in very limited ways, since it could not be used to confirm the truth of Islam or to instill faith but instead raised too many doubts. Hasan Hanafi, a noted Egyptian professor of philosophy of our time, has summarized his influence by writing: "al-Ghazali launched a conservative revolution that stifled this [prior] pluralism and transformed Islamic culture and society according to an absolute and state-enforced doctrine" (in Hanafi 2002, 72). Yet al-Ghazali, while denying the utility of philosophical speculation to underpin faith, respected it for its mathematical and astronomical advances and so did not condemn it altogether, saying instead that it should be confined to the few who could understand it and its limits adequately (Hodgson 1974, vol. 2, 180–83). Still another idea for the decline of Islam's "golden age" was the lack of social space for more neutral inquiry into nature, as there were very few patrons and no corporate-type entities, such as universities, available to support any such extrareligious investigation (Huff 1993, 47–84). Finally, there was also the problem of translation, another key influence. The rise of scholarship and science in early Islam was directly fed by the great period of translation, drawing from Greek, Syriac, and, to a lesser extent, Indian and Persian sources. By the fifteenth century, this process was long over and the number of individuals who knew both Arabic and Latin or any European vernaculars was extremely small, and even for purposes of trade refugees from the West were needed (Lewis 2002, 7, 45–47). Translations of Western books were almost nil up until the nineteenth century. Islam had essentially no knowledge of the European Renaissance or Scientific Revolution.

After al-Ghazali Islamic philosophy and even questioning of traditional religious orthodoxy did not stop entirely. This was especially the case in the Spain and the Maghreb, which had developed a somewhat separate intellectual culture from that of Baghdad and Persia. The Spanish Arab philosopher Ibn Rushd (1126–98), known in Europe as Averroes, produced exceptional summaries and commentaries on the works of Aristotle, as well as Plato's *Republic*. He further began what

Spinoza and others would later on do in Europe by writing that some of the Qur'an was allegory and not to be taken literally if it contradicted the truths arrived at by philosophical inquiry. Even a century later, there could still be great thinkers in the sciences, such as the polymath Nasir al-Din al-Tusi (1201–74), who wrote a number of important works on mathematics and astronomy and improved the Ptolemaic model of the solar system without, however, placing the Sun at the center. But overall, Ibn Rushd and al-Tusi came at the end of the great era of scholarship and science. In particular, Ibn Rushd's was a daring step that is strongly rejected by important Salafist thinkers up to our own day, notably Sayyid Qutb. Ironically, his influence was limited in his own society, in direct contrast to the enormous impact it had in Europe where it helped revive scholarly interest in Greek philosophy and science (Hourani 2002, 172–75).

The politics of the Islamic world in the early second millennium turned ever more against the kind of open intellectual speculation that had characterized the high point of Arab civilization. This happened as successive waves of tribal nomads who were relatively recent converts to Islam conquered its centers and sought to legitimize themselves by allying with conservative urban *ulama* (literally, "people of knowledge," learned legal scholars who are often influential leaders). These less educated nomads, the most important of whom were Turkic tribesmen, therefore imposed more puritanical, restrictive, and closed versions of Islam to show that they were good Muslims. There were, of course, periodic attempts to recapture the former openness. But typically political authorities backed unquestioning faith against such speculation, as did the religious urban masses in the main cities (Gellner 1983, 77–81).

Over the next centuries, as great transformation took place in Europe with the Renaissance, the Reformation, and the Enlightenment, Islamic learning stagnated and ceased to innovate or absorb much outside learning. Even as original a thinker as Ibn Khaldūn (1332–1406), the Tunisian Arab statesman, philosopher, economist, and historian, had no lasting influence. Like the great fifteenth-century Renaissance Italian Niccolò Machiavelli, Ibn Khaldūn broke away from explaining history in terms of divine influence and instead in terms of changing, human-driven social structures (Gellner 1983, 86–90; Ibn Khaldūn

1967, vii–xiv). He also perceived that even in his time the Europeans on the other side of the Mediterranean were making admirable important advances in philosophy, whereas for most of the Muslim world until the nineteenth century there was very little interest in what Europeans were thinking and writing (Kuran 2004, 134, 137–38).

In the Ottoman Empire, which at its height in the sixteenth and seventeenth centuries ruled the entire Middle East, North Africa, and southeastern Europe, elites began to notice the growing disparity between their military technology and that of the more advanced Europeans. By the end of the seventeenth century the Ottomans, having suffered serious military reverses, were worried. They even turned to Ibn Khaldūn's theories about why sedentary empires once built by vigorous nomads tended to get soft and decay to explain their problems (Kasaba 2009, 65; Lewis 1982/2001, 527–30 in Ayalon and Sharon 1986). This did not, however, lead to a greater understanding that it was a gradual shift toward increased tolerance and open inquiry in a few Western societies that was providing the impetus for innovation, and it was not until the nineteenth century that attempts at reform would go beyond "a search for the old forms that had been the underpinning of earlier Ottoman centuries." Until then there was no will at the center to push for reforms that displeased the religious authorities and might be unpopular with most elites (Faroqhi et al. 1994, 640).

More generally, by this time the intentional intellectual isolation from Christian Europe, including the lack of translation, had worked its damage. Moreover, according to the economist Timur Kuran, Islamic societies relied too much on stultified traditional schooling that discouraged original thought. Social customs were too strongly communal such that they discouraged the individualism that could produce innovative entrepreneurial activity as opposed to more established ways of making money. Merchants in even the most commercial cities never gained the kind of political strength that they established in the leading Italian, Dutch, and later other Western cities. Guilds that used their political clout to restrict innovation and competition were able to prevent change (Kuran 2004, 139–47).

This is not to say that such pressures against change were absent in western Europe and in the agrarian kingdoms and empires throughout the world. What happened in Europe was that the combination of greater individualism, urban merchant independence, and a few openings for greater tolerance and intellectual speculation broke through such restrictions (Chirot 1985). As this yielded the beginnings of some impressive technological changes, the more progressive societies became richer and more powerful, and this led to ever greater motives toward innovation. Had this not happened, no individual genius, not even a Spinoza, Descartes, Newton, Montesquieu, Hume, Smith, or Darwin, would have made much difference or even been allowed to write freely. At best, such innovators would have been quarantined or simply executed for heresy.

This very brief sketch is unable to offer a full explanation of what was unique about the West. But it does suggest why it is essential to think historically about the clear scientific backwardness of the Islamic world when it came into brutal contact with European colonialism in the eighteenth and nineteenth centuries and found itself far weaker than it had imagined.

Islamic Modernism

By the start of the nineteenth century it had become clear to many Muslim thinkers that something had to be done to catch up to the West, and in the hundred years that followed this became ever more obvious as European powers took control of almost all of the Muslim world. Russia conquered Central Asia and the Muslim Caucasus. The British extended their rule over all of greater India, including its very large Muslim population, as well as taking over vast Muslim parts of sub-Saharan Africa, of Malaya, and of the Persian Gulf emirates and gained effective control over Egypt and the Sudan. The Dutch extended their East Indies empire to include all of what is today Indonesia. The French conquered North Africa and the African Muslim territories not taken by the British. Italy seized Libya and parts of Somalia. After World War I the French and British divided up most of what had been left of the Arab portions of the Ottoman Empire. Only Turkey, Saudi Arabia, Yemen, Iran, and Afghanistan remained independent, though the latter two, like theoretically independent Egypt, were actually dominated by

Britain. This was such a humiliating, complete reversal of past history, when Muslim power had rivaled that of the West, that it obviously required reconsidering the validity of traditional religious beliefs.

The most prominent Muslim scholar to attempt to modernize Islam was Jamal al-Din al-Afghani (1838–98), who took the name al-Afghani to conceal the fact that he had been born as a Persian Shi'a. In the Sunni part of the Islamic world, which included approximately 90 percent of all Muslims, the writing of a Shi'a would have seemed less acceptable. Al-Afghani spent most of his career advising Sunni governments about reforming education and trying to demonstrate that Western science and education were compatible with Islam. He was most active in India, Afghanistan, the Ottoman Empire, and Egypt, but he also spent time in Paris where he learned more about the West, wrote, and lectured. He tried to convince Muslims that the scientific, philosophical advances of earlier centuries were something to be proud of and to which they needed to return. He also insisted that the West was a source of new knowledge that had to be included (Kurzman 2002, 103–10). In a speech he gave in Calcutta, India, in 1882, he said:

> Philosophy is the science that deals with the state of external beings, and their causes, reasons, needs, and requisites. It is strange that our *ulama* read . . . [al-Afghani cites a couple of orthodox, conservative Muslim scholars from the sixteenth and seventeenth centuries who were still being used to justify traditional rejection of "philosophy"] . . . and vaingloriously call themselves sages, and despite this they cannot distinguish between their left hand from their right hand, and they do not ask: Who are we and what is right and proper for us? They never ask the causes of electricity, the steamboat, and railroads. (quoted in Kurzman 2002, 105–6)

In 1883 the famous French historian and orientalist Ernest Renan suggested in a public lecture that in the golden age of Muslim science it was Greek and Persian influence that had made the key contributions, not Arab tradition, and this had only succeeded because Islam as a religion was still relatively unsure of itself and weak (Renan 1883). Once it felt more secure and strong, it rejected this cosmopolitan influence.

Al-Afghani was then living in Paris and responded by agreeing with Renan that Muslim societies had indeed become scientifically backward but countered that, after all, Christian societies had once been as well and that it was entirely possible for Muslims to modernize. Al-Afghani wrote:

> If it is true that the Muslim religion is an obstacle to the development of sciences, can one affirm that this obstacle will not disappear someday? How does the Muslim religion differ on this point from other religions? All religions are intolerant, each one in its own way. The Christian religion . . . has emerged from the first period to which I have just alluded; thenceforth free and independent, it seems to advance rapidly on the road to progress and science . . . I cannot keep from hoping that Muhammadan [a term no longer used but acceptable until not long ago] society will succeed someday in breaking its bonds and marching resolutely . . . after the manner of Western society. (quoted in Kurzman 2002, 108)

It is not entirely surprising that al-Afghani was repeatedly expelled from Muslim countries where he was serving as an advisor. However much he was renowned and some Muslim elites agreed with him, he sometimes sounded more like David Hume than a pious Muslim. He claimed to be a true Muslim, but it is quite obvious why a later fundamentalist like Sayyid Qutb insisted on returning to this theme to utterly reject the polluting influence of Greek and Persian influence and to condemn the long-gone age of Islamic cultural ascendancy.

Al-Afghani was hardly unique. Charles Kurzman's collection of writings by what he calls "modernist Islamists" from 1840 to 1940 includes a large number of intellectuals from throughout the Muslim world. Some were more religious, some less so, but all knew that something had to be changed if Muslims were to meet the competition from and counter the aggressive colonialism of the West. All of them agreed that the point was not to reject Islam or religion but to allow it to adapt. So why did the modernizing project fail?

By the 1930s, a bifurcation was occurring. The modernizing tendencies in Muslim societies were being captured by openly secular ideologies: nationalism, fascism, and socialism. On the other hand, there was a strong reaffirmation of conservative religiosity that rejected the need to imitate the West (Kurzman 2002, 26). The Muslim Brotherhood was founded in Egypt in 1928 to promote conservative Islamic values and mobilize them to fight British colonialism. At the same time a very conservative brand of Wahhabi Islam consolidated its hold on Saudi Arabia with the unification of that kingdom by Ibn Saud in the 1920s and 1930s. After World War II, as it became rich from its oil, Saudi Arabia was able to send out missionaries and influence the growth of its own brand of Islam. Modernizing Islam did not die a sudden death, however. It survived and gained ground in Indonesia, where it allied itself to the anticolonial nationalist cause, and it exists elsewhere (Hefner 2000, 2005). Nevertheless, it lost many of its potential supporters to secular ideologies, especially after the defeat of fascism in World War II, to socialist nationalism and Marxist-Leninist communism. For a time, especially from the 1940s to the late 1960s, it seemed that those secular modernizers would triumph over religious conservatism, but they did not. Instead, most of the secular modernizing projects, especially in the Arab Middle East, Iran, and Pakistan, failed to deliver the benefits they had promised, producing instead a number of public evils: corruption, oppression, poverty, and weakness in the face of the West's and, not least of all, Israel's own potent economic and military successes. All of this opened the way for the rise of conservative Islam, including the rise of extremist Salafism, as an alternative to secularizing modernization.

The Rise and Fall of Secular Nationalist Modernization

It is a tragedy for the Middle East's Muslim societies that secular modernization in most ways failed, except to a considerable extent in Turkey. This is most obviously the case for Arab societies but could be extended to Iran and south Asia as well. In Southeast Asia and Turkey, modernization and some form of secular reform did succeed to an extent, though even there the issue is not yet fully settled.

As far as Arab lands are concerned, modern nationalism was a reaction to British and French colonialism. After World War I and into the 1940s, proponents of nationalism, most prominently Sati al-Husri (1882–1968), developed a pan-Arabic philosophy that proclaimed the need for all Arabs to unite into an anticolonial, independent, single nation. First in Iraq and then in Syria, Husri, from the 1920s to the 1940s, was appointed to create school systems that taught its students to be pan-Arab nationalists and to reject European domination. Husri was inspired by German theories of nationalism that emphasized the unity of those with shared blood and language and the need, first propounded by the German philosopher Herder in the late eighteenth century, that each such nation deserved its own unified state. He also felt that even if most Arabs were Muslims, there were different kinds of Muslims, as well as Christians who were Arab, and that common blood and language were more important than religion in the modern world (Dawisha 2003, 49–74).

In Egypt and across North Africa and the Middle East, Arab nationalism that stressed the need for some sort of unity and modernization in order to overcome colonial power came from intellectuals trained in British and French ways, aware of European nationalism, and eager to enlist their own people in their cause. Because the colonial period also saw the rapid growth of cities and an uprooted migrant population that could be mobilized in those cities, it was inevitable that anticolonialism would ultimately unite a sufficient number of Arabs to throw out the Europeans. But this was only a first step. Liberated nations had to be made more prosperous and stronger. Always, there was tension between the pan-Arab ideologues and the more localized, particularly Egyptian forms of nationalism. However, new school systems, broader education, and anti-Western passions prevailed everywhere. After World War II, the rise of a Jewish Israeli state identified as a European colonial outpost provided a further unifying pan-Arab common cause (Dawisha 2003, 75–134).

In 1947 the Arab Socialist Ba'ath (Renaissance) Party was founded by three men: Michel Aflaq (introduced in chapter 5), a Damascus-born, French-educated Christian intellectual; his friend Salah al-Din al-Bitar, a Sunni Muslim from Damascus, who had also been to the Sorbonne; and Zaki Arsuzi, a Syrian Alawite and onetime Sorbonne student (Makiya 1989, 185–89). The party was secular, multiconfessional, pan-Arab, and socialist. (Alawites were considered a heretical Shi'a sect that combined elements of Islam, Christianity, and its own practices.) There could be no clearer example of how a group of highly educated intellectuals forging a new political philosophy directly influenced politics. Within a few decades, Ba'athists took power in Syria and Iraq. In Syria, an Alawite family, the Assads, assumed control in the name of this party in 1970 and continue (as of this writing, somewhat tenuously) to rule most of it. In Iraq, the Ba'ath first took over the government in 1963, and one of its members, Saddam Hussein, inspired by the writings of Aflaq, ruled from 1979 until he was overthrown by an American invasion in 2003.

Ba'athism was not the only such modernizing, secular party to take power. Gamal 'Abd al-Nasser (usually written as Gamal Abdel Nasser), who led the overthrow of the corrupt Egyptian monarchy in 1952 and became Egypt's dictator from 1954 until he died in 1970, espoused a similar socialist, nationalist philosophy and became a key rival of the Ba'ath for Arab allegiance. Sadly for Egypt, his ideas contained the same fatal flaws. The Ba'ath admired the Soviet Union, while rejecting Arab communist parties as not being loyal nationalists or sufficiently respectful of Islam (Makiya 1989, 250–53). Nasser did the same and differed from the Ba'ath chiefly because they both claimed to be the leaders of the Arab world, not because of significant ideological disagreements.

It was not just in Egypt, Syria, and Iraq that socialism became an ideal. The entire Third Worldist movement in Africa, Asia, and Latin America was enraptured by its promise. This was true whether the light shone on Maoist China, the Soviet Union, or the more nuanced version promoted by Tito in Yugoslavia. But in practice, what Third World regimes did was nationalize some of the more efficient parts of their economies against the will of many of their people, turning over state enterprises and purchasing boards to inept, corrupt bureaucracies. The results typically were economic stagnation and falling legitimacy, which necessitated greater repression to keep the regimes in power. If Iraq could temporarily escape this problem because of its oil wealth, Syria, Egypt, and most other Third World cases could not. From the start all these movements believed that a revolutionary elite deserved to run affairs and that it was counterproductive to have real elections.

Nasser once said that the Egyptian masses were "a caravan lost on a wrong path"; thus "it is our duty to lead the convoy back on the correct road ... [to] ... allow it to keep on its way" (Malley 1996, 102–3).

The ultranationalist side to the new philosophy in Egypt and the Ba'athist countries led to militarization and an aggressive posture toward Israel, which could be used as a rallying cry. This encouraged a series of wars with Israel, most dramatically the 1967 war that humiliated Nasser after his braggadocio about how well he had prepared Egypt for this confrontation. The problem was that Arab armed forces were run by the same corrupt and inept political allies of the dictators as the ones who were in charge of economic matters. They were good at suppressing internal dissent by mostly unarmed civilians but not up to the task of facing a modern army and air force (Ajami 1981).

Failures made all these regimes increasingly brutal and repressive, as this was the only way to stay in power. That opened the gate to something very different from what the secularizing modernizers had wanted. It became clear, in short, that these modernizers did not know their own societies very well, that a powerful internal element had been overlooked. It did not take long, that is, for Islamic religious fervor to grow and expand in rejection of the corrupt, oppressive, and religiously impure dictatorships (Malley 1996, 204–49; Owen 2012).

It needs to be emphasized that Iran's explicitly antisocialist and increasingly anti-Islamic modernization efforts led by its authoritarian shah (king, though he called himself the "King of Kings") were not successful either. On the contrary, the shah's modernization from above that benefited a relatively small elite and infuriated the large part of his population that remained devout also proved to be a disaster. In a sense, as it began to bear fruit in producing a modernizing middle class, the shah's boastful, expensively wasteful, repressively militaristic regime and nasty secret police that persecuted those who wanted more democracy alienated that very middle class that should have been his natural supporter (McDaniel 1996; Keddie and Richard 2006). When the shah was overthrown, it was the religious Shi'ite establishment, led by the noted Muslim conservative scholar and theologian Ayatollah Ruholla Khomeini (1902–89), who took power. (In Shi'a Islam, which dominates Iran, ayatollahs are the highest, most scholarly and intellectual interpreters of Islam and are its preeminent religious leaders. Sunni Islam lacks this structured and theologically authoritative hierarchy.)

Other similar failures led to the rise of extremist Muslim political forces as well, even where they were unable to seize power. In Algeria, the 1990s saw a terrible civil war between the corrupt military establishment and radical Islamists who had gained strength from the failures of the regime (Malley 1996; Souaïdia 2001). In Pakistan, repeated bouts of inept military rule, defeat in wars against India, failing government services, huge inequality, and massive corruption also fed religious extremism among those who felt that the promise of modernizing nationalism had failed (Talbot 2012). Even in relatively successful Tunisia, an authoritarian and increasingly corrupt secular dictator wound up being overthrown at the start of the Arab Spring that began in 2010 and spread throughout the Middle East (Noueihed and Warren 2012; Owen 2012). And in Turkey, the most secular, most advanced Middle Eastern Muslim nation, the flood of new rural and devout immigrants into the cities set the stage for the electoral victory of an Islamist party, albeit a more moderate one than those that came to the fore elsewhere in the Middle East but where the future of relations between secular modernizers and Islamists remains both contested and fraught with danger (White 2013).

One question that lingers over these developments is the role of oil. This, after all, was the principal reason for the West's interest in the region as well as the primary source of economic growth in many Muslim countries—Iran, Iraq, Algeria, Libya, Saudi Arabia, Kuwait, Qatar, United Arab Emirates, Oman, and Sudan (later on), with smaller but still important influence in Tunisia, Yemen, Egypt, and Syria. In the forty-year period between 1970 and 2010, more than $12 trillion of oil revenue went to these nations (British Petroleum 2014), yet poverty remains widespread and modernization very uneven. Oil wealth has not acted so much as a "curse" in these nations but as a tool of its leaders. There is no innate "evil" in oil or a necessary oil "curse." Rather, where there are ill effects these reflect poor leadership, skewed ownership structures that allow those in power to control all the revenues, and weak institutions (Luong and Weinthal 2010). The wealth has mainly gone to royal families, political leaders and their cronies, arms buying, forms of corruption, and, in a number of cases like Saudi Arabia and Iran, massive subsidies (for food, water, electricity, fuel) for the public in order to stymie calls for political and social reform. Thus the region's vast natural wealth has propped up and enriched regimes that have created few important opportunities for their people. In a significant way, oil wealth has provided a means for governments to avoid building modern economies, with education systems, expanded employment, and a high-level scientific and engineering culture. This reality has not been lost on the people themselves. Resulting despondency and frustration have had their own effects in urging more than a few toward religious extremism.

Such extremism, therefore, has a number of specific influences. But at the heart of it all is the fact that after more than a century and a half of attempted religious reforms, various experiments in modernization, the rise and fall of secular nationalism (socialist or not), and boastful claims that success was at hand, the main goals have not been achieved. Few of the Muslim economies are able to find employment for their huge number of youths. None can claim to have come close to catching up to the more advanced West or, in the case of Middle Eastern Arabs, to hated Jewish Israel. Even in the most successful Muslim societies, notably Turkey, Malaysia, and most recently Indonesia, conflict between secularism and Islam is far from resolved. Nor has it been in the very rich oil states of the Arabian Peninsula, chiefly Saudi Arabia, where that wealth has been used to maintain a rigidly conservative Islamic kind of rule.

THE RISE OF THE NEW SALAFISM: FROM MODERNISM TO QUTB AND AL-QAEDA

In Islam as in Christianity, there has long been a tradition of trying to purify what many saw as a corrupted and less authentic drift in belief. Each such movement claimed to be going back to some fundamental, original, true version of the religion based on the founding texts, the Bible or the Qur'an. Each time these purifying, fundamentalist attempts have also been opposed by various forces attached to all kinds of different versions of the religion, ranging from power holders whose orthodoxy was challenged by the reformers to many different kinds of heterodoxies. Over time, however, fundamentalist campaigns have actually been responding to, and were substantially shaped by, the present situation in which they arose. The ways in which the new versions of purifying reforms have arisen, whether in a Sunni form or in a very untraditional form in Shi'a Iran, have been no different.

Salafism, as mentioned earlier, refers to the "Salaf," the earliest generation of the Prophet Muhammad's followers. They are deemed to have been the best ever, least corrupted, true Muslims, and their astounding success in creating the basis of the vast early Muslim empire and spreading Islam so widely is ascribed to the purity of their faith. Salafists want Muslims to return to what they assume to have been this seventh-century version of Islam.

But just as the various forms of American Christian fundamentalism are actually modern and relatively recent, so are the several movements to purify, revive, and spread the true Islamic faith that have led to intensified violence. Salafists may claim to be traditionalists, but their strength lies in how they have reacted to the pressures of modernization and the contemporary weakness of their societies. As in the Christian case, much of the original impetus for such reformist movements came from the writings and proselytizing of scholarly intellectuals, until their messages spread to the wider public and gained an important following. Scholarly writing advocating Islamic reform has to show that it fully accepts Qur'anic scripture, though how it does that can be contentious (Cook 2000, 109–15).

A premodern starting point for twentieth-century Salafism is the writing of Ahmad Ibn Taymiyya (1263–1328), who lived in Damascus at a particularly troubled time. Islam had suffered the biggest defeat in its history at the hands of the Mongols, who, even after converting to Islam, were still viewed as foreign outsiders. They had conquered Muslim Persia and destroyed the last of the Abbasid Caliphate in Baghdad in 1258. Egypt and Syria, however, had been taken over by the Mamluks, slave soldiers consisting mostly of men from around the Black Sea or of Turkic speakers in Central Asia. They were widely used by Arab polities as warrior mercenaries. Seeking religious legitimacy, Mamluks enlisted the urban *ulama*, whose Islam was conservative and relatively purer than that of the rural peasant population. In 1260 the Mamluks defeated an invading Mongol army in Palestine and subsequently fought a series of wars with the Mongols, who proved unable to defeat them.

This was also the period of the late Christian Crusades, when these West Europeans still controlled much of coastal Palestine and Lebanon. In a series of wars the Mamluks managed to drive out these Christian Crusaders as well.

The late thirteenth century, therefore, witnessed much fighting against these two sets of outsiders, and Ibn Taymiyya reacted by insisting that only a very pure, original form of Islam should be practiced in order to restore Muslim greatness and that anyone, including rulers, who did not adhere to this prescription was not a true Muslim and therefore evil. By the twentieth century neither the Mongols nor the Mamluks were around, but the Crusaders, in the form of the intervening European (and later American) powers, were very much a presence. Muslims (as well as some of the invading Westerners) identified this new European incursion as a new kind of Christian Crusade. Ibn Taymiyya's texts became useful once more. The modern Salafists, chief among them Sayyid Qutb and an Indian Pakistani Muslim admired by Qutb, Sayyid Abul A'la Mawdudi (1903–79), cited his work as a guide to Muslims seeking to purify their religion in order to effectively fight back against the returned infidels (Toth 2013, 64, 70, 195–96, 306n32; Euben and Zaman 2009, 79–85).

It is not, however, possible to draw a straight line from Ibn Taymiyya to modern times, even if his writings were an inspiration. A more relevant, more immediate and influential intellectual origin of contemporary Islamic fundamentalism, strangely enough, was the modernist, relatively liberal main disciple of al-Afghani. His name was Muhammad Abduh (1849–1905). But perhaps this was not so strange. The ancestors of reactionary contemporary American evangelical thought, after all, were nineteenth-century Protestant social liberals who led the antislavery movement and sought to reconcile modern science with religion.

After studying with al-Afghani in Egypt, and later joining him in Paris in 1884, Abduh eventually returned to his native Egypt and was appointed a leader of al-Azhar, Sunni Islam's then (and still now) most

prestigious and influential theological university. Among the many reforms he proposed was a return to a purer understanding of the Qur'an.
He contended (as did al-Afghani) that a true reading of the Qur'an
would show that it demanded rational examination of the world and
the ability to adapt laws to existing and changing situations, and that
therefore the rigidity of much Muslim thinking and practice was not
the true religion (Kurzman 2002, 50–60). On science, he wrote:

> [H]ow is it that Muslims are content with so little and many in-
> deed have closed and barred the door of knowledge altogether,
> supposing thereby that God is pleased with ignorance and a ne-
> glect of study of His marvelous handiwork? . . . If Islam welcomes
> enquiry into its content, why is the Qur'an not read except by
> chanting, and even the majority of educated men of religion only
> know it very approximately? (quoted in Kurzman 2002, 59)

Abduh wanted to educate girls, modernize al-Azhar's curriculum,
and make Muslims more aware of the Qur'an's openness to knowledge
and discourse, telling them not to turn against their religion but to return it to its original character. He eventually became resigned to how
difficult it was to reform Egypt, or to free it from British domination,
and died a disappointed man (Toth 2013, 251–53). By the second half
of the twentieth century, the prevailing view of those who wanted
to return to the Qur'an to find the correct, original interpretation
had become almost entirely opposed to what Abduh had originally
wanted.

In part, this reversion was a reaction to the increasingly dependent
and manifestly weak situation in which most Muslim societies found
themselves after the collapse of the Ottoman Empire and the elimination of its last emperor, who had claimed the title of caliph. It no longer seemed that gradual reform would be sufficient to overcome colonialism and backwardness; furthermore, the rise of secular nationalism
threatened the very basis of Islam from within, so modernization itself
appeared to some as the enemy. But there was more—a profound social
change that was occurring throughout the Muslim world.

The Increasing Importance of Urban Islam

Ernest Gellner's analysis of modern Algeria offers a sociological explanation of the changes that have occurred in Islamic societies (Gellner 1983, 149–73). For a very long time the heart of the more learned, purer form of orthodox Islam has been urban. Rural societies, including both nomadic and peasant ones, tended to follow the leadership of various local saints and preachers whose religious leadership was often unorthodox or based on local beliefs and practices that overlapped with tribal allegiances and held communities together but were not more widely acceptable. As noted, it was common for conquering tribal federations of nomadic origin or slave mercenaries with no inherent legitimacy of their own to become rigorously orthodox in order to buttress their appeal to a wider constituency, including urban centers they needed to control. Islam has always had great respect for scholars, so that even illiterate rural tribesmen could be swayed by exceptionally persuasive learned scholars. In fact, many of the most successful religious brotherhoods were started by *ulama*, men who had studied in leading urban centers of knowledge and then gone back to rally more rural tribesmen to their cause while also converting them to greater orthodoxy. This pattern created a permanent tension in the Islamic world between more and less orthodox practices, between the purer versions of urban centers and more parochial, tribal forms.

Since the start of the twentieth century, a basic demographic change has occurred to alter this ancient dichotomy. What were once mostly rural societies have become far more urban as rural migrants have been drawn in by the greater job and mobility opportunities available in cities. And what was once widespread nomadism has drastically shrunk as it is increasingly unsustainable in the modern world. Thus as Islamic societies have urbanized, the more rigorous, orthodox kind of Islam has become more dominant than ever. This has occurred at the very time that secular modernization in most Muslim societies seems to have failed. It has come when the West, first Europe, then America and its perceived client state of Israel, have risen to be far richer and more powerful than Muslim states. The closer we get to the present, the more the hallmarks of these states, from sub-Saharan Africa to Pakistan and as far as parts of Southeast Asia, come to include widespread urban youth unemployment, economic frustration, and a kind of stifling stagnation. The way has thus been opened toward an ever greater insistence on a purer, more orthodox, and less varied kind of Islam. This has also meant that among the faithful there is less tolerance for those who are less rigorous and compliant with orthodoxy.

The Wahhabi Anomaly

After the assaults of September 11, 2001, on New York and Washington, it came to the attention of the world that fifteen of the nineteen terrorists involved were from Saudi Arabia. This was where the prevailing Muslim doctrine was inspired by an eighteenth-century Arab scholar and politically active, puritanical Salafist preacher, Muhammad Abd al-Wahhab (1703–92). At the time, what has since become the royal family of Saudi Arabia were local chieftains, whose leader, Muhammad bin Saud, formed a pact with al-Wahhab, who legitimized the Saudi conquest of most of Arabia in the name of purifying Islam and bringing it back to its roots. The first Saudi state was established on that basis. Despite future struggles, a close relationship with Wahhabist beliefs and practices thereafter persisted, down to the present day. The Saudi leadership was contested during the nineteenth century by Egyptian and Ottoman rulers and lost most of its power. But under the leadership of Abdulaziz Ibn Saud (1876–1953), the family fortunes revived and most of Arabia was reconquered, leading to the establishment of the present Saudi kingdom in 1932, with Wahhabism as its official religious doctrine. Given that this doctrine has ruled Saudi spiritual life ever since, while the country has remained a dynastic kingdom (since Ibn Saud's death in 1953, rule has passed to several of his sons in succession), the association of Islamic terrorism with Wahhabism remains plausible.

The reality, however, is more complicated. Some analysts (for example, DeLong-Bas 2004) have pointed out that al-Wahhab's actual writings are not nearly as bloodthirsty as the version of Islam that guided Osama bin Laden and his al-Qaeda terrorists and that, in any case, the eighteenth-century puritanical call for a return to the fundamental practices of early Islam had little or nothing to do with the West. Al-Wahhab himself railed against Ottoman corruption and laxness (with more than a little justification), not against Europeans. Indeed, the aim that most energized the original Saudi campaign was to drive Ottoman influence from the holy cities of Mecca and Medina. Al-Wahhab's reformism was part of a whole set of similar Reformation-type movements across the Muslim world, from West Africa to Java in the East Indies, in the late eighteenth and early nineteenth centuries. These came in response to a perception that Islam was drifting away from its original purity (Robinson 1982, 118–19).

This reformist wave was hardly the first in Islamic history. The ninth and tenth centuries had seen the rise of the Hanbali legal tradition, which established the most severe of Islam's juridical schools and to which al-Wahhab himself belonged. There were many other cases, as well, ranging from the Almohad Caliphate in Morocco and southern Spain in the twelfth century to the Mughal emperor Awrangzeb, who turned to the Naqshbandi order emphasizing greater purity of Islam in seventeenth-century India (Hodgson 1974, vol. 2, 269–71, vol. 3, 93–98). In almost all cases, as with Wahhabism, fundamentalist scholars and preachers sought to lead puritanical reform movements, denouncing Muslims who had become lax or had absorbed more tolerant non-Islamic traditions. This could involve converting a ruler to their cause, as in the case of Awrangzeb, or sometimes raising their own armies among less devout tribesmen, converting them, and leading them to form new states, as in the Almohad case where Moroccan Berber tribesmen were mobilized. A much later example occurred in northern Nigeria when Usman dan Fodio (1754–1817), an urban Fulani scholar, rallied the mostly nomadic Fulani throughout the region to conquer the "corrupt" Hausa city-states and found a Fulani empire. None of these particular examples was a modern response to the rise of the West. But by the early nineteenth century, the larger situation was rapidly changing.

At this point, Wahhabism was already somewhat out of touch. Still focusing on less pious Muslims, its leaders had failed to realize that the major challenge to Islam was now European expansion, which could (and did) lead to the colonization of almost the entire Muslim world.

Indeed, some of the more sophisticated reform movements of the time were much more aware of this new development. By the early twentieth century, Wahhabism was even more of an anachronism, especially as it was practiced in the Saudi kingdom (Hourani 2002, 349). Had it not been for the subsequent discovery of oil in the kingdom and the enormous amount of money that it provided the royal family, it is likely that a version of Wahhabism would never have become a global phenomenon influencing Muslims everywhere.

Although current Wahhabi religious leaders may claim they are pure traditionalists, what they practice is no longer the original version. It is something much newer and modern, dating from the second half of the twentieth century and grafted onto traditional Saudi Wahhabism in a most curious way. In this transformation, the writings of Sayyid Qutb and other extreme Salafist texts have been influential. How Qutb and other modern versions of Salafism have come to exercise so much power over the minds of so many Muslims is the real story of how violent anti-Westernism and antimodernism have flourished. Before we turn to this subject, however, a bit more needs to be said about the contemporary form of Wahhabism. For this, Gilles Kepel's analysis is exceptionally enlightening (2004, 152–96).

When Ibn Saud conquered most of Arabia after World War I, his kingdom was a heterogeneous collection of many tribes and diverse versions of Islam. To Western eyes, this diversity may seem unexpected, even striking; it shows, however, the degree of variability in Islam, as interpreted by different social groups up to modern times. In Saudi Arabia, Islam ranged from more open, cosmopolitan, and tolerant forms in the Hijaz (along the Red Sea Coast and including the holy cities of Mecca and Medina), to the severe orthodoxy of the Najd (the center of Arabia and the home of the Saudis), to the Shi'ite northeast (considered heretical by Wahhabis), and finally to the less strict and, especially with respect to women, less restrictive forms practiced by many Bedouin nomadic tribes. For the sake of national unity, the Saudis imposed their own strict orthodoxy throughout the kingdom, giving free reign to the Wahhabi *ulama*, at least up to a point. Ibn Saud did have to repress an uprising by the most extreme Wahhabis. They objected to his relations with the British who helped finance his conquests, but he regained favor by giving the *ulama* control over education and higher learning in the kingdom and imposing most of the puritanical rules on which they insisted. After World War II, British influence was replaced by America's and American oil companies that opened up the huge Saudi fields. As oil money started pouring in, the royal family gave ever more funding to the *ulama* in order to maintain a legitimacy that was increasingly tainted by their ever more lavish lifestyle and dependence on American support. The Saudi state encouraged Wahhabi missionary activity throughout the Muslim world both to keep its most activist Islamists busy outside the kingdom and to support more conservative religiosity throughout the Islamic world. Saudi Arabia also allowed the entry of Salafist Muslim scholars who were fleeing repression in the secularizing Arab states, particularly those ruled by Egypt's Nasser and the Ba'ath. This included Muhammad Qutb, the brother of Sayyid Qutb, who became a respected and influential professor of Islamic theology after his brother's execution by Egypt's Nasser in 1966. This also suited the Saudi rulers, whose greatest fear from the 1950s to the late 1970s was that their monarchy would be overthrown by Third Worldist revolutionaries who had taken power in other Arab countries. Devotion to strict Islam was seen as the best counterstrategy, particularly because within Saudi Arabia itself the state had become extremely dependent on Western technology and expatriate expertise to modernize its economy and run its petroleum production. But as Toby Jones has argued (2010), this created a permanent tension between the Wahhabi *ulama* and some conservative voices within the Saud family on the one hand and others in ruling circles who wanted to modernize the society but dared not push too far for fear of alienating their religious base. The result was that a new, ever stricter, and more reactionary form of Wahhabism was allowed to flourish in education, social, and cultural matters in order to continue with economic modernization. But that more fundamentalist, more puritanical Wahhabism was also increasingly deeply anti-Western.

In 1979 radical Islamists briefly took over the Grand Mosque in Mecca, the main site for the holy annual pilgrimage, killing many worshipers and security forces. They had to be crushed in an extended, bloody confrontation that lasted two weeks and ended in the beheading of sixty-three surviving militants. It was also in 1979 that the Iranian Islamic Revolution occurred, directly challenging Saudi religious legitimacy. This finally woke up the Saudis to the danger they had created. But by then, the situation was no longer what it had been in the earlier days of the kingdom. A rapidly rising urban population, youth unemployment, and growing inequality, combined with the power conservative clerics held over Saudi education, had contributed to creating a radicalized reactionary Islamist constituency. The ruling Saud family tried to placate the extremist *ulama* and their followers while also trying to keep extremism in check. Even more than thirty years later, in the early 2010s, the Saudi elite had not come to terms with what they had fostered and continued to subsidize. This has made their hold on power more precarious, but they see no way around what they have allowed to turn into a source of religious reaction and instability (Jones 2010, 236–44; Jones 2011). Be that as it may, the many missionaries, subsidized mosques, and financing of Salafist converts throughout much of the world, including in certain Western countries with Muslim immigrants, have done their work implanting the neo-Wahhabi, anti-Western synthesis throughout a great many Muslim communities.

These extremists are certainly a minority of Muslims, and it would be wrong to suggest that most Muslims support their most violent members (Kurzman 2011). Nevertheless, an ideologically committed minority can be a powerful force, particularly among the young, strongly influenced by a coherent, intellectually admired set of texts that can be interpreted by leaders in a way that has wide appeal. All extremist movements that have gained a measure of political power, from Marxism-Leninism to fascism to various forms of religious fundamentalism (modern as well as premodern), gained their importance through the work of inspired and committed minorities willing to struggle against more moderate majorities. That is why it is important to look at the inspirational intellectuals who laid the foundations of such movements.

The Tragedy of Sayyid Qutb and the Rise of Violent Salafism

Sayyid Qutb was born in 1906 in a rural Egyptian village south of Cairo. As an intelligent and ambitious boy, he received a good education, thoroughly Muslim but relatively modern, and succeeded in elevating himself into the ranks of the prestigious corps of schoolteachers. He became a talented writer whose literary commentary made him a minor celebrity in intellectual circles. Always inclined to be somewhat mystical, he wrote poetry as well. He seemed in most respects to be a pious, gentle man who remained devoted to his religion but who also accepted the modernizing ideas of reformers who wanted to revive Islam by incorporating Western ideas, science, and social change. He was an Egyptian nationalist who wished to have his country freed of British colonialism, something widely shared by almost all Egyptians.

By the 1940s, disappointed by Egypt's failure to turn its formal independence into genuine liberation from British domination and increasingly disgusted by the corruption he saw among Egypt's elite, Qutb began a slide toward radicalism. He denounced Western influence as inherently polluting because Europe had turned its back on religion in favor of soulless materialism and pleasure seeking. He began to see the introduction of such immorality as the root of Muslim societies' own failure to free themselves of colonialism, poverty, and inequality. By the late 1940s, he had become persuaded that the West was so hopelessly amoral and corrupt, particularly as was revealed by its rampant sexuality and commercialism, that it could only serve as a bad example. A heartfelt and true religion, he felt, was necessary to save a people from such degeneracy, and only Islam could fill that role. (For this and subsequent paragraphs, see Calvert 2010 and Toth 2013.)

In 1948, Qutb was sent to the United States to learn about its educational system in order to garner some lessons for Egyptian reform. He toured much of the country but spent the largest part of his time in the religious and rather conservative town of Greeley, Colorado, where he attended the Colorado State College of Education. Greeley was legally alcohol free, as were many other strongly Protestant (and Mormon) parts of the United States, and the late 1940s are not a time remembered by Americans as particularly sexually or otherwise loose, but by then the forty-two-year-old Qutb had already made up his mind about the West and America. Never comfortable with women, except for his mother, sisters, and a few very devout Islamist admirers, he never married and may never have had any physical relations with women. What he saw in America, where men and women interacted quite openly, was moral laxity, too much emphasis on sex, and churches that were more materialistic than truly religious. This, interestingly, was very close to the perception of fundamentalist Christian evangelicals as well, though without such an obsessive fear of female sexuality. Qutb considered American culture "primitive." Though he was not yet a proponent of violent jihad, he was starting to move in the direction of believing that only the original, pure form of Islam should be practiced and that winning over Muslims was going to be a struggle (Calvert 2010, 139–55). (Jihad literally means "struggle" and can be applied to individual struggle to attain a deeper faith as well as to the more warlike version Qutb and other Muslim radicals have increasingly favored. Depending on which part of the Qur'an one consults, either version appears possible.)

After Qutb returned to Egypt, his writing became more strident and more widely disseminated. He picked up from Sayyid Abul A'la Mawdudi, whose views had greatly influenced Muslim anticolonialism and anti-Westernism in India before independence and later in Pakistan, the notion of *jahiliyya*, that is, ignorance (Jalal 2008, 242–73). This term had been applied in the Qur'an to pre-Islamic Arabia because it had not yet been enlightened by the Prophet Muhammad's revelations. But the term was used by Mawdudi to describe modern Islamic societies that had abandoned the true, pure faith and so must be brought back to genuine Islam (Euben and Zaman 2009, 79–85). This became a key concept for Qutb. *Jahiliyya* was prevalent and had to be combatted because the political leaders and elites in Muslim countries had fallen under its sway. This was because they had succumbed to Western ideas. Qutb thus became a kind of religious Third World prophet urging unity against Western colonialism and imperialism but also against Israel, which he interpreted as an outpost of Western colonial domination. He began to inveigh against "Crusaders" and "Zionists," by which he meant all Christians and, according to his reading of the Qur'an, all Jews.

Third World anti-imperialism and anti-Westernism was, as we have seen, a growing movement that became the basis for nationalist, socialist, and frequently anti-Israeli sentiment throughout much of postcolonial Africa, Asia, and parts of Latin America. But Qutb's version was religious, not socialist, and increasingly antinationalist because he wanted all of Islam to unite, not just as a set of divided sovereign nations. He joined the Muslim Brotherhood (originally founded in 1928), whose ideas were similar but had not appealed to Qutb before his gradual conversion to Islamic radicalism.

The Muslim Brotherhood had grown since its founding, especially after World War II, when branches were established throughout the Arab world. Hassan Al-Bana, its founder, had been murdered by Egyptian government agents in 1949, but his program to use Islam as a source of unity against Western colonialism continued to spread. Qutb took this further by saying that not only supposedly Muslim Egypt but all existing Islamic societies were steeped in *jahiliyya* and so had to be transformed. He proposed that in order to free Muslims of all weakening defects it was necessary to reconvert the masses to original Islam. While Qutb became a leading promoter of the Brotherhood's ideas, he moved ever more toward its most radical segments, as opposed to the more moderate side that preferred compromise with the authorities.

Israel, since its victory against combined Arab armies in 1948, now occupied an important place in Qutb's thinking. In order to justify his increasingly visceral hatred of Jews, Qutb turned to a part of the Qur'an that told the story of how Muhammad, after his flight to Medina, had become an ally of prominent Jewish tribes there but then turned against them when they betrayed his trust. These Jews were therefore condemned as hypocrites and traitors whose men had to be exterminated. This was part of what some analysts have called Qutb's ever more "paranoid" thinking (Calvert 2010, 165–71).

In his most widely disseminated work, written near the end of his life, Qutb insisted that modern science and technology were acceptable, even if invented by the impure West, but not if taken to the point of trying to explain the origins of life and the universe, and certainly not if science were to be used as philosophy to expound on morality and the meaning of culture. To do so would deny God's role and inject materialist thinking into what ought to remain the proper domain of Islamic worship. Any attempt to use Western science to impinge on religious faith and Islamic culture was a deception meant to weaken Islam. He wrote:

[T]his statement about culture is one of the tricks played by world Jewry. Whose purpose is to eliminate all limitations, especially the limitations imposed by faith and religion, so that Jews may penetrate into body politic of the whole world and then may be free to perpetuate their evil designs. At the top of the lists of these activities is usury, the aim of which is that all the wealth of mankind end up in the hands of Jewish financial institutions which run on interest. (Qutb 1964, 111)

There was nothing unusual about such a statement. *The Protocols of the Elders of Zion* or the Argentine military dictatorship or, of course, the Nazis, among many others, would have concurred about the evil role of the Jews, who had become the standard-bearers of all that was iniquitous about modern capitalism.

For Qutb, however, it was not just Jews who were to blame but all of Western thinking. Here Qutb's mistrust of what was an essential part of Enlightenment thought, particularly the cultural liberalism that allowed free thinking about the origins and meaning of life and the universe, not to mention skeptical examination of religious dogma, was not particularly unique either. As Paul Berman's examination of antiliberalism in the modern world has suggested, Qutb's views were consistent with all of the totalitarian, violent movements, religious or not, that existed in the twentieth century. Qutb's version was particularly religious and Islamic, so that he rejected communism but also Western democracy because "it restricts God's domain to the heavens. . . . Freedom in a liberal society seemed to Qutb to be no freedom at all. That kind of freedom was merely one more expression of the hideous schizophrenia—the giant error that places the material world over here, and God over there" (Berman 2004, 80–81). In that sense, Qutb's dissatisfaction with the liberal separation of church and state was not very different from that of a good many conservative evangelicals who have viewed such separation as contrary to Scripture. By phrasing his hatred of the West, of Jews, and of Enlightenment liberalism in pious Muslim, Qur'anic terms, Qutb was able in his writings to appeal directly to discontented Muslims.

Such was especially true in *Milestones* (1964). This was meant for far wider distribution than his immense, more scholarly, multivolume textual analysis of the holy book, *In the Shade of the Qur'an*. In *Milestones*, he expressed his views in an easily understandable way that tied his rejections of Western thought and his disgust with Islam's failures to an improper or insufficiently careful reading of the Qur'an. Thus not only the West but also existing Muslim state institutions, including Egypt under Nasser, had to be combatted. The whole world was filled with ignorance, *jahiliyya*. Muslims had to return to the pure faith of the founder and his immediate followers. There should be freedom to choose the proper faith, he wrote, though he insisted that if illegitimate restrictions were removed, all of the world would naturally turn to Islam. Therefore, it was right to destroy those who stood in the way, that is, those who disagreed with pure Islam. The claim of "freedom" was therefore very conditional. Nor was it necessary to use centuries of scholarly accretions to the faith, especially those parts influenced by impure outside sources such as Greek or more recent Western philosophy. Only a return to the basic text was necessary, and every Muslim, not just an educated elite, would understand it (*Milestones* 40–41). No political system or material power should hinder the way of preaching Islam, but any that did should be destroyed. Enemies of Islam had to be either killed or else submit and relinquish power of any kind. This, Qutb said, was the true meaning of jihad, not the weak version that claims it should only be "defensive war," much less the mere struggle by individuals to attain a higher level of faith and morality (*Milestones* 57).

Why did this become so appealing to so many? Because, for a true believer, the rightful order of the world had been overturned. "Crusaders" and "Zionists" had taken over. The Qur'an, while it certainly has anti-Jewish and anti-Christian passages, also prescribes tolerance for those who pay a special tax and submit. Qutb did not disagree and insisted that Islam should not be forced on others as long as they were free to convert or, if not, agreed to submit. For most of Islam's history, the majority of Christians and Jews under its various empires and kingdoms were indeed tolerated, but only as long as they remained submissive (Cohen 1994). Since the nineteenth century, however, Christians had ruled Muslims and dominated them, and the once subservient Jews had created a powerful state in the middle of the Arab world. This should not have happened; it was nothing less than a violation of what the Qur'an had called for. Seeking an explanation from within his ever more radicalized faith, Qutb could only assume that what had gone wrong was part of a gigantic world plot that God had allowed to play out because His true believers had lost their way.

Qutb did not reach his most extreme positions, for which he is now famous and revered by his followers, until Third World revolutionary ideas came to power in the nations of Islam and dramatically failed to produce what they had promised. This was the tragedy that led to the rise of such a widespread Salafist radical movement, thus a ready audience for Qutb and others like him. Had the more secular Third Worldism of Nasser and the Ba'ath worked, Salafism would have continued to exist but not as such a widespread phenomenon.

In 1952, the Egyptian monarchy was overthrown by a military coup led by then colonel Gamal 'Abd al-Nasser, though it would be another two years before he assumed the title of president. At first the Muslim Brotherhood, which Qutb formally joined in 1953, supported Nasser. It gradually turned against him as it became evident that the military officers now in charge had a secular, modernizing Egypt in mind, not a religious one. In 1954 a member of the Brotherhood tried to assassinate Nasser but failed. Qutb and the main leadership of the movement had nothing to do with this, but Nasser took the opportunity to arrest thousands of members and break the organization. Qutb was arrested, tortured, and in 1955 sentenced to fifteen years in prison on trumped-up charges. Already a frail, unwell man, the needless brutalization he suffered and his observation of other tortures only accelerated his full radicalization. Strangely, or perhaps not so strangely, given his own increasing paranoia, he would later say that the plot to kill Nasser had actually been a "Zionist-Crusader" conspiracy to discredit and destroy the Brotherhood (Calvert 2010, 191–95).

As Nasser then seemed to move from triumph to triumph, nationalizing the Suez Canal and surviving a British-French-Israeli invasion that tried to overthrow him in 1956, he seemed to have won the game. The Muslim Brotherhood was marginalized; Nasser pushed through a popular land reform, created a new socialist bureaucracy to run the economy, allied himself with the Soviet Union, and built up a powerful armed force to confront Israel. It was not until 1967, a year after Nasser had Qutb executed by hanging, that the fantasy of all this was exposed when Egypt was crushed by Israel in the Six-Day War. Nasser died a broken man in 1970 and left a legacy of corruption, inefficiency, and economic stagnation entirely unable to accommodate the rapidly rising young population with a future. It was the incompetence and legacy of Nasserism, as well as of similar other Arab ideologies—Ba'athism in Syria and Iraq, as well as the Algerian military's and Muammar Qaddafi's version in Libya—that ultimately discredited Third Worldism in the Middle East and opened the way for a revival of Islamic extremism for which Qutb's prison writings would prove to be a shining inspiration (Ajami 1981).

Qutb remained in jail from 1955 to 1964 but under conditions relaxed enough to allow him to continue writing and to have his work published. He completed the volumes of his key work, *In the Shade of the Qur'an*, and finally *Milestones* (which includes key chapters from *In the Shade of the Qur'an*), both of which have become staples of late twentieth- and twenty-first-century Islamic thought. Controversial, heavily debated, admired by some and loathed by others, these books have been very widely cited and translated into many languages.

Briefly freed, Qutb was again arrested in 1965 for having knowledge of another anti-Nasser plot. By then *Milestones* was being widely read and was found in the possession of radical Islamists intent on overthrowing Nasser, and it was on that basis that Qutb was condemned to death. His hanging in 1966 made him a martyr whose fame has continuously spread since then. (An extraordinary video of a serene Sayyid Qutb, looking calm and almost saintly, being led to his execution is available on YouTube.) He was a small, quiet, sickly man dressed in a Western suit and tie, with large ideas that have gained a huge following. That Egypt's army was utterly defeated a year later by Israel must have come as no surprise to those convinced that Qutb was correct in labeling Nasser a *jahili*, a corrupted, ignorant, and inauthentic Muslim who was more like the evil biblical pharaoh portrayed in Exodus than a righteous leader of an Islamic people (Kepel 1993).

When Qutb was executed, the news deeply affected a pious fifteen-year-old Egyptian middle-class boy named Ayman al-Zawahiri. This boy became a medical doctor and one of the leaders of a very radical Egyptian Islamist group dedicated to the violent overthrow of the secular regime in power. After Nasser's death, the presidency was taken by Anwar Sadat, who, despite being quite religious himself, committed what was in the eyes of the Islamists the unpardonable sin of making peace with Israel. They managed to assassinate Sadat in 1981. By then Zawahiri had already been in Afghanistan to help the war against the Soviet Union's occupation force and its Afghan communist allies. He was not part of the assassination plot but knew about it, and he was arrested as an accessory to the crime. In prison he was further radicalized by the usual harsh conditions and torture, and once freed, he moved to Saudi Arabia where he linked up with Osama bin Laden, another, more famous, and much richer Afghan veteran. Together they ultimately founded al-Qaeda ("the base") and, after a series of other bombings and killings, plotted and organized the dramatic attacks of September 11, 2001, on New York and Washington. In all this, Zawahiri, the more scholarly and intellectual of the two, continued to be inspired by Qutb, except that the repeated failure of domestic plots in Egypt and Saudi Arabia convinced him that the war had to be carried abroad to weaken the Western defenders of corrupt Muslim elites. If the United States could be driven out of the Middle East, then Qutb's program of destroying evil Muslim regimes would become far more feasible (Kepel 2004, 70–107).

After Osama bin Laden was killed by American military action in 2011 while he was in his supposedly safe hiding place in Pakistan, Zawahiri, who is also securely in Pakistan, became the leader of al-Qaeda. Despite massive American intervention in wars in Iraq and Afghanistan, and continuing pursuit of al-Qaeda supporters in Pakistan, Yemen, Somalia, and other places, the organization has survived and been skillfully guided into spreading its influence throughout much of the Muslim world. It seeks alliances and provides doctrinal as well as some logistical guidance for radical Islamists in West, North, and East Africa, in the civil war in Syria, and for Sunni extremists in Iraq and Yemen and elsewhere in the Middle East, in Pakistan and Afghanistan, and to a lesser but still important degree in Muslim Southeast Asia. An even more extreme Salafist group split off from al-Qaeda while fighting in the Syrian civil war that began in 2011 and in 2014 conquered a substantial portion of Syria and Iraq. The Muslim Brotherhood, particularly its more radical part inspired by al-Qaeda, has also become an inspiration for alienated radicalized Muslim immigrants in Europe (Pargeter 2008; Pargeter 2013, 136–78).

It is wrong to pretend either that Qutb was an entirely singular figure towering above all other Islamic thinkers of the twentieth century or that his ideas have been uncontested. Many Islamists decry the extremism he advocated, and there have been many other influential theorists. But in part because of the clarity and powerful simplicity of *Milestones*, because its author led such an exemplary, clean life unencumbered by any hint of self-seeking or devious political maneuvering, and because of the way he was executed more for what he wrote and thought than anything he actually did, he has increasingly become the most cited of all Islamists by radical Salafists worldwide (Filiu 2011, 70, 136).

Just as Karl Marx was far from being socialism's only theoretician in the nineteenth century but gradually became its single leading light in the twentieth, so Qutb is well on his way to becoming the major theoretician of radical Islam in the twenty-first century. Whether his theories can ever become the basis of a functioning society is quite another matter, but we can speculate that wherever and whenever his followers attain power, if they ever do, their society will be dominated by such hatred and rejection of the Enlightenment that it will stand no chance of succeeding in the modern age. Already, because of the triumph of conservative Islam over the modernizers, most Muslim societies have fallen still further behind not only the West but also East Asia. Perhaps paradoxically, however, the further they fall behind, the more appealing Qutb's ideas will seem to those seeking a religious way out of that backwardness.

Is Iran Different? Ayatollah Khomeini's Vision

The rise of religious extremism in Iran, based on Shi'ite rather than Sunni Islam, had similar causes. There were many decades of felt humiliation at the hands of the West, first Europeans (Russians and British), then, after World War II, increasingly the Americans. A reformist prime minister in the early 1950s who tried to wrest control of Iran's oil resources from the Anglo Iranian Oil Company (now British Petroleum) was overthrown with the help of an American CIA plot in 1953. Power was handed back to Reza Pahlavi, the shah of Iran, who instituted an autocratic, arrogant regime that trampled on the religious sensitivities of his people and led to a rapid but uneven modernization from above, fueled by oil wealth. The shah's modernization, however, left out much of the population, increased inequality, and alienated the middle classes who wanted more democracy and less secret police. To top things off, the shah tolerated heretical versions of Islam, like the Bahai, and was a friend of Israel (Keddie and Richard 2006).

The shah was overthrown in 1979 and was replaced as ruler by the Ayatollah Ruholla Khomeini (1902–89). Ayatollahs are Shi'ite religious leaders whose learned scholarship qualifies them in the eyes of the clergy and the devout to become spiritual and politically influential leaders. Khomeini was a deeply intellectual theologian who developed unique theories about how leading Shi'a Islamic scholars should guide society so that it could become more thoroughly Muslim. But unlike Sayyid Qutb, Khomeini was a shrewd political leader who gained power and set up a republic ruled by clerics who followed his ideas. His was both a more elitist and a more practical ideology than Qutb's, one unlikely to attract Muslims who are not Shi'ite or, more specifically, backers of Iranian political ambitions. Far from promoting the notion that Muslim states should be superseded by a united caliphate, Khomeini proved himself to be a fervent nationalist intent on strengthening his state and using its religious influence to promote Iran as the greatest power in the Middle East.

Shi'a Islam split from the majority Sunni version in the seventh century when the descendants of Muhammad through his daughter Fatimah and her husband, Ali (who was also Muhammad's cousin), were denied the leadership of the growing Muslim empire. Ali eventually became the fourth caliph but ruled only for five years before being assassinated while praying. The Partisans (Shi'a) of Ali have since then disputed the legitimacy of Sunni political leadership and, in particular, since the Middle Ages have been waiting for a disappeared imam, or leader, to come back to life and lead them. There have been many varieties of Shi'a Islam, but its most important population centers are in Iran, Iraq, and Bahrain where Shi'as are in the majority. Substantial minorities also exist in Lebanon, Saudi Arabia, and Pakistan, with different varieties in Turkey, Syria, and Yemen. Outside of Iran in recent centuries Shi'a Muslims have mostly been despised minorities, but this changed dramatically in 1979 when Khomeini took power and used his religious credentials to make Iran a protector of all Shi'ites, thus creating a powerful set of allies across the Middle East (Ajami 1986; Nasr 2007). Without going into detail about their theological differences, we can say that over time, Shi'a and Sunni communities have become similar to ethnic groups competing for control of resources in modern states throughout the Middle East where they coexist. Nevertheless, they share much, as do all believing Muslims, above all faith that the Qur'an is a holy text. Many Shi'as also feel deep resentment toward Western colonialism and that somehow the rise of Israel is a particularly humiliating continuation of Western imperialist intrusion. Thus for these Shi'as the continuing weakness, corruption, and poverty of Muslim societies need to be remedied by strengthening, not abandoning, Islam.

Khomeini, however, was not what could properly be called a fundamentalist, and as an intellectual influence on Islamic extremism, he was very different from Qutb. He was, first of all, someone who believed that only a learned intellectual elite could properly interpret the Qur'an, unlike Qutb, who felt the true faith was accessible to everyone without mediation. Second, as mentioned, Khomeini was a nationalist whose main intent was to strengthen Iran in order to make it the center of Islam, not to abolish the modern nation-state in favor of a universal caliphate, as Qutb and his followers have wanted. In this sense, Khomeini was a distinct modernist who wished to have Iran enter the ranks of great nations and was willing to engage in strategies of power and subterfuge along the lines of those used by Western states. Khomeini's Iran certainly involved itself in international affairs and promoted Islamic unity, but it was more in the same style as Stalin's Cominform that sought to subordinate communist parties everywhere to Soviet domination and interests. The regime established by Khomeini has used mostly Shi'a allies to promote Iranian goals. Finally, Khomeini's philosophy created an entirely new kind of Shi'ite state run by clerical authority, led by himself and his chosen successor, Ayatollah Ali Khamenei. This state is meant to rule while Shi'a Islam waits for the final days that will come with the reappearance of the disappeared descendant of Ali, known as the Twelfth Imam, who vanished in the ninth century but will return to redeem the world. In the meantime, the government is to run a conventional autocratic state with very clear modern great power international ambitions throughout the Middle East, where it has become a protector of Shi'a communities and a leader in the fight against the West and Israel. The innovation proposed by Khomeini has been to denounce all secular political leadership as corrupt and unjust, something quite original in Iranian history, and to claim that the only worthy substitute is a regime guided by scholarly religious judges. Khomeini called this concept Velayat-e Faqih, jurisdiction over believers, and the chief judge, at first Khomeini himself, was to serve as the supreme guide. Khomeini was well aware of how completely original this was and "warned listeners that this 'true Islam' might sound 'strange.' After all, false ideas spread over the centuries by a conspiracy of Jews, imperialists, and royalists had taken a heavy toll." This would be righted by the proper if novel interpretation he proposed (Abrahamian 1993, 25 and more generally 13–38). By insisting on this particular view of the Qur'an and Hadith, Khomeini was not suggesting that any Muslim could just go back to the original texts, as learned analysis was necessary to uncover this as yet unperceived truth that had only emerged recently under his guidance.

In a way, Khomeini succeeded. The Iranian state he established in 1979 survives, still guided by his successor. It engages in terrorism as a tool of its ambitions and plays a major role in Middle Eastern politics. Its presidents, who have been far less powerful than the supreme religious leader, have varied over time, and one of them, Mahmoud Ahmadinejad (presided 2005–13), actually seemed to believe that the Twelfth Imam was coming soon. This was probably one of the reasons he lost the trust of the clerical establishment that is, on the whole, far more practical and intent on preserving the power and wealth it has accumulated. Other presidents have not insisted on this particular piece of dogma about the return of the awaited Twelfth Imam, but instead, the clerical regime has empowered its newly formed, increasingly corrupt elite with its own economic interests. It is therefore much more realistic than the kind of unachievable utopian dream put forth by Qutb.

The problem Iran faces, aside from whatever international complications in which it is involved, is that like Qutb and the whole array of Islamists, fundamentalist or not, who reject the West, it has shut itself off from the Western Enlightenment. But it wants to have a modern economy, the most advanced weapons (including, it would seem, nuclear ones), and all the accouterments of modernity except for intellectual freedom and a sense that some sort of separation between church and state is necessary to sustain innovative thinking and progress. In that sense it is not very different from what fundamentalist evangelicals in the United States want. It also resembles attempts in the twentieth century that were antireligious but wanted to merge modern science and technology with ideologically rigid governments that repressed freedom of thought.

Whether or not separating the two parts of the Enlightenment can work remains to be seen. Keeping modern technology and material progress while abandoning the political and moral side, the promotion of individual liberty, and the skepticism toward any absolutist doctrine may in the long run inhibit progress too much to be entirely viable. Or perhaps not. This was the key question and most dramatic confrontation of ideas in the twentieth century and will remain so in the twenty-first, not just with respect to Islam but throughout the world.

The Future of Anti-Enlightenment Religious Extremism

The dream of a utopian, pure, Salafist Islam that unites all the faithful and the Khomeini version of a Muslim world headed by a resurgent Iran are not the only extreme ideas floating around among Muslims in the early years of the twenty-first century. There is, as Jean-Pierre Filiu has pointed out, an increasing sense among many that the days of the Apocalypse are near. The collapse of authority in some Muslims states, the wars in Iraq, Afghanistan, Pakistan, and Syria, the rise of terrorism within Muslim societies, the seemingly unending and worsening tension between Muslims on the one hand and Christians and Jews on the other, the division within Muslim societies between various Islamic tendencies and between Islamists and more secular modernizers, and the general poverty, corruption, and injustice in the world all feed this fantasy. There is a Christian equivalent, as we saw in the previous chapter, and it is perhaps not surprising that it has much in common with the Muslim version. Indeed, the return of Jesus Christ plays an important role in the Muslim apocalypse, just as it does in the Christian version, though for Muslims Christ is recognized as having been a major prophet (not the son of God) whose valid preaching was, however, distorted and corrupted by later Christians and of course by Jews. Disturbing, however, is that among the several Muslim predictions for the "end of days," all share an obsessive anti-Semitism centered on the existence of Israel and the fact that it is supported by hated America (Filiu 2011). In the Muslim story, Israel is the very opposite of the holy site in the Christian Apocalypse—it is, instead, the ultimate evil that will be annihilated.

Though Qutb was certainly not one who had much to say about the end of days, much of his emphasis on the evils in today's world, on the need to combat Christians and Jews, on the revolutionary obligation to overthrow existing Muslim regimes, and on the mounting problems Muslims face in the world is consistent with millennial ideas. However unsettling, these realities reflect the truth that much of the Muslim world is deeply troubled. Too many of its societies have been misruled by foreign-imposed colonialism and then by the supposedly liberated regimes that followed. There is a large reservoir of angry young people frustrated by their inability to carve out a decent future. The humiliations of the past have been followed by new ones as the United States has intervened and Israel has thrived. The rightful order in which the true religion, Islam, should rule over much of the Earth has been overturned for the past two centuries, and there are no signs that this will change. So even while the large majority of Muslims everywhere may continue to wish for a better world without being either Salafists or violently inclined, there is little doubt that extreme doctrines will continue to find a receptive home. Among them, the writing and exhortations of

Sayyid Qutb will resonate, perhaps in simplified and more popularized accounts.

This, after all, is exactly what happened with the complex ideas of Marx and the reactionary thinkers who inspired fascism. Streamlined and taken over by politically shrewd believers, they managed to take power and dramatically threaten the very survival of the liberal Enlightenment. It is also the way in which successful revolutionary religious movements have established themselves in the past.

As we concluded in the last chapter, it is unlikely that the American version of Christian fundamentalism will ever gain as much success simply because the United States is not in nearly as sad a state of disrepair or even resentful despair as are most Muslim societies and because the liberal Enlightenment tradition has established strong institutional roots that cannot so easily be dismissed. In Muslim societies where no such roots have taken hold, it is a different matter.

The Power of Ideas
and the Importance of the Humanities

> The great object, in trying to understand history, political, religious, lit-
> erary or scientific, is to get behind men and to grasp ideas. Ideas have a
> radiation and development ... in which men play the part of godfathers
> and godmothers more than that of legitimate parents.
>
> LETTERS OF LORD ACTON

The world of the twentieth century was one built in substantial part
by the ideas of Adam Smith, Karl Marx, and Charles Darwin, by the
founders of American democracy, but also by the reactions against the
Enlightened vision of progress that they championed. There were, of
course, many other thinkers of merit who were part of these debates,
and we have not meant to presume that those we have analyzed were
alone. But they were vitally important and especially innovative and
thus merit particular attention.

Our twenty-first-century world continues to be deeply influenced
by Smith's and Darwin's ideas, and just as certainly by the debates about
democracy expressed by Thomas Jefferson and Alexander Hamilton, especially in the United States, which remains the world's premier power.
Karl Marx seems less important now than a few decades ago, though it
would be premature to dismiss his and Friedrich Engels's influence so
quickly and easily. Forms of socialist idealism retain the power to energize those who dislike or abhor the capitalist order that now prevails.
Versions of Marxist ideas are certain to regain their promise in some
parts of the world.

At the same time, reaction against the thinkers we have featured shows no signs of going away. Smith's conception of market capitalism as the best hope for a freer, more progressive society and the American Founders' liberal championing of democracy are far from universally accepted. Even among nations that now call themselves democracies, the realization of basic freedoms remains highly (some would say disappointingly) variable. As for Darwin's evolutionary theory, it continues to animate bitter resistance in our time, as it has since it first appeared. Nor does the Enlightenment's faith in the power of science and free thought as the means to find solutions to humanity's problems remain unchallenged. Karl Marx, who strongly believed that good social science could transform the world, would undoubtedly have been appalled to see how badly that notion was misused and perverted by regimes that claimed to be inspired by his theories. Meanwhile fascism, as it was practiced in the earlier twentieth century, is no longer with us in the same form. But a number of its major elements—ultranationalism, disdain for democracy and individual rights, autocratic and brutally murderous repression, and a tendency to celebrate force and xenophobia—remain highly potent forces today. Indeed they are, if anything, on the rise once more in the 2010s. The battle of ideas over these issues is very far from over, and it appears certain that the struggle will not be concluded in this new century, if ever.

Our analyses in this book are meant to show the great value to be gained by going back to the original texts in order to study the actual thought of seminal intellectuals and to better see where and how they were subsequently embraced (or enslaved) for distinct purposes. Only in this way can we bring to light their vast historical fertility, whose full extent we have not yet come near to exhausting. We would say, in fact, that such study is essential both for gaining a more complete understanding about the creation and spread of modern freedoms, plus the institutions to implement and protect them, and for comprehending the varied resistance to such freedoms and the reasons why this continues.

Though it is obvious that we prefer only some of the ideas we have discussed, we also recognize that within what we broadly called

Enlightenment liberalism there are enough possible interpretations and serious arguments, such as those between Jefferson and Hamilton, to easily encompass what are today called social democracy, liberalism, conservatism, and libertarianism. The Enlightenment was never about one set of ideas or interpretations. Writings that have created new modes of comprehending and shaping human society can hardly be exhausted by any single group of interpretations. We would insist, therefore, that at least some of the forms of reaction against these sets of ideas need respectful analysis. Even those that we find contemptible have to be treated seriously, with analytic distance, so that we may better understand where they come from and why they arise. Thus we are not trying to sway ideological opinions but are appealing to readers to take ideas seriously, to study them, and to understand their origins, meaning, and consequences.

The Complexity and Continuing Importance of Powerful Ideas

Our first three foundational thinkers, Smith, Marx, and Darwin, all left the modern era a different place than when they entered it. Their ideas have proven able to encourage diverse, at times even conflicting, interpretations by later intellectuals, political leaders, and institution builders. Indeed, we find that all of the thinkers highlighted in this book did not at all bequeath to posterity a collection of fixed concepts and obvious positions. Very much to the contrary. Books like *Wealth of Nations*, *Das Kapital*, and *Origin of Species* have within them a great diversity of stated and suggested viewpoints, not all of which are fully compatible with one another by any means. They present major, original, brilliantly groundbreaking ideas but with enough subtlety and complexity to provoke fierce debate down to the present day, even among their admirers. It is also why those who deeply oppose the ideas proposed by these works still address them, either directly or at least indirectly by inference. To attack the concept of free markets or the reality of genetic mutation is to do battle with *Wealth of Nations* or *Origin of Species* (we often say "argue against Adam Smith" or "Charles Darwin," but it is really their writings that are at issue). They are among the key foes to be combatted for anyone wanting to counter much of what has been progressive about modernity.

Powerful ideas have no copyright. The past two centuries give witness to concepts like "the invisible hand," "dialectical materialism," and "natural selection" being seized upon by an enormous range of individuals and groups to inspire new schools of thought, new views of social betterment, new policies, new forms of cultural expression, and new ways of understanding who we are as human beings in a fascinatingly complicated social and natural environment. Remaining deeply attached to the original ideas, but always led by their own understanding of them, these interpreters have been the more immediate agents of change over time. As we have seen in the chapters of this book, their impacts have been extremely varied, from the profoundly beneficial to the monstrously destructive. It is far too simple to attribute the cause for such impacts solely to the source texts themselves, to a small number of later commentators, or even to their reception in particular historical periods. But the major texts were at the start of it all and have remained key sources. It is the interaction of all these ingredients—the texts, their later interpreters, the way in which they influenced leaders and policies, how the understanding of them was affected by historical trends and events, and how they affected public opinion—that has been determining.

The reasons why Darwin's epochal work—and, indeed, his very name—came to be used on behalf of biology, laissez-faire economics, the "field" of eugenics, and then nationalist chauvinism can hardly be explained in a few paragraphs or pages. No less is this true of the expanded uses to which Darwin is put today. None of this, to be sure, dilutes or detracts from the immeasurable influence of original ideas themselves. The same may be said of Marx and Smith or, for that matter, of Jefferson and Hamilton, all of whose writings and opinions have also been put to many different uses ever since they appeared.

Adam Smith

Read carefully, Adam Smith favored both sides of what has since been grounds for an angry debate between two different groups of believers in the inherent value of capitalism as a progressive, efficient, and liberating way of organizing modern societies. On one side, there is his clear support for making free markets the single most important way of creating and spreading wealth. On the other are those who agree but also consider the role of governments vitally important because free markets are insufficient to provide all the necessary parts of a strong and good society.

Smith may not have used the image of the "invisible hand" often, but he certainly disapproved of attempts to limit the power of markets. He trusted the self-interest of the multitudes to come to the fairest and most productive ways of allocating goods and investing their capital. Individual self-interest and the spontaneous order that emerged from its free working were certainly deemed better than what governments usually did to control economies. Smith particularly disliked rules that served purely narrow interests, whether by guilds, by privileged social strata, by merchants seeking monopolies, or by governments that might hinder free trade. But at the same time, he wanted to help the poor, advance the working class, promote education, and get governments to invest in necessary public goods.

Smith was the founder of modern economics in that he understood much about the complex interactions of public and private interests and what was required to loosen the bonds of stultifying privilege and tradition. He shared the optimism of the eighteenth-century Enlightenment, whose values he synthesized and systematized in his own writing.

It is a disservice to Smith's memory, his work, and of course to our society to abandon one part of his thought to privilege the other. The self-interest operating through free markets to provide proper incentives for economic growth is crucial. To deny this because unfettered capitalism creates a whole set of its own problems is to miss the main point. All modern attempts to excessively curb market forces, most notably and extremely in communist economies, have resulted in stagnation, corruption, and ultimate failure.

Nevertheless, as recent economic analysis has shown, to neglect the other side of Smith's ideas is no less an error. Entirely free markets produce a concentration of capital, as the most efficient and ruthless take an increasing proportion of profits and learn to leverage their economic power into political power to protect their wealth. Inequality does, after all, increase until it produces political reactions from both Left and Right that threaten stability. Government action can counter this tendency toward rising inequality, as happened in the mid-twentieth century's main advanced capitalist economies, but without such intervention, inequality grows, as it has done most notably in the United States since the 1970s but almost everywhere else as well (Piketty 2014). Adam Smith did not predict exactly how modern economies would work—how could he at the very start of the Industrial Revolution? He did know, as some of his latter-day followers have failed to appreciate, that allowing too much inequality and too much influence going to powerful economic interests was not good for either prosperity or freedom.

Karl Marx

Karl Marx was outraged by the injustice he saw in the industrializing and most advanced parts of Europe in the mid-nineteenth century. He was hardly the only one. A host of reformers offered different solutions, and the most famous authors of novels in Great Britain and France, Charles Dickens and Victor Hugo, were equally scandalized.

What Marx offered, with the help of his great friend, editor, and supporter Friedrich Engels, was a systematic analysis of history and economics to explain the world that western Europe had come to be. He was right on many counts and wrong on many others. Capitalism does tend toward greater inequality unless democratic forces intervene to limit the power of capital. It does lurch from one crisis of excessive speculation and overproduction to another. In the early part of the twentieth century, industrial labor forces in advanced societies did organize themselves, though more to improve their situation through reform than to promote revolution. On the other hand, capitalism did not self-destruct and still shows no signs of doing so. Its ability to improve technology has proved to be astounding, though without the freedom of thought of the Enlightenment it is unlikely that this would have happened or continued. Market capitalism has proved itself to be far more resilient and adaptable to change than its critics, including Marx, ever believed. Marxism as a political ideology never took power through revolutions in advanced societies. Such revolutions took place only in relatively backward, poor ones where his ideas, modified and adapted by Lenin and later by Mao and a few other communist leaders, were harnessed to the forces of aggrieved nationalism, something that would have disappointed Marx in no small amount. In any case, where Marxism, mostly in the guise of Leninist and Maoist adaptations, did come to power, it produced economic systems that succeeded for a short time and then failed catastrophically. It also imposed cruel dictatorships and killed many tens of millions in the attempt to make Marxism work. This has considerably discredited Marx's ideas.

Such discredit does not in the least change the truth, though it is a dark one, that Marx's ideas had tremendous effects on the twentieth century. For a while it seemed as if Marxism-Leninism, adopted and further modified by Mao and the Chinese, would actually conquer the world, or large parts of it. That this did not happen, again, does not diminish in the least the power that Marx's work had.

Marxist analysis, flawed as it was, provided insights that are once again proving to offer some cautions about the nature of capitalism. His outrage about capitalism's production of inequality, today manifested most by the forces of antiglobalization and by strong antiliberal reaction, is shared by many. In all of its many forms, this kind of discontent offers few if any systematic analytic explanations better than Marxism, except for religious versions that deny modernity, science, and the whole Enlightenment tradition that Marx still believed in. Therefore, a newly revived form of Marxism that looks back to its originator is almost certain to appear and once again directly influence the world.

Charles Darwin

Charles Darwin's contribution to the creation of modern biology is unquestionable. But what about the social, political, and philosophical consequences of his theory of evolution?

However much Darwin would have disliked the ugly consequences of eugenics and racist interpretations that emerged in the late nineteenth and early twentieth centuries, we cannot deny that some of this did come from certain aspects of his writing and that in later works he leaned in that very direction without quite understanding where it might lead. Social Darwinism, a blend of Herbert Spencer's and Darwin's ideas, in many ways more a creation of the former than the latter (though often wrongly ascribed entirely to Darwin himself), is still alive and well. Some intellectuals and policymakers continue to believe that giving too much aid and comfort to the weak and poor only makes them less likely to adapt and save themselves. Theories that claim to see humanity divided into superior and inferior races, fighting with each other for resources, remain widespread from China to the United States. Even some versions that see the contest for domination and survival as one between competing cultures rather than genetically determined races interpret the world in terms of Social Darwinism.

No less have there been new attempts, in a wide variety of fields, to use natural selection as the explanatory scheme for human behaviors and emotions of every kind, from individual crimes to capitalism itself. Such Darwinian fundamentalism, as it has been called, is not new, though today the focus is not on evolution per se but its main mechanism, natural selection. We are witness once again to the belief, which Darwin himself came to partly share, that biology has the power to claim all things human and to deservedly take this domain away from nonscientific fields of knowledge, including the humanities.

This hardly means that we should reject Darwin, but as with our other major thinkers, we ought to remember that such great ideas hold within themselves contradictions and potential hazards as well as liberating insights. That is all the more reason to fully appreciate what Darwin actually wrote and meant.

There is no doubt that while some criticism of Darwin is based on purely antiscientific religiosity, one consequence of his work, as we have pointed out, has been to eliminate the divine from the history of life, including human beings. This was very much a part of the earlier seventeenth- and eighteenth-century Enlightenment's legacy, but Darwin put it in final terms that were impossible to neglect or dismiss. Evolutionary theory, therefore, continues to be deeply disturbing, particularly to the billions of people who find meaning and guidance in ideas that cast the world as God's holy creation and history itself as the unfolding of a sacred narrative. If all is just the outcome of random selection pressures, chance mutations, genetic drift, and asteroid impacts, what purpose is there in anything? In this sense, the Darwinian world system can only appear pessimistic. Claiming, as some extreme contemporary Darwinists do, that belief in God is just a foolish, willfully ignorant delusion completely neglects this larger reality. The contempt they show is simply one more indication that the struggles raging for the past 150 years will continue with no loss of intensity.

Combining Darwin's and the entire Enlightenment's scientific objectivity and rationalism with a humane philosophy that gives broader meaning to human life remains a work in progress that is very far from being completed. Going back to Darwin himself is a necessary step in this continuing search for answers.

DEMOCRACY AND AMERICA'S PLACE IN THE WORLD

The role of the United States in institutionalizing and then preserving Enlightenment liberalism against strong opposition in the twentieth century justifies our looking carefully at the founding of this unusual and unusually powerful country. Jefferson and Hamilton both agreed and deeply disagreed about how to interpret Enlightenment thought, with one favoring a weak central government and greater individual liberty, while the other believed in a stronger federal authority to make liberal economic and political ideals actually work. This debate continues unabated in the United States and in much of the rest of the democratic world.

Particularly important, however, is that these two thinkers represented two sides of the same Enlightenment thinking that characterized Adam Smith's work. Both Jefferson and Hamilton embraced the importance of free thought, of personal liberty, and of giving free markets a decisive role in economic policy. Undoubtedly Jefferson's hypocrisy about slavery, which he knew was wrong but on which he depended economically (as did his southern colleagues, including Madison and Washington), and America's failure to grapple properly with this issue from the start weaken our faith in his liberalism. Nevertheless, his ideas, as well as Hamilton's, shaped America's ultimate goals and idealism in ways that are wholly active today and will remain so.

The slavery issue resulted in a terrible American Civil War that was itself followed by a hundred years of racial segregation and denial of basic civil rights for those Americans who were not of European descent. But the ideas of democratic liberalism that fueled the Revolutionary generation and that eventually helped end slavery never went entirely away, though they have certainly suffered other periods of diminishment. Indeed, they remain at the heart of efforts to continue to improve the United States itself and as a potential inspiration to the rest of the world. If these ideas had not been powerful enough to see the nation through two world wars, a devastating depression, and the temptations of fascism, reactionary nationalism, and aggressive factionalism, they would long ago have vanished.

For better or, as some would have it, for worse, the United States of America remains the single most powerful nation on Earth in the early twenty-first century. Even if, as some believe, an alternate model is emerging in China—capitalist but authoritarian and undemocratic—the United States will remain in the forefront of the ideal developed by Enlightenment European philosophers and, as such, a model itself. In the twentieth century, fascist and communist models presented themselves as vital alternatives, but they failed, horribly and miserably. In the new century, there are religiously inspired alternative models, as well as the state capitalism, or "Chinese," way (Callahan 2013). We would not presume to predict which of these will still seem viable in the late twenty-first century. Nor is it possible to deny that the United States has too often failed its own ideals internationally, pursuing imperial-type aims in parts of the world near and far, into the twenty-first century. Such actions can tarnish the model of democratic liberalism presented by the United States, but they do not melt it down. America's own long-term goal, in a sense, remains the same as it was in the antebellum era: to better approach in reality its own ideals in mind. It is a fair bet that the ideas of freedom underlying American democracy, which are still primarily those of Enlightenment Europe, are not going to disappear so easily.

As far as the United States itself is concerned, it would be salutary in this time of bitter division (the 2010s) to go back to the Jefferson-Hamilton debates. Angry as they were, bitter as they could be, their shared love of liberty and their understanding that whether one believed in active or relatively inactive central government, excessive centralization of power was an evil of brutal consequence made it possible for compromises to emerge. Compared to how much of Europe at that time thought of government, Jefferson and Hamilton were not really so far apart in that both believed that no religion should be forced on a nation, that power should be treated with caution and have institutional barriers placed against its possible excesses, that scientific progress was key to promoting progress, that markets ought to be allowed to regulate most of the economy, and that educating the entire population in order to bring it into public affairs was essential. Both, in other words, believed in democracy. Learning how much they shared as well as why they so angrily disagreed would frame today's political controversies in a more moderate way and make compromise easier.

THE COUNTER-ENLIGHTENMENT

The Counter-Enlightenment has been and continues to be an inevitable reaction to the significant triumph of the Western Enlightenment itself. The French Revolution's excesses, from what appeared to be mob rule and the Reign of Terror to Napoleon's military dictatorship and his wars with all of Europe, animated a religious and monarchical reaction in favor of political and moral tradition. But as the nineteenth century went on, with all of its economic and social changes, it became increasingly obvious that calling for a return to the past was not enough. To mobilize opinion, it was necessary to propose a reaction that went beyond just wishing for the restoration of pre-Revolutionary times. Several different intellectual strands combined in the second part of the nineteenth century to produce the philosophical basis for a mass-based antiliberalism. In America, southern slavery and then the Jim Crow laws and the continued expansion into the West found an ideological justification in theories about "superior" and "inferior" races. Something very similar legitimized the aggressive push into a vastly expanded European imperialism into African and Asian colonies, especially by the domestically more liberal British and French states. Finally, the growing perception among many late nineteenth-century European intellectuals on both the Left and the Right that liberal capitalist democracy was alienating, corrupt, and irreparably hypocritical as well as unheroic, dull, and conventionally stuffy prepared the way for a number of influential philosophical statements calling for a new, more vigorous, antidemocratic, and even anti-Enlightenment reaction to cleanse societies of accumulated dysfunction.

The growing nationalism and colonial aggressiveness of European states that led to the catastrophe of World War I allowed this tendency to turn into disastrous political reaction in the 1920s and 1930s. Fascism arose not only in Europe but also in the Asian societies most attuned to Western progress, primarily Japan. By 1940, it seemed that outside the English-speaking world, most powerfully the United States and its eventual ally, Great Britain, the Enlightenment had died. In continental Europe itself only Switzerland and Sweden remained free and democratic. The rest of the Continent was ruled either by Hitler and his allies or by Stalin. In Latin America fascist ideas and various kinds of dictatorships prevailed, and in Asia Japanese imperialism was rampant. Africa and the Middle East were still mostly colonial holdings.

We know that in the end fascist powers were defeated, though at enormous cost. The ideas behind fascism, however, have hardly vanished, and just as it is important to understand where more liberal ideas come from, it is equally vital to know why and how fascist ideas developed and proliferated. New versions exist and are more likely to gain ground than to become obsolete.

Finally, we felt it necessary to treat two forms of religious extremism that also deny much if not all of the Enlightenment's liberating and progressive ideas. While it is clear that we do not agree with them, we insist that the ideas behind them have to be taken seriously and understood. They are not simple products of thoughtless and irrational emotion and superstition. There are reasons why they appeal. As with serious ideas that we favor, those that we may dislike need to be understood and respected as genuine.

Fascism

Fascism was the successful attempt to mobilize mass support in favor of reaction against the morality of the Enlightenment. There is no doubt that fascism in Italy, then later in Germany, responded to real failures of the liberal order. There was World War I, followed by the economic uncertainties of the 1920s, and of course the Great Depression of the 1930s. Either Marxist-Leninist communism as practiced by the new Soviet Union or Mussolini's and later Hitler's and the Japanese military's forms of fascism promised to solve these problems. In so doing, in these major countries as well as in offshoots in Latin America and in smaller European countries, as well as in Stalin's USSR on the Left, the basic principles of free thought, free markets, and respect for individual rights of the Enlightenment were explicitly rejected as weak, corrupt, and ineffective.

After World War II and the defeat of the fascist powers, it might have seemed that this sort of reaction on the Right was finished, but that is not the case. Widespread anti-Semitism and other forms of racism persist, ultranationalism is far from gone, and criticism of Western (now more American than British or French) liberalism remains persuasive to large parts of the world. The late twentieth-century failure of communism and of leftist, Marxist-inspired Third World ideology to solve the problems of former colonial regions has opened the way for a more rightward drift that again brings up some of the same tendencies as those that led to such a rejection of the Enlightenment in the early twentieth century.

In both Russia and China, autocratic, aggressive nationalism is a powerful intellectual force, and the combination of market economies, state interference, and favoritism of certain corrupt, politically connected large enterprises has actually re-created something surprisingly similar to the way in which Nazi Germany and fascist Italy ran their societies. Neither postcommunist Russia nor China, which still claims to be communist, would admit to being fascist, of course, but the rejection of democracy and of the West and the political intolerance they practice while trying to foster technological innovation and science might not seem so alien to the intellectual precursors of European fascism.

In lesser powers, too, particularly in the Middle East, in cases ranging from Erdoğan's Turkey to clerically dominated Iran to military rule in Egypt, something like this seems to prevail or to be heading in that direction, at least in the mid-2010s. In all these cases, the outcomes are far from predetermined, but what is striking is that many of the same arguments against democracy and Enlightenment liberty for both markets and individuals are back in fashion as they were in the first part of the twentieth century.

Going back to those earlier debates can be startling. By changing only a few phrases and references, they seem as relevant as ever.

Christian Fundamentalism

In the United States, many liberal intellectuals and scientists have found it astonishing that religious hostility to Enlightenment liberalism and modern science has actually grown over the past few decades. This has come from a large percentage of Christian evangelicals and their many organizations, which, since the 1970s, became engaged in reactionary political and social activism at a high level. Modern science, primarily but not exclusively in the form of Darwinian evolution, is strongly rejected by this cohort of religious Americans. The extension of rights to sexual minorities and the legal right of women to have abortions are seen as the spread of immoral, ungodly corruption that denies the teachings of the Bible and threatens the country in terms of its standing in God's eyes. Furthermore, this kind of religiosity, advanced by missionary work over decades, has met startling success in poorer parts of the world, especially in Latin America and Africa.

The origins and early development of American Protestant evangelicalism were quite different in outlook. Evangelicals embraced key ideas of the American Enlightenment, including individual liberty, religious freedom, and the separation of church and state. They proved an important support for the Revolution and, in the nineteenth century, became a major progressive force in their attempts to aid the poor, advance workers' and women's rights, and end slavery. The advance of industrialism and modernity in America they tended to view as aspects of God's kingdom in His chosen land; these aspects had to be accepted even as the problems they created called out for helpful interventions. But as it did in so many other domains, the Civil War brought a deep division among evangelicals. In the South, evangelical Protestantism retreated from modernity. It became associated in white churches with continuing resentment against the North, with racism and Jim Crow segregation, and with a distrust of modern progress. In other parts of the country, especially the Northeast, the progressive tradition in evangelicalism was revived in the late nineteenth century in a movement known as the social gospel.

Fundamentalism began as a direct reaction to the social gospel and to new and powerful evidence rejecting the inerrancy of the Bible. It demanded a return to the "fundamentals" of a supernatural Christianity and to Scripture as the literal word of God. By the 1920s, this reaction had permeated large parts of the South and portions of the Midwest as a militant movement seeking new laws against the teaching of evolution. It might have seemed by the mid-twentieth century, a generation after the famous Scopes "Monkey" Trial, that this kind of religiosity was doomed to obsolescence. But it returned as a political force as America itself became more conservative in the last decades of the century. By the early twenty-first century, allied in part with Catholics of the Religious Right and latching on to the many discontents of alienated white Americans who felt marginalized by the rise of minorities, by immigrants, and by highly educated, richer elites, fundamentalist evangelicals underwent a full-fledged revival of political influence, focused in the Republican Party.

What would happen if the ideas that underlie this phenomenon were to gain an upper hand in government? The United States would be transformed into something its Founders would never have found acceptable. The rejection of science in such areas as biology, geology, and climate research would be repellent to not only Jefferson and Hamilton but Madison, Franklin, Washington, Adams, Jay, and a host of others. The elevation of one sect of Christianity above all other religions, to the point where it had a dominant influence at the federal and state levels, would negate Enlightenment principles embedded in the Constitution and Declaration of Independence and, ironically, would go against what evangelicals themselves advocated in the Revolutionary era. While big government would be theoretically abjured, interference with personal rights in matters of family life would violate other long-held American values, as would the racially tinged fight against "foreign" influences and migrants.

Whether the trends of success for fundamentalism can spread much further in the United States may be doubtful. Its hardened answers to many questions have come to seem unhelpful to some younger evangelicals who perceive American society in the midst of new changes, with calls for expanded forms of social justice and compassion. The inevitable clash with the continuing strength of Enlightenment ideals regarding freedom of thought and acceptance of diverse viewpoints is bound to take its toll on fundamentalist intolerance. But there is no denying that, as a world force, the ideas that underlie this kind of religiosity also have their appeal and must be taken seriously. They have proven dynamic in certain ways, even as they have remained seemingly fixed. Here also, that is, the power of ideas and the need to understand their source, their strengths, and why they are persuasive to so many highlight the necessity to read and analyze foundational texts and commentaries.

Radical Islam

In the contemporary world there are few crucial problems that reflect so clearly the power of ideas as the rise and durability of extreme Muslim Salafism. The American "war on terror" has killed a substantial number of violent extremists and been waged against them in Afghanistan, Pakistan, and the Middle East. They have been attacked and repressed by numerous Muslim governments, as well as by Russia. But they continue to metastasize and to reappear in ever-new forms across large portions of Africa, the Middle East, and South and Central Asia. They are also seen as a threat in America and particularly in Europe where large Muslim immigrant minorities now live.

This brings up the quotation by Victor Hugo with which we began this book: "Invading armies can be resisted; invading ideas cannot be." It is not that Salafism will triumph in most Muslim countries, much less throughout the world. In the long run it may not succeed anywhere. But the idea of a holy war demanded by Allah is firmly implanted among active minorities. Treating it merely as some form of irrationality or as a pathological phenomenon that can be eradicated by brute force is to make the same mistake as all those who have sought through history to eliminate other powerful ideas by violent repression.

There are economic and sociopolitical reasons for Salafism's rise and persistence, but of equal or greater importance is the fact that behind it lies an idea about the proper role of Islam, of its place and destiny in the world, and who its real enemies are. No one better expressed this than Sayyid Qutb, who, a half century after his execution, continues to inspire millions, as does the almost equally influential Indian Pakistani cleric Abul A'la Mawdudi, who himself provided some of Qutb's ideas. To understand the sources of this ideology requires some knowledge of its historical background and the crucial texts that form its intellectual basis. Simplified and transmitted throughout the world, they will for a long time inspire more Salafists. As with Christian fundamentalism, at the heart of this many-headed movement is a system of thought that responds to real needs and hopes among its religious followers. In fact it is the decline and failure of secular and moderate reformism in so many Muslim societies that is behind this and will continue to be as long as there is no successful reform.

Christian and Muslim rejections of modernity, particularly their denial of the heart of Enlightenment liberalism, are strikingly similar in a number of areas, including the near paranoid sense by fundamentalists in both religions that they are surrounded by evil forces determined to exterminate their entire faith. Yet such comparison would certainly be anathema to both groups, who see each other as mortal enemies. They can never be allies because, for all the pretense that both have a common "Abrahamic" God and have incorporated some common elements of Judaism, they fervently disagree about which is the correct holy text, about the nature of Jesus Christ, and about who Muhammad really was. To Islamists (but many others too), Christianity was the religion of the European colonial exploiters and remains a part of the hateful West. Christianity and Islam are also bitter rivals in much of Africa, where extreme versions of both religions are gaining ground. Yet it is possible to see both as understandable, in some ways even legitimate, responses to the forces of modernization that appear to have disrupted, debilitated, and abandoned so many traditions and traditional understandings.

This is the basis of all anti-Enlightenment ideas, that modern liberalism has made the world a far worse place, corrupted and enfeebled. Therefore the original ideas behind it need to be refuted and replaced. The dream of a universal, peaceful, enlightened world promoted by the eighteenth-century Enlightenment philosophers remains a false dream, a dangerous mirage that must be destroyed. And the only way to obliterate it is by counterideas able to produce countervisions, including violent, extremist ones.

THE IMPORTANCE OF THE HUMANITIES

These considerations give rise to a conclusion, one that follows from everything presented in this book. Having discussed some of the most powerful and controversial ideas responsible for modern society, it seems clear that the humanities are absolutely essential to any system of higher education. Why? Because no program of learning that aims to engage and prepare students for the larger world, and for citizenship in that world, can do without the study, analysis, and critical evaluation of ideas—for all the many reasons that these chapters have endeavored to show. Such work is the stock and trade of the humanities and, to some degree, the social sciences. This means the fields of history, philosophy, literature, art, languages, classics—fields that teach skills related to the scrutiny of thought, how and where it originates, how it is expressed, how it should be assessed, and how it achieves influence. There is no substitute for these skills in comprehending the power of ideas. Nor do we see a surfeit of such skills among political leaders today and in recent years.

This leads to a second conclusion. One of the most important aspects of the humanities should be a focus on the history of ideas and the philosophical currents that inspire large social, economic, cultural, and political trends. Again, being able to critically read and understand foundational texts, to analyze belief systems, and to discover the complex arguments that have produced different movements, wars, institutions, national identities, and the like is required if we are to educate the young in ways most fitting to a new and challenging century. This is not simply because a well-educated person is a "better citizen" but because otherwise so much of what goes on in the world and around us remains obscure or confusing. Our world is ever more densely and immediately connected, especially through forms of communication. As it is, too much of what is important winds up being explained by superficial and simplistic generalization or by narrow, factional opinion.

We are not speaking here about the kinds of studies, influenced by postmodern thought, that have been widely practiced in humanities departments over the past several decades. That the dominance of such studies has been held responsible for a decline in this domain of teaching and learning is well-known. Our endeavor here is only partly related to this; we come neither to bury nor to rescue literary theory, cultural studies, and so forth. Our main objection to postmodern pedagogy and scholarship is their tendency to treat the Enlightenment, especially its love of reason, as a source of evils and to deny, therefore, the enormous positive powers it unleashed and the complex legacy these powers have had. Here is not the place to detail an argument that deserves full-scale historical analysis. Suffice it to say that our discussions in this book suggest it is no accident that an embrace of irrationalism put a number of brilliant canonical postmodern thinkers at the gates of the Counter-Enlightenment, most prominently Martin Heidegger, Carl Schmitt, Paul de Man, and Maurice Blanchot (Wolin 2004). All collaborated with fascism in their early years, though Blanchot, unlike the others, clearly changed his mind about fascism. (For a very good analysis about the relationship between postmodernism, irrationalism, and the Enlightenment, see Baker and Reill 2001.)

What we want to highlight is the need for study that will help better elucidate the realities of human experience in modern society. Critical reading and discussion of texts that have been immeasurably important in the creation of the modern world ought to be an essential part of higher education. The kind of approach to the humanities we think is essential—and which we have pursued, at an introductory level, in these pages—is not original, as many would agree, because part of what we propose was once taken as a given in major colleges and universities throughout the Western world. What we mean, however, would not be limited to a focus on the Enlightenment alone, far from it. Reading the ideas that have been opposed to the Enlightenment is as important as understanding those that have stemmed from it; they, too, must be understood and critiqued in a knowledgeable way. Thinkers of formidable influence over the past three centuries include many we have mentioned only briefly or not at all in this book. Some, far more than we have been able to treat, have not been Europeans or Americans though typically those from other regions have had to react, either favorably or against, Western ideas.

The humanities, we believe, should expand their subject matter to include major thinkers in all fields. This means analyzing the philosophical, political, and social ideas of economists, scientists, even mathematicians, not just of philosophers, authors, artists, and social theorists. Needless to say, this would include thinkers from all parts of the world, not only Europe and the United States. Nor would it be restricted to the eighteenth and nineteenth centuries.

The power intellectuals of many kinds have wielded in modern history is enormous and multifaceted. Their ideas lie at the heart of ideals, policies, and actions of those who have possessed political power. Their influence, not just on politics but also on the arts, on science, and on all our institutions, has been enormous. Without knowing what they hoped to achieve, what new sets of ideas they originated, and why they have been so influential as well as controversial, we have little chance to comprehend the world we have made and now live in. This may be only part of what the humanities can and should be about, but it gives back to that field significance and an argument for appreciation that have been in recent decline.

Ultimately we are left with the question of whether the liberal side of the Enlightenment will prove as resilient in the decades ahead as it has until now, even if the world will no longer be dominated by a few Western powers. Another way of posing the problem, as Lord Acton might have done, is to ask to what degree will intellectuals, leaders, and the general public today become the guardians, even the instruments, of ideas they refuse to examine deeply and to amend wisely. Would we all not be better served if they did? It is the work of a committed, engaged, and global intellectual history to deeply inform this issue, to take hold of the realities involved and reveal what they have to tell us about the world we have made.

BIBLIOGRAPHY

Abrahamian, E. 1993. *Khomeinism: Essays on the Islamic Republic*. Berkeley: University of California Press.

Adams, H. 1918. *The Education of Henry Adams*. New York: Houghton Mifflin.

Adanır, F. 2001. "Kemalist Authoritarianism and Fascist Trends in Turkey during the Interwar Period." In S. U. Larsen, ed., *Fascism outside Europe: The European Impulse against Domestic Conditions in the Diffusion of Global Fascism*. Boulder, CO: Social Science Monographs.

Agulhon, M. 1990. *La République*. Paris: Hachette.

———. 1995. *The French Republic, 1879–1992*. Oxford: Blackwell.

Ahamed, L. 2009. *Lords of Finance: The Bankers Who Broke the World*. New York: Penguin.

Ahmida, A. A. 2005. *Forgotten Voices: Power and Agency in Colonial and Postcolonial Libya*. New York: Routledge.

Ajami, F. 1981. *The Arab Predicament: Arab Political Thought and Practice since 1967*. Cambridge: Cambridge University Press.

———. 1986. *The Vanished Imam: Musa al Sadr and the Shia of Lebanon*. Ithaca: Cornell University Press.

———. 1998. *The Dream Palace of the Arabs: A Generation's Odyssey*. New York: Pantheon Books.

Akerlof, G. A., and R. J. Shiller. 2009. *Animal Spirits: How Human Psychology Drives the Economy, and Why It Matters for Global Capitalism*. Princeton: Princeton University Press.

Alexander, D., and R. L. Numbers, eds. 2010. *Biology and Ideology from Descartes to Dawkins*. Chicago: University of Chicago Press.

Allan, D. 1993. *Virtue, Learning, and the Scottish Enlightenment: Ideas of Scholarship in Early Modern History*. Edinburgh: Edinburgh University Press.

Amsden, A. H. 1989. *Asia's Next Giant: South Korea and Late Industrialization*. New York: Oxford University Press.

Anderson, B. R. 1983. *Imagined Communities: Reflections on the Origin and Spread of Nationalism*. London: Verso.

Applebaum, A. 2013. *Iron Curtain: The Crushing of Eastern Europe, 1944–1956*. New York: Doubleday.

Aristotle. 350 B.C.E. *Politics*. Vol. 4. Trans. B. Jowett. http://classics.mit.edu /Aristotle/politics.6.six.html.

Armitage, D. 2000. *The Ideological Origins of the British Empire*. Cambridge: Cambridge University Press.

———. 2007. *The Declaration of Independence: A Global History*. Cambridge, MA: Harvard University Press.

Armstrong, K. 2000. *The Battle for God*. New York: Knopf.

Aron, R. 1962. *The Opium of the Intellectuals*. New York: Norton.

———. 2002. *Le marxisme de Marx*. Paris: Librairie générale française.

Auerbach, J. A. 1999. *The Great Exhibition of 1851: A Nation on Display*. New Haven: Yale University Press.

Avrich, P. 1970. *Kronstadt, 1921*. Princeton: Princeton University Press.

———. 1972. *Russian Rebels, 1600–1800*. New York: Schocken Books.

Ayalon, D., and M. Sharon, eds. 1986. *Studies in Islamic History and Civilization: In Honour of Professor David Ayalon*. Jerusalem: Cana.

Bailyn, B. 1967/1992. *The Ideological Origins of the American Revolution*. Cambridge, MA: Belknap Press of Harvard University Press.

———. 2003. *To Begin the World Anew: The Genius and Ambiguities of the American Founders*. New York: Knopf.

———. 2013. *The Barbarous Years: The Peopling of British North America, Conflict of Civilizations, 1600–1675*. New York: Knopf.

Baker, K. M. 1975. *Condorcet: From Natural Philosophy to Social Mathematics*. Chicago: University of Chicago Press.

Baker, K. M., and P. H. Reill, eds. 2001. *What's Left of Enlightenment? A Postmodern Question*. Stanford: Stanford University Press.

Balmer, R. H. 2007. *Thy Kingdom Come: How the Religious Right Distorts the Faith and Threatens America, an Evangelical's Lament*. New York: Basic Books.

Barber, J., and M. Harrison. 2006. "Patriotic War, 1941 to 1945." In M. Perrie, D. C. Lieven, and R. G. Suny, eds., *The Cambridge History of Russia*. Cambridge: Cambridge University Press.

Bartholomew, J. R. 1989. *The Formation of Science in Japan: Building a Research Tradition*. New Haven: Yale University Press.

Baum, R. 1994. *Burying Mao*. Princeton: Princeton University Press.

Bayly, C. A. 2003. *The Birth of the Modern World, 1780–1914: Global Connections and Comparisons*. Malden, MA: Blackwell.

Becker, C. L. 1922. *The Declaration of Independence: A Study in the History of Political Ideas*. New York: Knopf.

Becker, G. S. 1992. *The Economic Approach to Human Behavior*. Chicago: University of Chicago Press.

Beecher, H. W. 1871. *The Life of Jesus, the Christ*. New York: J. B. Ford.

Beer, G. 2000. *Darwin's Plots: Evolutionary Narrative in Darwin, George Eliot, and Nineteenth-Century Fiction*. 2nd ed. Cambridge: Cambridge University Press.

Begley, L. 2009. *Why the Dreyfus Affair Matters*. New Haven: Yale University Press.

Bell, D. 1960. *The End of Ideology; on the Exhaustion of Political Ideas in the Fifties*. Glencoe, IL: Free Press.

———. 2001. *The Radical Right*. 3rd ed. New Brunswick, NJ: Transaction.

Beller, S. 1989. *Vienna and the Jews: 1867–1938: A Cultural History*. Cambridge: Cambridge University Press.

Benario, H. W. 1976. "Gordon's Tacitus." *Classical Journal* 72(2): 107–21.

Berend, T. I. 1998. *Decades of Crisis: Central and Eastern Europe before World War II*. Berkeley: University of California Press.

———. 2013. *An Economic History of Nineteenth-Century Europe: Diversity and Industrialization*. Cambridge: Cambridge University Press.

Bergère, M. 2000. *Sun Yat-sen*. Trans. J. Lloyd. Stanford: Stanford University Press.

Berlin, I. 1963. *Karl Marx: His Life and Environment*. London: Oxford University Press.

———. 2002. *Liberty: Incorporating Four Essays on Liberty*. Ed. H. Hardy, with an added essay by I. Harris. Oxford: Oxford University Press.

———. 2013. *The Power of Ideas*. Ed. H. Hardy. Princeton: Princeton University Press.

Berman, P. 2004. *Terror and Liberalism*. New York: Norton.

Bernasconi, R., and T. L. Lott. 2000. *The Idea of Race*. Indianapolis: Hackett.

Bernstein, E. 1993. *The Preconditions of Socialism*. Ed. and trans. H. Tudor. Cambridge: Cambridge University Press.

Berry, C. J. 1997. *Social Theory of the Scottish Enlightenment*. Edinburgh: Edinburgh University Press.

Bezirgan N. A. 1988. "The Islamic World." In T. F. Glick, ed., *The Comparative Reception of Darwinism*, 375–87. Chicago: University of Chicago Press.

Bessel, R. 2009. "The First World War as Totality." In R. J. Bosworth, ed., *The Oxford Handbook of Fascism*, 52–69. Oxford: Oxford University Press.

Bix, H. P. 2000. *Hirohito and the Making of Modern Japan*. New York: HarperCollins.

Black, E. 2008. *War against the Weak: Eugenics and America's Campaign to Create a Master Race*. New York: Dialog Press.

Blackstone, W. E. 1878. *Jesus Is Coming*. New York: Fleming H. Revell.

Blaug, M. 1986. *Great Economists before Keynes: An Introduction to the Lives & Works of 100 Great Economists of the Past*. Brighton, Sussex: Wheatsheaf Books.

Blouet, B. W. 1987. *Halford Mackinder: A Biography*. College Station: Texas A&M University Press.

Bob Jones Univ. v. Simon, 416 U.S. 725 (1974).

Bonnell, V. E. 1986. *The Russian Worker: Life and Labor under the Tsarist Regime*. Berkeley: University of California Press.

Boothroyd, P., and P. X. Pham. 2000. *Socioeconomic Renovation in Viet Nam: The Origin, Evolution, and Impact of Doi Moi*. Singapore: Institute of Southeast Asian Studies.

Boswell, J. 1769. *An Account of Corsica: The Journal of a Tour to That Island and Memoirs of Pascal Paoli*. 3rd ed. London: Edward and Charles Dilly.

Bosworth, R. J., ed. 2009. *The Oxford Handbook of Fascism*. Oxford: Oxford University Press.

Bottomore, T. B. 2002. *The Frankfurt School and Its Critics*. London: Routledge.

Bowler, P. J. 2009. *Evolution: The History of an Idea*. 3rd ed. Berkeley: University of California Press.

Bracher, K. D. 1995. *Turning Points in Modern Times: Essays on German and European History*. Cambridge, MA: Harvard University Press.

British Petroleum. 2014. "Energy Outlook." http://www.bp.com/en/global/corporate/about-bp/energy-economics/energy-outlook.html.

Broadie, A. 2001. *The Scottish Enlightenment: The Historical Age of the Historical Nation*. Edinburgh: Birlinn.

——, ed. 2003. *The Cambridge Companion to the Scottish Enlightenment*. Cambridge: Cambridge University Press.

Browne, J. 1996. *Charles Darwin: A Biography*. Vol. 1, *Voyaging*. Princeton: Princeton University Press.

——. 2002. *Charles Darwin: A Biography*. Vol. 2, *The Power of Place*. Princeton: Princeton University Press.

——. 2006. *Darwin's Origin of Species: A Biography*. London: Atlantic Books.

Buchan, J. 2006. *The Authentic Adam Smith: His Life and Ideas*. New York: Norton.

Bulhof, Ilse N. 1988. "The Netherlands." In Thomas F. Glick, ed., *The Comparative Reception of Darwinism*, 269–306. Chicago: University of Chicago Press.

Bulmer, Michael. 2003. *Francis Galton: Pioneer of Heredity and Biometry*. Baltimore: Johns Hopkins University Press.

Burbank, J., and F. Cooper. 2010. *Empires in World History: Power and the Politics of Difference*. Princeton: Princeton University Press.

Burke, E. 1997. "Reflections on the Revolution in France." In J. Z. Muller, ed., *Conservatism: An Anthology of Social and Political Thought from David Hume to the Present*, 83–122. Princeton: Princeton University Press.

Butler, D., and G. Butler. 2000. *Twentieth-Century British Political Facts*. New York: St. Martin's Press.

Caldwell, B. J., C. Menger, and M. Barnett. 1990. *Carl Menger and His Legacy in Economics*. Durham: Duke University Press.

Callahan, W. A. 2013. *China Dreams: 20 Visions of the Future*. New York: Oxford University Press.

Calvert, J. 2010. *Sayyid Qutb and the Origins of Radical Islamism*. New York: Columbia University Press.

Carlyle, A. 1860. *The Autobiography of the Rev. Dr. Alexander Carlyle*. 2nd ed. London: William Blackwood and Sons.

Carnegie, A. 1889. "Wealth." *North American Review* 148(391): 653–57.

Caron, F. 1985. *La France des patriotes de 1851 à 1918*. Paris: Fayard.

Carsten, F. L. 1967. *The Rise of Fascism*. Berkeley: University of California Press.

Chan, A. L. 2001. *Mao's Crusade: Politics and Policy Implementation in China's Great Leap Forward*. Oxford: Oxford University Press.

Cheng, N. 1987. *Life and Death in Shanghai*. New York: Grove Press.

Chernow, R. 2005. *Alexander Hamilton*. New York: Penguin.

Cherry, C., ed. 1998. *The New Israel: Religious Interpretations of American Destiny*. Chapel Hill: University of North Carolina Press.

Chirot, D. 1980. "The Corporatist Model and Socialism." *Theory and Society* 9(2): 363–81.

———. 1985. "The Rise of the West." *American Sociological Review* 50(2): 181–95.

———. 1986. *Social Change in the Modern Era*. San Diego: Harcourt Brace Jovanovich.

———. 1995. "Modernism without Liberalism: The Ideological Roots of Modern Tyranny." *Contention* 5(1): 141–66.

———. 1996. *Modern Tyrants: The Power and Prevalence of Evil in Our Age*. Princeton: Princeton University Press.

Chirot, D., and A. Reid, eds. 1997. *Essential Outsiders: Chinese and Jews in the Modern Transformation of Southeast Asia and Central Europe*. Seattle: University of Washington Press.

Clarke, P. F. 2009. *Keynes: The Rise, Fall, and Return of the 20th Century's Most Influential Economist*. New York: Bloomsbury Press.

Cobb, M. 2006. "Heredity before Genetics: A History." *Nature Reviews Genetics* 7(12): 953–58.

Cohen, M. R. 1994. *Under Crescent and Cross: The Jews in the Middle Ages*. Princeton: Princeton University Press.

Cohen, M., and N. Fermon, eds. 1996. *Princeton Readings in Political Thought: Essential Texts since Plato*. Princeton: Princeton University Press.

Cohen, S. F. 1973. *Bukharin and the Bolshevik Revolution: A Political Biography, 1888–1938*. New York: Knopf.

Colp, R. 1974. "The Contacts between Karl Marx and Charles Darwin." *Journal of the History of Ideas* 35(2): 329–38.

Cook, M. 2000. *The Koran: A Very Short Introduction*. Oxford: Oxford University Press.

Cosmides, L., and J. Tooby. 1997. "Evolutionary Psychology: A Primer." http://www.psych.ucsb.edu/research/cep/primer.html.

Courtois, S., and M. Kramer. 1999. *The Black Book of Communism: Crimes, Terror, Repression*. Cambridge, MA: Harvard University Press.

Crackel, T. J. 1989. *Mr. Jefferson's Army: Political and Social Reform of the Military Establishment, 1801–1809*. New York: New York University Press.

Cumings, B. 1982. "Corporatism in North Korea." *Journal of Korean Studies* 4(1): 269–94.

———. 2010. *The Korean War: A History*. New York: Modern Library.

Cunningham, N. E. 2000. *Jefferson vs. Hamilton: Confrontations That Shaped a Nation*. Boston: Bedford/St. Martin's.

Cuvier, G. 1998. *Georges Cuvier, Fossil Bones, and Geological Catastrophes: New Translations and Interpretations of the Primary Texts*. Ed. M. J. Rudwick. Chicago: University of Chicago Press.

Dahl, R. A. 2000. *On Democracy*. New Haven: Yale University Press.

Darwin, C. 1846. *Geological Observations on South America*. London: Smith, Elder, & Co.

———. 1859. *On the Origin of Species by Means of Natural Selection, or the Preservation of Favoured Races in the Struggle for Life*. London: John Murray.

———. 1871. *The Descent of Man*. Vols. 1–2. London: John Murray.

———. 1872. *The Expression of Emotions in Man and Animals*. London: John Murray.

———. 1887. *The Life and Letters of Charles Darwin, Including an Autobiographical Chapter: In Three Volumes*. Vols. 1–3. Ed. F. Darwin. London: John Murray.

———. 2002. *The Complete Work of Charles Darwin Online*. Ed. J. Van Wyhe. http://darwin-online.org.uk/EditorialIntroductions/vanWyhe_notebooks.html.

Darwin, C. 1845. *Journal of Researches into the Natural History and Geology of the Countries Visited during the Voyage of H.M.S. Beagle*. 2nd ed. London: John Murray.

Darwin, C., and N. Barlow. 1958. *Autobiography: With Original Omissions Restored*. London: Collins.

Davenport, C. B. 1911. *Heredity in Relation to Eugenics*. New York: Henry Holt.

Davies, S., and J. R. Harris. 2005. *Stalin: A New History*. Cambridge: Cambridge University Press.

Davis, D. B. 1975. *The Problem of Slavery in the Age of Revolution, 1770–1823*. Ithaca: Cornell University Press.

Dawisha, A. I. 2003. *Arab Nationalism in the Twentieth Century: From Triumph to Despair*. Princeton: Princeton University Press.

———. 2009. *Iraq: A Political History from Independence to Occupation*. Princeton: Princeton University Press.

Dawkins, R. 1976. *The Selfish Gene*. Oxford: Oxford University Press.

———. 2006. *The God Delusion*. Boston: Houghton Mifflin.

Dawood, N. J. 1967. Introduction to I. Khaldūn and F. Rosenthal, ed., *The Muqaddimah: An Introduction to History*. New York: Pantheon Books.

Dawson, G. 2010. *Darwin, Literature and Victorian Respectability*. Cambridge: Cambridge University Press.

de Maistre, J. 1814. "Essay on the Generative Principle of Political Constitution and of Other Human Institutions." In J. Z. Muller, *Conservatism: An Anthology of Social and Political Thought from David Hume to the Present*, 136–45. Princeton: Princeton University Press.

De Wever, B. 2009. "Belgium." In R. J. Bosworth, ed., *The Oxford Handbook of Fascism*, 470–88. Oxford: Oxford University Press.

DeLong-Bas, N. J. 2004. *Wahhabi Islam: From Revival and Reform to Global Jihad*. Oxford: Oxford University Press.

Dennett, D. C. 1995. *Darwin's Dangerous Idea: Evolution and the Meaning of Life*. New York: Simon and Schuster.

Destutt de Tracy, A. 1817. *A Treatise on Political Economy; to which is prefixed a supplement to a preceding work on the understanding, or Elements of Ideology; with an analytical table, and an introduction on the faculty of the will . . . Translated from the unpublished French original.* Trans. T. Jefferson. Georgetown, DC: Joseph Milligan.

Deutscher, I. 1963. *The Prophet Outcast: Trotsky.* Vols. 1–3. London: Verso.

Dewey, J. 1910. *The Influence of Darwin on Philosophy, and Other Essays in Contemporary Thought.* New York: Henry Holt.

Dikötter, F. 2010. *Mao's Great Famine: The History of China's Most Devastating Catastrophe, 1958–62.* London: Bloomsbury.

Dittmer, L. 1974. *Liu Shao-ch'i and the Chinese Cultural Revolution: The Politics of Mass Criticism.* Berkeley: University of California Press.

Dixon, A. C., ed. 1910. *The Fundamentals: A Testimony to the Truth.* 12 vols. Chicago: Testimony Publishing Company.

Dobzhansky, T. 1937. *Genetics and the Origins of Species.* New York: Columbia University Press.

Domke, D. and S. Coe. 2010. *The God Strategy: How Religion Became a Political Weapon in America.* New York: Oxford University Press.

Dreisbach, D. L. 1997. " 'Sowing Useful Truths and Principles': The Danbury Baptists, Thomas Jefferson, and the 'Wall of Separation.' " *Journal of Church and State* 39(3): 455–501.

Drumont, É. 1886. *La France juive: Essai d'histoire contemporaine.* Paris: C. Marpon and E. Flammarion.

Duke, B. 2013. "Remembering Forty Years of Abortion." Ethics and Religious Liberty Commission of the Southern Baptist Convention. http://erlc.com/article/remembering-forty-years-of-abortion.

Dwyer, J. A. 1998. *The Age of the Passions: An Interpretation of Adam Smith and Scottish Enlightenment Culture.* East Linton: Tuckwell Press.

Eckes, A. E. 1995. *Opening America's Market: U.S. Foreign Trade Policy since 1776.* Chapel Hill: University of North Carolina Press.

Edwards, J. 1737. *A Faithful Narrative of the Surprising Work of God in the Conversion of Many Hundred Souls in Northhampton.* Christian Classics Ethereal Library.

Edwards, J. 1839. *The Works of Jonathan Edwards, A.M.* Ed. E. Hickman. Vols. 1–2. London: William Ball.

Eisenhower Presidential Library and Museum. N.d. "Civil Rights: The Little Rock School Integration Crisis." http://eisenhower.archives.gov/research/online_documents/civil_rights_little_rock.html.

Ellis, J. J. 1998. *American Sphinx: The Character of Thomas Jefferson*. New York: Knopf.

———. 2002. *Founding Brothers: The Revolutionary Generation*. New York: Knopf.

Elshakry, M. 2009. "Global Darwin: Eastern Enchantment." *Nature* 461(29): 1200–1201.

———. 2013. *Reading Darwin in Arabic*. Chicago: University of Chicago Press.

Emden, C. J. 2008. "Carl Schmitt, Hannah Arendt, and the Limits of Liberalism." *Telos* 142:110–34.

———. 2010. *Friedrich Nietzsche and the Politics of History*. Cambridge: Cambridge University Press.

Engel v. Vitale, 370 U.S. 421 (1962).

Euben, R. L., and M. Q. Zaman, eds. 2009. *Princeton Readings in Islamist Thought: Texts and Contexts from al-Banna to Bin Laden*. Princeton: Princeton University Press.

Faroqhi, S., D. Quataert, B. McGowan, and S. Pamuk. 1994. *An Economic and Social History of the Ottoman Empire*. Cambridge: Cambridge University Press.

Faye, E. 2009. *Heidegger: The Introduction of Nazism into Philosophy in Light of the Unpublished Seminars of 1933–1935*. New Haven: Yale University Press.

Ferling, J. E. 2013. *Jefferson and Hamilton: The Rivalry That Forged a Nation*. New York: Bloomsbury Press.

Ferro, M. 1993. *Nicholas II: Last of the Tsars*. New York: Oxford University Press.

Feser, E., ed. 2006. *The Cambridge Companion to Hayek*. Cambridge: Cambridge University Press.

Fieldhouse, D. K. 1972. "Imperialism: An Historiographic Revision." In K. E. Boulding and T. Mukerjee, *Economic Imperialism: A Book of Readings*. Ann Arbor: University of Michigan Press.

Filiu, J. 2011. *Apocalypse in Islam*. Trans. M. B. DeBevoise. Berkeley: University of California Press.

Fink, C., P. Gassert, and D. Junker. 1998. *1968: The World Transformed*. Cambridge: Cambridge University Press.

Fitzhugh, G. 1857/1960. *Cannibals All! or, Slaves without Masters*. Cambridge, MA: Belknap Press of Harvard University Press.

Fitzpatrick, S. 2008. *The Russian Revolution*. Oxford: Oxford University Press.

Foster, S. 2014. *British North America in the Seventeenth and Eighteenth Centuries*. Oxford: Oxford University Press.

Freedom House. 2014. "Freedom in the World 2014." http://www.freedomhouse
    .org/report/freedom-world/freedom-world-2014#.UxzP_lxLr1o.

Freud, S. 1952. *An Autobiographical Study*. Ed. J. Strachey. New York: Norton.

Friedman, M. 1962/2002. *Capitalism and Freedom*. Chicago: University of Chicago Press.

Friedman, M., and A. J. Schwartz. 1963. *A Monetary History of the United States, 1867–1960*. Princeton: Princeton University Press.

Fukuyama, F. 1992. *The End of History and the Last Man*. New York: Free Press.

Galbraith, J. K. 1955/1980. *Economics and the Art of Controversy*. New Brunswick, NJ: Rutgers University Press.

Galton, F. 1869. *Hereditary Genius: An Inquiry into Its Laws and Consequences*. London: Macmillan.

"A Game of Catch-up." 2011. *The Economist*. September 24. http://www
    .economist.com/node/21528979.

Gellner, E. 1981. *Muslim Society*. Cambridge: Cambridge University Press.

———. 1983. *Nations and Nationalism*. Ithaca: Cornell University Press.

———. 1992. *Postmodernism, Reason and Religion*. London: Routledge.

Gibbard, A. 1992. *Wise Choices, Apt Feelings: A Theory of Normative Judgment*. Cambridge, MA: Harvard University Press.

Glenny, M. 1996. *The Fall of Yugoslavia: The Third Balkan War*. 3rd rev. ed. New York: Penguin.

———. 2000. *The Balkans: Nationalism, War, and the Great Powers, 1804–1999*. New York: Viking.

Gliboff, S. 2008. *H. G. Bronn, Ernst Haeckel, and the Origins of German Darwinism: A Study in Translation and Transformation*. Cambridge, MA: MIT Press.

Glick, T. F., ed. 1988. *The Comparative Reception of Darwinism: With a New Preface*. Chicago: University of Chicago Press.

Glick, T. F., M. Puig-Samper, and R. Ruiz. 2001. *The Reception of Darwinism in the Iberian World: Spain, Spanish America, and Brazil*. New York: Spring.

Gobineau, J. 1853–55. "Essai sur l'inégalité des races humaines." http://classiques
    .uqac.ca/classiques/gobineau/essai_inegalite_races/essai_inegalite_races
    .html.

Goldfield, D. R. 2012. *America Aflame: How the Civil War Created a Nation*. New York: Bloomsbury Press.

Gordon, L. P. 1976. *Woman's Body, Woman's Right: Birth Control in America*. New York: Viking.

Gossett, T. F. 1997. *Race: The History of an Idea in America*. New York: Oxford University Press.

Gottschall, J., and D. S. Wilson. 2005. *The Literary Animal: Evolution and the Nature of Narrative*. Evanston, IL: Northwestern University Press.

Gould, S. J. 1981. *The Mismeasure of Man*. New York: Norton.

———. 1997. "Darwinian Fundamentalism." *New York Review of Books* 44:34–37.

Gray, J. 1996. *Isaiah Berlin*. Princeton: Princeton University Press.

Grant, M. 1916. *The Passing of the Great Race*. New York: Scribner's.

Greenfeld, L. 1993. *Nationalism: Five Roads to Modernity*. Cambridge, MA: Harvard University Press.

Gregor, A. J. 1969. *The Ideology of Fascism: The Rationale of Totalitarianism*. New York: Free Press.

Griswold, C. L., Jr. 1999. *Adam Smith and the Virtues of Enlightenment*. Cambridge: Cambridge University Press.

Haakonssen, K. 1996. *Natural Law and Moral Philosophy: From Grotius to the Scottish Enlightenment*. Cambridge: Cambridge University Press.

Hacker, J. D. 2011. "A Census-Based Count of the Civil War Dead." *Civil War History* 57(4): 307–48.

Hadley, J. 1996. *Abortion: Between Freedom and Necessity*. Philadelphia: Temple University Press.

Hall, D. D. 1990. *Worlds of Wonder, Days of Judgment: Popular Religious Belief in Early New England*. Cambridge, MA: Harvard University Press.

Halsall, P. 1997. "Modern History Sourcebook: Vietnamese Declaration of Independence, 1945." http://www.fordham.edu/halsall/mod/1945vietnam.html.

———.1998. "Modern History Sourcebook—Karl Pearson: National Life from the Standpoint of Science, 1900." http://www.fordham.edu/halsall/mod/1900pearsonl.asp.

Hamilton, A. 1791. "Report on Manufactures." www.constitution.org/ah/rpt_manufactures.pdf.

———. 2001. *Writings*. Ed. J. B. Freeman. New York: Literary Classics of the United States.

Hamilton, A., J. Jay, and J. Madison. 2001. *The Federalist: A Collection*. Ed. G. W. Carey. Indianapolis: Liberty Fund.

Hanafi, H. 2002. "Alternative Conceptions of Civil Society: A Reflective Islamic Approach." In H. S. Hasmi, ed., *Islamic Political Ethics: Civil Society, Pluralism, and Conflict*, 56–75. Princeton: Princeton University Press.

Hannaford, I. 1996. *Race: The History of an Idea in the West*. Washington, DC: Woodrow Wilson Center Press.

Hartz, L. 1955. *The Liberal Tradition in America: An Interpretation of American Political Thought since the Revolution*. New York: Harcourt, Brace.

Harvey, D. 1990. *The Condition of Postmodernity: An Enquiry into the Origins of Cultural Change*. Oxford: Blackwell.

Hashmi, S. H. 2012. *Just Wars, Holy Wars, and Jihads: Christian, Jewish, and Muslim Encounters and Exchanges*. New York: Oxford University Press.

Hatch, N. O. 1991. *The Democratization of American Christianity*. New Haven: Yale University Press.

Hawkins, M. 1997. *Social Darwinism in European and American Thought, 1860–1945: Nature as Model and Nature as Threat*. Cambridge: Cambridge University Press.

Hayek, F. A. 1944/2007. *The Road to Serfdom: Text and Documents: The Definitive Edition*. Ed. B. Caldwell. Chicago: University of Chicago Press.

———. 1960/2011. *The Constitution of Liberty: The Definitive Edition*. Chicago: University of Chicago Press.

Heckscher, E. F. 1934. *Mercantilism*. London: Allen and Unwin.

Hefner, R. W. 2000. *Civil Islam: Muslims and Democratization in Indonesia*. Princeton: Princeton University Press.

———. 2005. *Remaking Muslim Politics: Pluralism, Contestation, Democratization*. Princeton: Princeton University Press.

Heller, A. C. 2009. *Ayn Rand and the World She Made*. New York: Nan A. Talese/Doubleday.

Heng, L., and J. Shapiro. 1984. *Son of the Revolution*. New York: Vintage.

Henretta, J. A. 1996. *The Origins of American Capitalism: Collected Essays*. Lebanon, NH: Northeastern University Press.

Herschel, J. F. 1987. *A Preliminary Discourse on the Study of Natural Philosophy: A Facsimile of the 1830 Edition*. Chicago: Chicago University Press.

Himmelfarb, G. 1959. *Darwin and the Darwinian Revolution*. Garden City, NY: Doubleday.

Hirschman, A. O. 1977. *The Passions and the Interests: Political Arguments for Capitalism before Its Triumph*. New Haven: Yale University Press.

———. 1991. *The Rhetoric of Reaction: Perversity, Futility, Jeopardy*. Cambridge, MA: Belknap Press of Harvard University Press.

Hitler, A. 2003. *Hitler's Second Book*. Ed. G. L. Weinberg. Trans. K. Smith. New York: Enigma Books.

Hobsbawm, E. J. 1962. *The Age of Revolution: Europe, 1789–1848*. London: Weidenfeld and Nicolson.

———. 1987. *The Age of Empire, 1875–1914*. New York: Pantheon Books.

———. 1996. *The Age of Capital: 1848–1875*. London: Weidenfeld and Nicolson.

———. 2002. *Age of Extremes: The Short Twentieth Century, 1914–1991*. London: Michael Joseph.

Hobson, J. A. 1902. *Imperialism: A Study*. London: G. Allen and Unwin.

Hodge, C. 2005. *Systematic Theology*. Vol. 1. http://www.ccel.org/ccel/hodge /theology1.html.

Hodge, M.J.S. 2008. *Before and After Darwin*. Farnham: Ashgate.

Hodgson, M. G. 1974. *The Venture of Islam: Conscience and History in a World Civilization*. Vols. 1–3. Chicago: University of Chicago Press.

Hofstadter, R. 1955. *Social Darwinism in American Thought*. New York: Knopf.

Holborn, M. 1981. *Sociology: Themes and Perspectives*. London: Collins.

Holmes, S. 1993. *The Anatomy of Antiliberalism*. Cambridge, MA: Harvard University Press.

Hont, I., and M. Ignatieff, eds. 1985. *Wealth and Virtue: The Shaping of Political Economy in the Scottish Enlightenment*. Cambridge: Cambridge University Press.

Hoppen, K. T. 1998. *The Mid-Victorian Generation, 1946–1886*. Oxford: Oxford University Press.

Horn, P. L. 1989. *Marquis de Lafayette*. New York: Chelsea House.

Hosking, G. A. 1997. *Russia: People and Empire, 1552–1917*. Cambridge, MA: Harvard University Press.

Hourani, A. 1983. *Arabic Thought in the Liberal Age, 1789–1939*. Cambridge: Cambridge University Press.

———. 2002. *A History of the Arab Peoples*. Cambridge, MA: Belknap Press of Harvard University Press.

Howe, D. W. 1991. "The Evangelical Movement and Political Culture in the North During the Second Party System." *Journal of American History* 77(4): 1216–39.

———. 2007. *What Hath God Wrought: The Transformation of America, 1815–1848*. New York: Oxford University Press.

Howland, D. 2000. "Society Reified: Herbert Spencer and Political Theory in Early Meiji Japan." *Comparative Study of Society and History* 42:67–83.

Huang, K. 2008. *The Meaning of Freedom: Yan Fu and the Origins of Chinese Liberalism*. Hong Kong: Chinese University Press.

Huff, T. E. 1993. *The Rise of Early Modern Science: Islam, China, and the West.* Cambridge: Cambridge University Press.

Hughes, H. S. 1961. *Consciousness and Society: The Reorientation of European Social Thought, 1890–1930.* New York: Vintage Books.

Hume, D. 1739. *A Treatise of Human Nature.* Vol. 1. London: John Noon.

———. 1826. *The Philosophical Works of David Hume.* Vols. 1–4. Online Library of Liberty. Edinburgh: Adam Black and William Tait.

Hunt, T. 2009. *Marx's General: The Revolutionary Life of Friedrich Engels.* New York: Metropolitan Books.

Hutcheson, F. 1726. *An Inquiry into the Original of Our Ideas of Beauty and Virtue.* London: J. Darby.

———. 1755/1968. *A System of Moral Philosophy.* New York: A. M. Kelley.

Ibn Khaldūn. 1967. *The Muqaddimah: An Introduction to History.* Ed. F. Rosenthal. New York: Pantheon Books.

Institute for the Study of American Evangelicals. 2012. "How Many Evangelicals Are There?" http://isae.wheaton.edu/defining-evangelicalism/how-many -evangelicals-are-there/.

Ioanid, R. 2000. *The Holocaust in Romania: The Destruction of Jews and Gypsies under the Antonescu Regime, 1940–1944.* Chicago: Ivan R. Dee.

Irwin, D. A. 1996. *Against the Tide: An Intellectual History of Free Trade.* Princeton: Princeton University Press.

Israel, J. 2001. *Radical Enlightenment: Philosophy and the Making of Modernity, 1650–1750.* Oxford: Oxford University Press.

———. 2006. *Enlightenment Contested: Philosophy, Modernity, and the Emancipation of Man, 1670–1752.* Oxford: Oxford University Press.

———. 2011. *A Revolution of the Mind: Radical Enlightenment and the Intellectual Origins of Modern Democracy.* Princeton: Princeton University Press.

Jacob, F. 1993. *The Logic of Life: A History of Heredity.* Trans. B. E. Spillmann. Princeton: Princeton University Press.

Jacobson, D. L. 1965. *The English Libertarian Heritage.* Indianapolis: Bobbs-Merrill.

Jacques, M. 2009. *When China Rules the World: The End of the Western World and the Birth of a New Global Order.* New York: Penguin.

Jalal, A. 2008. *Partisans of Allah: Jihad in South Asia.* Cambridge, MA: Harvard University Press.

James, W. 1880. "Great Men and Their Environment." *Atlantic Monthly* (October): 441–59.

Janos, A. C. 2000. *East Central Europe in the Modern World: The Politics of the Borderlands from Pre- to Postcommunism*. Stanford: Stanford University Press.

Jay, M. 1986. *Marxism and Totality: The Adventures of a Concept from Lukács to Habermas*. Berkeley: University of California Press.

Jefferson, T. 1904. *The Works of Thomas Jefferson*. Vols. 1–12. Ed. P. L. Ford. New York: G. P. Putnam's Sons.

——. 1984. *Writings*. Ed. M. D. Peterson. New York: Literary Classics of the U.S.

——. 2013. *The Best of the Online Library of Liberty No. 40: Thomas Jefferson, "The Declaration of Independence" (1776)*. Indianapolis: Liberty Fund.

Jefferson, T., and T. J. Randolph. 1829. *Memoirs, Correspondence, and Private Papers of Thomas Jefferson: Late President of the United States*. Vols. 1–4. London: H. Colburn and R. Bentley.

Jenkins, P. 2002. *The Next Christendom: The Coming of Global Christianity*. New York: Oxford University Press.

Johnson, C. 1962. *Peasant Nationalism and Communist Power: The Emergence of Revolutionary China*. Stanford: Stanford University Press.

——. 1982. *MITI and the Japanese Miracle: The Growth of Industrial Policy, 1925–1975*. Stanford: Stanford University Press.

Johnson, S. 1913. *The Works of Samuel Johnson*. Vols. 1–16. Troy, NY: Pafraets Book.

Jones, A. H. 1980. *Wealth of a Nation to Be: The American Colonies on the Eve of the Revolution*. New York: Columbia University Press.

Jones, G. 1980. *Social Darwinism and English Thought: The Interaction between Biological and Social Theory*. Brighton: Humanities Press.

Jones, P., and A. S. Skinner, eds. 1992. *Adam Smith Reviewed*. Edinburgh: Edinburgh University Press.

Jones, T. C. 2010. *Desert Kingdom: How Oil and Water Forged Modern Saudi Arabia*. Cambridge, MA: Harvard University Press.

——. 2011. *Counterrevolution in the Gulf*. Washington, DC: United States Institute of Peace.

Jordan, D. S. 1903. *The Blood of the Nation: A Study of the Decay of Races through Survival of the Unfit*. Boston: American Unitarian Association.

Judt, T. 1986. *Marxism and the French Left: Studies in Labour and Politics in France, 1830–1981*. Oxford: Clarendon Press.

Judt, T. 1992. *Past Imperfect: French Intellectuals, 1944–1956*. Berkeley: University of California Press.

————. 2005. *Postwar: A History of Europe since 1945*. New York: Penguin Press.

Kant, I. 1784/2006. *Toward Perpetual Peace and Other Writings on Politics, Peace, and History (Rethinking the Western Tradition)*. 2nd ed. Ed. P. Kleingeld. Trans. D. Colclasure. New Haven: Yale University Press.

Karier, T. M. 2010. *Intellectual Capital: Forty Years of the Nobel Prize in Economics*. New York: Cambridge University Press.

Kasaba, R. 2009. *A Moveable Empire: Ottoman Nomads, Migrants, and Refugees*. Seattle: University of Washington Press.

Katznelson, I. 2013. *Fear Itself: The New Deal and the Origins of Our Time*. New York: Liveright.

Kautsky, J. H. 1967. *Political Change in Underdeveloped Countries: Nationalism and Communism*. New York: Wiley.

Keddie, N. R. 1968. *An Islamic Response to Western Imperialism*. Berkeley: University of California Press.

Keddie, N. R., and Y. Richard. 2006. *Modern Iran: Roots and Results of Revolution*. New Haven: Yale University Press.

Kennan, G. F. 1960. *Soviet Foreign Policy, 1917–1941*. Princeton: Van Nostrand.

————. 1979. *The Decline of Bismarck's European Order: Franco-Russian Relations, 1875–1890*. Princeton: Princeton University Press.

Kennedy, P. M. 1980. *The Rise of the Anglo-German Antagonism, 1860–1914*. London: Allen and Unwin.

————. 1987. *Rise and Fall of the Great Powers: Economic Change and Military Conflict from 1500 to 2000*. New York: Random House.

Kepel, G. 1993. *Muslim Extremism in Egypt: The Prophet and Pharaoh*. Berkeley: University of California Press.

————. 2004. *The War for Muslim Minds: Islam and the West*. Cambridge, MA: Belknap Press of Harvard University Press.

Kern, S. 2010. *The Jeffersons at Shadwell*. New Haven: Yale University Press.

Kershaw, I. 1999. *Hitler*. New York: Norton.

Kersten, R. 2009. "Japan." In R. J. Bosworth, ed., *The Oxford Handbook of Fascism*, 526–44. Oxford: Oxford University Press.

Kevles, D. J. 1985. *In the Name of Eugenics: Genetics and the Uses of Human Heredity*. Berkeley: University of California Press.

Keynes, J. M. 1936/2009. *The General Theory of Employment, Interest and Money*. New York: Classic Books America.

————. 1963. *Essays in Persuasion*. New York: Norton.

Kiernan, B. 2008. *The Pol Pot Regime: Race, Power, and Genocide in Cambodia under the Khmer Rouge, 1975–79*. 3rd ed. New Haven: Yale University Press.

Kindleberger, C. P. 1973. *The World in Depression, 1929–1939*. London: Penguin.

Kinealy, C. 1997. *A Death-Dealing Famine: The Great Hunger in Ireland*. Chicago: Pluto Press.

Kirby, J. 2001. *The Josh Kirby Discworld Portfolio*. London: Paper Tiger.

Kirby, W. C. 1984. *Germany and Republican China*. Stanford: Stanford University Press.

Knight, A. W. 1993. *Beria: Stalin's First Lieutenant*. Princeton: Princeton University Press.

Knott, S. F. 2002. *Alexander Hamilton and the Persistence of Myth*. Lawrence: University Press of Kansas.

Kohn, H. 1944. *The Idea of Nationalism: A Study in Its Origins and Background*. New York: Macmillan.

———. 1955. *Nationalism: Its Meaning and History*. Princeton, NJ: Van Nostrand.

Kokutai No Hongi. 1937/1949. Cambridge, MA: Harvard University Press. Originally published by Japan's Ministry of Education (Monbushō).

Kornai, J. 1992. *The Socialist System: The Political Economy of Communism*. Princeton: Princeton University Press.

Kramer, A. 2009. "The First World War as Cultural Trauma." In R. J. Bosworth, ed., *The Oxford Handbook of Fascism*, 32–51. Oxford: Oxford University Press.

Kropotkin, P. A. 1910. *Mutual Aid: A Factor of Evolution*. London: Heinemann.

Kukathas, C. 2006. "Hayek and Liberalism." In E. Feser, ed., *The Cambridge Companion to Hayek*, 182–207. Cambridge: Cambridge University Press.

Kuran, T. 2004. *Islam and Mammon: The Economic Predicaments of Islamism*. Princeton: Princeton University Press.

Kurzman, C., ed. 2002. *Liberal Islam: A Source Book*. New York: Oxford University Press.

———. 2011. *The Missing Martyrs: Why There Are So Few Muslim Terrorists*. Oxford: Oxford University Press.

Kydland, F. E. 1995. *Business Cycle Theory*. Brookfield, VT: E. Elgar.

Laats, A. 2010. *Fundamentalism and Education in the Scopes Era: God, Darwin, and the Roots of America's Culture Wars*. New York: Palgrave Macmillan.

Lamarck, J. B. 1914. *Zoological Philosophy: An Exposition with Regard to the Natural History of Animals*. New York: Macmillan.

Lambert, F. 2008. *Religion in American Politics: A Short History*. Princeton: Princeton University Press.

Lankov, A. N. 2013. *The Real North Korea: Life and Politics in the Failed Stalinist Utopia*. New York: Oxford University Press.

Laqueur, W. 1996. *Fascism: Past, Present, and Future*. New York: Oxford University Press.

———. 2006. *The Changing Face of Anti-Semitism: From Ancient Times to the Present Day*. New York: Oxford University Press.

Lardy, N. R. 1983. *Agriculture in China's Modern Economic Development*. Cambridge: Cambridge University Press.

———. 2002. *Integrating China into the Global Economy*. Washington, DC: Brookings Institution Press.

———. 2006. *China: The Balance Sheet: What the World Needs to Know Now about the Emerging Superpower*. New York: Public Affairs.

———. 2008. *Debating China's Exchange Rate Policy*. Washington, DC: Peterson Institute for International Economics.

———. 2009. *China's Rise: Challenges and Opportunities*. Washington, DC: Peterson Institute for International Economics.

Larsen, S. U. 2001. *Fascism outside Europe: The European Impulse against Domestic Conditions in the Diffusion of Global Fascism*. Boulder, CO: Social Science Monographs.

Larson, B., and F. Brauer. 2009. *The Art of Evolution: Darwin, Darwinisms, and Visual Culture*. Hanover, NH: Dartmouth College Press.

Larson, E. J. 1997. *Summer for the Gods: The Scopes Trial and America's Continuing Debate Over Science and Religion*. New York: Basic Books.

———. 2007. *A Magnificent Catastrophe: The Tumultuous Election of 1800, America's First Presidential Campaign*. New York: Free Press.

Lary, D., and S. R. MacKinnon. 2001. *The Scars of War: The Impact of Warfare on Modern China*. Vancouver: University of British Columbia Press.

Lawrence, M. A., and F. Logevall, eds. 2007. *The First Vietnam War: Colonial Conflict and Cold War Crisis*. Cambridge, MA: Harvard University Press.

Lazitch, B., and M. M. Drachkovitch. 1972. *Lenin and the Comintern*. Stanford: Hoover Institution Press.

Leffler, M. P. 2007. *For the Soul of Mankind: The United States, the Soviet Union, and the Cold War*. New York: Macmillan.

Lemon v. Kurtzman, 403 U.S. 602 (1971).

Lenin, V. I. 1902. *What Is to Be Done?* http://www.marxists.org/archive/lenin/works/1901/witbd/i.htm.

———. 1939. *Imperialism, the Highest Stage of Capitalism: A Popular Outline*. New York: International Publishers.

Levine, G. L. 1988. *Darwin and the Novelists: Patterns of Science in Victorian Fiction*. Cambridge, MA: Harvard University Press.

Lewis, B. 1982/2001. *The Muslim Discovery of Europe*. New York: Norton.

———. 2002. *What Went Wrong? The Clash between Islam and Modernity in the Middle East*. New York: Oxford University Press.

Lewontin, R. C., S. P. Rose, and L. J. Kamin. 1984. *Not in Our Genes: Biology, Ideology, and Human Nature*. New York: Pantheon Books.

Licht, W. 1995. *Industrializing America: The Nineteenth Century*. Baltimore: Johns Hopkins University Press.

Lifton, R. J. 1986. *The Nazi Doctors: Medical Killing and the Psychology of Genocide*. New York: Basic Books.

Lightman, B. V. 1997. *Victorian Science in Context*. Chicago: University of Chicago Press.

Lincoln, A. 1858. "House Divided Speech." http://www.abrahamlincolnonline.org/lincoln/speeches/house.htm.

Lindgren, J. R. 1973. *The Social Philosophy of Adam Smith*. The Hague: Martinus Nijhoff.

Lipset, S. M., and G. Marks. 2000. *It Didn't Happen Here: Why Socialism Failed in the United States*. New York: Norton.

Locke, J. 1690/1988. *Two Treatises of Government*. Ed. P. Laslett. Cambridge: Cambridge University Press.

———. 1764. *The Two Treatises of Civil Government*. Ed. T. Hollis. London: A. Millar.

———. 1824. *The Works of John Locke in Nine Volumes*. 12th ed. Vols. 1–9. London: Rivington.

Logevall, F. 2000. *The Origins of the Vietnam War*. Harlow: Longman.

Love, J. L. 1996. *Crafting the Third World: Theorizing Underdevelopment in Rumania and Brazil*. Stanford: Stanford University Press.

Lovejoy, A. O. 1936. *The Great Chain of Being: A Study of the History of an Idea*. New York: Harper.

Lucas, R. E. 1995. *Studies in Business-Cycle Theory*. Cambridge, MA: MIT Press.

———. 2002. *Lectures on Economic Growth*. Cambridge, MA: Harvard University Press.

Luong, P. J., and E. Weinthal. 2010. *Oil Is Not a Curse: Ownership Structure and Institutions in Soviet Successor States*. New York: Cambridge University Press.

Lutz, D. S. 1992. "European Works Read and Cited by the American Founding Generation." In *A Preface to American Political Theory*, 159–64. Lawrence: University Press of Kansas.

Luxemburg, R. 2003. *The Accumulation of Capital*. London: Routledge.

Lyell, C. 1830/1990. *Principles of Geology*. Vols. 1–3. Chicago: University of Chicago Press.

MacFarquhar, R., and M. Schoenhals. 2006. *Mao's Last Revolution*. Cambridge, MA: Belknap Press of Harvard University Press.

Macpherson, W. J. 1995. *The Economic Development of Japan, 1868–1941*. Cambridge: Cambridge University Press.

Magnuson, N. A. 1977. *Salvation in the Slums: Evangelical Social Work, 1865–1920*. Metuchen, NJ: Scarecrow Press.

Maier, P. 1997. *American Scripture: Making the Declaration of Independence*. New York: Knopf.

———. 2010. *Ratification: The People Debate the Constitution, 1787–1788*. New York: Simon and Schuster.

Makiya, K. [Samir al-Khalil]. 1989. *Republic of Fear: The Inside Story of Saddam's Iraq*. New York: Pantheon Books.

Malley, R. 1996. *The Call from Algeria: Third Worldism, Revolution, and the Turn to Islam*. Berkeley: University of California Press.

Malone, D. 1974. *Jefferson and His Time*. Vols. 1–6. Boston: Little, Brown.

Malthus, T. R. 1807. *An Essay on the Principle of Population*. Vols. 1–2. London: T. Bensley.

Mandeville, B., and F. B. Kaye. 1924. *The Fable of the Bees; or, Private Vices, Publick Benefits*. Vols. 1–2. Oxford: Clarendon.

Manent, P. 1995. *An Intellectual History of Liberalism*. Princeton: Princeton University Press.

Mannheim, K., L. Wirth, and E. Shils. 1936. *Ideology and Utopia: An Introduction to the Sociology of Knowledge*. London: K. Paul, Trench, Trubner & Co.

Manuel, F. E. 1995. *A Requiem for Karl Marx*. Cambridge, MA: Harvard University Press.

Marsden, G. M. 1991. *Understanding Fundamentalism and Evangelicalism*. Grand Rapids, MI: W. B. Eerdmans.

———. 2006. *Fundamentalism and American Culture*. New York: Oxford University Press.

Marty, M. E. 1989. *Religion and Republic: The American Circumstance*. Boston: Beacon Press.

Marty, M. E., and R. S. Appleby. 1992. *The Glory and the Power: The Fundamentalist Challenge to the Modern World*. Boston: Beacon Press.

Maruyama, M., and I. I. Morris. 1969. *Thought and Behavior in Modern Japanese Politics*. London: Oxford University Press.

Marx, A. W. 1998. *Making Race and Nation: A Comparison of South Africa, the United States, and Brazil*. Cambridge: Cambridge University Press.

Marx, K. 1835. "Reflections of a Young Man on the Choice of a Profession." http://www.marxists.org/archive/marx/works/1837-pre/index.htm.

———. 1871/1940. *The Civil War in France*. New York: International Publishers.

———. 1967. *The Eighteenth Brumaire of Louis Bonaparte*. New York: International Publishers.

———. 1977. *Karl Marx: Selected Writings*. Ed. D. McLellan. Oxford: Oxford University Press.

———. 1995. *Capital: A New Abridgement*. Ed. D. McLellan. Oxford: Oxford University Press.

Marx, K., and E. J. Hobsbawm. 1965. *Pre-capitalist Economic Formations*. New York: International Publishers.

Mattar, P. 1988. *The Mufti of Jerusalem: Al-Hajj Amin al-Husayni and the Palestinian National Movement*. New York: Columbia University Press.

Maxson, C. H. 2006. *The Great Awakening in the Middle Colonies*. Whitefish, MT: Kessinger.

Mayr, E. 1985. *The Growth of Biological Thought: Diversity, Evolution, and Inheritance*. Cambridge, MA: Belknap Press of Harvard University Press.

———. 1993. *One Long Argument: Charles Darwin and the Genesis of Modern Evolutionary Thought*. Cambridge, MA: Harvard University Press.

McCraw, T. K. 2012. *The Founders and Finance: How Hamilton, Gallatin, and Other Immigrants Forged a New Economy*. Cambridge, MA: Belknap Press of Harvard University Press.

McCulloch, J. R. 1856. *A Select Collection of Early English Tracts on Commerce*. London: Political Economy Club.

McCusker, J. J., and R. R. Menard. 1991. *The Economy of British America, 1607–1789*. Chapel Hill: University of North Carolina Press.

McDaniel, T. 1988. *Autocracy, Capitalism, and Revolution in Russia*. Berkeley: University of California Press.

———. 1996. *The Agony of the Russian Idea*. Princeton: Princeton University Press.

McDonald, F. 1978. "Founding Father's Library: A Bibliographical Essay." *Literature of Liberty: A Review of Contemporary Liberal Thought* 1(1): 4–15.

McLellan, D. 1859/1977. Preface to K. Marx, *Capital: A Critique of Political Economy*, 389. New York: Vintage Books.

———. 1995. *The Thought of Karl Marx: An Introduction*. London: Papermac.

McLoughlin, W. T. 1980. *Revivals, Awakenings, and Reform*. Chicago: University of Chicago Press.

McNally, D. 1988. *Political Economy and the Rise of Capitalism: A Reinterpretation*. Berkeley: University of California Press.

McNeill, W. H. 1963. *The Rise of the West: A History of the Human Community*. Chicago: University of Chicago Press.

Melamed, Y. Y., and M. A. Rosenthal. 2010. *Spinoza's "Theological-Political Treatise": A Critical Guide*. Cambridge: Cambridge University Press.

Menand, L. 2002. *The Metaphysical Club: A Story of Ideas in America*. New York: Farrar, Straus and Giroux.

Mencken, H. L. 2006. *A Religious Orgy in Tennessee: A Reporter's Account of the Scopes Monkey Trial*. New York: Melville House.

Merikoski, I. A. 2002. "The Challenge of Material Progress: The Scottish Enlightenment and Christian Stoicism." *Journal of the Historical Society* 11(1): 55–76.

Michels, R. 1915. *Political Parties: A Sociological Study of the Oligarchical Tendencies of Modern Democracy*. New York: Hearst's International Library.

Milgate, M., and S. C. Stimson. 2009. *After Adam Smith: A Century of Transformation in Politics and Political Economy*. Princeton: Princeton University Press.

Mill, J. S. 1956. *On Liberty*. Indianapolis: Bobbs-Merrill.

Miller v. California, 413 U.S. 15 (1973).

Miller, P. 1953. *The New England Mind: From Colony to Province*. Cambridge, MA: Belknap Press of Harvard University Press.

Milner, R. 2009. *Darwin's Universe: Evolution from A to Z*. Berkeley: University of California Press.

Mirabeau, comte de, H. 1764. *Philosophie rurale, ou Économie génerale et politique de l'agriculture*. Vols. 1–2. Amsterdam: Les Libraires Associés.

Mitchell, S. 1996. *Daily Life in Victorian England*. Westport, CT: Greenwood Press.

Mitter, R. 2013. *China's War with Japan, 1937–1945: The Struggle for Survival*. New York: Allen Lane.

Mokyr, J. 2010. *The Enlightened Economy: An Economic History of Britain, 1700–1850*. New Haven: Yale University Press.

Montgomery, W. 1988. "Germany." In T. F. Glick, ed., *The Comparative Reception of Darwinism*, 81–115. Chicago: University of Chicago Press.

Montefiore, S. S. 2004. *Stalin: The Court of the Red Tsar*. New York: Knopf.

Montesquieu, baron de, C. 1748/1989. *The Spirit of the Laws*. Cambridge: Cambridge University Press.

Moore, B. 1966. *Social Origins of Dictatorship and Democracy: Lord and Peasant in the Making of the Modern World*. Boston: Beacon Press.

Moreno, P. D. 2013. *The American State from the Civil War to the New Deal: The Twilight of Constitutionalism and the Triumph of Progressivism*. Cambridge: Cambridge University Press.

Morgan, P. 2009. "Corporatism and the Economic Order." In R. J. Bosworth, *The Oxford Handbook of Fascism*, 150–65. Oxford: Oxford University Press.

Morris, E. 2001. *The Rise of Theodore Roosevelt*. New York: Modern Library/Random House.

Mosca, G. 1939. *The Ruling Class*. Edited and revised by A. Livingston. New York: McGraw-Hill.

Mosse, G. L. 1966. *Nazi Culture: Intellectual, Cultural, and Social Life in the Third Reich*. New York: Grosset and Dunlap.

Mossner, E. C. 2001. *The Life of David Hume*. 2nd ed. Oxford: Oxford University Press.

Mossner, E. C., and S. Ross, eds. 1987. *The Correspondence of Adam Smith*. Oxford: Clarendon Press.

Muller, J. Z., ed. 1997. *Conservatism: An Anthology of Social and Political Thought from David Hume to the Present*. Princeton: Princeton University Press.

———. 2010. *Capitalism and the Jews*. Princeton: Princeton University Press.

Muller-Wille, S., and H. Rheinberger. 2007. *Heredity Produced: At the Crossroads of Biology, Politics, and Culture, 1500–1870*. Cambridge, MA: MIT Press.

Murray, G. 1997. *Vietnam: Dawn of a New Market*. New York: St. Martin's Press.

Nash, G. B. 1979. *The Urban Crucible: Social Change, Political Consciousness, and the Origins of the American Revolution*. Cambridge, MA: Harvard University Press.

Nasr, S. V. 2007. *The Shia Revival: How Conflicts within Islam Will Shape the Future*. New York: Norton.

National Abortion Federation. 2010. "Clinic Violence: Violence Statistics." http://www.prochoice.org/about_abortion/violence/violence_statistics .html.

Nekola, J. C. 2013. "The Malthusian-Darwinian Dynamic and the Trajectory of Civilization." *Trends in Ecology & Evolution* 28(3): 127–30.

Nelson, R. R., and S. G. Winter. 1985. *An Evolutionary Theory of Economic Change*. Cambridge, MA: Belknap Press of Harvard University Press.

Neumann, F. L. 1944/1963. *Behemoth: The Structure and Practice of National Socialism.* New York: Octagon Books.

Newport, F., and J. Carroll. 2005. "Another Look at Evangelicals in America Today." December 2. http://www.gallup.com/poll/20242/Another-Look-Evangelicals-America-Today.aspx.

Newport, K.G.C. 2000. *Apocalypse and Millennium: Studies in Biblical Exegesis.* Cambridge: Cambridge University Press.

Niekerk, C. 2004. "Man and Orangutan in Eighteenth-Century Thinking: Retracing the Early History of Dutch and German Anthropology." *Monatshefte* 96(4): 477–502.

Nietzsche, F. W. 1954. *The Philosophy of Nietzsche: Thus Spake Zarathustra, Beyond Good and Evil, The Genealogy of Morals, Ecce Homo, The Birth of Tragedy.* New York: Modern Library.

Nisbet, R. 1980. *History of the Idea of Progress.* New York: Basic Books.

Noll, M. A. 1992. *A History of Christianity in the United States and Canada.* Grand Rapids, MI: W. B. Eerdmans.

———. 2005. *America's God: From Jonathan Edwards to Abraham Lincoln.* New York: Oxford University Press.

———. 2010. *The Rise of Evangelicalism: The Age of Edwards, Whitefield, and the Wesleys.* New York: InterVarsity Press.

Nolte, E. 1965. *Three Faces of Fascism: Action Française, Italian Fascism, National Socialism.* New York: Holt, Rinehart and Winston.

Nord, D. P. 2007. *Faith in Reading: Religious Publishing and the Birth of Mass Media in America.* New York: Oxford University Press.

Noueihed, L., and A. Warren. 2012. *The Battle for the Arab Spring: Revolution, Counter-revolution and the Making of a New Era.* New Haven: Yale University Press.

Numbers, R. L. 2006. *The Creationists: From Scientific Creationism to Intelligent Design.* Cambridge, MA: Harvard University Press.

Nunca Más: The Report of the Argentine National Committee on the Disappeared. 1986. New York: Farrar, Straus and Giroux.

Otsubo, S., and J. R. Bartholomew. 1998. "Eugenics in Japan: Some Ironies of Modernity, 1883–1945." *Science in Context* 11(3–4): 545–65.

Owen, R. 2012. *The Rise and Fall of Arab Presidents for Life.* Cambridge, MA: Harvard University Press.

Oz-Salzberger, F. 2003. "The Political Theory of the Scottish Enlightenment." In A. Broadie, ed., *The Cambridge Companion to the Scottish Enlightenment*, 157–77. Cambridge: Cambridge University Press.

Packenham, R. A. 1992. *The Dependency Movement: Scholarship and Politics in Development Studies*. Cambridge, MA: Harvard University Press.

Paley, W. 1809. *Natural Theology; or, Evidences of the Existence and Attributes of the Deity Collected from the Appearances of Nature*. 12th ed. London: J. Faulter.

Pangle, T. L. 1990. *The Spirit of Modern Republicanism: The Moral Vision of the American Founders and the Philosophy of Locke*. Chicago: University of Chicago Press.

Pargeter, A. 2008. *The New Frontiers of Jihad: Radical Islam in Europe*. Philadelphia: University of Pennsylvania Press.

———. 2013. *The Muslim Brotherhood: From Opposition to Power*. London: Saqi Books.

Passmore, K. 2009. "The Ideological Origins of Fascism before 1914." In R. J. Bosworth, ed., *The Oxford Handbook of Fascism*, 11–31. Oxford: Oxford University Press.

Patterson, D. 2011. *A Genealogy of Evil: Anti-Semitism from Nazism to Islamic Jihad*. Cambridge: Cambridge University Press.

Paul, D. B. 1995. *Controlling Human Heredity: 1865 to the Present*. Atlantic Highlands, NJ: Humanities Press International.

Paxton, R. O. 2009. "Comparisons and Definitions." In R. J. Bosworth, ed., *The Oxford Handbook of Fascism*, 547–65. Oxford: Oxford University Press.

Payne, S. G. 1966. "Spain." In H. Rogger and E. J. Weber, eds., *The European Right: A Historical Profile*, 168–207. Berkeley: University of California Press.

———. 1999. *Fascism in Spain, 1923–1977*. Madison: University of Wisconsin Press.

———. 2008. *Franco and Hitler: Spain, Germany, and World War II*. New Haven: Yale University Press.

Perliger, A. 2012. *Challengers from the Sidelines: Understanding America's Violent Far-Right*. West Point, NY: The Combating Terrorism Center.

Perry, E. J. 1980. *Rebels and Revolutionaries in North China, 1845–1945*. Stanford: Stanford University Press.

Peterson, M. D. 1975. *Thomas Jefferson and the New Nation: A Biography*. New York: Oxford University Press.

Peukert, D. 1987. *Inside Nazi Germany: Conformity, Opposition, and Racism in Everyday Life*. New Haven: Yale University Press.

Pew Forum on Religion and Public Life, Pew-Templeton Global Religious Futures Project. 2011. *Global Christianity: A Report on the Size and Distribution of the World's Christian Population*. Washington, DC: Pew Research Center.

Phillipson, N. 2010. *Adam Smith: An Enlightened Life*. New Haven: Yale University Press.

Piketty, T. 2014. *Capital in the Twenty-First Century*. Cambridge, MA: Harvard University Press.

Pincus, L. 1996. *Authenticating Culture in Imperial Japan: Kuki Shūzō and the Rise of National Aesthetics*. Berkeley: University of California Press.

Pincus, S. 2009. *1688: The First Modern Revolution*. New Haven: Yale University Press.

Pipes, R. 1990. *The Russian Revolution*. New York: Knopf.

Pitts, J. 2005. *A Turn to Empire: The Rise of Imperial Liberalism in Britain and France*. Princeton: Princeton University Press.

Polanyi, K. 1944/2001. *The Great Transformation*. Boston: Beacon Press.

Pope, A. 1734. *An Essay on Man*. Epistle I. www.poetryfoundation.org/poem /174165.

Porter, R. 1978. "Gentlemen and Geology: The Emergence of a Scientific Career, 1660–1920." *Historical Journal* 21:809–36.

Poulantzas, N. A. 1974. *Fascism and Dictatorship: The Third International and the Problem of Fascism*. London: NLB Books.

Proctor, R. 1988. *Racial Hygiene: Medicine under the Nazis*. Cambridge, MA: Harvard University Press.

Prothero, S. 2003. *Jesus as Icon: How the Son of God Became an Icon in America*. New York: Farrar, Straus and Giroux.

Pusey, J. R. 1983. *China and Charles Darwin*. Cambridge, MA: Council on East Asian Studies, Harvard University.

———. 2009. "Global Darwin: Revolutionary Road." *Nature* 462(984): 162–63.

Qutb, S. 1964/n.d. *Milestones*. Cedar Rapids, IA: The Mother Mosque Foundation.

Rable, G. C. 2010. *God's Almost Chosen Peoples: A Religious History of the American Civil War*. Chapel Hill: University of North Carolina Press.

Rae, J. 1895/1990. *Life of Adam Smith*. 2nd ed. London: Macmillan.

Raleigh, D. J. 2006. "The Russian Civil War, 1917–1922." In M. Perrie, D. C. Lieven, and R. G. Suny, eds., *The Cambridge History of Russia*. Cambridge: Cambridge University Press.

Rauschenbusch, W. 1917. *A Theology for the Social Gospel*. New York: Abingdon Press.

Raymond, J. 2003. *Pamphlets and Pamphleteering in Early Modern Britain*. Cambridge: Cambridge University Press.

Reagan, L. J. 1997. *When Abortion Was a Crime: Women, Medicine, and Law in the United States, 1867–1973*. Berkeley: University of California Press.

Renan, E. 1883. *L'islam et la science*. Montpellier: L'Archange minotaure.

Richards, R. J. 2008. *The Tragic Sense of Life: Ernst Haeckel and the Struggle over Evolutionary Thought*. Chicago: University of Chicago Press.

Riley, D. J. 2010. *The Civic Foundations of Fascism in Europe: Italy, Spain, and Romania, 1870–1945*. Baltimore: Johns Hopkins University Press.

Ritvo, L. B. 1990. *Darwin's Influence on Freud: A Tale of Two Sciences*. New Haven: Yale University Press.

Robbins, C. 1959. *The Eighteenth-Century Commonwealthman*. Cambridge, MA: Harvard University Press.

Robinson, F. 1982. *Atlas of the Islamic World since 1500*. New York: Facts on File.

Rock, D. 1993. *Authoritarian Argentina: The Nationalist Movement, Its History, and Its Impact*. Berkeley: University of California Press.

Rodogno, D. 2009. "Fascism and War." In R. J. Bosworth, eds., *The Oxford Handbook of Fascism*, 239–58. Oxford: Oxford University Press.

Rogers, J. A. 1988. "Russia: Social Sciences." In T. F. Glick, ed., *The Comparative Reception of Darwinism*, 256–68. Chicago: University of Chicago Press.

Rogger, H., and E. J. Weber, eds. 1966. *The European Right: A Historical Profile*. Berkeley: University of California Press.

Rosenblatt, H. 2009. *The Cambridge Companion to Constant*. Cambridge: Cambridge University Press.

Ross, I. S. 1998. *On the Wealth of Nations: Contemporary Responses to Adam Smith*. London: St. Augustine's Press.

Rossiter, C. 1953. *Seedtime of the Republic: The Origin of the American Tradition of Political Liberty*. New York: Harcourt, Brace.

Rothschild, E. 2001. *Economic Sentiments: Adam Smith, Condorcet, and the Enlightenment*. Cambridge, MA: Harvard University Press.

Rousseau, J-J. 2005. *The Plan for Perpetual Peace, On the Government of Poland, and Other Writings on History and Politics*. Trans. C. Kelly. Hanover, NH: Dartmouth College Press.

Rudwick, M. 2007. *Bursting the Limits of Time: The Reconstruction of Geohistory in the Age of Revolution*. Chicago: University of Chicago Press.

Ruse, M. 1999. *The Darwinian Revolution: Science Red in Tooth and Claw*. 2nd ed. Chicago: University of Chicago Press.

Saint-Hilaire, É. G. 1835. *Études progressives d'un naturaliste, pendant les années 1834–1835*. Paris: Roret.

Samuelson, P. 1948/1967 and 1948/1973. *Economics: An Introductory Analysis*. 7th and 9th eds. New York: McGraw-Hill.

Samuelson, P. A., and W. D. Nordhaus. 1944/2009. *Economics*. 19th ed. New York: McGraw-Hill.

Sassoon, D. 2007. *Mussolini and the Rise of Fascism*. London: HarperPress.

Schmitt, C. 1933. "Public Law in a New Context." In G. L. Mosse, ed., *Nazi Culture: Intellectual, Cultural, and Social Life in the Third Reich*, 323–26. New York: Grosset & Dunlap, 1966.

Schram, S. R. 1969. *Marxism and Asia*. New York: Allen Lane.

Schwarcz, V. 1986. *The Chinese Enlightenment: Intellectuals and the Legacy of the May Fourth Movement of 1919*. Berkeley: University of California Press.

Schwartz, B. I. 1989. *The Secret Speeches of Chairman Mao: From the Hundred Flowers to the Great Leap Forward*. Cambridge, MA: Council on East Asian Studies, Harvard University.

Scofield, C. I. 1917. *The Scofield Reference Bible*. New York: Oxford University Press.

Secord, J. A. 2003. *Victorian Sensation: The Extraordinary Publication, Reception, and Secret Authorship of Vestiges of the Natural History of Creation*. Chicago: University of Chicago Press.

Segev, T. 2000. *One Palestine, Complete: Jews and Arabs under the British Mandate*. London: Little, Brown.

Sernett, M. C. 1975. *Black Religion and American Evangelicalism: White Protestants, Plantation Missions, and the Flowering of Negro Christianity, 1787–1865*. Metuchen, NJ: Scarecrow Press.

Shanin, T. 1972. *The Awkward Class: Political Sociology of Peasantry in a Developing Society: Russia, 1910–1925*. Oxford: Clarendon.

Shapin, S. 1996. *The Scientific Revolution*. Chicago: University of Chicago Press.

Shapiro, F. R. 2006. *The Yale Book of Quotations*. New Haven: Yale University Press.

Shapiro, J. 2001. *Mao's War against Nature: Politics and the Environment in Revolutionary China*. Cambridge: Cambridge University Press.

Sher, R. B. 2004. "New Light on the Publication and Reception of the Wealth of Nations." *Adam Smith Review* 1:3–29.

Sheridan, E. R. 2002. *Jefferson and Religion*. Chapel Hill: University of North Carolina Press.

Shirk, S. L. 2007. *China: Fragile Superpower*. New York: Oxford University Press.

Skidelski, R. 1994. *John Maynard Keynes*. Vol. 2, *The Economist as Savior*. New York: Penguin.

———. 2010. *Keynes: The Return of the Master*. New York: Public Affairs.

Skinner, A. S. 2003. "Economic Theory." In A. Broadie, ed., *The Cambridge Companion to the Scottish Enlightenment*, 178–204. Cambridge: Cambridge University Press.

Skoble, A. J., and T. R. Machan. 1999. *Political Philosophy: Essential Selections*. Upper Saddle River, NJ: Prentice Hall.

Skya, W. 2009. *Japan's Holy War: The Ideology of Radical Shintō Ultranationalism*. Durham: Duke University Press.

Sloman, L., and P. Gilbert. 2000. *Subordination and Defeat: An Evolutionary Approach to Mood Disorders and Their Therapy*. Mahwah, NJ: Lawrence Erlbaum.

Slotkin, J. S. 1965. *Readings in Early Anthropology*. Chicago: Aldine.

Sluga, G. 2009. "The Aftermath of War." In R. J. Bosworth, ed., *The Oxford Handbook of Fascism*, 70–87. Oxford: Oxford University Press.

Smith, A. 1776. *An Inquiry into the Nature and Causes of the Wealth of Nations*. London: Strahan and T. Cadell.

———. 1904. *An Inquiry into the Nature and Causes of the Wealth of Nations*. Ed. E. Cannan. Library of Economics and Liberty. London: Methuen. http://www.econlib.org/library/Smith/smWN.html.

———. 1976–87. *The Glasgow Edition of the Works and Correspondence of Adam Smith*. Vols. 1–7. Indianapolis: Oxford University Press.

———. 1984. *The Theory of Moral Sentiments*. Ed. D. D. Raphael and A. L. Macfie. Indianapolis: Liberty Fund.

Smith, C. 2006. *Adam Smith's Political Philosophy: The Invisible Hand and Spontaneous Order*. London: Routledge.

Smith, S. A. 2006. "The Revolutions of 1917–1918." In M. Perrie, D. C. Lieven, and R. G. Suny, eds., *The Cambridge History of Russia*. Cambridge: Cambridge University Press.

Snow, E. 1961. *Red Star over China*. New York: Grove Press.

Snyder, T. 2010. *Bloodlands: Europe between Hitler and Stalin*. New York: Basic Books.

Solonari, V. 2010. *Purifying the Nation: Population Exchange and Ethnic Cleansing in Nazi-Allied Romania*. Washington, DC: Woodrow Wilson Center Press.

Somit, A., and S. A. Peterson. 1997. *Darwinism, Dominance, and Democracy: The Biological Bases of Authoritarianism*. Westport, CT: Praeger.

Sorel, G., and J. Jennings. 1999. *Reflections on Violence*. Cambridge: Cambridge University Press.

Souaïdia, H. 2001. *La sale guerre: Le témoignage d'un ancien officier des forces de l'armée algérienne*. Paris: Découverte.

Spence, J. D. 1990. *The Search for Modern China*. New York: Norton.

———. 1997. *God's Chinese Son: The Taiping Heavenly Kingdom of Hong Xiuquan*. New York: Norton.

Spencer, H. 1851. *Social Statics: Or the Conditions Essential to Human Happiness*. London: John Chapman.

Spencer, H. 1885. *The Man versus the State*. London: Williams and Norgate.

Spener, P. J. 1964. *Pia desideria*. Trans. T. G. Tappert. Minneapolis: Fortress Press.

Stalin, J. V. 1939. *History of the Communist Party of the Soviet Union (Bolsheviks): Short Course*. New York: International Publishers.

Stebbens, R. E. 1988. "France." In T. F. Glick, ed., *The Comparative Reception of Darwinism*, 117–64. Chicago: University of Chicago Press.

Steinberg, J. 1996. *Why Switzerland?* Cambridge: Cambridge University Press.

Stern, A. 2005. *Eugenic Nation: Faults and Frontiers of Better Breeding in Modern America*. Berkeley: University of California Press.

Sternhell, Z. 1986. *Neither Right nor Left: Fascist Ideology in France*. Trans. D. Maisel. Berkeley: University of California Press.

Sternhell, Z., M. Sznajder, and M. Ashéri. 1994. *The Birth of Fascist Ideology: From Cultural Rebellion to Political Revolution*. Trans. D. Maisel. Princeton: Princeton University Press.

Stewart, D. 1858. "Account of the Life and Writings of Adam Smith." In W. Hamilton, ed., *The Collected Works of Dugald Stewart*. Vol. 10. Edinburgh: Thomas Constable.

———. 1980. "Dugald Stewart's Account of Adam Smith." In I. S. Ross, D. D. Raphael, and A. S. Skinner, eds., *Adam Smith: Essays on Philosophical Subject*. Oxford: Oxford University Press.

Stoeffler, F. E. 1965. *The Rise of Evangelical Pietism*. Leiden: E. J. Brill.

Storing, H. J., ed. 1981. *The Complete Anti-Federalist*. Vol. 1. Chicago: University of Chicago Press.

Streeck, W., and K. Yamamura. 2001. *The Origins of Nonliberal Capitalism: Germany and Japan in Comparison*. Ithaca: Cornell University Press.

Swartz, D. 2012. "Embodying the Global Soul: Internationalism and the American Evangelical Left." *Religions* 3(4): 887–901.

Talbot, I. 2012. *Pakistan: A New History*. New York: Columbia University Press.

Taylor, C. 2007. *A Secular Age*. Cambridge, MA: Belknap Press of Harvard University Press.

Taylor, J. 2009. *The Generalissimo: Chiang Kai-shek and the Struggle for Modern China*. Cambridge, MA: Belknap Press of Harvard University Press.

Taylor, M. W. 1992. *Men versus the State: Herbert Spencer and Late Victorian Liberalism*. Oxford: Oxford University Press.

Teichgraeber, R. F., III. 1987. " 'Less Abused than I Had Reason to Expect': The Reception of *The Wealth of Nations* in Britain." *Historical Journal* 30(2): 337–66.

Thaxton, R. 2008. *Catastrophe and Contention in Rural China: Mao's Great Leap Forward Famine and the Origins of Righteous Resistance in Da Fo Village.* Cambridge: Cambridge University Press.

Thilly, F. 1909. "Friedrich Paulsen's Ethical Work and Influence." *Ethics* 19(2): 141–55.

Tilly, C. 1992. *Coercion, Capital, and European States: AD 990–1992.* Cambridge, MA: Blackwell.

———. 2007. *Democracy.* Cambridge: Cambridge University Press.

Timerman, J. 1982. *Prisoner without a Name, Cell without a Number.* New York: Vintage.

Tismaneanu, V. 2012. *The Devil in History: Communism, Fascism, and Some Lessons of the Twentieth Century.* Berkeley: University of California Press.

Tocqueville, A. 2004. *Democracy in America.* Ed. A. Goldhammer. New York: Library of America.

Todes, D. 2009. "Global Darwin: Contempt for Competition." *Nature* 462(5): 36–37.

Toth, J. 2013. *Sayyid Qutb: The Life and Legacy of a Radical Islamic Intellectual.* Oxford: Oxford University Press.

Treitschke, H. G. von. 1879. "Unsere Aussichten." *Preußische Jahrbücher* 44(5): 559–76.

Trenchard, J., and T. Gordon. 1737. *Cato's Letters; or, Essays on Liberty, Civil and Religious, and Other Important Subjects.* Vols. 1–4. London: Printed for W. Wilkins, T. Woodward, J. Walthoe, and J. Peele.

Trotsky, L. 1937. *Stalinism and Bolshevism: Concerning the Historical and Theoretical Roots of the Fourth International.* New York: Pioneer.

Tucker, R. C. 1977. *Stalinism: Essays in Historical Interpretation.* New York: Norton.

Turner, H. A. 1996. *Hitler's Thirty Days to Power: January 1933.* Reading, MA: Addison-Wesley.

U.S. Census Bureau. 2014. "History." http://www.census.gov/history/.

Van Maarseveen, H., and G. Van der Tang. 1978. *Written Constitutions: A Computerized Comparative Study.* Dobbs Ferry, NY: Oceana Publications.

Verdery, K. 1991. *National Ideology under Socialism: Identity and Cultural Politics in Ceaușescu's Romania.* Berkeley: University of California Press.

Vidal, F., M. Buscaglia, and J. J. Vonèche. 1983. "Darwinism and Developmental Psychology." *Journal of the History of the Behavioral Sciences* 19(1): 81–94.

Vincent, M. 2009. "Spain." In R. J. Bosworth, eds., *The Oxford Handbook of Fascism,* 362–79. Oxford: Oxford University Press.

Vogel, E. F. 1989. *One Step ahead in China: Guangdong under Reform*. Cambridge, MA: Harvard University Press.

Von Hagen, M. 2006. "World War I, 1914–1918." In M. Perrie, D. C. Lieven, and R. G. Suny, eds., *The Cambridge History of Russia*. Vol. 3. Cambridge: Cambridge University Press.

Vucinich, A. 1988. *Darwin in Russian Thought*. Berkeley: University of California Press.

Wakeman, F. E. 1975. *The Fall of Imperial China*. New York: Free Press.

Walker, D. A. 2006. *Walrasian Economics*. New York: Cambridge University Press.

Wallace, A.R. 1871. *Contributions to the Theory of Natural Selection: A Series of Essays*. London: Head, Hole and Co.

Wallerstein, I. M., R. Collins, M. Mann, G. M. Derlugian, and C. J. Calhoun. 2013. *Does Capitalism Have a Future?* New York: Oxford University Press.

Wallis, J. 1995. *The Soul of Politics: Beyond "Religious Right" and "Secular Left."* New York: Harcourt Brace.

Washington, G. 1892. *The Collected Writings of George Washington*. Vols. 1–14. New York: G. P. Putnam's Sons.

———. 1997. *Writings*. Ed. J. H. Rhodehamel. New York: Library of America.

Watanabe, M., and O. T. Benfrey. 1990. *The Japanese and Western Science*. Philadelphia: University of Pennsylvania Press.

Weber, E. J. 1966. "Romania." In H. Rogger and E. J. Weber, eds., *The European Right: A Historical Profile*, 501–74. Berkeley: University of California Press.

Weiner, A. 2001. *Making Sense of War: The Second World War and the Fate of the Bolshevik Revolution*. Princeton: Princeton University Press.

Weiner, D. R. 2000. *Models of Nature: Ecology, Conservation, and Cultural Revolution in Soviet Russia*. Bloomington: Indiana University Press.

Werth, B. 2009. *Banquet at Delmonico's: Great Minds, the Gilded Age, and the Triumph of Evolution in America*. New York: Random House.

Westad, O. A. 2003. *Decisive Encounters: The Chinese Civil War, 1946–1950*. Stanford: Stanford University Press.

Whitaker, N. 1770. *A Funeral Sermon, on the Death of the Reverend George Whitefield: Who Died Suddenly at Newbury-Port, in Massachusetts-Bay, . . . September 30, 1770*. Boston: Samuel Hall.

White, G. 1989. *Developmental States in East Asia*. New York: St. Martin's Press.

White, J. B. 2013. *Muslim Nationalism and the New Turks*. Princeton: Princeton University Press.

Wien, P. 2006. *Iraqi Arab Nationalism: Authoritarian, Totalitarian, and Profascist Inclinations, 1932–1941.* London: Routledge.

Williams, D. K. 2010. *God's Own Party: The Making of the Christian Right.* Oxford: Oxford University Press.

Wills, G. 1992. *Lincoln at Gettysburg: The Words That Remade America.* New York: Simon and Schuster.

Wilson, E. O. 1975. *Sociobiology: The New Synthesis.* Cambridge, MA: Harvard University Press.

———. 1998. *Consilience: The Unity of Knowledge.* New York: Vintage Books.

Winch, D. 1978. *Adam Smith's Politics: An Essay in Historiographic Revision.* Cambridge: Cambridge University Press.

Wolin, R. 2004. *The Seduction of Unreason: The Intellectual Romance with Fascism. From Nietzsche to Postmodernism.* Princeton: Princeton University Press.

Wood, E. M. 2012. *Liberty and Property: A Social History of Western Political Thought from Renaissance to Enlightenment.* London: Verso.

Wood, G. S. 1992. *The Radicalism of the American Revolution.* New York: Knopf.

———. 1998. *The Creation of the American Republic, 1776–1787.* Chapel Hill: University of North Carolina Press.

———. 2007. *Revolutionary Characters: What Made the Founders Different.* New York: Penguin.

———. 2009. *Empire of Liberty: A History of the Early Republic, 1789–1815.* Oxford: Oxford University Press.

Woodside, A. 1976. *Community and Revolution in Modern Vietnam.* Boston: Houghton Mifflin.

Wootton, D. 2010. *Galileo: Watcher of the Skies.* New Haven: Yale University Press.

Xiao, X. 1995. "China Encounters Darwinism: A Case of Intercultural Rhetoric." *Quarterly Journal of Speech* 81(1): 83–99.

Yang, J. 2012. *Tombstone: The Great Chinese Famine, 1958–1962.* Introduction by E. Friedman and R. MacFarquhar. Trans. S. Mosher and J. Guo. New York: Farrar, Straus and Giroux.

Young, R. M. 1985. *Darwin's Metaphor: Nature's Place in Victorian Culture.* Cambridge: Cambridge University Press.

Ziadat, A. A. 1986. *Western Science in the Arab World: The Impact of Darwinism, 1860–1930.* New York: Macmillan.

INDEX

decline of, 330; emergence of, in Italy and Germany, 309–16; European spread of movements of, 322–25; Great Depression and, 124–25; imperialism and elitist theories, effects of, 305–8; intellectual roots of, 295–98; Japanese, 317–18; Middle East, Arab nationalists, anticolonial intellectuals, and, 327–31; as "neither left nor right," 309, 332; overview, 430–31; Paxton's definition of, 323; philosophical support and intellectual appeal of, 331–35; remaining elements of, 419; revolutionary, violent upheaval required by, 309–10; Romanian, 318–20; Spanish, 323–24; World War I and, 308–9. *See also* anti-Semitism; Nazism

Fawcett, Rachel, 229

Faye, Emmanuel, 335

Feder, Gottfried, 321

federalism. *See* democracy, Jeffersonian vs. Hamiltonian; Hamilton, Alexander, Jr.

Federalist Papers (Hamilton, Madison, and Jay), 234–39

Federal Reserve, 67, 271

Ferla, Salvatore, 326

feudal mode of production, 90–91

Filiu, Jean-Pierre, 415

Finney, Charles, 346

First International, 104, 123

fossils, 157

Foucault, Michel, 145

France: anti-Semitism in, 301–2; Asian communism and, 124; Charles X, overthrow of, 288; Colbertism, 29; colonialism, 126, 138; communism in, 126; Darwin and, 179; Dreyfus Affair, 302; fascism in, 309, 322; French Revolution, 92–93, 97, 285–87, 288–89; Marx on Napoleon III coup (1851), 118; nationalism and, 294, 297; Smith on,

45; socialism and communism in, 104, 106–7, 126; Tocqueville on democracy and, 274; trade agreements with England, 53; World War I and, 107

Franco, Francisco, 323–24

Frankfurt School, 145

Franklin, Benjamin, 219, 221, 253, 343

freedom. *See* liberty

free exchange, markets, and trade: "liberalism" and worship of, 75–76; Physiocrats on, 29; Smith on, 45–46, 48, 55, 56. *See also* commerce; Smith, Adam

French and Indian War (Seven Years' War), 26, 222–23

French Communist Party, 124

French Enlightenment, 27, 37

French Revolution, 92–93, 97, 285–87, 288–89

French SFIO (French Section of the Workers' International), 104

Freud, Sigmund, 203–4, 327

Friedman, Milton, 57–58, 68, 72–73

Fukuyama, Francis, 10

"Full Vindication of the Measures of Congress" (Hamilton), 230–31

fundamentalism, Darwinian, 206–7

fundamentalism, Islamic. *See* Salafist (fundamentalist) Islam

fundamentalism and evangelicalism, Christian: abortion issue, 368–71, 373, 378; biblical authority and inerrancy and, 340, 352, 354–55, 362, 370–71; black evangelicalism, 350–51; distinction between, 337–38; in early twentieth century, 360–63; education and, 360–61, 364–65, 375–76; "evangelical" as term, 338; "fundamentalist" as term, 358–59; *The Fundamentals* (Dixon), 358–60, 374; in global context, 339–41;

Jefferson, Martha Skelton, 249–50, 252
Jefferson, Peter, 248
Jefferson, Thomas: American Revolution
  and, 224; busts at Monticello, 264;
  Danbury Baptists, response to, 258–59;
  Darwin and, 249; evangelicals and,
  344–45; Hamilton, differences and
  commonalities with, 219–20, 265–68,
  275–76; incongruities in, 245–46;
  as intellectual, 226, 246; letters of,
  222, 247–48, 260, 263–64; life of,
  245, 248–50, 252; national political
  career, 251; "negative liberty" and, 276;
  presidency and addresses, 262–63, 273;
  Shay's Rebellion, response to, 266; on
  slavery, 254–55, 275; Virginia political
  career and reforms, 250, 255–57. See also
  democracy, Jeffersonian vs. Hamiltonian
Jefferson, Thomas, writings of:
  Autobiography, 246, 248; Bill for
  Establishing Religious Freedom, 257–58;
  A Bill for the More General Diffusion
  of Knowledge, 256; Declaration of
  Independence, 252–54, 360; The Life
  and Morals of Jesus of Nazareth, 259;
  Notes on the State of Virginia, 246–47,
  252, 254–55; Report on Commerce, 260;
  A Summary View of the Rights of British
  America, 247, 251
Jenkins, Philip, 340
"Jesus Film, The," 339
Jesus Is Coming (Blackstone), 355
Jevons, William Stanley, 59
Jews and Jewish communities: in Argentina,
  326; Bergson and, 297; genocide
  against, 313, 319; Marx and Jewish
  identification, 82, 107; Marx and Jewish
  prophetic tradition, 100; premillennial
  Dispensationalism and, 356; in Russia,
  115, 117; Spinoza and Dutch Jews, 283;
  in Vienna, 314. See also anti-Semitism;
  Israel

Johnson, Samuel, 255
Jones, Toby, 401
Jordan, David Starr, 195
Journal of Researches (Voyage of the Beagle)
  (Darwin), 163–64
Judt, Tony, 145–46
Jungle, The (Sinclair), 201

Kansas-Nebraska Act (1854), 269
Kant, Immanuel, 13, 16, 326
Kato Hiroyuki, 186, 187, 188
Kaunda, Kenneth, 138
Kennedy, John F., 246, 364
Kepel, Gilles, 400
Keynes, John Maynard, 3, 56, 57, 64–67
Khamenei, Ayatollah Ali, 414
Khmer Rouge, 141–42
Khomeini, Ayatollah Ruholla, 391–92,
  412–14
Khrushchev, Nikita, 121, 146
Kim Il Sung, 141
Kim Jong Il, 141
Kim Jong Un, 141
Kindleberger, Charles, 66
King, Martin Luther, Jr., 365
Kingsley, Charles, 175
Knott, Stephen, 277
Kokutai No Hongi ("the fundamentals"),
  317–18
Koop, C. Everett, 369
Kosciusko, Thaddeus, 222
Kropotkin, Peter, 182–83
Kuki Shūzō, 317–18
Kurzman, Charles, 387
Kydland, Finn, 69

labor, division of: Engels on Darwin and,
  181; Hamilton on, 242; Marx on, 88;
  Smith on, 43–44, 47, 50
labor movements and unionism as threat to
  Marxism, 108
Labour Party of Great Britain, 104